The Jaws Book

The Jaws Book

New Perspectives on the Classic Summer Blockbuster

Edited by
I. Q. Hunter and Matthew Melia

BLOOMSBURY ACADEMIC
NEW YORK • LONDON • OXFORD • NEW DELHI • SYDNEY

BLOOMSBURY ACADEMIC
Bloomsbury Publishing Inc
1385 Broadway, New York, NY 10018, USA
29 Earlsfort Terrace, Dublin 2, Ireland

BLOOMSBURY, BLOOMSBURY ACADEMIC and the Diana logo are trademarks of
Bloomsbury Publishing Plc

Cover design by Eleanor Rose | Cover image: *Jaws*, 1975, dir. Steven Spielberg
© Collection Christophel / ArenaPAL www.arenapal.com

Library of Congress Cataloging-in-Publication Data
Names: Hunter, I. Q., 1964– editor. | Melia, Matthew, editor. |
Gottlieb, Carl, writer of foreword.
Title: The Jaws book : new perspectives on the classic summer blockbuster /
edited by I.Q. Hunter and Matthew Melia ; foreword by Carl Gottlieb.
Description: New York, NY : Bloomsbury Academic, 2020. |
Includes bibliographical references and index.
Identifiers: LCCN 2020009263 | ISBN 9781501347528 (hardback) |
ISBN 9781501347542 (pdf) | ISBN 9781501347535 (ebook)
Subjects: LCSH: Jaws (Motion picture : 1975) | Thrillers (Motion
pictures)–United States–History and criticism. | Action and adventure
films–United States–History and criticism. | Horror films–United
States–History and criticism. | Motion pictures–Production and
direction–United States. | Motion pictures–United
States–History–20th century.
Classification: LCC PN1997.J343 J39 2020 | DDC 791.43/72–dc23
LC record available at https://lccn.loc.gov/2020009263

ISBN: HB: 978-1-5013-4752-8
PB: 978-1-5013-7386-2
ePDF: 978-1-5013-4754-2
eBook: 978-1-5013-4753-5

Typeset by Newgen KnowledgeWorks Pvt. Ltd., Chennai, India

To find out more about our authors and books visit www.bloomsbury.com
and sign up for our newsletters.

Contents

Illustrations

Tables

Foreword

Carl Gottlieb

Once upon a time in Hollywood a long long time ago in a different galaxy, there was something called the Studio System. It was already failing but still in operation when Universal Studios and the Zanuck/Brown Company agreed that Peter Benchley's best-selling novel *Jaws* would make a good summer popcorn movie. They also agreed that an emerging talent named Steven Spielberg, already under contract to the studio, would be the right guy to direct it. Steven, in turn, thought I should be in the film – as an actor and television comedy writer with improvisational experience, I could help out with crowd scenes and work with local actors who had little or no experience.

At the same time, Steven wanted very much to rewrite the existing script, and we discussed it in detail with an eye towards how we'd change it. Three weeks before principal photography was to begin, I met with Richard Zanuck and David Brown and Steven Spielberg at the Bel-Air hotel for a Sunday brunch, which turned into high tea after we had spent hours discussing the script. It was only twenty days before commencement of principal photography and hardly enough time to rework the entire screenplay.

It was agreed that Steven and I had a good take on the revisions, so I quit my job as a story editor of a successful TV series (*The Odd Couple*), got on a plane with Steven to Boston and Martha's Vineyard, Massachusetts, and began immediately reworking, rethinking and rewriting the screenplay. The process would continue through months of anguished technical difficulties and the resulting screenplay as filmed became the movie we all know as *Jaws*, and which I have come to think of as the Fish Movie that changed my life.

For 'The Record', a large part of which you are holding in your hands in this volume: In the summer of 1974, when *Jaws* was made, it was a studio picture made as a popcorn summer movie to be released in 1975, filling out a release schedule that was conventional for the times. What happened next could not have been predicted, was unforeseen and changed movie history and exhibition patterns for the next 45 years – the movie doubled its budget and schedule and jeopardized the careers of everyone connected to it. How, Why, Who and What actually happened is explored here in refreshing academic detail, by dedicated scholars of film-making. Enjoy!

Carl Gottlieb co-wrote *Jaws, Jaws 2* and *Jaws 3-D*, as well as *The Jerk, Dr. Detroit* and *Caveman*, which he also directed. *The Jaws Log*, his classic account of the film's production, is the biggest selling 'making of' book in publishing history.

Acknowledgements

The editors would like to thank all the contributors to *The Jaws Book* for their patience, enthusiasm, timely response to enquiries and the high quality of their chapters.

Nine chapters in *The Jaws Book* began as presentations at the *Jaws 40th Anniversary Symposium* on 17 June 2015 at De Montfort University, Leicester, UK. We wish to thank DMU's Cinema and Television History Research Institute (CATHI) and Centre for Adaptations for generously funding the symposium and thereby making this book possible. Thanks are also due to Nicholas Blatt, Callum Coombe, Elizabeth Castaldo Lundén, Daniel Massie, Adam O'Brien and Conor Wigert, who presented excellent papers at the symposium, and especially to Carl Gottlieb, who gave a memorably gracious, witty and informative interview via Skype and contributed a Foreword to *The Jaws Book*.

We would like to express our sincere gratitude to Katie Gallof at Bloomsbury for commissioning *The Jaws Book* and being the most supportive and understanding of editors and to Erin Duffy for seeing the book through to publication.

Special thanks to Wieland Schwanebeck, in whose edited collection, *Der weisse Hai Revisited: Steven Spielbergs Jaws und die Geburt eines amerikanischen Albtraums* (Berlin: Bertz + Fischer, 2015), Chapters 13 and 14 originally appeared. They are reprinted here with Wieland's kind permission, in translated and slightly revised versions.

Notes on Contributors

Nathan Abrams is Professor in Film at Bangor University where he also directs the Centre for Film, Television and Screen Studies. His most recent books are *Stanley Kubrick: New York Jewish Intellectual* (2018) and (with Robert Kolker) *Eyes Wide Shut: Stanley Kubrick and the Making of His Final Film* (2019). He is also editing (with I. Q. Hunter) *The Bloomsbury Companion to Stanley Kubrick*.

Emilio Audissino is a film scholar and a film musicologist at the University of Southampton, who holds one PhD in History of Visual and Performing Arts from the University of Pisa, Italy, and one PhD in Film Studies from the University of Southampton, UK. He specializes in Hollywood and Italian cinema, and his interests are film analysis, screenwriting, film style and technique, comedy, horror and film sound and music. He has published journal articles, book chapters and encyclopaedia entries on the history and analysis of films from the silent era to contemporary cinema. He is the author of the monograph *John Williams's Film Music: 'Jaws', 'Star Wars', 'Raiders of the Lost Ark' and the Return of the Classical Hollywood Music Style* (2014), the first book-length study in English on the composer, and the editor of the collection of essays, *John Williams. Music for Films, Television and the Concert Stage* (2018). His book *Film/Music Analysis. A Film Studies Approach* (2017) concerns a method to analyse music in films that blends neoformalism and gestalt psychology. He is also an active screenwriter.

Warren Buckland is Reader in Film Studies at Oxford Brookes University. He is the author of *Directed by Steven Spielberg: Poetics of the Contemporary Hollywood Blockbuster* (2006). His other publications include *Wes Anderson's Symbolic Storyworld* (2019); two edited collections on puzzle films, *Hollywood Puzzle Films* (2014) and *Puzzle Films: Complex Storytelling in Contemporary Cinema* (2009); plus several volumes on film theory, including *The Routledge Encyclopedia of Film Theory* (co-edited with Edward Branigan, 2014), *Film Theory: Rational Reconstructions* (2012), *Studying Contemporary American Film* (co-authored with Thomas Elsaesser, 2002) and *The Cognitive Semiotics of Film* (2000).

Vincent Campbell is an associate professor of media and communication at the University of Leicester. He has written articles on science documentaries for journals such as *Environmental Communication* and *Public Understanding of Science* and is the author of *Science, Entertainment and Television Documentary* (2016).

Robert Geal is Lecturer in Film and Television Studies at the University of Wolverhampton, UK. He has published papers and book chapters on film adaptation; debates in film theory; representations of race in American television; gender and sexuality in animation; and spectacle in science fiction in journals including *Literature/ Film Quarterly*, *New Review of Film and Television Studies*, *Film International* and *Adaptation*.

Sheldon Hall is a Senior Lecturer in Stage and Screen Studies at Sheffield Hallam University, UK. He has contributed to many books and journals on aspects of American and British history and is the author of *Zulu: With some Guts behind It – The Making of the Epic Movie* (2014), co-author of *Epics, Spectacles, and Blockbusters: A Hollywood History* (2010) and co-editor of *Widescreen Worldwide* (2010). He is currently writing *Armchair Cinema: Feature Films on British Television* for publication by Tomahawk Press.

I.Q. Hunter is Professor of Film Studies at De Montfort University, Leicester, UK, author of *British Trash Cinema* (2013) and *Cult Film as a Guide to Life* (2016), and editor or co-editor of twelve books, including *Pulping Fictions* (1996), *Trash Aesthetics* (1997), *British Science Fiction Cinema* (1999), *British Comedy Cinema* (2012), *Science Fiction Across Media: Adaptation/Novelization* (2013) and *The Routledge Companion to British Cinema* (2017). He is currently co-editing *The Bloomsbury Companion to Stanley Kubrick* (2021) with Nathan Abrams and writing *Psychomania* (2021) for Auteur's Devil's Advocates series.

Neil Jackson is Senior Lecturer in Film Studies at the University of Lincoln, UK and is the co-editor of *Snuff: Real Death and Screen Media* (2016). He recently contributed 'Bigger Than a Payphone, Smaller Than a Cadillac' to *Grindhouse: Cultural Exchange on 42nd Street and Beyond* (edited by Austin Fisher and Johnny Walker) and an article on *Forced Entry* (1972) to the *Porn Studies* journal. He has also contributed an article on the cultural significance of the pornographer to *The Routledge Companion to Media, Sex and Sexuality* (2018) (edited by Clarissa Smith, Feona Attwood and Brian McNair). He has also recently contributed the two-part article, 'Sex Work at the BBFC', to the *Screening Sex* academic blog (www.screeningsex.com). His chapter 'Hardcore and Rough on the Outside' will soon appear in *Shockers!: The '70s Cinema of Trash, Terror and Sexploitation* (edited by Xavier Mendik and Julian Petley) and his article on *A Serbian Film* (2010) will appear in *New Blood: Framing Horror in the 21st Century* (edited by Eddie Falvey, Joe Hickinbottom and Jonathan Wroot). He is currently preparing *Combat Shocks*, a study of the representation of the Vietnam War in exploitation cinema, for Bloomsbury.

Peter Krämer is a Senior Research Fellow in Cinema and TV in the Leicester Media School at De Montfort University (Leicester, UK). He is the author or editor of nine academic books, including *The New Hollywood: From Bonnie and Clyde to Star Wars* (2005) and *The Hollywood Renaissance: Revisiting American Cinema's Most Celebrated Era* (2018, edited with Yannis Tzioumakis).

Matthew Leggatt is Lecturer in English and American Literature at the University of Winchester. His recent publications include the monograph *Cultural and Political*

Nostalgia in the Age of Terror (2018) and the journal article 'Another World Just out of Sight: Remembering or Imagining Utopia in Emily St. John Mandel's *Station Eleven*' (2018). He is currently editing a collection on nostalgia in contemporary film and television for SUNY.

Felix Lempp currently works as a research assistant in the German Department at the University of Hamburg. He holds an MA degree in German Literature from the Albert-Ludwigs-Universität Freiburg (2016) and passed the first state examination for German and History at the Catholic University of Eichstätt-Ingolstadt (2013). His research interests include making of narratives in various media, the theory and practice of contemporary drama and theatre, spatial theory in literary studies and intercultural literature.

Kathleen Loock is a postdoctoral researcher at the John F. Kennedy Institute for North American Studies, Freie Universität Berlin. She has co-edited the collection *Film Remakes, Adaptations, and Fan Productions: Remake/Remodel* (with Constantine Verevis, 2012), edited the special issues 'Serial Narratives' for *LWU: Literatur in Wissenschaft und Unterricht* (2014) and 'American TV Series Revivals' for *Television & New Media* (2017), and co-edited the special issue 'Exploring Film Seriality' for *Film Studies* (with Frank Krutnik, 2017). Her other publications include journal articles and book chapters on film remakes, sequels and seriality in film and television. She is currently writing a book on the cultural and industrial history of Hollywood's remaking practice.

Matthew Melia is a Senior Lecturer in Film, English Literature and Media at Kingston University, UK. His research interests lie in the work of Stanley Kubrick and Ken Russell and he is currently working on the production history of *A Clockwork Orange* and Russell's unmade films and projects. He is also currently putting together the book *Refocus: The Films of Ken Russell* (2021). He also has a personal and academic interest in cult cinema and the western and is a contributor to the forthcoming book *Reframing Cult Westerns: From The Magnificent Seven to The Hateful Eight* (2020).

Nigel Morris retired from the University of Lincoln in 2019 as Associate Professor in Media Theory after two decades in the School of Film and Media. He wrote *The Cinema of Steven Spielberg: Empire of Light* (2007) and edited *A Companion to Steven Spielberg* (2017) and a Spielberg special issue of the *New Review of Film and Television Studies* (2009). Deviser of Lincoln's BA (Hons) in Film & Television, he has published on fiction film, national cinemas and broadcasting. Current research includes a proposed monograph exploring realism in film and television fiction.

Murray Pomerance is an independent scholar living in Toronto. He is the author of *Virtuoso: Film Performance and the Actor's Magic* (2019), *A Dream of Hitchcock* (2019), *Cinema, If You Please: The Memory of Taste, the Taste of Memory* (2018) and numerous other titles. He edits the 'Horizons of Cinema' series at SUNY and the 'Techniques of the Modern Image' series at Rutgers.

Daniel Varndell teaches English Literature at the University of Winchester, UK. He is the author of *Hollywood Remakes: Deleuze and the Grandfather Paradox* (2014) and has published more recently on the films of Hal Hartley and Michael Haneke and on the screen performances of John Barrymore and Peter Sellers. His forthcoming monograph looks at etiquette and torture in film performance.

Linda Ruth Williams is Professor of Film at Exeter University and Co-Investigator of the AHRC-funded research project Calling the Shots: Women and Contemporary UK Film Culture 2000–2015. She has written five books, including *The Erotic Thriller in Contemporary Cinema* (2005) and the forthcoming *Steven Spielberg's Children*, as well as editing and co-edited several other volumes including *Contemporary American Cinema* (2005). She researches gender and cinema, post-1960 American cinema, censorship and sexuality, and contemporary British film culture. Since 2007 she has co-curated the *Screenplay* Film Festival in Shetland, has also co-curated film seasons at the NFT Southbank, was one of the founders of the New Forest Film Festival and has served as chair of the Edinburgh International Film Festival Short Film Jury and as a Jury member at the Strasbourg European Fantastic Festival and the Golden Trailer Awards. In 2019 she was visiting fellow at Corpus Christi College, Cambridge, and visiting scholar of the Centre for Film and Screen, Cambridge University.

Introduction

I. Q. Hunter and Matthew Melia

This year Steven Spielberg's *Jaws* (1975), one of the most popular and important films in the history of Hollywood, turns 45.

Widely regarded as the first 'summer blockbuster', *Jaws* grossed $7.06 million in the three days after its release on 20 June 1975, went into profit after ten days and would go on to gross $260 million domestically.[1] By 10 September 1975, it had beaten records set by *The Sound of Music* (1965) and *The Godfather* (1972) and become the first film to earn over $100 million in domestic rentals (the money paid by exhibitors to the distributor).[2] Overtaking *The Exorcist* (1973) as the most successful film of all time, *Jaws* eventually grossed around $480 million worldwide[3] and set the scene for a new type of 'high-concept' action film, one capable of 'being reduced successfully to a single image' and designed for ease of marketing to the widest possible audience.[4] After the success of *Jaws* and then *Star Wars* (1977), which surpassed *Jaws* with a worldwide gross of $775 million,[5] fantasy blockbusters in the mode of what Peter Krämer calls 'the family-adventure movie' became the defining Hollywood output.[6] Such big-budget 'event' films would become a Spielberg trademark in films like *Close Encounters of the Third Kind* (1977), *E.T.: The Extra-Terrestrial* (1982) and *Jurassic Park* (1993), the film that came closest to recapturing *Jaws*' blend of horror, suspense and nature run wild.

The significance of *Jaws* to American cinema cannot be over-emphasized. *Jaws* launched the career of the most successful director in history – after its success Columbia green-lit *Close Encounters* and Spielberg would get final cut for the rest of his career[7] – and set a vertiginously high standard for blockbuster entertainment. Yet even though *Jaws*' production history and promotion strategies have received wide critical coverage, few books are devoted exclusively to analysing the film itself.[8] In fact till recently little scholarship – let alone sympathetic scholarship – addressed issues of form and meaning in Spielberg's films as opposed to their commercial impact and supposed complicity in dumbing down Hollywood.[9]

The Jaws Book takes a fresh look at the original summer blockbuster, questioning some myths, analysing themes and formal strategies, and tracking the legendary film's cultural footprint. In the current age of mega-expensive and expansive digital cinematic universes and fast and furious franchising, the time is right for new perspectives on this much loved classic movie that not only kept people off the beaches but decisively moved the needle of American popular cinema and culture.

Selling the shark

Peter Benchley's first novel, *Jaws*, was still in galleys when up-and-coming producers, Richard Zanuck and David Brown, paid $175,000 for the film rights, including $25,000 for Benchley to write the screenplay.[10] Steven Spielberg, whose first feature, *The Sugarland Express* (1974), was produced by Zanuck and Brown, came across the galley proofs in their office and asked for a copy.[11] Armed with concept drawings by production designer Joe Alves, Zanuck and Brown pitched the movie to Universal, with which they had a distribution deal, hired Spielberg to direct and started pre-production even before the book's publication in January 1974.[12]

Although *Jaws* the novel became a bestseller and shifted three and a half million copies by early 1975, *Jaws* the movie was nevertheless a risky production.[13] Spielberg was still a relatively young contract director at Universal, albeit with two TV movies behind him, *Duel* (1971) and *Something Evil* (1972), as well as the as yet unreleased *The Sugarland Express*.

The lead actors had featured in some of the biggest recent hit films, but they were not themselves superstars and major box office draws. Roy Scheider was recognizable to audiences through his role in *The French Connection* (1971); Richard Dreyfuss's most notable appearance had been in *American Graffiti* (1973); and British actor Robert Shaw was best known as the villain, Red Grant, in the Bond movie, *From Russia with Love* (1963), and as Doyle Lonnegan in Zanuck and Brown's *The Sting* (1973). More worrying, *Jaws* would be the first film shot on the ocean rather than in tanks on a studio lot, and there was no guarantee that the proposed hydraulic shark would be convincing on-screen.[14]

The producers and Benchley therefore began promoting the book as soon as it was published and plugged the film relentlessly long before its release date. As Michael Pye noted in the *Sunday Times*:

> Eight months before the film opened, producers and author did the rounds of radio and TV chat shows to sell the book, already an established best seller. One month before the opening, even Verna Fields, who as editor would usually have no part in any film promotion, was on tour to sell the film. The Press coverage, with careful leaks, included a *Time* magazine front cover.[15]

Brown told Jim Harwood of *Variety*:

> We sent copies to people who talk to other people, like headwaiters and cab drivers. We adapted the artwork from the book to the artwork of the film promotion. By the time we sneaked the film in Dallas, we didn't even need to name it in the ad. We put in the logo of the sharks teeth and the swimming girl and 3000 came out in a hailstorm![16]

Zanuck and Brown dedicated a promotional tour exclusively to the novel to keep the film in the public consciousness '"during the arid space" between the finish of photography last September and the June release':[17]

Zanuck and Brown have been closely involved in promoting the paperback … The pair recently returned from a six city tour sponsored by Bantam, instead of the usual film oriented public appearances, they took the route normally used by authors, appearing in bookstores, radio-TV talkshows and interviews with literary editors.[18]

Meanwhile, Benchley wrote the first three or so drafts of the screenplay, which incorporated Spielberg's suggestions.[19] Playwright Howard Sackler then did five weeks of uncredited rewrites, instituting major changes from the novel and contributing the idea and a version of Quint's Indianapolis speech, which was subsequently reworked by John Milius (according to some accounts) and Robert Shaw.[20] At Zanuck's and Brown's insistence the book's adulterous affair between Ellen Brody and Matt Hooper and a Mafia subplot were excised to streamline the story into two acts and make it more suitable for a family audience.[21] To write the final version, Spielberg enlisted actor and television comedy writer, Carl Gottlieb, who had a small role in *Jaws* as newspaper editor, Harry Meadows.[22] Gottlieb would continue to rework the screenplay on location amid a high-pressure chaos of improvisation, daily rehearsals and nightly rewrites.[23] Some of the film's most celebrated lines were apparently ad-libbed, such as Brody's 'You're going to need a bigger boat'. In fact, Spielberg later claimed – somewhat implausibly – that

all the dialogue for *Jaws* came from improvisation because I was not one hundred percent happy with the script that I had developed and was responsible for. I was very happy with the structure, but not with some of the characterizations and dialogue. So I sat with these three talented actors at my house every day, and we improvised and rehearsed till we found a way to play the scene.[24]

In the end the screenplay was credited to Benchley and Gottlieb, though at no point did they actually collaborate.[25]

Location shooting began at Martha's Vineyard off Massachusetts in May 1974, while Ron and Valerie Taylor filmed additional footage of real great whites at Dangerous Reef, South Australia. The production was famously one of the most troubled in film history, as Gottlieb recounts in his classic first-hand account, *The Jaws Log*, and had all the ingredients for a terrific behind the scenes movie like *The Disaster Artist* (2017) or *Dolemite Is My Name* (2019).[26] (In fact, Ian Shaw, Robert's son, dramatized it in a stage play, *The Shark Is Broken*, at the Edinburgh Fringe in 2019.[27]) The shoot was extended from thirty-five days to over five months, wrapping finally in September 1974, while the budget more than doubled to $8 million.[28] There were tensions within the cast, notably between Dreyfuss and Shaw, who was frequently drunk. The mechanical shark, Bruce (named after Spielberg's lawyer), frequently refused to work, causing Spielberg to rechristen it (probably apocryphally) the 'Great White Turd'. Bruce's failure to perform was ultimately to the film's benefit. As Spielberg said, keeping the shark mostly off-screen made him work less like Ray Harryhausen and more like Alfred Hitchcock,[29] so that *Jaws* became a 'less-you-see-the-more-you-get-thriller'.[30]

After some cuts to mollify the censors *Jaws* was released with a remarkably lenient PG rating and a warning on the poster that the film might be 'too intense' for minors. Reviews were cautious. Many top critics, such as Roger Ebert, recognized Spielberg's mastery of technique and storytelling: '*Jaws* is a sensationally effective action picture, a scary thriller that works all the better because it's populated with characters that have been developed into human beings we get to know and care about.'[31] Others, like Molly Haskell in *The Village Voice*, complained that 'you feel like a rat, being given shock treatment',[32] while Charles Champlin of the *Los Angeles Times* hated the film as 'a coarse-grained and exploitive work which depends on excess for its impact' and called Shaw a 'Poor Man's Captain Ahab'.[33] Penelope Gilliatt in *The New Yorker* unfavourably compared *Jaws* with *Rollerball* (1975), which came out five days before. She wrote:

> The scriptwriters are Peter Benchley and Carl Gottlieb. The stars (one swallowed) are Robert Shaw, Richard Dreyfuss and Roy Scheider. The shark is plastic. The film is punk ... *Jaws* is a foolish exercise in special effects, not to be mistaken for sci-fi; 'Rollerball' is ideological sci-fi, but politically as purblind as any film dealing in augury as I have seen' both films are dependent on sorts of grossness, lassitude, and blood lust that they break their necks to create in us. Without our compliance, which we could contemplate withholding, they would be non-negotiable goods.[34]

Jaws nevertheless quickly became a cultural phenomenon. Soon after its release Pye commented on the film's ubiquity and what he termed '*Jaws*-consciousness', noting the role of the studio in managing public awareness of the film through promotions and tie-in merchandising (an area that *Star Wars* would develop exponentially):

> On the back of the shark, Universal studios, who made the film, have launched T shirts, bike bags, beach towels, pyjamas, knee stockings and plastic cups; outside New York, a discotheque called *Jaws* has opened, complete with stuffed shark; real estate advertisements in Los Angeles feature natural lakes with a guarantee 'No Jaws Here'
> ... The Studio has meticulously counted 35 political cartoons based on the *Jaws* poster in which the Shark has played roles from Ronald Reagan to Soviet submarines, and the innocent victim has been President Ford, the Statue of Liberty, Individual Rights and Congressional Ineffectiveness ... Unofficial merchants have offered plastic shark's fins for wearing on the back while swimming, shark jaws at $50 (£23) and ice cream flavours named Finnilla, Jawberry and Sharkalate.[35]

Three days prior to the film's opening, the studio 'unleashed its TV advertising campaign nationwide to cover all 464 cinemas [409 in the US and 55 in Canada] where the film was to open'.[36] Universal spent $1.8 million on pre-release advertising and $700,000 on TV spots.[37] This concentrated 'three day blitz' of 'front-loading' was intended to 'knock the nation over the head' – a strategy that the studio considered a success.[38] Rather than a staggered release to build an audience by word of mouth, the film was opened wide, a policy of saturation booking more usually associated with exploitation cinema. This is credited as one of the film's key innovations, though an initial intention to open even wider in 800–1000 cinemas simultaneously was scrapped.[39] In fact none of these strategies was new but the campaign brought them together 'into an eye-catching strategic synthesis and exploited them to the maximum'.[40] As a result,

> *Jaws* became the definitive modern blockbuster as both large-scale production value and box office attraction, profiting from enormous promotion and publicity as well as ancillary benefits ... *Jaws* doubled the stock value of MCA, Universal Studio's owner, which had already risen following positive previewing.[41]

Jaws won Oscars for sound mixing, John Williams's score and Verna Fields's editing – she was widely rumoured by insiders to have 'saved the film'[42] – though it lost to *One Flew over the Cuckoo's Nest* (1975) in the category of Best Picture. Remarkably, Spielberg was not even nominated as best director.

Interpreting and assessing *Jaws*

The film's success and the ensuing *Jaws*mania suggested that it had tapped into *something* significant and reviewers were eager to read it as a zeitgeist movie.

The secret to the film's success lies in the simplicity of the pulp material, which included, as David Brown put it, 'A little bit of *Peyton Place*, a hint of Moby Dick, and a dollop of underwater *Godfather*', but it also draws from the great American literary tradition.[43] Its narrative of man-against-nature owes much to the myth of the frontier and the wilderness as well as Hemingway's *The Old Man and the Sea* (1951), Melville's *Moby-Dick* (1851) and maybe even Jack London's *Call of the Wild* (1903). *Jaws* engages both high and low cultural taste. In many ways, it is an updated 1950s exploitation 'creature feature'.

Gottlieb has admitted the influence of both William Castle's gimmicky horror movies and *The Thing from Another World* (1951),[44] while Spielberg said they were simply trying to make a Roger Corman picture.[45] Like *Godzilla* and other 1950s monsters, the shark comes to embody the anxieties and fears of the nuclear age and the devastation of the atom bomb, which Quint helped to deliver in 1945. At the same time *Jaws* belongs to the early 1970s 'revenge of nature' horror cycle along with *Frogs* (1972) and *Phase IV* (1974), though it is striking that contemporary reviews didn't refer to it as a horror film; Roger Ebert, for example, called it an adventure film and Vincent Canby, science fiction.[46] *Jaws* also plausibly aligns with the disaster movie cycle that began with *Airport* (1970) and peaked with *The Towering Inferno* (1974) and *Earthquake* (1974), and it inspired such hybrids of the revenge of nature and disaster cycles as *King Kong* (1976) and *The Swarm* (1978).[47] Indeed this generic indeterminacy – adventure, horror, science fiction, small-scale disaster film, Hitchcockian thriller – doubtless increased *Jaws*' box office appeal because, as Nigel Morris remarks, it avoided alienating potential viewers ... Hybridity ... offers a potentially wider tonal range, possibly enriching the permutations of emotional, visceral or intellectual impact for any individual viewer – as the hugely varying range of critical interpretations seems to confirm – while ensuring different but compatible satisfactions, and hence a successful excursion, for couples and groups.[48]

Jaws quickly attracted deeper readings of varying plausibility from critics seeking cultural and political significance in its massive success.[49] This 'feeding frenzy for semioticians' inspired many a 'half-assed autopsy' – as Mayor Vaughn puts it – on the fish, the director and the audience.[50] Critics have seen in the film an archetypal confrontation between man and uncontrollable nature that plays upon primal fears such as the engulfing sea and the unique horror of being eaten. Freudian subtexts are certainly easy to spot. Consider the image of a giant phallic shark ripping into a naked girl in the opening scene while a boy lies drunk on the beach moaning 'I'm coming, I'm coming'. Propelled by the unforgettable threatening (chomping) two-note heartbeat of John Williams's score, *Jaws* reaches down into our unconscious and disturbs anxieties around parenthood, childhood, gender and masculinity, sexuality, rape and castration. As Mark Kermode wrote at the time of *Jaws*' fortieth anniversary:

> First things first; *Jaws* is not about a shark. It may have a shark in it – and indeed all over the poster, the soundtrack album, the paperback jacket and so on. It may have scared a generation of cinemagoers out of the water for fear of being bitten in half by the 'teeth of the sea'. But the underlying story of *Jaws* is more complex than the simple terror of being eaten by a very big fish.[51]

Interpretations of the film particularly linked it to Watergate and the Vietnam War. After all it was released in the same year as the war drew to a close and the year after the resignation of President Richard Nixon, who is embodied in the film by lookalike Mayor Vaughn and his attempted cover-up of the shark attacks. Vietnam is allegorized, perhaps, in the scenario of American masculinity out of its depth against an unseen enemy, and the traumatized home front, by the death of Alex Kinter and his mother's grief at officialdom's indifference to the lives of the young (see Melia's chapter). Or maybe, as Fidel Castro declared, the film is in fact a cunning metaphor for capitalism, with the Mayor and the shark equally amoral and rapacious in tearing apart the American Dream.[52] Critics dwelled too on the sexual politics of a 'movie in which sex and violence are, if not indistinguishable forms of oral aggression, then certainly the source of kindred thrills' and diagnosed symptoms of misogyny and anti-feminist backlash (see Morris's chapter).[53] Consensus has gelled around the film's conservatism and nostalgia for the certainties of the patriarchal family: 'Today – especially in light of Spielberg's obsessive focus on the defence and reconstitution of the nuclear family throughout his subsequent films – *Jaws*' reauthorisation of a conservatively conceived middle-class patriarchal masculinity ... seems very much more apparent'.[54]

The unprecedented box office success of *Jaws* incited countless imitations and encouraged trends towards 'sequelitis' and franchising. The first sequel *Jaws 2* (1978), essentially a teen film, generated over $50 million in rentals and was the fifth highest earning film of the year.[55] *Jaws 3-D* (1983), on which Gottlieb also worked, was an excuse to fit a sequel around the latest cinematic fad. The final sequel, the awful but endearingly quirky *Jaws: The Revenge* (1987), asked the audience to buy into the conceit that the original shark's family was pursuing a vendetta against the Brodys (see Loock's chapter).[56] Meanwhile, unlicensed rip-off 'Jawsploitation' films proliferated from the United States (*Grizzly* [1976], *Piranha* [1978], *Orca* [1977]) to Mexico (*Tintorera* [1977]) and Italy (*Tentacles* [1977] and *The Last Shark* [1981], which copied *Jaws* so closely that Universal sued).[57] *Jaws* partly inspired the slasher film cycle of the late 1970s and early 1980s – the extended point-of-view shot that opens *Halloween* (1978) resembles the shark's-eye perspective at the start of *Jaws*.[58] *Alien* (1979) – essentially 'Jaws-in-Space' – also showcases a killer motivated by pure instinct, delays full view of the creature and relies on a variety of Hitchcockian scare-tactics. Though *Jaws* itself escaped the indignity of being remade, the *Jaws*ploitation film has re-emerged since the 1990s to take advantage of the cheapness and convenience of digital special effects, with such films as *Deep Blue Sea* (1999), *The Reef* (2010), *Bait* (2012), the *Sharknado* series (2013–18), *The Shallows* (2016), *47 Meters Down* (2017) and *The Meg* (2018).

While *Jaws* has now achieved classic status – and a 98 per cent Rotten Tomatoes score – its place in film history is more ambiguous, at any rate from the perspective of many film scholars. The 'New Hollywood' that is conventionally dated to *Bonnie and Clyde* (1967) and *The Graduate* (1967) is sometimes divided into two periods, roughly a Golden Age 'Renaissance' of radical films from 1967 to 1975 followed by a populist 'New New Hollywood' kick-started by *Jaws*, *Star Wars* and family-friendly hits like *Grease* (1978) and *Superman* (1978).[59] *Jaws* has in fact many elements of the earlier, edgier period, such as violence, exploitation influences, a largely male cast and a focus on testing masculinity, but its happy ending and the defeat of threats to the nuclear family look forward to the later family-adventure movies (see Krämer's chapter). Many scholars and critics have blamed *Jaws* and *Star Wars* for ushering in a reconstituted and much more conservative studio system churning out multiplex superhits for kids and fixated by opening weekends (see Nigel Morris's chapter). Effectively ending the critically lionized Renaissance of the early 1970s, *Jaws* supposedly marked the decline into what Robin Wood, most scathing of these politically minded critics, called the 'Lucas-Spielberg Syndrome' whose ideological project is to infantilize both films and filmgoers.[60] According to Wood, in 'films catering to the desire for regression to infantilism',[61] Spielberg's sincerity is 'unaccompanied by anything one might reasonably term intelligence, and in fact incompatible with it'.[62] *Easy Riders, Raging Bulls*, Peter Biskind's popular history of the New Hollywood, repeated the charge for the benefit of a wider readership. Spielberg and Lucas, he wrote, 'were infantilising the audience, reconstituting the spectator as child, then overwhelming him and her with sound and spectacle, obliterating irony, aesthetic self-consciousness, and critical reflection'.[63] The result, according to Jonathan Kirshner, was the cultural downgrading of cinema and the irksome sidelining of critical gatekeepers:

movies opening everywhere at once ... aggressively marketed and highly dependent on the first few weeks of grosses, were less reliant on the opinions of cinephiles and the influence of serious critics. Talking about movies, and, worse, arguing about them, would become less important.[64]

Despite scholars' long-established condescension towards Spielberg, hostility towards his films has diminished sharply in recent years.[65] The critical standing of *Jaws* in particular is now higher than ever. Many younger film scholars, brought up on Spielberg and often unembarrassed fans of *Jaws* and *Star Wars*, retain little of the older generation's nostalgia for art cinema and visceral distaste for blockbuster movies and their mass audiences. Moreover, rather than a popcorn movie of crude shocks and jolts, *Jaws* now seems a precision-engineered masterpiece of classical film-making, whose deep focus compositions, painstakingly blocked long takes, subtly controlled palette and sensational editing have only started to be fully acknowledged and studied. Critics are finally starting to take serious account of Spielberg's precocious 'visual mastery'[66] as well as the remarkable craft of Gottlieb's screenplay, Fields's editing, Williams's music, the ensemble acting and the cinematography by Bill Butler and Michael Chapman.

The Jaws Book

Part One of *The Jaws Book* takes the long view of the film. The first two chapters examine and frankly complicate *Jaws'* status as the first summer blockbuster. Peter Krämer considers its cultural and historical position in relation to the Hollywood Renaissance of 1967–75 and the 'New New Hollywood' of blockbusters and franchises, and offers a personal reflection on his own history with the film. Assessing their statuses as adaptations and original works, he compares *Jaws* with *Star Wars*, which he judges the real game changer in engaging young woman and children as well as young men and thereby recapturing the family audience for Hollywood films. Suggesting a new line of research, Krämer highlights *Jaws'* ecological dimension and its emphasis on mothers, the maternal and Mother Earth.

Sheldon Hall's chapter uses primary archival research to question many of the myths about the film's release and distribution, such as its being the first summer blockbuster and the first major film to open wide with saturation booking and a TV advertising campaign. Arguing that *Jaws* was the culmination of existing industry trends rather than a sudden breakthrough, he clarifies the film's place in the development of Hollywood's characteristic practices.

Turning to issues of form and aesthetics, Warren Buckland extends his research into editors' contribution to the Hollywood Renaissance by analysing the problems encountered on *Jaws* by 'Mother cutter' Verna Fields.[67] Referencing the normative conventions described in Karel Reisz and Gavin Millar's *The Technique of Film Editing*, Buckland highlights *Jaws'* technical and formal innovations, notably the interplay of restricted narration and point-of-view shots and the meticulous use of continuity and shot flow in the final chase scene. Emilio Audissino meanwhile focuses on another Oscar-winning triumph of the film, John Williams's score, arguing that one of its key roles is to 'materialize' the shark and make up for the mechanical Bruce's technical inadequacies. He notes that the score does this with striking honesty – when we hear the celebrated *da-da-da-da* 'shark ostinato' the shark is always 'present', but when we do not, the shark is never there. Williams's 'neoclassical' score also brilliantly captures the different 'spirits' of the film's two acts: the first is a horror film with the shark as protagonist, and the second, buoyed by 'pirate music', a seaborne adventure story. Although Williams's score for *Star Wars* is usually credited with reviving symphonic music in films, Audissino shows that *Jaws* was crucial for demonstrating that traditional scoring could strengthen and not merely complement narratives.

Nigel Morris's chapter provides an overview of *Jaws*' critical heritage and reveals how *Jaws* and Spielberg himself became hostages in a culture war over the fate of the New Hollywood and the ideological function of blockbuster cinema. As noted above, Spielberg's reputation especially among academic film critics used to be remarkably low, even after – indeed especially after – his rebranding as a serious *auteur* with *Schindler's List* (1993). As Morris says elsewhere, 'Spielberg, because of *Jaws*, is blamed for dumbing-down movies, and for the shortcomings of other directors' products, whether high-concept blockbusters or exploitative imitations'.[68] Morris investigates how *Jaws*, always a popular favourite in spite of critical ambivalence or disdain, achieved its current extremely high reputation even among film scholars – a reputation to which Morris's own revisionist books on Spielberg have significantly contributed. He also shows that the critical agenda on *Jaws* was rapidly established in the early reviews, especially in relation to Watergate, Vietnam and gender politics.

Murray Pomerance's richly allusive chapter, by contrast, is an 'unorthodox foray' and very deep dive into the mysteries of *Jaws*, which offers a set of new theoretical frameworks for understanding it. Taking the maw of the shark as his point of departure, Pomerance considers the film's cunningly musical manipulation of temporality as well as unexpectedly reading it in alignment with van Gogh, von Hoffmannstahl and Samuel Beckett.

Part Two of *The Jaws Book* mostly centres on interpretations, which for once do not cluster around Watergate, Vietnam and the politics of gender. With considerable wit and audacity, Nathan Abrams's chapter sets out to excavate *Jaws*' unacknowledged Jewish subtexts. Remarking that little has been written about Spielberg as director of specifically Jewish films beyond *Schindler's List* and *Munich* (2005), Abrams argues that *Jaws*, like Stanley Kubrick's films, is resplendent with coded intimations of Jewishness.[69] By 'reading Jewish', Abrams shows that *Jaws* serves up a smorgasbord of possible Jewish interpretations, from the shark representing the tough Israeli Jew in the wake of the Yom Kippur War to Hooper's role as a brave Jewish outsider coming to the rescue of the gentiles.

Linda Ruth Williams draws on her extensive research into children and family in Spielberg's films to examine how, contrary to popular belief, they are not cosy or child-friendly worlds.[70] She explains that Spielberg provocatively exploits and threatens his child characters and, in *Jaws* (as in *Jurassic Park* and others), breaks cinematic taboo by presenting them essentially as meat. At such moments, Spielberg refuses the mantle of family director and assumes the identity of an exploitation director.

Robert Geal offers a comparative discussion of *Jaws* and Spielberg's other great monster movie, *Jurassic Park*. He explores the films as theoretical battlegrounds that invite competing, conflicting and overlapping theoretical approaches, in this case poststructuralist and cognitive ones. Interrogating Stephen Heath's poststructuralist analysis of *Jaws* in the essay 'Jaws, Ideology and Film Theory' and his presentation of cinema as a machine of ideology and masochism, Geal considers *Jaws*' self-reflexivity and its challenge to the allegedly passive cinematic spectator.[71] He considers how the (visual) absence of the mechanical shark in *Jaws* and the fetishization of the dinosaurs and their technological means of creation in *Jurassic Park* are used to elicit audience reaction.

A trio of chapters sets *Jaws* in its historical and generic contexts. Matthew Leggatt interrogates the atomic and nuclear contexts of *Jaws* against the historical backdrop of the sinking of the *USS Indianapolis* recalled in Quint's monologue and analyses how the film encodes the anxieties of the Cold War and the post-Hiroshima nuclear age. *Jaws* is ultimately about confronting disaster, and as with so many of Spielberg's films the inescapable reference point is the Second World War. Daniel Varndell, by contrast, relates *Jaws* to an even most distant historical point, the nineteenth century and its Romantic tradition, which associates seafaring with 'suffering, pain, separation and loss'. Addressing themes of lostness, displacement and territoriality, as well as changing depictions of the beach, Varndell unpicks how *Jaws* updates the representation of seafaring as a voyage of self-discovery and comments on 'the inexorable expansion of capitalism' and the tensions of an increasingly globalized world.

The western is one genre to which Spielberg has so far not contributed – unless you count the opening scenes of *Indiana Jones and the Last Crusade* (1989). Matthew Melia's chapter, however, argues that the western is a definite albeit largely unacknowledged presence in *Jaws*. As well as featuring visual and aural references to classic westerns including *High Noon* (1952) and *Rio Bravo* (1959), *Jaws* is indebted to the genre's iconic frontier spaces and narratives of chivalric virtue and adventure in the wilderness. Like the revisionist westerns of the New Hollywood, such as *The Wild Bunch* (1969) and *McCabe and Mrs. Miller* (1971), *Jaws* ironizes the myths of male heroism imprinted on the genre even as it reclaims the lost romantic ideal of American masculinity represented by Hawksian male bonding.[72]

The final part of the book ventures beyond *Jaws* to address the sequels and wider questions around the film's afterlife and cultural impact. Katherine Loock uses *Jaws* as a prism for understanding the problems and politics of remaking in Hollywood sequels. After an historical analysis of 'sequelitis', she addresses the use of repetition, 'one-upmanship' and textual continuity in the *Jaws* franchise, which struggled to work meaningful variations on the hopelessly constraining set-up of man versus fish. Felix Lempp's chapter critically engages with the creation and perpetuation of myths around the film's production in Gottlieb's *The Jaws Log* and two 'making-of' documentaries. Interrogating these accounts of heroic problem-solving in the face of hostile elements and islanders and the whims of a mechanical shark, Lempp reveals how the making-ofs' narrative strategies remediate myths of the film's creation in their own visual and narrative language. The making-ofs, he argues, 'stage the very production processes they pretend to describe objectively'.

Although *Jaws* is not usually classed as a cult movie,[73] Neil Jackson's chapter offers a case study of *Jaws* as the object of a creative but distinctly ambivalent mode of cult worship. Focusing on a French fan film, *Jaws: The Sharksploitation Edit* (2009), Jackson debates how far this mischievous act of 'artistic vandalism' works as a subversive form of adaptation and relates 'its processes of textual desecration and transformation' to mainstream *Jaws*ploitation films. He asks whether such an unauthorized fan interaction re-enforces the film's cultural position or as an editorial intervention disrupts the film's narrative, structure and interpretative meanings and relocates it as grindhouse exploitation.

In the final chapter, Vincent Campbell discusses the crucial relationship between *Jaws* and nature documentaries about sharks and, in particular, the film's use as a framing device on the Discovery channel's *Shark Week*. Campbell also considers how Ron and Valerie Taylor's *Blue Water, White Death* (1971), the first documentary to record extensive footage of great white sharks on camera, not only inspired Benchley's novel but also lent a visual style to the footage that the Taylors filmed for *Jaws*. He also discusses how *Jaws*' demonization of sharks impacted, very badly indeed, on the global shark population.[74]

This book cannot hope, and does not pretend, to be comprehensive. There is still much research to be done on *Jaws*, especially research grounded in primary and archival resources. Eagerly we await, for example, empirical studies of *Jaws* fandom, audience memories, the screenplay's development and the distribution, exhibition and reception of the film outside the United States. *The Jaws Book* certainly aims to encourage such research, but the chief purpose of these new perspectives is to invite fans and scholars alike to look afresh at Spielberg's masterpiece and celebrate one of the greatest achievements of Hollywood cinema.

Notes

1   https://www.the-numbers.com/movie/Jaws#tab=box-office (accessed 9 December 2019).

2   Elizabeth Guider, '"Jaws" Phenom Took Bite of History', *Variety* 12–16 June 2006: 6. See Sheldon Hall's chapter and this useful overview: Michael Coate, 'The Game Changer: Celebrating *Jaws* on Its 40th Anniversary', *The Digital Bits*, 22 June 2015, http://thedigitalbits.com/columns/history-legacy-showmanship/remembering-jaws-40th?showall=1 (accessed 3 December 2019).

3   Nigel Morris, *The Cinema of Steven Spielberg: Empire of Light* (London: Wallflower, 2007), 44.

4   Justin Wyatt, *High Concept: Movies and Marketing in America* (Austin: University of Texas Press, 1994), 112. Cf. Marco Cucco, 'The Promise Is Great: The Blockbuster and the Hollywood Economy', *Media, Culture & Society* 3, no. 2 (2009): 219.

5   https://www.the-numbers.com/movie/Star-Wars-Ep-IV-A-New-Hope#tab=summary (accessed 3 December 2019).

6   *Jaws'* status as a 'family-adventure film' is up for debate and is discussed in Peter Krämer's chapter. On the family-adventure movie, see Krämer, 'Would You Take Your Child to See This Film? The Cultural and Social Work of the Family-Adventure Movie', in Steve Neale and Murray Smith, eds, *Contemporary Hollywood Cinema* (London: Routledge, 1998), 294–311; and Krämer, 'The Impact of *Star Wars*', *Pure Movies*, 16 March 2014, https://www.puremovies.co.uk/columns/the-impact-of-star-wars/ (accessed 4 December 2019). On the blockbuster, 'the audiovisual product that best represents today's Hollywood', see Cucco, 'The Promise Is Great'.

7   'Jaws: The Groundbreaking Summer Blockbuster'.

8   On *Jaws* the film rather than its production history, see Nigel Andrews, *Jaws: The Ultimate A-Z (Bloomsbury Movie Guide)* (London: Bloomsbury, 1999); Antonia Quirke, *Jaws* (London: British Film Institute, 2002); and Wieland Schwanebeck, ed., *Der weisse Hai Revisited: Steven Spielbergs Jaws und die Geburt eines amerikanischen Albtraums* (Berlin: Bertz + Fischer, 2015).

9   Notable recent books on Spielberg include Morris, *The Cinema of Steven Spielberg*; Lester D. Friedman, *Citizen Spielberg* (Urbana: University of Illinois Press, 2006); Warren Buckland, *Directed by Steven Spielberg: Poetics of the Contemporary Hollywood Blockbuster* (New York: Continuum, 2006); James Kendrick, *Darkness in the Bliss-Out: A Reconsideration of the Films of Steven Spielberg* (New York: Bloomsbury Academic, 2014); Adrian Schober and Debbie Olson, eds, *Children in the Films of Steven Spielberg* (Lanham, MD: Lexington, 2016); Molly Haskell, *Steven Spielberg: A Life in Films* (New Haven, CT: Yale University Press, 2017); Adam Barkman and Antonio Sanna, eds, *A Critical Companion to Steven Spielberg* (Lanham, MD: Lexington, 2019); Linda Ruth Williams, *Steven Spielberg's Children* (New Brunswick, NJ: Rutgers University Press, forthcoming); and, the most comprehensive, Nigel Morris, ed., *A Companion to Steven Spielberg* (Chichester: Wiley Blackwell, 2017).

10 Carl Gottlieb, *The Jaws Log*, 30th Anniversary Expanded Edn (London: Newmarket, 2005, Kindle), Chapter Three; Howard Sounes, *Seventies: The Sights, Sounds and Ideas of a Brilliant Decade* (London: Simon & Schuster, 2006), 222–3. See also Ted Morgan, 'Sharks: The Making of a Best Seller', in Robert Atwan, Barry Orton and William Vesterman, eds, *American Mass Media: Industries and Issues* (New York: Random House, 1978), 140–50.

11 Joseph McBride, *Steven Spielberg: A Biography* (New York: Faber & Faber, 1997), 230.

12 Dennis L. Prince, *Joe Alves: Designing Jaws* (London: Titan, 2019), 12.

13 Andrews, *Jaws*, 20.

14 Prince, *Joe Alves*, 65.

15 Michael Pye, 'Enter the Shark', *Sunday Times*, 3 August 1975. Unpaginated clipping on *Jaws* microfiche in BFI (British Film Institute) Reuben Library.

16 *Variety*, 4 June 1975. Unpaginated clipping on *Jaws* microfiche in BFI (British Film Institute) Reuben Library.

17 Ibid.

18 Ibid.

19 Gottlieb, *The Jaws Log*, Chapter Four; Donald R. Mott and Cheryl McAllister Saunders, *Steven Spielberg* (London: Columbus, 1986), 32.

20 Andrews, *Jaws*, 27. Carl Gottlieb's detailed account of the speech's gestation, from Sackler's draft screenplay to Shaw's final version, is given in the expanded edition of *The Jaws Log*, note to Chapter Eleven. He is clear that Milius did *not* write the speech.

21 Sounes, *Seventies*, 223. See also I. Q. Hunter, 'Spielberg and Adaptation', in Nigel Morris, ed., *A Companion to Steven Spielberg* (Chichester: Wiley Blackwell, 2017), 212–26. At the *Jaws 40th Anniversary Symposium*, Gottlieb described the film as having (unusually) just two acts, but others, such as Warren Buckland in this book and Gottlieb himself in *The Jaws Log*, claim that there are in fact three.

22 Gottlieb, *The Jaws Log*, Chapter Five.

23 McBride, *Steven Spielberg*, 239; Mott and Saunders, *Steven Spielberg*, 33. See also John Baxter, *Steven Spielberg: The Unauthorised Biography* (London: HarperCollins, 1997), 129–32; and Friedman, *Citizen Spielberg*, 162.

24 Susan Royle, 'Steven Spielberg in His Adventures on Earth', *American Premiere*, 10 July 1982: 23–4.

25 Andrews, *Jaws*, 43.

26 As well as Gottlieb, *The Jaws Log*, these books exhaustively recount the film's production: Edith Blake, *On Location … on Martha's Vineyard: The Making of the Movie Jaws* (New York: Ballantine, 1976); Patrick Jankiewicz, *Just When You Thought It Was Safe: A Jaws Companion* (Albany: BearManor Media, 2009); and Matt Taylor, *Jaws: Memories from Martha's Vineyard*, expanded 2nd edn (London: Titan, 2012).

27 https://themalestrom.com/interviews/the-shark-is-broken-ian-shaw/ (accessed 9 December 2019).

28 Sounes, *Seventies*, 229.

29 ' "Jaws": The Groundbreaking Summer Blockbuster That Changed Hollywood, and Our Summer Vacations, Forever', *Cinephilia & Beyond*, n.d.: https://cinephiliabeyond. org/jaws-groundbreaking-summer-blockbuster-changed-hollywood-summer-vacations-forever/ (accessed 4 December 2019).

30 McBride, *Steven Spielberg*, 249.

31 Roger Ebert, review of *Jaws*, *Chicago Sun-Times*, 1 January 1975, https://www. rogerebert.com/reviews/jaws-1975 (accessed 4 December 2019).

32 Quoted in ibid., 256.

33 Champlin's original review of 20 June 1975 is archived here: https://www.latimes. com/entertainment/herocomplex/la-et-hc-jaws-original-review- 20150619-story.html (accessed 4 December 2019).

34 Penelope Gilliatt, rev. of *Jaws*, *New Yorker*, 7 July 1975. Unpaginated clipping on microfiche in BFI (British Film Institute) Reuben Library.

35 Pye, 'Enter the Shark'.

36 Ibid.

37 McBride, *Steven Spielberg*, 255.

38 Pye, 'Enter the Shark'.

39 Baxter, *Steven Spielberg*, 140; Cucco, 'The Promise Is Great', 216, 221.

40 Barry Langford, *Post-Classical Hollywood: Film, Industry, Style and Ideology since 1945* (Edinburgh: Edinburgh University Press, 2010), 156.

41 Morris, *The Cinema of Steven Spielberg*.

42 McBride, *Steven Spielberg*, 252.

43 Andrews, *Jaws*, 29.

44 Emilio Audissino, *John Williams's Film Music: Jaws, Star Wars, Raiders of the Lost Ark, and the Return of the Classical Hollywood Music Style* (Wisconsin: University of Wisconsin Press, 2014), 108.

45 Peter Biskind, *Easy Riders, Raging Bulls: How The Sex 'N' Drugs 'N' Rock 'N' Roll Generation Saved the World* (London: Bloomsbury, 1998), 265. See also Roger

Corman, with Jim Jerome, *How I Made a Hundred Movies in Hollywood and Never Lost a Dime* (Cambridge, MA: Da Capo Press, 1998), xi.

46 Jason Zinoman, *Shock Value: How a Few Eccentric Outsiders Gave Us Nightmares, Conquered Hollywood, and Invented Modern Horror* (London: Duckworth Overlook, 2012), 175–6.

47 See Hall's chapter and J. Hoberman, '*Nashville* contra *Jaws*, or "The Imagination of Disaster" Revisited', in Thomas Elsaesser, Alexander Horwath and Noel King, eds, *The Last Great American Picture Show: New Hollywood Cinema in the 1970s* (Amsterdam: Amsterdam University Press, 2004) 195–222.

48 Morris, *The Cinema of Steven Spielberg*, 57.

49 See Friedman, *Citizen Spielberg*, 163–4; and Morris, *The Cinema of Steven Spielberg*, 48–57.

50 Andrews, *Jaws*, 143.

51 Mark Kermode, '*Jaws*, 40 years on: "One of the truly great and lasting classics of American cinema"', *The Observer*, 31 May 2015, https://www.theguardian.com/film/2015/may/31/jaws-40-years-on-truly-great-lasting-classics-of-america-cinema (accessed 4 December 2019).

52 Andrews, *Jaws*, 118; McBride, *Steven Spielberg*, 255.

53 Hoberman, '*Nashville* contra *Jaws*', 213.

54 Langford, *Post-Classical Hollywood*, 154–5.

55 Richard Nowell, *Blood Money: A History of the First Teen Slasher Film Cycle* (New York: Continuum, 2011), 127.

56 See also I. Q. Hunter, '*Jaws: The Revenge* and the Production of Failure', *Continuum: Journal of Media and Cultural Studies*, 33, no. 6 (2019): 677–91.

57 On *Jaws*ploitation movies, see Denis Lotti, 'Mare Monstrum: il riverbero di Jaws nei sequel illegittimi: mockbuster, imitazioni, ripoff (e documentary) di produzione italiana (1976–1995)', *Cinergie, il cinema e le altri arti*, 7 (2015): 96–104, https://cinergie.unibo.it/article/view/6976/6712 (accessed 4 December 2019); and I. Q. Hunter, *Cult Film as a Guide to Life: Fandom, Adaptation and Identity* (New York: Bloomsbury, 2016), 77–96.

58 Nowell, *Blood Money*, 92–3.

59 See Peter Krämer and Yannis Tzioumakis, 'Introduction', in Krämer and Tzioumakis, eds, *The Hollywood Renaissance: Revisiting American Cinema's Most Celebrated Era* (New York: Bloomsbury, 2018), xvii. See also Peter Krämer, *The New Hollywood: From Bonnie and Clyde to Star Wars* (London: Wallflower, 2005), 90.

60 Robin Wood, *Hollywood from Vietnam to Reagan* (New York: Columbia University Press, 1986). See also McBride, *Steven Spielberg*, 259; and Friedman, *Citizen Spielberg*, 176–9.

61 Wood, *Hollywood*, 175.

62 Ibid., 178.

63 Biskind, *Easy Riders, Raging Bulls*, 344.

64 Jonathan Kirshner, *Hollywood's Last Golden Age: Politics, Society, and the Seventies Film in America* (Ithaca: Cornell University Press, 2012), 214.

65 See Andrew M. Gordon, *Empire of Dreams: The Science Fiction and Fantasy Films of Steven Spielberg* (Lanham, MD: Rowman & Littlefield, 2008, Kindle), 'Introduction'.

66 Friedman, *Citizen Spielberg*, 169.

67 Warren Buckland, 'The Film Editors who Invented the Hollywood Renaissance: Ralph Rosenblum, Sam O'Steen and Dede Allen's *Bonnie and Clyde* (1967), in Krämer and Tzioumakis, eds, *The Hollywood Renaissance*, 19–34.

68 Morris, *The Cinema of Steven Spielberg*, 47.

69 On 'reading Jewish' with reference to Kubrick, see Nathan Abrams, ' "A Double Set of Glasses" Stanley Kubrick and the Midrashic Mode of Interpretation', in Saer Maty Ba and Will Higbee, eds, *De-Westernizing Film Studies* (London: Routledge, 2012), 141–51.

70 Williams, *Steven Spielberg's Children*. See also Linda Ruth Williams, ' "Who Am I, David?": Motherhood in Spielberg's Dramas of Family Dysfunction', in Morris, ed. *A Companion*, 243–57.

71 Stephen Heath, '*Jaws*, Ideology and Film Theory', *Times Higher Education Supplement* (26 March 1976); reprinted in Bill Nichols, ed., *Movies and Methods*, vol. 2 (Berkeley: University of California Press, 1985).

72 See also Friedman, *Citizen Spielberg*, 165–6.

73 But see the Preface to Hunter, *Cult Film*, for an autobiographical account of unabashed *Jaws* cult fandom.

74 See McBride, *Steven Spielberg*, 249; Nancy Knowlton and Wendy Benchley, 'The State of Sharks, 40 Years after *Jaws*', *Smithsonian.com* 11 August 2014, https://www.smithsonianmag.com/science-nature/state-sharks-40-years-after-jaws- 180952309/ (accessed 4 December 2019).

Part One

Production, Reception and Style

1

'She was the first': The place of *Jaws* in American film history

Peter Krämer

The forty-fifth anniversary of the original release of *Jaws* in the United States is an appropriate occasion to consider its place in American film history and also to reflect on the paths we, as film scholars, have taken to arrive at our current thinking about this movie. So I want to take this opportunity for some personal and professional reflections before – sharklike, as it were – I get to the academic 'meat' of this essay.

Where was I in June 1975? The brief answer is: *not* in the cinema watching *Jaws*. This is not altogether surprising because I was still living in West Germany at the time, where the film was released only in September 1975, and even then I, being only 14 years old, was not allowed to see it because it was rated '16'. I am not sure whether I had even *wanted* to see *Jaws*. I vaguely remember that at some point in the mid-1970s I developed an aversion against the very idea of 'big' Hollywood movies, at least among current releases.

One of the first Film Studies books I read, and one of the reasons for my decision to study film at university, was a German translation of James Monaco's *How to Read a Film* (first published in the United States in 1977). I was very pleased to find out a few years later that in 1979 Monaco had also published a book about contemporary Hollywood, *American Film Now*. It largely confirmed my distrust of Hollywood's biggest hits. Monaco's comprehensive study of the major Hollywood studios and the conglomerates they belonged to, of the ways films were made and marketed, of important aesthetic and generic trends as well as of key film-makers since the late 1960s set out to demystify American cinema: 'The current governing myth has it that we are undergoing a Hollywood Renaissance – a rebirth. Yet, it seems to me, that – for the most part – American film in the seventies has a better reputation than it deserves.'[1]

In formulating his critique, Monaco referred to *Jaws* on several occasions[2] and, referencing the name the crew had given to the film's shark, went as far as characterizing what he perceived to be the main problem with contemporary Hollywood cinema as 'the Bruce esthetic':

The Bruce esthetic is visceral – mechanical rather than human. Films like *Jaws* that fit it are machines of entertainment, precisely calculated to achieve their effect – at the box office as well as inside the theater. Their model is the amusement-park rollercoaster. ... Bruce movie machines have effectively driven out smaller, more idiosyncratic film projects of the sort that would rather interest an audience than viscerally excite it.[3]

As a film student, first in Germany and then in the UK, and as a film scholar I hardly read anything throughout the 1980s and early 1990s which did *not* critique contemporary Hollywood cinema along these or closely related lines. Then, in 1993, Thomas Schatz's wonderfully succinct and incisive chapter on 'The New Hollywood' in *Film Theory Goes to the Movies*, an important collection on contemporary American cinema, expanded and deepened Monaco's critique, using some of the same terminology, for example, when he wrote that across the 1970s, 'we see films that are increasingly plot-driven, increasingly visceral, kinetic, and fast-paced'.[4] Like Monaco, Schatz also referred to a 'renaissance' (or rather: a renaissance 'of sorts') in American cinema: 'with the 1966 breakdown of Hollywood's Production Code and the emergence in 1968 of the new ratings system ... filmmakers were experimenting with more politically subversive, sexually explicit, and/or graphically violent material'.[5] Schatz interpreted Hollywood's 'penchant for innovation in the late 1960s and early 1970s' as a sign of 'the studios' uncertainty and growing desperation' in the face of a series of catastrophic big-budget flops which had led to estimated overall losses in excess of half a billion dollars from 1969 to 1971.[6]

In Schatz's account, Hollywood's financial recovery was closely associated with a series of massive hit movies from *The Godfather* (1972) onwards, and it is this recovery and this hit series which is at the heart of what he called 'The New Hollywood', a term he used to characterize mainstream American cinema since the 1970s.[7] Even more so than Monaco, Schatz focused on the importance of *Jaws* by declaring: 'If any single film marked the arrival of the New Hollywood, it was *Jaws*.'[8] It is important to emphasize here that, like Monaco, Schatz did *not* see *Jaws* as the beginning of a new era in Hollywood history, just as the most perfect incarnation of the New Hollywood. Indeed, he noted that, '[i]n many ways, the film simply confirmed or consolidated various existing industry trends and practices', thus making sure that these trends and practices would dominate for decades to come.[9]

By the time I read Schatz's essay, I had belatedly embarked on my own investigation of Hollywood's biggest box office hits in the United States, inspired by the work of the German film historian Joseph Garncarz.[10] Finally watching the big hits from the 1970s and 1980s which I had missed during their original release, I soon identified a pattern that I thought other scholars (including Monaco and Schatz) had not paid sufficient attention to. Most of the biggest hits from 1977 onwards were films which appeared to be addressed to, and successful with, an all-inclusive family audience, comprising cinema's core audience of teenagers and young adults, as well as younger children and their parents. Because these films tended to take their characters (and their audiences) on fantastic adventures and also tended to focus on familial (or quasi-familial) relationships, I labelled them 'family-adventure movies'. Interestingly, *Jaws* and many other big hits of the decade before 1977, notably *The Exorcist* (1973), did not fit into this category, mainly because they did not seem to be addressed to, and successful with, family audiences. I did not make much of this observation at the time, but it became the foundation of much of my later work on recent American film history.

I first presented the results of my research on American hit patterns at a conference entitled 'Hollywood since the Fifties: A Post-Classical Cinema?', organized by Steve Neale at the University of Kent in July 1995. I think I was not the only scholar who experienced this conference as a turning point in scholarship on contemporary Hollywood, because it brought together a wide range of approaches and was, by and large, much less judgemental than most previous academic work on the subject. The papers presented at that conference, including my paper on family-adventure movies, were published in 1998 in the edited collection *Contemporary Hollywood Cinema*.[11] By this time, I had also published a long essay on the relationship between film and television in the United States, which not only went all the way back to the late nineteenth century but also aimed to identify an important shift in the media landscape between the 1970s and the 1980s.[12]

In addition, 1998 saw the publication, in *The Oxford Guide to Film Studies*, of an essay I had written a couple of years earlier about the long-running debates among film critics and scholars about the end of the 'classical' era in American film history and the beginning of a new era which, referring to the immediate post-war decades or to the period from the 1960s to the 1980s, had variously been labelled 'the baroque', 'Hollywood in transition', the 'Hollywood Renaissance', the 'New Hollywood' or 'post-classical' Hollywood.[13] Apart from finding that journalistic and academic commentators as well as industry insiders had talked for almost *five* decades about the end of the studio system and of classical film-making, I noticed that, in addition to Monaco and Schatz, many other scholars had made strong and compelling claims about important aesthetic and industrial shifts across the 1960s and *again* in the 1970s. Both 1967, the year in which a *Time* cover story identified a 'renaissance' in American cinema, and 1975, the year of *Jaws*, were identified as the start of new eras. Although critics saw sharp contrasts between these two different post-classical eras (1967–75 versus 1975 to the present), confusingly, both were often referred to in the literature as 'New Hollywood'.

In the late 1990s, I began with an attempt to integrate my research on American cinema since the late 1940s into a monograph, using, much as Schatz had done in 'The New Hollywood' (and Garncarz in his work on German cinema), the biggest hits at the American box office as my main focus.[14] It is at this point that I was finally willing to suggest that the periodization which had been proposed by other scholars had to be slightly amended, because the most important turning point in 1970s Hollywood cinema was the release of *Star Wars* in 1977, heralding the dominance of the family-adventure movie for decades to come, not the release of *Jaws* in 1975. I first presented this argument in 1999 at the 18th annual conference of the International Association for Media and History, which had 'Television and History' as its theme.[15] Since this particular paper was never published I want to revisit it here. In fact, the remainder of this essay follows it quite closely by first discussing major shifts in the technological, industrial and discursive context of American moviemaking in the mid-1970s, and then examining the marketing, reception and audience address of *Jaws*, before concluding with a brief analysis of the marketing, reception and audience address of *Star Wars*.

American media in the mid-1970s

The American entertainment industry is characterized by both corporate continuity and constant flux. Throughout much of the twentieth century, the same few corporations dominated the cinema, broadcasting, the record business and related industries. Yet the ways in which these corporations conceptualized their audiences and the products and services they provided for them as well as their internal organization and external alliances shifted dramatically over the years. Such shifts responded, among other things, to the opportunities afforded by new media technologies to demographic trends and to changes in the leisure time habits and preferences of the American population.[16]

The mid-1970s were a period of important change for American media industries and audiences. Until the mid-1970s, the three television networks ABC, CBS and NBC, broadcasting through their affiliate stations, had been the main providers of audiovisual entertainment for the American population. In return for reaching the majority of the population for several hours every day with advertising messages, the networks collected huge sums of money from advertisers. In order to keep audiences glued to their TV sets, the networks bought the broadcast rights for pre-recorded programmes produced by studios located in and around Los Angeles.

The biggest of these studios also produced films for theatrical release into the nation's cinemas. In fact, for studios such as Paramount, Fox, Universal, Columbia, MGM, United Artists and Warner (but *not* for Disney), the theatrical distribution of feature films was the single most important source of income. It is true that these films reached their largest audiences when shown by the networks a few years after their theatrical release, yet the licensing fees the studios received for such broadcasts were only a fraction of theatrical revenues. Thus, the big studios were dependent on the theatrical market which was highly volatile. While, after a catastrophic decline between the mid-1940s and a historical low point in 1971, overall attendance figures were beginning to recover in the mid-1970s, revenues for individual films continued to be difficult to predict, and many of the studios' most expensive movies sustained substantial losses.

A possible solution for the studios' financial fragility was new delivery systems for their product. In fact, ever since the first experimental television boom of the late 1920s, the studios had been trying to take control of various television technologies, so as to be able either to set up their own advertising-based networks or to make domestic users pay directly to the studios for filmed entertainment delivered into their homes via cable. By the 1950s, the studios had lost their battle for control of television to the existing radio networks and resigned themselves to a subsidiary role as the main programme suppliers for networks and independent TV stations while continuing to concentrate on their theatrical market.

However, technological developments in the mid-1970s gave studios another chance to gain direct access to domestic consumers. In 1975, SATCOM I, the first commercially available geostationary satellite, was launched, and transmission via this satellite allowed the Time Inc. subsidiary Home Box Office (HBO) to become the first nationwide pay-cable service, specializing in live sports and theatrical features. In 1975, Japanese consumer electronics giant Sony introduced the first affordable home video machines, which sold in large numbers and were primarily used for time-shifting (recording TV programmes for later viewing), yet also created a new market for the selling and renting of feature films. The studios' response to the emergence of these new delivery systems for their product was contradictory, seeing pay-cable and video not only as a competition for their theatrical market but also as a complementary source of income, if they could manage to get a substantial share of the money consumers were willing to pay for the viewing of feature films in the comfort of their homes. An easily overlooked, yet crucial part of Hollywood's response to new technologies was its reconceptualization of the audience, which was also based on the industry's analysis of important demographic trends.

To illustrate this, I want to discuss a prescient article published by A. D. Murphy in the entertainment industry's 'bible' *Variety* in August 1975 under the title 'Audience Demographics, Film Future'.[17] Murphy pointed out that Hollywood studios conceived of cinema and television, of the theatrical audience and the home audience, as two separate markets: the former was mostly young and dominated by males, the latter was older and dominated by females. According to Murphy, by 1975 this separation was no longer viable for two main reasons. Firstly, in the mid-1970s the baby boomers (born between 1946 and 1964) were beginning to reach the age (of about 25) at which previous generations had tended to stop going to the movies regularly. Thus, cinemas were threatened with the loss of their main audience in the late 1970s and early 1980s. However, the newly dominant group of 25- to 34-year-olds (predicted to increase by 50 per cent between 1970 and 1980) was 'bearing fewer children, and often at more advanced ages than their parents' and hence they might not stop going to the movies after all, if only Hollywood could refrain from making movies 'strictly for the young'.[18] Second, Murphy suggested that the expected rapid diffusion of pay-cable channels in the late 1970s would be based mainly on the appeal of movies, and consumption within the home, traditionally a familial space dominated by women, would therefore become ever more important for the producers of theatrical features. Murphy concluded: 'What it boils down to is that most films may again be made for a truly mass audience – a paying audience both in theatres and in homes.'[19]

Murphy's speculations were confirmed by a 1976 Gallup poll about the future uses of new media technologies.[20] The poll found that pay-TV and video were most likely to be used for film viewing. Furthermore, frequent cinemagoers would be the heaviest users of pay-TV and video, extending their interest in movies from theatres into their homes, without abandoning their cinema-going habit. Therefore, rather than concentrating on a core audience of young males, *Variety* again urged Hollywood to take the tastes of ageing baby boomers and their children into account[21] and to create an integrated cross-gender, cross-age, cross-media movie audience – in Murphy's words 'a truly mass audience'. As I now want to show, *Star Wars* perfectly fit this agenda, but *Jaws* did not.

Jaws

When *Jaws* was released in the United States on 20 June 1975, industry expectations were high. Like many of Hollywood's biggest hits up to this point, *Jaws* was based on a bestselling novel. Five million copies of the paperback edition of Peter Benchley's novel had been sold since its publication in January 1974, and sneak previews for the film had met with very positive responses.[22] *Jaws* was widely advertised on television and released in 464 cinemas at once, an unusually large number for this time, and it quickly broke all box office records in the United States.[23]

Critical responses to the film were mixed. The *New Yorker*, for example, saw *Jaws* as 'a foolish exercise in special effects' dependent on 'grossness, lassitude, and bloodlust that they break their necks to create in us'.[24] *Variety*, on the other hand, called it an '[e]xcellent filmization of the book', characterized by a 'literate screenplay' and 'consummate suspense, tension and terror'.[25] The paper also related *Jaws* to previous films about animal attacks such as *The Birds* (1963) and a resurgence in monster movies.[26] Similarly, *Time*'s cover story 'Summer of the Shark' argued that *Jaws* was 'part of a bracing revival of high adventure films and thrillers', comparing it to disaster movies such as *Earthquake* (1974) and horror films such as *The Exorcist* in terms of their emotional effectiveness, yet arguing that, unlike those films, 'it is quite a good movie', mainly because its violence was less explicit and direct: '*Jaws* is vicarious, not vicious, a fantasy far more than an assault'.[27] Still, the magazine could not help drawing a parallel between the film and its featured attraction: 'If the great white shark that terrorizes the beaches of an island summer colony is one of nature's most efficient killing machines, *Jaws* is an efficient entertainment machine.' Furthermore, the experience of the film was described in distinctly masculine terms as a courageous confrontation with one's own fears, based on identification with the film's three male protagonists: 'It is a dread dream that weds the viewer's own apprehensions with the survival of the heroes. It puts everyone in harm's way and brings the audience back alive ... [T]he only thing you have to fear is fear itself'.[28]

While the film was hugely popular, there was concern that it focused too exclusively on the cinema's core audience of young males. An audience survey published in January 1974 had characterized this core audience as follows:

> Today's movie-goer is a very special breed of individual. First of all he is an active person. He is young, above average education, above average income. He works hard and he plays hard. He is apt to find vacations so important that he considers them a necessity. He travels more. He buys books and wants to know what's going on.[29]

While the male pronoun is not used here to refer only to males, there was, as Murphy noted in *Variety*, certainly a strong male bias in the film industry's conception of its theatrical audience at that time.

Jaws can be said to address this typical (male) cinemagoer in a number of ways. Not only is the film based on a book, but, more important, both the film and the source novel carefully reference and rework one of the great classics of American literature, another archetypal story of man confronting the great white one: *Moby-Dick*. With its theme of nature taking revenge on a corrupt capitalist society, and its intricate referencing of America's deployment of nuclear bombs in the Second World War, the film also engages with topical debates about ecology and technological hubris, thus being able to flatter educated viewers. More specifically, in the rich young scientist Matt Hooper (Richard Dreyfuss) the film offers upscale viewers a direct object of identification.

Hooper is placed at one end of a spectrum of masculine types, at the other end of which the film places the archaic figure of the shark hunter Quint (Robert Shaw). Situated between these two extremes is the film's main protagonist, the displaced New York cop Martin Brody (Roy Scheider), an Everyman who has to leave his domestic surroundings behind to confront the shark and his own fear of the water. Bonding with, and learning from, both Quint and Hooper, Brody overcomes his fears, kills the shark and regains a masculinity which quiet family life and corrupt politics have threatened to take away from him. The film ends with a re-masculinized Brody chatting with his new friend Hooper, who has been stripped of all of his sophisticated technology and his arrogance, while Quint, whose archaic masculinity (based on social isolation and the desire to hunt and kill) is unsuitable for modern times, has been killed by the shark, who is a distorted mirror image of him.

Jaws, then, negotiates male desire for action outside the confines of family and community life, and it offers itself as an equivalent to the adventure that revitalizes Brody and Hooper. In the same way that Brody and Hooper have to confront the shark, viewers have to confront *Jaws*; Brody has to overcome his fear of water by going out onto the sea, and viewers have to overcome their fear of the film, in which they immerse themselves for the duration of the screening; the shark attacks its screaming victims in the water much like the film sneaks up on audiences in the dark of the auditorium, making them scream. In other words, the film suggests that Brody and Hooper's journey from civilization to nature, from safety to danger, from comfort to adventure is equivalent to the audience's journey from their homes to the cinema and from the reality of the theatre auditorium into the fantasy on the screen.

More generally, the film ingeniously inserts itself into the familiar ritual of people going on trips during their vacations. The film's action takes place in the days running up to the Fourth of July weekend, the biggest holiday weekend of the summer season, as the dialogue explicitly states, and it shows thousands of people gathering on Amity Island for fun and adventure. Unusually for Hollywood's big releases up to this point, *Jaws* was released towards the end of June, rather than during the Christmas season, and the time of its release thus exactly mirrored the time at which its action takes place, and the people gathering on the beach mirrored those gathering in the cinema auditorium. The film implicitly put forward a proposition to its audience: instead of going to the beach, spend your summer holiday with a trip to the cinema. In fact, the huge success of *Jaws* helped to turn the summer into Hollywood's primary season for the release of its big action-adventure films.

The parallels drawn in *Jaws* between the beach and the cinema, between the film characters' confrontation with the shark and the audience's confrontation with the film itself, are particularly obvious in its opening sequence, which also emphasizes the film's specific appeal to a young male audience and its potential alienation of other audience groups. Replicating the main appeal of the poster for the film, which featured a naked woman being approached from below by a huge shark, the film itself begins with a sexual tease for men and the enactment of the vicarious violation of a woman. Before any human characters appear on the screen, the viewer is forced into an optical identification with the shark, whose movements underwater the camera reproduces. The movements which are only vaguely menacing at this point will soon turn into a direct, extremely violent attack on a female. It is reasonable to suggest that this may be a particularly uncomfortable position for a female spectator to adopt.

Following the opening underwater scene, the film then shifts to a group of young people amusing themselves at night on the beach. A woman lures one of the men away from the crowd with what appears to be the promise of a sexual encounter. By leaving the crowd behind and moving closer to the water, the young man enters the realm of the film's generic fantasy, in which his fears and desires will be played out for him. This is also the suggestion made by the poster trying to lure prospective audiences into the cinema. In the film, the woman undresses and jumps into the water, while the young man is too drunk to get undressed and follow her. The woman is then attacked by the shark, which, as we later find out, bites off the lower part of her body. While the woman screams in the water, the young man lies on the beach, mumbling: 'I'm coming. I'm coming.' The shark attacks precisely where the young man cannot perform; the young woman's hoped-for screams of ecstasy are replaced by screams of pain and terror. At the end of this violent mockery of a sexual encounter, the young man rolls over and falls asleep.

Thus, on all levels, *Jaws* appealed very specifically to adolescent males and young male adults, and at the same time the film was in danger of alienating other audience segments. Women are initially introduced as sexual teases and potential victims of shark attacks and do not have much of a role in the rest of the film, which focuses on the trials and tribulations of its three male protagonists, their encounters with the shark, their bonding with each other and their posturing in front of each other, which is most comically realized in the scene where the drunken men compare shark-inflicted wounds and Brody has not much to show (except perhaps his scar from an appendicitis). *Woman's Wear Daily* commented that *Jaws* was '[t]he perfect movie for anyone with a larger-than-life castration complex'.[30] Thus, the film appeared to be too hostile to, or ignorant of, women and too obsessed with male fears and desires to be of much interest to female audiences.

Furthermore, in audience surveys women have consistently expressed their dislike of horror and other action-oriented genres as well as X-rated material and their preference for comedy, love stories, drama and musicals.[31] In the above quoted 1974 survey, for example, when asked which kind of movie they were most likely to choose when going to the cinema, 32 per cent of the women said comedy (as opposed to 23 per cent of the men) and 26 per cent said love story (as opposed to 2 per cent of the men); only 7 per cent listed westerns (as opposed to 22 per cent of the men) and less than 0.5 per cent listed war films (as opposed to 9 per cent of the men). When asked about their least preferred type of film, 43 per cent of the women said X-rated movies (as opposed to 25 per cent of the men), 26 per cent said horror (as opposed to 21 per cent of the men) and 14 per cent said war films (as opposed to 7 per cent of the men). While hardly any women objected to love stories and musicals, each was named by 13 per cent of the men as their *least* favourite genre.

With its absence of a love story and its focus on the violent attacks of a horrific monster, with its almost exclusive emphasis on male action and male bonding in the second half of the film and its tantalizing glimpses of female nudity both on the poster and in the opening sequence, *Jaws* would appear to be very much at odds with female tastes. At the same time, most of these filmic elements also made *Jaws* unsuitable for children, and there was some concern about its PG rating, which only demanded that children had to be advised by their parents about attending this film but did not require them to be accompanied by an adult. It was felt that perhaps this was not enough of a warning.[32]

In fact, the reception of *Jaws* was informed by an ongoing debate about Hollywood's neglect of child and female audiences in favour of an increasingly exclusive focus on young males. In 1972 a *Variety* headline declared: 'Children Too Have Film Rights'.[33] In the same year, the paper lamented the fact that in recent years Hollywood's theatrical releases had ignored women, who had previously been considered as the film industry's most important target audience. By the early 1970s, however, cinema-going had become 'increasingly dominated by the male breadwinner's choice of screen fare' with the result that 'most b.o. [box office] hits of recent times barely feature women in supporting roles', while often containing generous helpings of sex and violence.[34] *Jaws* certainly fit *Variety*'s description of Hollywood's typical box office fare since the late 1960s.

One of the consequences of Hollywood's focus on theatrical releases that specifically appealed to young males, yet might alienate other audience groups, was that television broadcasts of recent releases became increasingly problematic. In the light of television's appeal to family audiences, and specifically to women, recent Hollywood films were either wholly inappropriate for broadcasting or they had to be substantially re-edited. Encouraged by the excellent ratings for previous features made specifically for television rather than theatrical release, in the early 1970s the three networks began to invest heavily in telefilm production and replaced their regular movie nights with a series of made-for-TV films, which were both cheaper for the networks and more popular with their audiences.[35] In the light of these developments, then, it becomes clear that *Jaws*, despite its huge success, did in fact exemplify the trend towards the increasing fragmentation of the mass audience – with cinemas and television catering for different audience segments, defined primarily in terms of gender and age.

In sharp contrast with *Jaws*, *Star Wars* demonstrated two years later that it was indeed possible to make films again for 'a truly mass audience', as A. D. Murphy had demanded in his 1975 article. By reaching out to audience segments which *Jaws* ignored or alienated, specifically older people, women and children, *Star Wars* was able to surpass *Jaws'* record-breaking box office returns by another 25 per cent in its initial release, and in subsequent years it was going to increase its lead over *Jaws* with numerous re-releases and sequels.[36]

Star Wars

Market research conducted before the release of *Star Wars* indicated that on the basis of the film's title and a basic description of its content, young males expressed strong interest in *Star Wars*, whereas women and older people were put off by the film's classification as Science Fiction, associated primarily with cold technology and the absence of human interest, and its emphasis on military battle.[37] The marketing campaign developed from this research sought to counter the resistance of women and mature audiences by highlighting Princess Leia and her relationship with the male protagonist Luke Skywalker in posters and by elevating the apparently juvenile Science Fiction story through references to Greek myths and classic fairy tales, declaring *Star Wars* to be a modern myth. The marketing campaign for the film's May 1977 release was primarily and highly successfully aimed at the cinema's core audience of 12- to 24-year-olds and secondarily at the 25–35 age group, while the campaign for the film's first re-release in July 1978 managed to attract the over-35s with the promise of a nostalgic recreation of their childhood movie experiences at Saturday matinees. In addition, the unexpected huge success of the film's merchandising indicated that *Star Wars* was also very popular with younger children, an audience that the main marketing campaign had more or less ignored.

The film was designed to engage such diverse audiences right from the start, partly by delaying the appearance of the young male hero for a long time, focusing instead on his main opponent Darth Vader, on Princess Leia and on the comic duo of two rather childish robots, C-3PO and R2-D2, and also by addressing the spectators directly, positioning them as an enchanted audience for the retelling of an age-old story. After the 20th Century-Fox logo and fanfare, the black screen shows only the film's tag line: 'A long time ago in a galaxy far, far away ....' This line merges *Star Wars'* Science Fiction setting with its aspirations to being a mythical tale, and it reworks the familiar fairy-tale opening 'Once upon a time ...', so as to remind both the children and the adults in the audience of the stories they may have first been told by their mothers when they were very young.

This is followed by John Williams's *Star Wars* theme and an expository text scrolling across the screen. While this text talks of civil war between good rebels and an evil empire and of the stolen plans for the empire's most dangerous weapon, it does not mention any of the male warriors by name and instead concludes with a paragraph highlighting the agency and centrality of the film's female protagonist: 'Pursued by the Empire's sinister agents, Princess Leia races home aboard her starship, custodian of the stolen plans that can save her people and restore freedom to the galaxy....' The next sequence repeats this duality, on the one hand presenting the battle between spaceships and between anonymous soldiers and on the other hand focusing on the agency of

Princess Leia who appears to hide the stolen plans in R2-D2, who together with his companion C-3PO promptly saves them from the empire's clutches by launching an escape pod towards the planet below, while Leia stays on board and is captured after a brief fight. The scene culminates with an encounter between Leia and her masked opponent Darth Vader.

Afterwards, the film focuses on the clumsy movements and childish squabbling of the two robots after their landing on the desert planet. This scene carefully replicates the empty, abstracted landscape and the comical anthropomorphic beings, so dependent on each other and yet always fighting with each other, which are characteristic of many children's cartoons. In this way, quite unlike *Jaws*, the opening sequence of *Star Wars* makes a sustained effort to engage women and children as well as young males.

In addition to this careful appeal to diverse audience segments, *Star Wars* also presented its epic story as a family affair. Luke Skywalker is first presented as a young man eager to follow in the footsteps of his apparently dead father who was a warrior. Yet he is held back by his uncle (who has raised him), until Luke's wish to break free from him is tragically fulfilled when the empire's stormtroopers searching the planet for the two robots kill both his adoptive parents. Fortunately, Luke has already acquired a substitute father in Obi-Wan Kenobi, who is going to turn him into a knight, and he has also been assigned a military mission: to save Princess Leia and the known universe from domination by the evil empire. In the sequels, of course, the familial nature of the story is foregrounded even more when Leia turns out to be Luke's sister and Darth Vader his father.

Thus, in 1977 *Star Wars* successfully responded to the demand made by A. D. Murphy two years earlier that Hollywood should again produce films for an integrated mass audience, overcoming the divisions between different genders and age groups, and also being able to perform equally well on the big screen in movie theatres and on the small screen in people's homes. In fact, *Star Wars* provided a model for other film-makers of exactly how this could be achieved, namely by addressing its spectators as members of a family and by turning the epic adventure presented on the screen into a family affair. As mentioned earlier, I have labelled this model 'family-adventure movie', arguing that the majority of the top grossing films since the late 1970s, both in cinemas and on video (and later DVD), fit into this category.[38]

Conclusion

As mentioned earlier, this essay closely follows a paper I presented in 1999, and it does so because, by and large, I stand by the earlier analysis. However, partly as a result of my further work on the career and films of Steven Spielberg[39] and of my engagement with the work on *Jaws* of other scholars, notably Rich Glanville,[40] I would now want to add another layer.

If we shift emphasis from the film's prologue on the beach and its second half on the ocean to the scenes taking us from Chief Brody waking up to the moment he finally decides to go on a shark hunt, and if we also compare the film to the novel, we can easily see that it is much closer to the model of the 'family-adventure movie' than I have given it credit for (certainly closer than the novel is). This shift in focus reveals that the film tells the story of an initially rather weak, unreliable, easily corruptible father who a grieving mother, justifiably, holds responsible for the death of her young son and who almost gets his own son killed by the shark. When he goes on his big adventure, he does so because he finally lives up to his professional and familial responsibilities.

What is more, the poster, especially the version carrying the tagline 'She was the first', begins to look very different from this perspective. At first sight it seems to promise the violation of a whole series of young women by a giant, phallic shark. Yet, looking back on it after having seen the whole film, during which, after the prologue, only males are killed, with the most phallic of these males, Quint, having the lower half of his body swallowed by the shark, the poster's image of its huge mouth comes to represent male fears of female power (what *Woman's Wear Daily* labelled 'castration complex'). It is not only a kind of *vagina dentata* – a vagina with teeth – but also, arguably, a projection of the importance of the maternal.

After all, when the men compare scars on the boat, Hooper speculates that the tattoo Quint had removed spelled 'mom', after he himself has revealed that his deepest wound is a broken heart, caused by a woman who he might have hoped to become the mother of his children. This ties in with Brody's chastisement by a grieving mother and also perhaps with his initial fear of the ocean, which, one might say, is a maternal force, insofar as it has given rise to life on Earth and also can be seen to symbolize the womb from which we all have emerged. This in turn is closely connected to the film's ecological dimension and its foregrounding of the theme of male hubris (meddling with the very building blocks of Mother Nature to construct nuclear bombs). In addition to referring to the female victim, 'She was the first' thus could take on a whole range of new meanings, with regard to mothers, Mother Earth and Mother Nature. This may sound excessively speculative, but I do think that this line of analysis can be quite productive, especially when considering the films with which Spielberg and George Lucas revolutionized American (and indeed world) cinema from 1977 onwards.

Notes

1   James Monaco, *American Film Now: The People, the Power, the Money, the Movies* (New York: Plume, 1979), first page of unpaginated preface.
2   Indeed, *Jaws* is the second film title, after *Taxi Driver* (1976), mentioned in the book (on the third page of the preface).
3   Monaco, *American Film Now*, 50.
4   Thomas Schatz, 'The New Hollywood', in Jim Collins, Hilary Radner and Ava Preacher Collins, eds, *Film Theory Goes to the Movies* (New York: Routledge, 1993), 23. Schatz explicitly discusses Monaco's work on p. 19.
5   Ibid., 14–15.
6   Ibid., 13.
7   Ibid., 16–17.
8   Ibid., 17.

9   Ibid., 19.

10 Garncarz had begun a systematic analysis of German box office charts in the late 1980s. His first English-language publication in this field was 'Hollywood in Germany: The Role of American Films in Germany 1925–1990', in David W. Ellwood and Rob Kroes, eds, *Hollywood in Europe: Experiences of a Cultural Hegemony* (Amsterdam: VU University Press, 1994), 94–135.

11 Peter Krämer, 'Would You Take Your Child to See This Film? The Cultural and Social Work of the Family-Adventure Movie', in Steve Neale and Murray Smith, eds, *Contemporary Hollywood Cinema* (London: Routledge, 1998), 294–311.

12 Peter Krämer, 'The Lure of the Big Picture: Film, Television and Hollywood', in John Hill and Martin McLoone, eds, *Big Picture, Small Screen: The Relations between Film and Television* (Luton: John Libbey Media, 1996), 9–46.

13 Peter Krämer, 'Post-classical Hollywood', in John Hill and Pamela Church Gibson, eds, *The Oxford Guide to Film Studies* (Oxford: Oxford University Press, 1998), 289–309.

14 This eventually resulted in Peter Krämer, *The New Hollywood: From* Bonnie and Clyde *to* Star Wars (London: Wallflower, 2005).

15 Peter Krämer, ' "A Truly Mass Audience": Movies and the Small Screen in the Mid-1970s', 18th Conference of the International Association for Media and History, 'Television and History', Leeds, July 1999.

16 For a general overview, see Krämer, 'The Lure of the Big Picture'. The following paragraphs draw on this essay.

17 A. D. Murphy, 'Audience Demographics, Film Future', *Variety*, 20 August 1975: 3.

18 Ibid.

19 Ibid.

20 Frank Segers, 'Gallup Check Re Likes: Theatre, and/or, Homes', *Variety*, 25 May 1977: 13.

21 James Harwood, 'Films Gotta Cater to "Aging" Audience', *Variety*, 23 February 1977: 7.

22 Jim Harwood, 'Anticipated Success Mutes Squawks On Costs, Rental Terms', *Variety*, 4 June 1975, unpaginated clipping on *Jaws* microfiche in the British Film Institute (BFI), London.

23 Schatz, 'The New Hollywood', 18. It should be noted that if re-releases and ticket price inflation are taken into account, *Jaws*' earnings at the US box office were exceeded, according to *Variety* estimates from the late 1970s, by those of *Gone with the Wind* and *The Sound of Music*. Cobbett Steinberg, *Film Facts* (New York: Facts on File, 1980), 3.

24 Penelope Gilliatt, Review of *Jaws*, *New Yorker*, 7 July 1975, unpaginated clipping on *Jaws* microfiche, BFI.

25 Review of *Jaws*, *Variety*, 18 June 1975, reprinted in George Perry, *Steven Spielberg* (London: Orion, 1998), 106–7.

26 Joseph McBride, 'More Sharks, Other Killers Due; Jaws Quickens Monster Spree, Recall Fatal Frogs, Bugs, Bees', *Variety*, 30 July 1975, unpaginated clipping on *Jaws* microfiche, BFI.

27 'Summer of the Shark', *Time*, 23 June 1975, unpaginated clipping on *Jaws* microfiche, BFI.

28 Ibid.

29 'Movie Going and Leisure Time', Newspaper Advertising Bureau, January 1974, contained in file MFL x n.c. 2,101 no. 4, Billy Rose Theater Collection, New York Public Library at Lincoln Center, New York.

30 Review excerpted in Christopher Tookey, *The Critics' Film Guide* (London: Boxtree, 1994), 407.

31 Cf. Peter Krämer, 'A Powerful Cinema-going Force? Hollywood and Female Audiences since the 1960s', in Melvyn Stokes and Richard Maltby, eds, *Identifying Hollywood's Audiences: Cultural Identity and the Movies* (London: BFI, 1999), 98–112.

32 See, e.g., the slightly defensive conclusion of the *Variety* review (reprinted in Perry, *Steven Spielberg*, 107): 'The domestic PG rating attests to the fact that implicit dramaturgy is often more effective than explicit carnage.'

33 Jerry Lewis, 'Children Too Have Film Rights', *Variety*, 5 January 1972: 32. Cf. Peter Krämer, '"The Best Disney Film Disney Never Made": Children's Films and the Family Audience in American Cinema since the 1960s', in Steve Neale, ed., *Genre and Contemporary Hollywood* (London: BFI, 2002), 183–98.

34 'Pld 4-Hanky "Women's Market" Pix, Far, Far from 1972 "Year of Woman"', *Variety*, 30 August 1972: 5.

35 See Gary Edgerton, 'High Concept, Small Screen: Reperceiving the Industrial and Stylistic Origins of the American Made-for-TV Movie', *Journal of Popular Film and Television* 19, no. 3 (Fall 1991): 114–27.

36 Schatz, 'The New Hollywood', 22.

37 This and the following paragraphs is based on Olen J. Earnest, '*Star Wars*: A Case Study of Motion Picture Marketing', *Current Research in Film* 1 (1985): 7–13.

38 In addition to Krämer, 'Would You Take Your Child to See This Film?' and '"The Best Disney Film Disney Never Made"', see my following two publications: '"It's Aimed at Kids – the Kid in Everybody": George Lucas, *Star Wars* and Children's Entertainment', *Scope: An Online Journal of Film Studies*, December 2001, https://www.nottingham. ac.uk/scope/documents/2001/december-2001/kramer.pdf, last accessed 4 June 2019; and 'Disney and Family Entertainment', in Michael Hammond and Linda Ruth Williams, eds, *Contemporary American Cinema* (Maidenhead: Open University Press, 2006), 265–72, 275–9.

39 See, e.g., Peter Krämer, 'Steven Spielberg', in Yvonne Tasker, ed., *Fifty Contemporary Filmmakers* (London: Routledge, 2002), 319–28; and Peter Krämer, 'Spielberg and Kubrick', in Nigel Morris, ed., *A Companion to Steven Spielberg* (Chichester: Wiley-Blackwell), 195–211.

40 Rich Glanville's work is as yet unpublished.

2

Not the first: Myths of *Jaws*

Sheldon Hall

Looking up references to *Jaws* in a couple of dozen standard sources produces a remarkable degree of consensus: certain themes recur ceaselessly. These themes, which are found in scholarly studies as well as in popular journalistic and fan-based accounts of the film, are so insistent that they form a coherent, consistent mythology – a mythology in the sense of both a plausible narrative or 'biographical legend' (assuming a film can be said to have a biography) and a set of beliefs that have been taken for granted as a way of discussing the film and understanding its significance. In particular they revolve around a set of supposed 'firsts' that are the subject of this chapter.

The notion that *Jaws* was a watershed marking the end of one era (the 'New Hollywood' of auteurs and quasi-art films financed and released by major studios) and the beginning of another (the New 'New Hollywood' of big-budget action pictures and technological spectacle) recurs throughout both the critical literature and the popular discourse:

> If any single film marked the arrival of the New Hollywood, it was *Jaws*, the Spielberg-directed thriller that recalibrated the profit potential of the Hollywood hit, and redefined its status as a marketable commodity and cultural phenomenon as well. The film brought an emphatic end to Hollywood's five-year recession, while ushering in an era of high-cost, high-tech, high-speed thrillers.[1]

> If there was a single day when the era ended, it was June 21, 1975, just after two landmark films had appeared on the respective covers of *Time* and *Newsweek*.

> *Newsweek*'s cover film was *Nashville*, thought by some to be the film of the decade, but it was not the one that changed Hollywood forever. *Jaws* was.[2]

> The film created a sensation and with it Universal initiated the era of the blockbuster feature film, and forever altered the Hollywood film landscape.[3]

> *Jaws* was the first big-budget Hollywood film to be given both saturation television advertising and to be released from the start in a large number of cinemas.[4]

> *Jaws* (1975) was the first proto-blockbuster to deploy exploitation pre-release marketing tactics and saturation booking.[5]

The reputation of *Jaws* as the seminal blockbuster, as we know that term today, is beyond dispute. This was the start of the event movie; this was where the marketing of films blurred into military strategy.[6]

At mid-decade, Steven Spielberg's much-delayed production *Jaws* redefined the meaning of a blockbuster in the modern era. It was the first studio-planned national wide release, with a TV saturation ad campaign, licensing, and merchandising. It was also the first summer blockbuster, setting a precedent for all other summer blockbusters to follow.[7]

Jaws was the first in a new genre, the summer blockbuster movie. ... It marked a turning point in the business.[8]

For many, the release of *Jaws* in 1975 constitutes the true birth of New Hollywood. A huge film in so many ways, not least its box office receipts, *Jaws* has been credited with inventing the concept of the summer blockbuster, the must-see 'event' movie cut to the measure of the big screen, a sure-fire draw that would take families away from their TV sets.[9]

In 1975, Steven Spielberg's thriller *Jaws* ushered in a new era of filmmaking when it transformed the usually low-earning period of the summer break into a prime time for profit making.[10]

It was the first film to break the $100 million mark in box office takings and, for two years (up until the release of *Star Wars* in 1977), it remained the most successful box office hit in movie history. It also ushered in the age of the contemporary summer blockbuster.[11]

Jaws changed the business forever ....[12]

Jaws proved to be a genuine industry watershed, marking the birth of the New Hollywood in several crucial ways. ... *Jaws* sparked a widespread industry recovery that was fuelled primarily by a new breed of blockbuster.[13]

Synthesizing the above-quoted accounts (which could no doubt be added to exponentially), five main themes, or myths, emerge as standard. *Jaws* is said to be the:

1. First film to gross $100 million at the US box office
2. First blockbuster movie
3. First summer blockbuster
4. First big-budget major-studio film to be TV-advertised
5. First big-budget major-studio film to open wide

Each of these claims contains a grain of truth; otherwise, they would not have gained such strong purchase as they have. But they should not be accepted at face value. My own position echoes another comment by Thomas Schatz (author of the first and last of the above quotations), when at one point in his seminal 1993 article on 'The New

Hollywood' he noted in passing of *Jaws*: 'In many ways, the film simply confirmed or consolidated various existing industry trends and practices.'[14] This seems to me to get at the truth of the matter. Contrary to the mythology, *Jaws* did not appear out of nowhere to start a new and unprecedented cinematic ethos; rather, it emerged directly or indirectly out of industry practices with a long prior history which it refined, reworked or – to use a common current term – rebooted. I want therefore to develop and expand upon Schatz's insight by taking each of the above five myths in turn and attempting to demonstrate how they are all at best exaggerations, at worst distortions, of longer developments in commercial distribution, exhibition and promotion of which *Jaws* was as much a culmination as a breakthrough.

1. First film to gross $100 million at the US box office

The figure of $100 million has a talismanic significance in accounts of *Jaws*. It is offered as tangible, self-explanatory proof of the film's importance, condensed into an easily comprehended figure. Thus a multi-authored volume claims that '*Jaws* became the first film in motion picture history to earn over $100 million' and Warren Buckland states that it was 'the first film to break the $100 million mark in box office takings'.[15] Douglas Gomery tells us more specifically that it 'earned more than $100 million at the box office in six months', while Justin Wyatt notes that subsequently '$100 million became a benchmark for the blockbuster'.[16] But $100 million in what, exactly? What does this magical figure actually betoken?

In fact, *Jaws* was not the first film to gross $100 million *at the box office*. Rather, it was the first to earn $100 million in *distributor rentals* from the domestic, that is, North American (US and Canadian), market. *Grosses* are the monies taken at theatre box offices before any deductions by exhibitors or 'off-the-top' disbursements to revenue participants (such as stars with a cut of the gross from 'the first dollar'). *Rentals* are the proportion of box office takings – a proportion which may vary from one film to another, from one cinema to another or indeed from one week of a film's release to another – that are passed on to the distributor. These are the revenues available to pay off the film's production, distribution and marketing costs, as well as the distributor's fees, interest on the production loan and numerous other charges and expenses. Before the collection of national data directly from cinemas, there was not always a reliable way of knowing a film's total theatre earnings. In the late stages of a film's release (when bookings would be made for the payment of flat fees rather than a percentage of takings, as was common in early runs) theatres might not bother to report their takings to distributors, so there might be no accurate record of total ticket sales.

Until the late 1990s therefore, unless particular theatres were under discussion it was standard practice for trade journals such as *Variety* to refer to rentals rather than grosses because they provided a clearer index of a film's potential profitability. But because modern sources tend to cite grosses rather than rentals (a concept that is less easily understood than combined ticket sales), figures from the past which refer to rentals are often mistaken as grosses and vice versa. *Variety*'s A. D. Murphy noted in an article specifically related to *Jaws*:

> It is a common error in and out of the trade to confuse b.o. [grosses] with rentals. Boxoffice figures are meaningful in the early stages of release of a film in order to gauge its initial impact in given situations at a given time. But over time, rentals become the most meaningful parameter.[17]

Web sites such as the Internet Movie Database (IMDb) and Wikipedia are especially prone to this confusion, mixing up the different types of data or failing to identify which is which, and sometimes multiplying rental figures to estimate grosses without being explicit about doing so. In one of his later pieces, 'Tom' (*sic*) Schatz is again clearer than most commentators in noting that *Jaws* was 'the first film to gross over $200 million at the box office and to return over $100 million in rental receipts to its distributor – still the measure of a blockbuster hit'.[18]

As Michael Coate has observed, several films before *Jaws* had earned a domestic box office *gross* of $100 million in the United States and Canada, beginning with *The Sound of Music* (1965) and followed by *Gone with the Wind* (first released in 1939, but surpassing $100 million thanks to its 1967 reissue), *The Godfather* (1972), *The Sting* (1973) and *The Exorcist* (1973).[19] *The Sound of Music* was also the first film to earn over $100 million in world rentals. These five were the benchmark predecessors that *Jaws* had to beat in order to achieve its record revenues (however they were calibrated). Universal made a point of this by taking out a front-page advertisement in *Variety* each time one of them was surpassed until *Jaws* took the top spot from *The Godfather* on 5 September 1975. The advertisement noting this milestone also listed the domestic rentals of the earlier films as reported by *Variety* at the start of the year (but not of *Jaws* itself): *The Exorcist*, $66,300,000; *The Sting*, $68,450,000; *Gone with the Wind*, $70,179,000; *The Sound of Music*, $83,891,000; *The Godfather*, $85,747,184.[20]

Variety reported in its news columns that *Jaws* had passed the $100 million gross milestone on 23 August 1975, the film's fifty-ninth day of release, when Universal claimed the domestic theatre gross stood at $100,375,045.[21] But the studio declined to disclose rental figures at this stage. Murphy predicted in December 1975 that *Jaws* would be the first film to reach $200 million in *worldwide* rentals, but it was not until *Variety*'s year-end report in January 1976 that *Variety* estimated a *domestic* rental over $100,000,000: the initial figure published was $102,650,000, which two weeks later was amended to $104,000,000.[22] At this point the journal also reported that *Jaws* had surpassed *The Godfather* to achieve the highest worldwide rental to date, with a global total of $132,000,000 by January 1976 (overseas release having started in October 1975, but with most territories including the UK opening in December).[23] Updates of the film's total domestic rentals regularly appeared in the paper's annual charts of 'All-Time Film Rental Champs', reflecting additional revenues from reissues, and in January 1985 *Variety* issued its most precise U.S./Canadian rental figure yet: $129,961,081.[24] This was doubtless based on information received directly from the distributor, as other Universal titles were similarly updated with exact figures. They included Steven

Spielberg's *E. T. the Extra-Terrestrial* (1982), the first film to earn a domestic rental over $200 million, with a reported total at this stage of $209,976,989.

2. First blockbuster movie

Douglas Gomery has been especially insistent that *Jaws* was 'the first true blockbuster' and that with its release MCA-Universal and its chairman Lew Wasserman had 'initiated the era of the Hollywood blockbuster'.[25] But if that was the case, one wonders what people had been talking about when referring to blockbusters over the previous three decades. In fact, by 1975, 'blockbuster' was an old and familiar term, used outside of trade circles and even by the general public.[26] *Jaws* may have modified understanding of the concept, but it certainly did not create the category of blockbuster.

The word itself was first used in 1943, both extra-cinematically (it originated as the nickname given to a large bomb capable of destroying a city block, first deployed militarily in that year) and in its colloquial application to movies. Initially 'blockbuster' was used as a thematically appropriate metaphor to describe war-related films, beginning most appositely with RKO's *Bombardier* (1943). But after the Second World War, from about 1948 onwards, it was used analogically to denote films of considerable (commercial) power, size and impact. It therefore became added to a lexicon of terms which historically have been used to refer to films of particular industrial importance because of their exceptional cost, the exceptional marketing strategies used to promote them or their exceptional box office success. Earlier such terms have included feature, special, superspecial and roadshow, among others, most of which have fallen into disuse except by film historians.[27]

Moreover, in the 1950s 'blockbuster' came to refer not just to a particular kind of film but to a whole industrial strategy associated with the *regular* production of big-budget, heavily promoted films, distinct from more routine offerings and differentiated from other cultural and entertainment forms such as television (though the word blockbuster was sometimes used to describe these other forms too).[28] This strategy came to define the post-war, 'post-classical' or 'post-studio' era, reflecting changes in leisure patterns and in film consumption, as well as new or enhanced distribution and exhibition modes, such as the increased number of films presented as special 'roadshow' attractions in the late 1950s and 1960s. Traditional genres like the western, war film and musical were upgraded with higher budgets and technological enhancements such as colour and widescreen formats, while at the same time more marginal, mostly low-budget genres such as horror and science fiction experienced a resurgence with an increased number of productions, often made independently and sometimes deemed 'exploitation' pictures for the way in which heavy promotion aimed to turn them into mainstream successes. The taken-for-grantedness of blockbusters as both a production category and an industrial strategy can be seen in the pervasive presence of the word in magazine articles and trade-paper reports throughout the 1950s and 1960s, with titles such as '1958: Year of blockbusters', 'The Theory and Practice of Blockbusting' and 'Blockbusters or bust?'.[29]

Thus, when *Jaws* made its appearance in mid-1975 there was a ready-made conceptual category in which to place it rather than its inventing a new one. Indeed, there were several such categories available: another was 'disaster film', the most recent generic variant of the blockbuster, in which all-star casts were consumed by conflagrations or caught up in mid-air collisions, natural cataclysms and all manner of collective crises. *Jaws*, with its scenario of a community beset by an oceanic threat on its doorstep, leading to scenes of mass panic on a beach, also fitted this established template. Although there were significant recent predecessors such as *Krakatoa, East of Java* (1969), *Airport* (1970) and *The Poseidon Adventure* (1972), the disaster film really established itself as a recognized industry trend in the autumn of 1974, which saw the release in close succession of *Airport 1975* (1974), *Earthquake* (1974) and *The Towering Inferno* (1974), all spectacular successes. *Earthquake* and the *Airport* films were produced and released by MCA-Universal, which must clearly have known blockbusters when it saw them (as it had also done the previous year with *The Sting*). Some critics placed *Jaws* squarely within this disaster cycle; writing in the UK, six months after its US opening, Gordon Gow noted that the film was 'on a par in masochistic magnetism with *The Towering Inferno*', and Tom Milne commented: 'While it hardly merits the status of No. 1 box office *Jaws* is a perfectly acceptable, and sometimes genuinely exciting, entry in the disaster stakes.'[30] James Monaco's *Sight and Sound* review focused on the film's commercial achievement, identifying it with an already established pattern: Hollywood, he noted, was 'becoming increasingly oriented towards the large-budget, pre-sold adventure movie'.[31] In other words, *Jaws* was continuing a trend rather than creating one.

3. First summer blockbuster

The argument in favour of *Jaws* being the 'first' summer blockbuster is likely a response to the setting and subject matter of the film itself as much as to its seasonal timing. The story of course takes place at a coastal holiday resort during a summer vacation, with the key beach set piece occurring over the July Independence Day weekend. This synergy was surely not lost on Universal, whose decision to open the film on 20 June and to design a release pattern which kept it in circulation throughout July and August was certainly a triumph of scheduling and marketing. But as we shall see later, the success of that strategy depended partly on *limiting* the film's release – again, contrary to the mythology.

The summer months (especially July and August) were traditionally regarded as a lean time by distributors and exhibitors. Throughout the 'classical' studio era, the distributors designated their business year by seasons rather than by calendar year, and for most companies the annual season began in September and ended in August (20th Century-Fox was an exception, organizing its business year from August to July). Thus the optimum time to launch the new season's line-up was in the fall (television's annual seasons are comparable in this regard). Exhibitors, however, often complained that they were denied a steady stream of top pictures throughout the year and were sometimes left with a product shortage in the summer months, when they were forced to play out the end-of-season period with 'extended runs, repeat engagements or reissues' unless the distributors decided to open some of their new season's product early.[32] Even the industry's all-time peak year for attendance, 1946, was affected by a summer slump, though in its case this was 'merely a drop in biz from super-sensational to mildly terrific'.[33]

Summer was also, of course, the holiday period when leisure-seekers enjoyed outdoor activity in preference to movies. The first Monday in September is a national holiday, Labor Day, and this is often seen as marking the end of the summer vacation period. But hot weather also meant problems for many theatres, particularly those in southern and Midwestern states, which often closed in summer not only to allow their own staff a vacation but also because sweltering heat made some indoor theatres inhospitable. Even Broadway first-run houses could struggle in a heat wave.

Some of these conditions changed over time, however. The spread of air conditioning was credited by *Variety* in 1936 for a major upturn in summer business, with 'air-cooled theatres' offering a positive alternative to outdoor heat ('Instead of a bugaboo, hot weather has become an asset').[34] That summer saw the release of one of the decade's biggest hits, MGM's *San Francisco* (1936), which opened in July and played its metropolitan first runs through August. Its total domestic rental of $2,868,000 was surpassed among 1930s releases to that point only by the same studio's *The Great Ziegfeld* (1936). The following summer MGM enjoyed almost as great a success with another Clark Gable vehicle, *Saratoga* (1937).[35]

These films also reflected the industry's, and the country's, emergence from the Depression, though they were followed by a further recession. During the wartime boom years, exceptional conditions led to an alleviation of expected patterns of a summer drop-off, which *Variety* attributed to 'distributors' willingness to release top product immediately instead of waiting for the start of the new season; high wages in war-related industries, benefiting nearby communities; [and] shortage of gasoline keeping holiday-makers at home'.[36] The 1946 'seasonal dip' prior to a record fall could also be explained by local factors, including 'the great urge to get away from it all, denied for four years of gas rationing and travel restrictions'.[37]

The related post-war rises of car ownership and the drive-in theatre helped account for the increased importance of the summer season in the 1950s and 1960s. Open-air theatres after sundown attracted family groups as well as out-of-school teenagers on dates. While most roadshows were launched in the spring or fall seasons, films aimed at the family market (e.g. Walt Disney's) were often released in the summer and other holiday periods, when they found a ready audience of pre-teens and parents. Big-budget films which went into wide release in summer months included United Artists' *Trapeze* (1956), which earned the 'largest single week's gross in the history of the motion picture business' when generally released in 405 theatres in July 1956 following pre-release runs the previous month; and UA's *The Vikings* (1958), which after opening at Easter went wide during the summer, with '1,000 bookings aimed for during three weeks, mainly to break around [the] July 4 holiday'.[38] These two films were released with domestic inventories of 600 and 700 prints, respectively. Summer was also often the period when many roadshow films went into general release – that is, when they became more widely available to regular exhibitors after completing their exclusive, reserved-seat runs in metropolitan showcase theatres. For example, *The Longest Day* (1962), launched as a roadshow in select engagements in October 1962, enjoyed its 'first wave' of general release on 450 prints in summer 1963, followed by a period of withdrawal and then a further wave of 450 theatres in June 1964.[39]

By 1957, in fact, the previous received wisdom on the relative 'doldrums' of the summer had been reversed. In June of that year, *Daily Variety* reported that 'the trade is anxiously awaiting the anticipated summer pickup. The months of July and August have traditionally become the peak business period for the motion picture industry'.[40] This was despite the fact that air conditioning, now common in homes, was less of an attraction in theatres than it had been twenty years before and despite the increased number of pastimes that offered alternative distractions. One of the few advantages that cinema had over competing leisure options was that the summer months were now TV's doldrums.

4. First big-budget major-studio film to be TV-advertised

Although the Hollywood studios initially regarded the post-war advent of network television mainly as a threat through its competition for audiences and were slow to exploit the new medium as an opportunity for advertising and promotion, some publicists recognized its potential early on. One was Terry Turner, who as head of exploitation at RKO used advertising on local TV stations to sell the 1952 reissue of *King Kong* (1933) and helped it to gross more than twice than on its original release; significantly, those territories where TV was available yielded better results than those where it was not.[41] Subsequently as a freelancer Turner oversaw many similar campaigns and in trade press articles he advocated the greater use of television as a promotional tool. In 1959, Turner noted that television advertising had still not yet been fully exploited and in particular that the film industry had 'made very little effort to find the right technique to apply it to the so-called "big" pictures and get bigger and better results'.[42]

Some studios did this selectively in the 1960s, using national TV ads as well as local ones, though the latter were more common. A 1965 trade advertisement by 20th Century-Fox proclaimed 'the first sustained, continuing buy by a major motion picture company', involving 189 one-minute commercials aired every week during 'Major-League Championship Baseball' and 'Nightlife' on the national ABC TV network. Among the films thus promoted were such major releases as *The Sound of Music, Those Magnificent Men in Their Flying Machines, The Agony and the Ecstasy, Von Ryan's Express* (all 1965) and *Our Man Flint* (1966). With this strategy, Fox claimed that 'a new era was born in motion picture advertising! … Here at last is the pre-sell … the deep-sell … the continuing-sell exhibitors have been crying for'.[43] This was, however, advertising on only one network on a limited number of shows.

According to another trade advertisement ten years later, Universal's campaign for *Jaws* was 'the Biggest National prime-time T.V. Spot campaign in Motion Picture

History!', with twenty-three thirty-second spots aired at prime time every night between 17 and 20 June on all three national networks.[44] Unusually, exhibitors were required to contribute to the costs of this TV advertising as part of their bids for the right to play the picture in its opening engagements.[45] Undoubtedly, this was the most extensive and expensive TV-spot campaign to date, with a reported $700,000 spent on TV ads. Even so, it was not the first. In fact, Universal itself had already been using similar TV-advertising strategies with recent releases such as *Airport 1975*, as had other studios with other films. But the most important precursor was Columbia's *Breakout* (1975), which had in effect pretested the strategy one month before *Jaws*.[46]

That it was not a foolproof method of promotion was demonstrated by the next major release on which Universal attempted to repeat its own formula. The western *Rooster Cogburn* (1975), bringing back John Wayne in his Oscar-winning role from Paramount's *True Grit* (1969) and casting him for the first and only time opposite Katharine Hepburn, was the subject of a similar promotional and distribution campaign as *Jaws*. A trade advertisement listed the common elements:[47]

Pre-sold property
Prime-time TV spot campaign
Double truck full color
Super saturation

Yet when it opened in October the same year, *Rooster Cogburn*'s box office performance was mediocre, earning only $4.8 million in domestic rentals. Effective as it was when allied to the right product, national TV advertising and the other marketable ingredients did not produce a magic formula that could be applied to any film. *Variety*'s year-end report noted the lesson to be learned: 'When John Wayne and Katharine Hepburn can't lure them in, only a shark can.'[48]

5. First big-budget major-studio film to open wide

'Saturation' releases are commonly associated with so-called exploitation pictures – that is to say, films whose success depends on the marketizing (exploiting) of topical or sensational subject matter, rather than those which are merely 'exploitative' in the everyday sense. Industry wisdom has it that wide-release distribution and exhibition strategies were traditionally used for low-budget stinkers, aiming to make a quick hit-and-run before word got around about their poor quality or failure to deliver on the promises of their advertising. While undoubtedly there was some truth in this, it was not the only reason for wide releasing, which has a longer and more complex history than might be supposed. Another reason for wide or 'instant' releases was to capitalize on presumed 'want-to-see', either created artificially through elaborate promotional campaigns or because the ingredients of the film already had built-in public awareness by being 'pre-sold' – for example, through the presence of an established star, the use of extensive pre-release publicity or by being based on a well-known literary property. In any of these cases, there would be an audience ready and waiting for whom the gradual build-up of word-of-mouth was unnecessary or even counterproductive.[49]

There were two basic kinds of wide releases: intensive regional saturation, in which a large number of prints and theatre bookings were targeted on a particular area (such as a city, state or broader region); and simultaneous nationwide releasing, in which a large number of theatres in different areas across the country gained 'instant' access to a film. Among the earliest films to be given local saturation bookings were Charlie Chaplin's short comedies for the Mutual Corporation. Beginning with *The Floorwalker* (1916), between 200 and 300 prints (several times the number for an ordinary short or feature) were used for each of the sixteen Mutual pictures made by the star comedian in 1916–17. In the case of the three-reeler *A Dog's Life* (1918), released by First National, 160 prints were used in Greater New York alone, while 200 prints were used for territorial bookings of Chaplin's first full-length feature, *The Kid* (1921).[50] In the early sound era, Warner Bros. and RKO Radio both established a policy of 'day and date' releases in which around 300 prints of new sound films such as Warners' *The Desert Song* (1929) and RKO's *Cimarron* (1931) were made available to first-run exhibitors in major cities simultaneously with Broadway pre-release engagements.[51]

The seemingly antithetical distribution strategies of roadshowing (associated primarily with prestige pictures) and saturation releasing were sometimes used in alternation for particular films, depending on the territory or the stage of release. David O. Selznick's epic western *Duel in the Sun* (1946) opened as an exclusive roadshow in Los Angeles in late 1946, but was saturation-released the following summer in territories such as Greater New York, Texas and California. Shortly afterwards, 20th Century-Fox opened its bestseller adaptation *Forever Amber* (1947) nationwide with 475 prints, reported as one of the largest print orders at that time. Both of these films were successively the most expensive films yet made, each costing more than *Gone with the Wind* (1939), though neither enjoyed much critical acclaim.

Most major studios used both regional saturation and wide national releases throughout the 1950s, often for horror and science-fiction pictures such as Warners' *The Beast from 20,000 Fathoms* (1953), which opened in 614 theatres in its first two weeks of release.[52] But westerns and other films with rural settings were also often given saturation treatment in the south and Midwest: Warner Bros. claimed a record 651 simultaneous openings for *The Boy from Oklahoma* (1954).[53] In the late 1950s and early 1960s, showman and producer-distributor Joseph E. Levine specialized in large-scale releases of Italian costume adventures and Japanese creature features, supported by extravagant advertising campaigns; it is probably pictures such as these – most notably *Hercules* (1958) – that are responsible for the common association of wide releases with lowbrow trash. But Levine later applied the same principle to big-budget pictures such as the Harold Robbins adaptation *The Carpetbaggers* (1964), released nationwide by Paramount in over 700 prints to considerable box office success, though again with little esteem.[54] Some companies even opted for simultaneous global first runs. MGM's *The V.I.P.s* (1963) was planned for simultaneous release in 2,000 theatres in 750 cities around the world, which would have made it the 'biggest mass release ever in film history'. *Variety* reported it as opening in '172 theatres in 89 cities of

30 countries' outside the United States and Canada.[55] Five years later, Paramount's *Barbarella* (1968) was launched simultaneously 'in 41 nations, in over 1,000 theatres' worldwide.[56]

Also in the mid-1960s, United Artists developed a strategy of multiple first runs, a policy it called Premiere Showcase, which was subsequently taken up by other distributors. It was used on a wide range of pictures, most successfully the James Bond series. The Bond films were typically released with 500–600 prints for the domestic market. *Diamonds Are Forever* (1971), for example, opened at the end of the year in 104 theatres in thirty-three US and Canadian territories, including twenty-eight theatres in New York and nineteen in New Jersey, plus fifty-seven situations in twenty-five overseas cities.[57] In the summer of 1973, UA struck 600 prints for the Bond film *Live and Let Die* (1973), 550 for the musical *Tom Sawyer* (1973) and 450 for the general release of *Last Tango in Paris* (1972), which had opened as a roadshow.[58] Two years later, UA had 500 prints ready for the summer release of *The Return of the Pink Panther* (1975) while *Jaws* was waiting in the wings.[59] But the widest simultaneous domestic release of any major-studio film until the 1980s came in May 1975. One month before the release of *Jaws*, Columbia's Charles Bronson vehicle *Breakout* opened in more than 1,300 U.S. and Canadian theatres, in what a trade ad described as 'the most spectacular saturation blitz of any motion picture'.[60]

What is most remarkable about the wide release of *Jaws*, in the light of the claims often made about it and in the context of predecessors such as these, is that it could so easily have been much wider – that it was not, in fact, as wide as had initially been intended. There have been a number of published accounts, including Spielberg's own, of the aftermath of the film's second, enormously successful, public preview at Long Beach on 28 March 1975, attended by a cadre of Universal executives including MCA president Lew Wasserman.[61] In a post-screening debriefing, Wasserman instructed his distribution staff to cut back on a release strategy planned to include around 1000 simultaneous theatre openings (the exact number varies from one account to another). Rather than saturating the market in order to ensure a quick return on investment, Wasserman wanted the film to remain in circulation throughout the summer, in extended engagements that would extract the maximum possible revenue from each booking. In order to do that, the number of bookings was substantially reduced from the initial estimate to avoid 'milking' the picture too quickly and thereby reducing its theatrical life. Those theatres eventually chosen to receive the picture in the first wave of openings (409 in the United States, 55 in Canada) had to guarantee a minimum twelve-week run. So although there were ultimately more than 1,000 prints in domestic circulation, theatre engagements were added gradually throughout the summer and fall as the film gathered momentum rather than saturating the opening weeks.

Wasserman's motivation for this revised strategy was surely his recognition that, unlike a majority of exploitation pictures, *Jaws* delivered on the promise of its advertising, as manifested in the audience reaction that night. As a consequence, the wide-release strategy for big-budget studio pictures gained greater credibility, even if the film had not in fact introduced it. In the first of a still-continuing series of annual box office commentaries published in the US magazine *Film Comment*, Stuart Byron drew specific attention to

> Universal's unique distribution pattern for *Jaws*. It used to be that the opening of a movie everywhere at once was a signal to most of the public that the picture was a stiff …. But in opening at 500 theatres in late June, *Jaws* was the ultimate beneficiary of a trend toward so-called 'wide' openings, with attendant saturation advertising campaigns centered on television.[62]

As a consequence of *Jaws*, Byron noted,

> the psychological effects of this particular way of releasing a picture have been neutralized; the public accepts or rejects a film released this way, as the case may be. And this is an interesting development. It has been little noticed that the history of film distribution in America is the history of the neutralization of release patterns; a method of 'throwing away' a movie is transformed into a way of indicating its importance.[63]

Conclusion

If an 'event movie' is understood as meaning the kind of film which becomes a cultural phenomenon or a must-see attraction, then we need to look back as far as *The Birth of a Nation* (1915) for the most significant predecessor of *Jaws*. But if we restrict our attention to the New Hollywood era, then much of what has been claimed for *Jaws* can also be said, in some respects more convincingly, of one of the immediately preceding blockbusters against which its performance was often compared: *The Godfather*.

Researcher Michael Coate has tabulated all 464 opening engagements of *Jaws*, in an online article which convincingly refutes the myth of its nationwide opening as representing any kind of record.[64] Coate's listings show that only five cities had simultaneous bookings in three or more theatres, and only thirteen had two concurrent runs; the rest were exclusive engagements in their respective communities, albeit in multiple cities and towns in each state. This was the *Godfather* policy almost exactly, on an only slightly larger scale. Paramount president Frank Yablans rejected the term 'saturation' as a description of his simultaneous national release strategy for *The Godfather*, which involved booking the film into a small number of theatres in each area for twelve-week runs to maximize potential. Beginning with around 400 engagements opening in February 1972, the film's release expanded to involve around 1000 prints in circulation by the end of the year.[65] This anticipated many of the key features of the *Jaws* distribution strategy, which has little in common with the kind of mass coverage, opening on a 1000 or more screens, which only became commonplace in the 1980s and largely thanks to the influence of other films besides *Jaws*, including the remake of *King Kong* (1976).[66]

Jaws, then, had many ancestors; it borrowed from the promotional and distribution strategies developed for many films over the previous three decades, refining, enhancing, combining and synthesizing them with peculiar effectiveness. Not only in the way it did this but also in the spectacular degree of its commercial success, *Jaws* undoubtedly set a new benchmark for box office performance and persuaded subsequent films' distributors to emulate its example. It anticipated many later developments in, for example, the increased importance of wide releases of big-budget films in the summer and other holiday seasons. More than most films, it has served as a reference point for contemporary blockbuster cinema. It is important, influential, impressive and of continuing relevance. But it was not the first.

Notes

1 Thomas Schatz, 'The New Hollywood', in Jim Collins, Hilary Radner and Ava Preacher Collins, eds, *Film Theory Goes to the Movies* (New York: Routledge, 1993), 17.
2 Janet Maslin, 'Film: Golden Ages; Just before They Invented the Blockbuster', *New York Times*, 1 May 1994; online at http://www.nytimes.com/1994/05/01/movies/film-golden-ages-just-before-they-invented-the-blockbuster.html.
3 Douglas Gomery, 'Hollywood Corporate Business Practice and Periodizing Contemporary Film History', in Steve Neale and Murray Smith, eds, *Contemporary Hollywood Cinema* (London: Routledge, 1998), 51.
4 Geoff King, *New Hollywood Cinema: An Introduction* (London: I.B. Tauris, 2002), 55.
5 Linda Ruth Williams, 'Exploitation Cinema', in Pam Cook, ed., *The Cinema Book*, 3rd edn (London: BFI/Palgrave Macmillan, 2007), 300.
6 Ryan Gilbey, *It Don't Worry Me: The Revolutionary American Films of the Seventies* (New York: Faber and Faber, 2003), 85.
7 Alex Ben Block and Lucy Autrey Wilson, eds, *George Lucas's Blockbusting* (New York: It Books/HarperCollins, 2010), 508.
8 Connie Bruck, *When Hollywood Had a King: The Reign of Lew Wasserman, Who Leveraged Talent into Power and Influence* (New York: Random House, 2003), 343–4.
9 Mark Shiel, 'The Seventies: Introduction', in Linda Ruth Williams and Michael Hammond, eds, *Contemporary American Cinema* (Maidenhead: Open University Press/McGraw-Hill, 2006), 117.
10 Daniel Borden, Florian Duijsens, Thomas Gilbert and Adele Smith, *Film: A World History* (London: Herbert Press, 2008), 306.
11 Warren Buckland, *Directed by Steven Spielberg: Poetics of the Contemporary Hollywood Blockbuster* (New York: Continuum, 2006), 86.
12 Peter Biskind, *Easy Riders, Raging Bulls: How the Sex 'n' Drugs 'n' Rock 'n' Roll Generation Saved Hollywood* (London: Bloomsbury, 1998), 278.
13 Tom Schatz, 'The Studio System and Corporate Hollywood', in Paul McDonald and Janet Wasko, eds, *The Contemporary Hollywood Film Industry* (Malden, MA: Blackwell, 2008), 19–20.
14 Schatz, 'The New Hollywood', 19.
15 Borden, Duijsens, Gilbert and Smith, *Film: A World History*, 306; Buckland, *Directed by Steven Spielberg*, 86.

16 Gomery, 'The Hollywood Blockbuster: Industrial Analysis and Practice', 72; Justin Wyatt, 'From Roadshowing to Saturation Release: Majors, Independents, and Marketing/Distribution Innovations', in Jon Lewis, ed., *The New American Cinema* (Durham: Duke University Press, 1998), 79.

17 A. D. Murphy, 'Sockeroo *Jaws* Gross: What about Rentals?', *Variety*, 27 August 1975, 7.

18 Schatz, 'The Studio System and Corporate Hollywood', 20.

19 Coate, '*Jaws* ... Happy 35th!'

20 The advertisement was published in *Variety* on 24 September 1975, 48; the box office report had appeared as 'Updated all-time film champs', *Variety*, 8 January 1975, 26.

21 Murphy, 'Sockeroo *Jaws* Gross: What about Rentals?'.

22 A. D. Murphy, '*Jaws* Spectacular B.O. Thrust to Top $300-Mil in Global Rentals', *Variety*, 10 December 1975, 5; Robert B. Frederick, 'Terror-joy of *Jaws*: $102,650,000', *Variety*, 7 January 1976, 18; A. D. Murphy, 'Universal Pics Make Film history', *Variety*, 21 January 1976, 1.

23 Anon., 'Reprise as to *Jaws*', *Variety*, 21 January 1976, 102. Overseas opening dates are listed in Michael Coate, '*Jaws* ... Happy 35th!', *Cinema Treasures*, posted 18 June 2010; online at http://cinematreasures.org/blog/2010/6/18/jaws-happy-35th.

24 Anon., 'All-Time Film Rental Champs (of U.S.-Canadian Market)', *Variety*, 16 January 1985, 28.

25 Douglas Gomery and Clara Pafort-Overduin, *Movie History: A Survey*, 2nd edn (New York: Routledge, 2011), 284–5; Douglas Gomery, 'The Hollywood Blockbuster: Industrial Analysis and Practice', in Julian Stringer, ed., *Movie Blockbusters* (London: Routledge, 2003), 72.

26 For extended discussions of the etymological origins, applications and implications of the term, see Charles R. Acland, 'Senses of Success and the Rise of the Blockbuster', *Film History*, 25, nos 1–2 (2013); and Sheldon Hall, 'Pass the Ammunition: A Short Etymology of "Blockbuster"', in Andrew B. R. Elliott, ed., *The Return of the Epic Film: Genre, Aesthetics and History in the 21st Century* (Edinburgh: Edinburgh University Press, 2014).

27 For further discussion of these terms, see the Introduction to Sheldon Hall and Steve Neale, *Epics, Spectacles, and Blockbusters: A Hollywood History* (Detroit: Wayne State University Press, 2010).

28 See, e.g., *Variety*'s headline 'NBC-TV's blockbustin' lineup', 22 August 1951, 31.

29 Gene Arneel, '1958: Year of Blockbusters', *Variety*, 7 January 1959; Penelope Houston and John Gillett, 'The Theory and Practice of Blockbusting', *Sight and Sound*, Spring 1963; William Fadiman, 'Blockbusters or Bust?', *Films and Filming*, February 1963.

30 Gordon Gow, '*Jaws*' (review), *Films and Filming*, January 1976, 31; Tom Milne, '*Jaws*' (review), *Monthly Film Bulletin*, December 1975, 264.

31 James Monaco, '*Jaws*' (review), *Sight and Sound*, Winter 1975–6, 56.

32 *Variety*, 15 July 1942, 5, 25.

33 *Variety*, 29 May 1946, 3.

34 *Variety*, 16 September 1936, 5.

35 *Variety*, 5 July 1939, 3, 12.

36 *Variety*, 22 July 1942, 6.

37 *Variety*, 3 July 1946, 1, 20.

38 *Variety*, 11 July 1956, 18; 19 February 1958, 4.

39 *Variety*, 26 June 1963, 7; advertisement, 20 November 1963, 5.

40 *Daily Variety*, 26 June 1957, 1, 3.

41 *Variety*, 21 January 1953, 20.

42 *Variety*, 8 April 1959, 17.

43 Advertisement, *Variety*, 28 April 1965, 14.

44 Advertisement, *Variety*, 9 April 1975, 10–11.

45 *Variety*, 16 April 1975, 3.

46 See Biskind, *Easy Riders, Raging Bulls*, 278.

47 Advertisement, *Variety*, 23 July 1975, 14–15.

48 Robert B. Frederick, 'Terror-joy of "Jaws": $102,650,000', *Variety*, 7 January 1976, 18.

49 On the tradition of wide releasing, see: Brian Hannan, *In Theaters Everywhere: A History of the Hollywood Wide Release, 1917–2017* (Jefferson: McFarland, 2018).

50 *Variety*, 26 April 1918, 45; Hall and Neale, *Epics, Spectacles, and Blockbusters*, 45; *Variety*, 11 March 1921, 33.

51 Hall and Neale, *Epics, Spectacles, and Blockbusters*, 97.

52 Advertisements, *Variety*, 27 May 1953, 12, and 1 July 1953, 12–13.

53 Advertisement, *Variety*, 27 January 1954, 21.

54 *Variety*, 24 June 1974.

55 *Variety*, 17 July 1963, 22; 18 September 1963, 19.

56 Advertisement, *Variety*, 4 September 1968, 12–13.

57 *Variety*, 15 December 1971, 13; advertisement, 22 December 1971, 26.

58 *Variety*, 13 June 1973, 4.

59 *Variety*, 11 June 1975, 4.

60 *Variety*, 7 May 1975, 40.

61 See, e.g., Bruck, *When Hollywood Had a King*, 342–3; Dade Hayes and Jonathan Bing, *Open Wide: How Hollywood Box Office Became a National Obsession* (New York: Hyperion/Miramax, 2004), 159–60; Joseph McBride, *Steven Spielberg: A Biography* (New York: Faber and Faber, 1997), 258.

62 Stuart Byron, 'First Annual Grosses Gloss', *Film Comment*, March–April 1976, 30.

63 Ibid.

64 Michael Coate, 'The Game Changer: Celebrating "Jaws" on Its 40th Anniversary', online at http://www.thedigitalbits.com/columns/history-legacy--showmanship/remembering-jaws-40th.

65 *Variety*, 17 November 1971, 4.

66 Connie Bruck also notes *The Godfather* as the model for *Jaws*: *When Hollywood Had a King*, 343–4. On their immediate successors, see Hall and Neale, *Epics, Spectacles, and Blockbusters*, 213.

3

Cutting to the chase: Editing *Jaws*

Warren Buckland

*In looking back over that final act of the movie, the seagoing sequence that took two
and a half months to shoot and doubled the budget, [Spielberg] was right in recalling
the pain, the frustration, the physical hardship, and the dogged weariness that went
into making those last few reels.*[1]

In the summer of 1975 *Time* magazine was not alone in praising *Jaws* for its 'technically
intricate and wonderfully crafted' film-making, achieved via 'subtly correct camera
placement and meticulous editing'.[2] Yet, the chaos and complexity of the shooting
schedule, especially the final action sequence (chasing and killing the shark), is now
legendary, with the non-functioning mechanical shark the main culprit. In her account
of events, the film's editor Verna Fields also mentions the difficulties of filming on
the open sea, which led to mix-ups in scene numbers and continuity (particularly the
number of barrels used to track the shark), and problems with matching the look of
water, sky and lighting conditions from one shot to the next, which were sometimes
filmed months apart.[3] The gulf between chaotic shooting schedule and the resulting
'technically intricate and wonderfully crafted' film led to the suggestion that the film
was 'saved' by Fields (the veteran editor who began her career in 1944 as assistant sound
editor on Fritz Lang's *Woman in the Window*). Fields played down this suggestion,[4] yet
the studio backing the film, Universal, promoted her to an executive role, and she won
an Oscar for her work on *Jaws*.

Some directors leave editors little to do, for they plan their films down to the last
shot or they do not shoot much coverage (shoot the same action from several different
camera set-ups), while other directors shoot an enormous amount of coverage and
leave the editor to choose the best angles (as well as the best takes). Film editor Ralph
Rosenblum experienced both scenarios. He opens his memoir *When the Shooting
Stops ... The Cutting Begins* with an account of how William Friedkin abandoned *The
Night They Raided Minsky's* (1968) after seeing the first cut, leaving Rosenblum to sort
through the forty hours of footage to rescue the film.[5] Rosenblum also discusses the
opposite situation, of having little footage to work with. Early in his career he edited
the low-budget gangster film *Pretty Boy Floyd* (1960), which he says consisted mainly
of scenes of two characters talking: 'For each scene, I was provided with a long shot
of the two actors and close-ups of each.'[6] Rosenblum's job simply involved editing

together the two close-ups and the establishing shot. There was very little creative leeway, resulting in a simple, mechanically edited film.

Verna Fields's experience was different. She preferred to work closely with directors, joining films at the production stage.[7] *Jaws* was no exception: she was on location and assembled a rough cut of the first two acts of the film during production, and edited the final act (the chase sequence at sea) back in Hollywood. In an interview with Fields, Joseph McBride notes that

> her editing as well as her advice in all areas of filmmaking were acknowledged as crucial to the success of such key 1970s films as Peter Bogdanovich's *What's Up, Doc?* [1972] and *Paper Moon* [1973], George Lucas's *American Graffiti* [1973], and Steven Spielberg's *Jaws*, for which she won an Academy Award.[8]

And screenwriter-actor Carl Gottlieb (who was also on location during the filming of *Jaws*) points out that 'Steven enjoys close supervision of editing and is one of a breed of filmmakers who must see every edit, collaborate on every cut, and live with a picture from the initial planning through the final release print.'[9] Rather than try to single out the work of editor and director, I shall instead examine the editing in *Jaws* from technical and perceptual standpoints, in order to determine the significance of continuity editing in the final chase sequence.

Method

My method integrates into formal analysis the knowledge of film craft, or basic filmic techniques, embedded in part in film-making manuals. Karel Reisz and Gavin Millar's *The Technique of Film Editing* remains the seminal text for understanding the film editor's normative conventions and thinking processes.[10] Drawing upon this technical knowledge creates an expanded mode of formal analysis, one based on a specialized understanding of how film-makers think and work. This expanded type of criticism raises new issues to address when writing about films – issues practitioners face and solve on a day-to-day basis in making films.

The director, cinematographer and editor work to create a seemingly effortless 'shot flow', whereby the final shots fit together in terms of continuity and physical changes. Roy Thompson identifies four types of continuity across cuts within a scene: continuity of content, of movement, of position and sound.[11] Physical changes across cuts include: symmetry, shot scale, camera angle and movement (movement of actors within the shot and/or camera movement). In terms of cinematography, critics frequently discuss camera placement, but not always in terms significant to the director – its placement inside or outside the 'circle of action', or the decision-making process that leads to the judgement to switch from one to the other.

In regard to technical editing knowledge, the ratio of camera set-ups to shots in a scene is significant in narrative cinema. Rarely is a set-up used only once in a scene. More often, a set-up is fragmented into several shots. How many set-ups does a director use in a scene, and how many shots does the editor create from those set-ups? Is the scene built upon discontinuity from shot to shot (cutaways, inserts) or is it based on the continuity of action from shot to shot? Does the editor allow dialogue to carry over a cut, or does he/she cut during a pause? What editing conventions does the editor rely on to create a sense of continuity (analytical cuts, directional continuity, eyeline matches, match on action cuts, shot/reverse shots, point-of-view [POV] editing)? Many of these editing conventions are planned before filming begins (they are everyday decisions made by directors and editors). However, when shooting a documentary or when filming on location, it is impossible to rigidly follow a storyboard due to unexpected factors. But Reisz observes that action sequences do at least offer the editor some leeway:

> In assembling an action sequence the editor works with a much greater degree of freedom than in more static scenes where dialogue plays the predominant role. In a dialogue scene most of the visuals form an essential and unavoidable counterpart to the words and the editor is constantly tied down by the continuity of the words when cutting the picture. The visuals are anchored from the moment they are shot: the editor is merely able to choose between alternative shots and to time the cuts to the greatest dramatic effect.[12]

Action sequences are not usually hampered by synchronized dialogue, although the action sequence still needs to create a logical series of actions, achieved via a cumulative progression of a series of shots.

Technical innovations in *Jaws*

Jaws displays a number of formal and technical innovations: (1) it effectively combines suspense, curiosity and surprise; (2) it employs off-screen space for dramatic purposes; (3) it uses unattributed or delayed POV shots from the shark's perspective; (4) it places the camera on the water's surface; (5) it has a memorable score; and (6) the editing of the final chase sequence exceeds the sum of its parts.

In this chapter I focus on the final innovation but will give a brief overview of the others. The film's narrational strategies, especially the carefully planned shifts from restricted to omniscient narration, control the flow of story information to spectators, generating surprise, curiosity and suspense. In restricted narration, important story information is withheld and is only revealed much later. If the spectator is not informed that crucial information was withheld, surprise is created when it is eventually revealed. But if the spectator is given hints and clues about the withheld information, curiosity is created. The spectator's restricted knowledge of story events is usually mirrored in a central character, such as a detective who, in attempting to piece together a crime, experiences curiosity and surprise when he or she uncovers the crucial information. In omniscient narration, by contrast, the spectator is conferred crucial story information, which is not initially conveyed to some or all of the characters. This results in a discrepancy of knowledge between character(s) and spectator, creating anticipation and suspense.[13]

Noël Burch defines the fundamental opposition in film space as that between on-screen and off-screen spaces.[14] On-screen space names the space inside the film frame, and off-screen space lies beyond the film frame, which is divided into six segments: the four spaces beyond each frame line, a fifth space (the space behind the camera) and a sixth space (the space hidden within the film frame). In *Jaws*, Spielberg uses off-screen space (especially the sixth space) proficiently to create surprise (when, e.g., the shark suddenly emerges from the water, most famously when Brody is on the *Orca* boat throwing bait into the sea to attract the shark[15]). In addition, Spielberg signals the off-screen presence of the shark via yellow barrels, which are attached to harpoons fired into the shark from a harpoon gun. The barrels act as an important on-screen stand-in for the off-screen shark.

Spielberg also presents the opposite scenario: the film is punctuated by POV shots from the shark's perspective as it approaches unsuspecting victims (a moment of omniscient narration), although the shark's appearance is delayed, making the POV shot initially unattributed. What this means is that the origin of the glance (the shark) is not initially shown, but the glance itself is shown.

In regard to innovative cinematography and camera placement, neither the screenplay (by Peter Benchley and Carl Gottlieb) nor Tom Wright's storyboards conceived of filming parts of *Jaws* underwater from the shark's perspective; nor did they conceive of filming at water level. The latter technique was made possible by cinematographer Bill Butler's invention of the water box. In response to a question about why he used the water box, he said:

> The reason for using the water box is that you then have the ability to get the camera right at water level. You can literally let the water level rise up to the bottom of the lens without getting the camera wet. That's the only reason: just to keep the camera dry. It's nothing more than a square box; it looks like a fish tank. It has a solid bottom and the front is glass so that you can set a camera down in it.[16]

Butler's water box closely aligns spectators to the events in the water; it increases their psychological engagement with the film's events by placing them on the water's surface, inside the circle of action.

John Williams's score accompanies these innovative visual aspects of the film (precise camera placement and its movement through the water, representing the shark's POV). Giorgio Biancorosso argues that the accompaniment is literal: the first shark attack in the opening scene consists of several unattributed underwater POV shots accompanied by the 'Jaws theme', 'an *ostinato* motive consisting of the alternation of two notes'.[17] Biancorosso goes on to argue that 'it is only when we see the consequences of the upwardly moving shot, at the sound of the victim's screams, that the [musical] motive is wedded once and for all, if in retrospect, to [the shark]'.[18] The musical motive therefore comes to represent the shark's presence, filling in for the absence of the glance's origin in the unattributed POV shot.

How to edit a chase scene

Karel Reisz devotes Section 2 of *The Technique of Film Editing* to the practice of editing particular types of film sequences, beginning with the action sequence. He uses the chase at the end of Jules Dassin's *Naked City* (1948) as an example. Reisz determines 'how the editor has contrived [to create a] perfectly lucid continuity'[19] via the following techniques:

- Cross-cutting between pursued (the criminal Garza) and pursuer (the policeman Halloran).
- Cut away from pursuit to the police chief (Muldoon).
- Variation in the rate of cutting to underline the changing tension in the action.
- Repetition of camera set-ups (pursued then pursuer traverse the same location filmed in the same manner; such repetition creates textual cohesion).
- Directional movement within the shot (characters run towards/away from camera; they run into or out of screen space).
- Each cut switches attention by showing a different location.

Reisz argues that the key to a chase sequence is not rapid editing, as is commonly assumed, but the switch to a different location with each cut (a technique that incorporates the first two techniques, cross-cutting and cutaways). Paul Weatherwax, the editor of *Naked City*,

> has not cut the passage particularly fast, but has concentrated in switching the action around quickly among the three participants, in order to give the impression of the smoothly co-ordinated action of the two police contingents working together against the criminal.[20]

In the central part of the chase, 'each cut takes us to another part of the action: there are no cuts which continue the action of the previous shot'.[21] This switching of attention (which is also a form of omniscient narration) creates the impression of fast action. There are in fact two pieces of action taking place: pursuer–pursued, plus Muldoon and his men. The chase sequence systematically cuts from the pursued to the pursuer and then to Muldoon.

Cuts in action

The third act of *Jaws* comprises a chase sequence consisting of nine (loosely defined) scenes spread over 50 minutes (see Table 3.1). In this third act, the action is pared down to two possible outcomes: death of the shark/death of Quint, Hooper and Brody. Negative tension is created by the severity of this future event. The second option seems more probable, which is gradually realized when the *Orca* begins to sink, Quint is killed and Hooper disappears; but in the film's final state of affairs, the options are

Table 3.1 Act Three of *Jaws*

1.	Out at sea. Early signs of tension between Quint, Hooper and Brody.
2.	The shark is hooked on the fishing line but escapes.
3.	The shark surfaces and attacks the *Orca*.
4.	In the cabin, Quint, Hooper and Brody drink and exchange stories. The shark attacks.
5.	Quint and Hooper begin to repair the *Orca*, but the shark attacks again by dragging the *Orca* and then chasing it; the *Orca* begins to sink.
6.	Hooper goes into the water in a cage, but fails to kill the shark; instead, the shark almost kills Hooper.
7.	The shark kills Quint and almost kills Brody, but Brody manages to kill the shark by shooting at the air tank in its mouth.
8.	Hooper resurfaces and swims back to shore with Brody.
9.	Shot of the coastline with Brody and Hooper in the background reaching the shore. End credits.

reversed, for Brody succeeds in killing the shark and Hooper reappears, dissipating the negative tension.[22]

Within scene 5 of the third act we can identify a conventionally edited chase (1.41:03 to 1.43.47 on the DVD). This segment of film, comprising thirty-one shots and lasting 164 seconds, is united around a continuous piece of action, in which the shark chases the *Orca*. The segment begins with a shot of Quint starting up the engine and Hooper saying 'He's chasing us. I don't believe it' and ends when the chase is over, with Brody and Hooper staring off-screen at the shark (see Table 3.2). These thirty-one shots can be grouped into seven types (defined in terms of content) (see Table 3.3):

1. Quint is in the foreground of this series of shots, with Hooper in the middle ground on the left and Brody in the middle ground on the right. These six shots are evenly distributed throughout the first half of this segment. The camera position is the same – that is, the same camera set-up is used and is divided into six shots, although the framing changes slightly, for the three barrels the shark is dragging along can be seen in the background of the final four shots – 7, 11, 13, 16 (see Figure 3.1).
2. The *Orca* is filmed either from the stern (shots 2, 5, 20, 29) or the bow (shots 10, 17), either with a still camera (2, 5, 29) or a moving camera (10, 17 and 20).
3. Similarly, the barrels are filmed from several angles: coming towards the camera (3, 12, 29), moving away from the camera (5, 30) and filmed from the side (18). The segment as a whole therefore consists of repetition (the six shots of group [a]) and variation (different shots of the boat and barrels).
4. Brody and Hooper are filmed together on two occasions: in profile looking off-screen left at the barrels (shot 6) and filmed facing the camera (looking off-screen at the barrels) (shot 31). In this final shot they do not appear in the frame together, but successively, as the camera moves from Brody down to Hooper (Figures 3.2 and 3.3).

Table 3.2 The thirty-one shots of scene 5

1. Quint + Brody + Hooper	17. *Orca*
2. *Orca*	18. Barrels
3. Barrels	19. Tachometer
4. Quint + Brody + Hooper	20. *Orca*
5. *Orca* + barrels	21. Hooper
6. Brody + Hooper	22. Hooper
7. Quint + Brody + Hooper + barrels	23. Engine cover (explosion)
8. Tachometer (RPM gauge)	24. Brody
9. Hatch	25. Quint
10. *Orca*	26. Hooper
11. Quint + Brody + Hooper + barrels	27. Engine cover
12. Barrels	28. Quint and Hooper
13. Quint + Brody + Hooper + barrels	29. *Orca* and barrels
14. Tachometer	30. Barrels (+ Brody)
15. Hatch	31. Brody and Hooper
16. Quint + Brody + Hooper + barrels	

Table 3.3 Seven types of shots in scene 5

1.	Quint + Brody + Hooper	6 shots: 1, 4, 7, 11, 13, 16
2.	The *Orca* filmed from the water	6 shots: 2, 5, 10, 17, 20, 29
3.	The three barrels	4 shots: 3, 12, 18, 30
4.	Brody and Hooper	2 shots: 6, 31
5.	The gauge	3 shots: 8, 14, 19
6.	The hatch and engine cover	4 shots: 9, 15, 23, 27
7.	Additional shots on the *Orca*	6 shots: 21, 22, 24, 25, 26, 28

5. Close-ups of the tachometer (RPM gauge) are linked to Quint's awareness (he is aware of the tachometer directly in front of him, which he occasionally glances at).

6. But shots of the hatch, where smoke begins to billow, do not represent any character's awareness; the three men on the boat do not see this event. Instead, these shots (9, 15) constitute omniscient narration and create suspense by giving the spectator more information than the characters, thereby setting up a hierarchy between the spectator and characters. (Quint can surmise that the engine is under pressure, but he can infer this from watching the tachometer, not from observing the hatch, which he cannot see from his position on the boat.)

7. Shot 23 continues to involve the camera. The engine explodes, and the cover moves rapidly towards the camera, almost hitting it. In fact, the engine explodes at the end of shot 22; the explosion in shot 23 is either a second explosion or, more

Figure 3.1 Quint (Robert Shaw) looks off-screen towards the space behind the camera (the camera is still but the boat is moving). *Jaws* (1975). © Universal Pictures.

Figure 3.2 Brody (Roy Scheider) looks off-screen towards the space behind the camera (the camera is moving but the boat is still). *Jaws* (1975). © Universal Pictures.

likely, the same explosion filmed from a different angle and with a slight temporal overlap (less than half a second), which increases the explosion's effectiveness.

In shot 24 Brody is shown reacting to the explosion, but he does nothing. In shot 25 Quint grabs the fire extinguisher to put out the fire. He is filmed in close up and moves very close towards the camera. By the time the shot ends, he is exiting screen right, facing the camera just a few inches from it. In shot 26 Hooper gathers together his diving equipment, and in shot 27 Quint puts out the fire in the engine. Shots 21–27 switch the action around by cutting between the three men in their own spaces carrying out their own tasks, in contrast to the key establishing shot (a), repeated six times in the first half of the segment, which unites the three men and the shark in the

Figure 3.3 Hooper (Richard Dreyfuss) looks off-screen towards the space behind the camera (the camera is moving but the boat is still). *Jaws* (1975). © Universal Pictures.

same shot. The final shots mark the end of this segment, of the *Orca* stationary in the water and the shark swimming past, watched by Brody and Hooper.

As with the chase in *Naked City*, in *Jaws* moving towards/moving away from the camera is a significant structuring principle. In both films, the camera is not observing from a distance outside the circle of action, but is inside the circle of action. In shot 2, the *Orca* begins close to the camera but quickly moves away from it; in shot 3, the barrels move at great speed towards the camera, and the shot ends with the frame almost completely filled by the three barrels. These two shots therefore mark the beginning of the chase via the inversion of dynamic movement within the frame, divided by a 180-degree cut: the boat moves rapidly away from the camera/cut 180 degrees/the barrels move rapidly towards the camera.

This inverted dynamic movement, linked by a 180-degree cut, is mirrored in shots 21–22 of Hooper: in 21, he moves away from the camera and in shot 22 he moves towards the camera (where he jumps into some water in the boat's hull, splashing the camera, which is on the surface of the water in the water box). These two shots of Hooper are also linked via a 180-degree cut – but an inward cut, not outward. (In an inward 180-degree cut, the same subject is filmed, first from one side and then from the other side. In an outward 180-degree cut, the camera moves 180 degrees and points in the opposite direction, as is the case with shots 2–3.)

The first and last shots of this segment create textual cohesion by inverting one another. In shot 1 (Figure 3.1) Quint looks off-screen towards the camera – to what Burch called the fifth space, the space behind the camera (in this instance, the boat's bow). The camera is still but the boat is moving. In shot 31 Brody and Hooper look off-screen towards the camera – to the space behind the camera (in this instance, the boat's stern). The camera is moving but the boat is still (Figures 3.2 and 3.3). This segment is punctuated by a specific event: Quint begins to steer the *Orca* to shore but burns out the engine, which explodes, incapacitating the boat and its crew. The segment is therefore divided into a 'before' and 'after': before the explosion, the space is united via the frame (the three men and the shark appear in the same shot) or via overlapping space and eyeline matches. After the explosion the space is fragmented, as each man occupies a separate space and the film cuts from one space to another space.

Continuity

Continuity of content, movement, position and sound is maintained in this segment via several techniques. Firstly, there is the overlap of space between successive shots:

- 90-degree cuts (shots 5, 6, 7)
- Analytic cuts (shots 12–13)
- 180-degree internal cuts (shots 21–22: Hooper filmed from the back on the deck/ Hopper filmed from the front inside the cabin)
- Spielberg maintains spatial unity of the pursuit by keeping pursuer–pursued in the same frame (in shots 5, 7, 11, 13, 16, 29 and 30).

In a 90-degree cut, parts of the same space appear on-screen in successive shots, but are filmed from a different (90-degree) angle. It is the overlap of space and repetition of content from one shot to the next that helps to maintain continuity. In shot 5, Brody and Hooper appear in the background of a very long shot, staring out to sea towards the camera. In shot 6, the camera moves 90 degrees to film Brody and Hooper in profile staring out to sea. In shot 7 the camera moves 90 degrees again, this time facing Quint steering the boat, with Brody and Hooper in the middle ground looking out to sea; they are now filmed from their back. In all three shots the action is continuous, but this action is filmed from successive 90-degree angles. The change from one shot to the next is not confusing, for the cuts maintain the physical geography of the space and the spectator's orientation in relation to that space.

In an analytic cut the camera points in the same direction, along the same axis; only the scale of the shot changes. Shot 12 shows the barrels from the perspective of the *Orca*'s stern (but without showing the boat), and shot 13 shows the same action, but this time with the boat and crew in the foreground of the shot.

Second, a few of the shots are linked via an eyeline match: between shots 2–3 and 5–6 (Brody and Hooper/eyeline match/the barrels, on both occasions); and 13–14 (Quint/eyeline match/the tachometer). There is no overlap of space or action; instead, the successive shots are linked by the eyeline of an on-screen character looking off-screen, which motivates a cut to the off-screen object the character sees.

Third, in terms of match on action cuts, Hooper's movement is matched over the cuts between shots 21–22 and 28–29; the movement of the barrels continues over shots 29–30; in shot 6 Brody stands up and in shot 7 the movement is completed (although it is possible to argue that the movement was completed just before the cut). The match on action draws attention away from the cut by maintaining the continuity of the action across the cut.

And fourth, in regard to sound, music and dialogue, orchestral music accompanies shots 1 to 6; the 'Jaws theme' is prominent when the barrels appear in shot 3, linking the barrels to the shark. Diegetic sound dominates from shots 7 to 24 – the sound of the boat's engine is continuous across the cuts, up to the moment the engine explodes. Shots 7 to 24 also contain fragments of synchronized dialogue and of Quint singing. When Quint grabs the fire extinguisher (shot 25), the orchestral music again takes over. There is no dialogue editing in this segment – that is, no dialogue cutting points, no speaking across cuts; instead, the dialogue is contained within the shots where it is spoken, with the exception of Quint's singing, which covers shots 16–20: 16) Quint on-screen, 17) long shot of the *Orca*, 18) the barrels, 19) close up of the tachometer and 20) long shot of the *Orca*. The singing is constant, steady and continuous, even though the camera's distance from Quint varies significantly from shot to shot. Only in shot 16 is there direct synchronization of Quint's lips and the song. In this instance, the *Jaws* action segment under analysis confirms Reisz's observation, quoted above, that 'in assembling an action sequence the editor works with a much greater degree of freedom than in more static scenes where dialogue plays the predominant role'.

The continuity techniques identified in this segment of thirty-one shots from *Jaws* are deployed throughout the entire third act. In addition, shot/reverse shot is used in scene 4 (Quint, Hooper and Brody drink and exchange stories), with Quint and Hooper initially in the main shots and Brody in the reverse shots, until Brody joins Quint and Hooper just before the shark attacks. Shot/reverse shot is also used extensively in scene 6 (Hooper goes into the water in a cage, although there is no dialogue editing, only Hooper speaking while he is on-screen) and scene 7 (confrontation between Quint/ the shark and then Brody/the shark).

Continuity of content, movement, position and sound, created via a cumulative progression of carefully edited shots, is key to the success of the film's third act – 'carefully edited' not only in terms of continuity techniques but also in regard to the type of shots used, where they are placed and how many times they appear. In other words, the success of the film's chase sequence is dependent on how the shots fit together to create shot flow.

Conclusions

In the classical Hollywood film *Naked City*, the editor's primary goal was to create and maintain continuity in order to convey the physical details of the scene (to maintain geographical location, consistent character movement and direction, plus the spectator's orientation in relation to the location and the characters). But in his analysis of the film's final chase sequence, Reisz points out that the continuity is not exact, because the pursuer–pursued appear to be very close to one another, running past the same spot in quick succession (the background is very similar). This is in fact more pronounced than Reisz states, for the pursuer–pursued run past the exact same spot more than once. Yet, this is not noticeable on first viewing, for spectators simply follow the action.

Shot 30 of the *Jaws* segment analysed in this chapter can be cited as an exception to the segment's reliance on continuity editing, for the shark is seen moving in the opposite direction in relation to the *Orca*. Of course, it could have turned around while the action focused on Quint, Hooper and Brody on the boat, but no image shows the shark changing direction. Nonetheless, the sudden change in direction is not jarring, for the shark had time to change direction (the change in direction is not instantaneous, which would have been jarring).

The third act of *Jaws* is plagued by another continuity issue: number of harpoons + barrels fired into the shark. The *Orca* has five barrels displayed prominently on the bow. In scene 3 of act 3, Quint fires one harpoon + barrel into the shark. In scene 5, he fires a second harpoon + barrel into the shark, and then the *Orca* chases the shark. However, only one barrel is visible in the water. Moments later, Quint fires a third harpoon + barrel, but only two are visible in the water, while three of the five barrels are visible on the boat. The shark then begins to drag the *Orca* along, and Quint's response is to fire another harpoon, this time while standing at the boat's stern (the other times he was standing on the bow). Quint's position creates a dramatic shot, for the barrel attached to the harpoon smashes through the window of the cabin, hits Brody in the face (knocking off his glasses) before it lands in the water. But we only see three barrels in the water, and two on deck, even though Quint has fired four harpoons + barrels at the shark. In scene 8 Brody and Hooper use the two remaining barrels (although there should only be one left) as flotation aids as they swim to shore.

This reveals what more than one professional editor has claimed – that continuity is not the only concern when joining shots together and choosing the cutting point. Cutting should primarily enhance the drama of the story, while technical accuracy is secondary. For example, Richard Pepperman argues that editors should cut 'for value and impact – not matches'.[23] Editing needs to serve and enhance the dramatic situation of each scene, rather than mechanically follow rules of continuity. This principle has been taken to the extreme in what Steven Shaviro calls 'post-continuity' cinema (Michael Bay, Tony Scott), in which 'a preoccupation with immediate effects trumps any concern for broader continuity – whether on the immediate shot-by-shot level, or on that of the overall narrative'.[24] Spatial geography and continuity are relegated while delivering a series of shocks to spectators is privileged.

Joseph P. Magliano and Jeffrey M. Zacks identified three degrees of continuity in editing: 'edits that are continuous in space, time, and action; edits that are discontinuous in space or time but continuous in action; and edits that are discontinuous in action as well as space or time'.[25] Edits following the conventions of continuity editing do not hinder the perception of actions and events, while discontinuities in space and/ or time have minor effects (the changes in space and time become noticeable but do not disrupt the comprehension of actions and events). After all, each cut by its very nature creates an instantaneous displacement in space (and sometimes in time), which is only partly disguised by the techniques of continuity editing – directional continuity, match on action, eyeline match, sound bridge, etc. (Here I disagree with Magliano and Zacks, for no cut is continuous in space.) But discontinuity of action suggests an event boundary – the end of one event and the beginning of another. If the same action is presented in a discontinuous manner, it can lead to confusion. Magliano and Zacks conclude that the primary aim of continuity editing is therefore to maintain the continuity of action and events within scenes, with the continuity of space and time in themselves of secondary importance, a conclusion reached by other cognitive psychologists.[26] The coherence of the text is therefore less important than the coherence of the represented actions and events. Post-continuity can thereby be defined in terms of what Magliano and Zacks call 'edits that are discontinuous in action as well as space or time'. The inconsistency of harpoons + barrels in *Jaws* is a borderline case: on the one hand it signifies an inconsistency in the action, while on the other hand it remains secondary to the stark narrative conflict between the shark/the three men on the boat. Spectators attending to the film's narrative events are engaged with this conflict, not with idly counting barrels, especially in a medium where perception is temporally constrained (the next shot usually arrives within a matter of seconds). In addition, one study of eye tracking in narrative film (replicated in other studies) concluded that the spectator's region of interest (the part of the screen they focus on) is on average around 12 per cent of the entire screen, usually the centre.[27] What this means is that, when viewing a film in real time, spectators tend to focus on the 10–12 per cent of the screen where the main action is unfolding. We can transpose this observation from spectacle to narrative, which similarly creates a narrow zone of interest that focuses attention on key actions and events rather than all actions and events taking place on-screen. In *Jaws*, the *number* of barrels (although not the barrels themselves) would tend to fall outside this narrow zone of narrative interest.

Nonetheless, there are notable differences between scenes that employ techniques of continuity editing and those that violate these techniques. Magliano and Zacks suggest that scenes violating the conventions of continuity editing are not remembered as well as scenes that follow the conventions (for it is more difficult to construct a mental representation of the actions and events), and that discontinuous scenes lead to an increase in eye movement.[28] Of course, each cut necessarily creates discontinuity and heightens the spectator's visual attention, as he or she searches for the main point of interest after the cut, but the techniques of continuity editing disguise the cut and thereby minimize discontinuity and eye movement.

From the short analysis carried out in this chapter, and from the experiments carried out by cognitive psychologists, we can conclude that shot flow and strict adherence to the conventions of continuity editing are not necessary for the basic comprehension of actions and events in a narrative film, but that they nonetheless constitute 'added value' that can be appreciated by film-makers and *cinephiles* – such as the *Time* reviewer who found *Jaws* to be a 'wonderfully crafted' film due to the way it exploited basic filmic techniques such as camera placement and editing.

Notes

1   Carl Gottlieb, *The Jaws Log*, expanded edition (New York: Newmarket Press, 2012), 143.

2 Anon., 'Summer of the Shark', *Time*, 105, no. 26 (23 June 1975). Academic Search Complete, EBSCOhost (accessed 25 July 2018).

3 See Joseph McBride, 'The Editor: Verna Fields', in Joseph McBride, ed., *Filmmakers on Filmmaking: The American Film Institute Seminars on Motion Pictures and Television, Volume 1* (Los Angeles: J.P. Tarchner, 1983), 144. For another informed eyewitness account of the film's final action sequence, see Gottlieb, *The Jaws Log*, especially 162–3.

4 See McBride, 'The Editor: Verna Fields', 144.

5 Ralph Rosenblum, with Robert Karen, *When the Shooting Stops ... the Cutting Begins: A Film Editor's Story*, new edition (Cambridge, MA: Da Capo Press, 1986), 11–30.

6 Rosenblum, *When the Shooting Stops*, 135.

7 See McBride, 'The Editor: Verna Fields', 141–2; and Gottlieb, *The Jaws Log*, 103–4.

8 McBride, 'The Editor: Verna Fields', 139.

9 Gottlieb, *The Jaws Log*, 104.

10 Karel Reisz and Gavin Millar, *The Technique of Film Editing*, 2nd edn (London: Focal Press, 1968). Reisz wrote the first part of this book (13–272) and Gavin Millar wrote the second part (279–387). In this chapter I will only be quoting from Reisz's section.

11 Roy Thompson, *Grammar of the Edit* (Oxford: Focal Press, 1993), 48–9.

12 Reisz, *The Technique of Film Editing*, 84.

13 For a detailed analysis of the concepts of 'surprise', 'curiosity' and 'suspense', see William Brewer, 'The Nature of Narrative Suspense and the Problem of Rereading', in Peter Vorderer, Hans J. Wulff and Mike Friedrichsen, eds, *Suspense: Conceptualizations, Theoretical Analyses, and Empirical Explorations* (Mahwah, NJ: L. Erlbaum Associates, 1996), 107–27.

14 Noël Burch, *Theory of Film Practice*, translated by Helen R. Lane (Princeton, NJ: Princeton University Press, 1981), 17–31.

15 This moment in the film in fact creates a combination of surprise (the spectator and Brody were unaware of the shark's presence just below the surface of the water) and a few seconds of suspense (for the spectator briefly sees the shark before Brody sees it, for he is facing away from the water).

16 Bill Butler, in Dennis Schaefer and Larry Salvato, *Masters of Light: Conversations with Contemporary Cinematographers* (Berkeley: University of California Press), 91.

17 Giorgio Biancorosso, 'The Shark in the Music', *Music Analysis*, 29, no. 1/3 (2010): 306.

18 Ibid., 309.

19 Reisz, *The Technique of Film Editing*, 74.

20 Ibid., 76.

21 Ibid.

22 As with all narratives, there cannot be a sense of satisfaction and relief if the negative tension does not exist. See Dolf Zillmann, 'The Psychology of Suspense in Dramatic Exposition', in Vorderer et al., *Suspense*, 199–231 (especially 220–7).

23 Richard Pepperman, *The Eye Is Quicker. Film Editing: Making a Good Film Better* (Studio City, CA: Wiese), 27.

24 Steven Shaviro, *Post-Cinematic Affect* (Winchester: Zero Books, 2010), 123. See also Steven Shaviro, 'Post-Continuity: An Introduction', in Shane Denson and Julia Leyda, eds, *Post-Cinema: Theorizing 21st-Century Film* (Falmer: REFRAME Books, 2016), 51–64.

25 Joseph P. Magliano and Jeffrey M. Zacks, 'The Impact of Continuity Editing in Narrative Film on Event Segmentation', *Cognitive Science*, 35 (2011): 1489.

26 In their experimental study of eye movements following cuts, Filip Germeys and Géry d'Ydewalle conclude that:

> important changes in the visual scene, due to the changed camera position, do not really disturb the viewer. The experiment provides evidence against the hypothesis that violating editing rules causes large degrees of confusion or ruins the representation of a scene. In terms of visual perception, the Formal Editing Principle (Hollywood editing rules), which emphasizes smooth transitions between shots, does not need to be followed strictly; the findings are thus more in agreement with the modern viewpoint which states that perceptual inconsistencies between shots are easily overcome by the narrative structure of the movie. (Filip Germeys and Géry d'Ydewalle, 'The Psychology of Film: Perceiving Beyond the Cut', *Psychological Research* 71 [2007]: 465)

27 Robert B. Goldstein, Russell L. Woods and Eli Peli, 'Where People Look When Watching Movies: Do All Viewers Look at the Same Place?' *Computers in Biology and Medicine* 37 (2007): 957–64.

28 Magliano and Zacks, 'The Impact of Continuity Editing', 1511, and references in Ed Tan, 'Film-Induced Affect as a Witness Emotion', *Poetics* 23 (1994): 28, n. 19.

4

'The shark is not working' – But the music is: Scoring a hit with *Jaws*

Emilio Audissino

Jaws was a high-stakes gamble for Steven Spielberg. A budding film director with a substantial track record of television works despite his young age, including the sensational *Duel* (1971), and one feature-length film, *The Sugarland Express* (1974), Spielberg strenuously lobbied to get the *Jaws* director's chair, and he eventually got at the helm.[1] While *The Sugarland Express* was not designed to be a box office champion, *Jaws* was, in the wake of the fame of Peter Benchley's best seller. The film had to be a hit.

Trying to make the shark work

Two pre-production choices put the outcome seriously at risk. Spielberg insisted that the maritime shoots be done on location, in the open sea rather than in some studio tank. The advantage of location filming was increased realism and hence increased make-believe. The (big) disadvantage was the significantly lesser control one could have over the open-sea set. To this artistic decision another threatening variable was added: the mechanical shark. The protagonist of the story, the shark had to be shown: 'the story and the movie required that you see a boat, and men, and a shark, all in the same shot, on the surface of an ocean with an open horizon', explained screenwriter Carl Gottlieb.[2] A full-size animatronic of a Great White was needed. The veteran special-effects wizard Robert A. Mattey came out of retirement to accept the challenge. No mechanical creature of such complexity and size had been manufactured before, and since Mattey had managed to build a convincing giant squid for *20,000 Leagues under the Sea* (1954), he seemed the only one up to the task. Unfortunately, time pressure prevented conclusive trials and proper tests. 'Bruce' – this was the animatronic's moniker, after Spielberg's lawyer – was not ready to face the brutal attacks of the ocean and salt water. From the very first moment it was placed into the sea water, it became clear to everybody that Bruce would not work. The mechanics jammed continuously and Bruce – when not sinking – was unreliable and mostly unusable.[3] With Bruce requiring constant repairs – on location – and costs piling up, the producers even considered shutting down the production. Bruce's malfunctioning made the estimated budget of $8.5 million soar to $11 million and the 55-day production schedule inflate to 150 days.[4] Among crew members, a nickname for the derailing film started to circulate: 'Flaws'.[5]

Spielberg soldiered on and kept rewriting and shooting anyway. Since the 'leading character' was indisposed, he resorted to an array of placeholders to indicate the shark's presence: piers torn and dragged away; air barrels previously fixed to the beast's back to signal its presence underneath, point-of-view shots of the shark – so it could be conveniently kept off-screen – and, of course, a fin that travelled across the water surface. Indeed, in the 124-minute film,[6] eventually the shark can only be glimpsed at 60' and it finally shows up only at 78', totalling a mere 4' of screen time. Necessity is the mother of invention, which applies to the arts too. Or, to borrow from Rudolf Arnheim, it is the technical limitations of the medium that make art possible, 'a necessity of which the artist makes a virtue'.[7] In hindsight, it was Bruce's constant technical failures and its forced visual absence that made *Jaws* the thriller masterpiece we all know. As acknowledged by Spielberg himself and the producers, keeping the shark hidden gave the film its true edge and terrorizing appeal.[8] No sophisticated animatronic or advance CGI (computer-generated imagery) can beat what is 'the world's most powerful graphics chip, imagination', to resort to a non-scholarly but very effective citation from *The Big Bang Theory*'s Sheldon Cooper.[9] Of all the several very effective signs that the film employed to reveal the presence of the beast while at the same time keeping it visually hidden for our imagination to fill in, music is the most effective.

Enter John Williams

Before *Jaws*, John Williams and Steven Spielberg had previously collaborated on only one project, *The Sugarland Express*. The young director had had his eyes on Williams for a long time:

> I'm a soundtrack collector and I collected scores of great composers. … And for many years there was like a drought. A lot of the great old composers like Dimitri Tiomkin and Max Steiner were no longer writing music any more. … There was just a real loss of pure symphonic film music. And then when I heard *The Reivers* [1969] and *The Cowboys* [1972] I said, 'My God, this guy must be eighty years old!' … I really thought, 'Maybe he's some guy who's eighty years old, who maybe wrote the greatest scores of his life.' And I wanted to know who this guy was and I met this young man named John Williams. … I was amazed! You know, 'It's a rebirth, film music is back. It's alive! Hallelujah!'[10]

If *The Sugarland Express* was 'a first date', *Jaws* was when the actual artistic 'marriage' between Spielberg and Williams took place. Here John Williams demonstrated not only his musical versatility and proficiency but also his profound dramaturgic understanding of what type of sound the film at hand intrinsically needs. From *Jaws* onwards, Williams has been one of Spielberg's most trusted collaborators, always able to devise the one right solution for any specific film problem: 'John has transformed and uplifted every movie that we've made together', praised Spielberg.[11]

Williams has a strongly visual approach to the conceptualization of his film scores, an approach that is inevitable when music adheres to the film as tightly as his music typically does. Consequently, he is used to *not* reading scripts:

> It's like when you read a novel: you envisage the locales, you cast the players in your mind. That's the reason, I think, why people are so often disappointed by film versions of novels they have read – they don't conform to their preconceptions.[12]

He further explains his modus operandi:

> I will sit down and look at the film with the director. … I'd like to have a pristine reaction to film, as a reader would to a novel, to not know what comes on the next page. Because that first impression of surprise, shock, excitement, boredom if it dips, because that sense of ebb, flow and tempo is best gotten from a viewer who doesn't really know what to expect next.[13]

Hence Williams generally does not commence working on a film until a workprint is ready to be 'spotted'– this is the Hollywood jargon for when a director and composer view a draft edit of the film and decide which parts require music and which don't and also write down the precise timing, duration, contour and dynamics of the parts to be scored. Williams's reaction to the film was positive: 'I came out of the screening so excited. I had been working for nearly 25 years in Hollywood but had never had an opportunity to do a film that was absolutely brilliant. … *Jaws* just floored me.'[14] It is customary that directors and editors, when the film is assembled, resort to a 'temp track', a selection of repertoire music, either from the concert canon or from other film scores. This selection provides guidance to the editor to shape the pace and the rhythmic configuration of a sequence, or serves as an inspiration for the creation of a specific mood. Since music is something difficult to verbalize, the temp track is also helpful, during the meeting with the composer, to give an indication of the kind of music the director has in mind. With *Jaws*, of course, the required mood was one of tension and thrill, and Spielberg had found (or *thought* he had found) an appropriate example to show Williams what music the film called for:

> I had actually cut in one of John's own pieces of music for the opening titles. That was John's title theme from Robert Altman's film *Images* [1972]. So I cut in a section that was a lovely piano solo with some very ominous strings in the background that would probably have been wonderful for a movie about a hunting. And I thought it was playing against the obvious primal feelings that run very deep through *Jaws*. When Johnny heard it, though, he just didn't go for it at all.[15]

As in the case of *Psycho* (1960) – when Bernard Herrmann ignored Hitchcock's indication about leaving the shower murder unscored[16] – here too the composer knew better. Explains Williams: 'Most of the discussions I had with Steven at that point were about the shark. The challenge was to find a way to characterize something that's underwater with music rather than with sound effects'[17] – unlike, for example, the choice that would be made for *Piranha* (1978), in which the deadly voracity of the school of fish is rendered through a buzz sound, an aggressive static noise. Williams's solution, contrary to Spielberg's idea, was exactly to build on those 'primal feelings' depicted in the film. When Williams invited Spielberg to his house to give the director a foretaste of the film's main theme, he played, with just two fingers on the lower keys of the piano, the now-famous *da-da-da-da dum-da-da-da dum-da-da-da da-da-da-da …*:

> When Johnny played me the *Jaws* score on the piano, I thought he was pulling my leg. … And he played it again. And then he played it until I stopped laughing. I had a more esoteric idea musically in mind. He said, 'The sophisticated approach you would like me to take isn't the approach you took with the film I just experienced'.[18]

Williams devised a musical equivalent of the beast, not a melody as Spielberg would have expected but rather the primitive rhythmic simplicity of an *ostinato*: a hammering and unrelenting repetition of two notes, periodically broken by a third accented one (see Figure 4.1).

The ostinato gives music a motor quality, an immediate feeling of something in motion. In this case the pattern is made more refined by that third accented note, which is like a stronger propulsive thrust, and gives the whole patter an increased drive and momentum. Those bass notes also recall the heartbeat, the primordial rhythm of life, 'the pounding of a heart under great stress' in Giorgio Biancorosso's words, which identifies the creature depicted by the motif as primitive and driven by very basic and implacable instincts.[19] Williams reminisces:

> I fiddled around with the idea of creating something that was very … brainless, … like the shark. All instinct … Meaning something [that] could be very repetitious, very visceral, and grab you in your gut, not in your brain. Remember, Steven didn't have the computer shark. He only had his rubber ducky, so the simple idea of that bass ostinato, just repeating those two notes and introduce a third note when you don't expect it and so on. It could be something you could play very softly, which would indicate that the shark is far away when all you see is water. Brainless

Figure 4.1 Transcription of John Williams, Shark Motif #1 (ostinato), © 1975 BMI, published by USI B Music Publishing, administered by Songs of Universal, Inc., from *Suite from Jaws*, printed by Hal Leonard, 'John Williams Signature Edition', 04490414, mm. 12–14 [used in compliance with the U.S. Copyright Act, Section 107].

music that gets louder and gets closer to you, something is gonna swallow you up.[20] I thought that altering the speed and volume of the theme, from very slow to very fast, from very soft to very loud, would indicate the mindless attacks of the shark.[21]

This musical intuition would prove seminal to turn the 'rubber ducky' into a credibly threatening sea monster.

Making the shark work

Why has the *da-da-da-da* ostinato proven so effective? Much has been written on this celebrated musical motif. For example, K. J. Donnelly has stated that 'the music ... does not merely signify [the shark's] presence, it *is* its presence',[22] and Jerrold Levinson pinpointed it as 'the only reliable signifier of the shark'.[23] These two definitions already frame the exceptional importance of this shark ostinato within the film: the music is so central that it is actually one of the film's characters and, as per this status, when the ostinato is there, the shark *is* there. Indeed, numerous false alarms and childish pranks – like the fake-fin caper – take place in the film, but the ostinato is heard *only* when the shark is actually in the vicinity. In this sense, the shark ostinato is a rare instance of intellectual honesty in horror/thriller scoring. A typical device in horror/ thriller is to exploit music to trick audiences into experiencing a climactic suspense that eventually leads nowhere: the monster is not there even if apparently intimated by music. Music creates false alarms to help narration keep the viewer, sadistically, in a state of constant suspense – and often the monster/killer jumps out from behind a dark corner totally unannounced by music, with a startle-inducing surprise effect.[24] Williams's score, on the contrary, is openly honest: when we hear the shark ostinato, the beast is there; when there is no music, there is no shark. In circumstances in which the shark is merely mentioned or feared, Williams employs another motif, a horn-and-tuba three-note *motto* – for example, featured in the scene in which Brody studies a book about shark attacks. The central musical interval of this shark motto is the tritone or augmented fourth, a dissonant interval traditionally associated with evil, the 'diabolus in musica' (see Figure 4.2).[25]

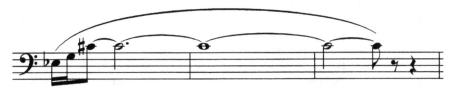

Figure 4.2 Transcription of John Williams, Shark Motif #2 (motto), © 1975 BMI, published by USI B Music Publishing, administered by Songs of Universal, Inc., from *Suite from Jaws*, printed by Hal Leonard, 'John Williams Signature Edition', 04490414, mm. 16–18 [used in compliance with the U.S. Copyright Act, Section 107].

The second shark motif is showcased during the Indianapolis-story sequence in particular. Quint, the leader of the shark-hunt expedition, tells his horrific experience as a survivor of the *USS Indianapolis*, torpedoed during the Second World War: of the 1,196 crew members, only 317 men survived, many of the victims having been eaten alive by sharks. The shark motto is masterfully introduced to highlight the most gruesome details of Quint's tale, while the shark ostinato, on the other hand, is never used, because there is some talking about sharks going on, but *the* titular shark is not physically there.

The aforementioned 'intellectual honesty' in the use of the shark ostinato is fundamental to the dramaturgical strategy of the score. The shark ostinato does not merely accompany some actions or help characterize something/someone – as most film music does. Music *materializes* the shark itself. In the absence of the animatronic that should have played that part, the music had to step in, as an understudy would have in the event of the star's illness. The music had to be the shark. The most in-depth analysis of this 'presentational' quality of the shark ostinato is by Giorgio Biancorosso, who particularly focuses on the first half of the film, in which this ostinato plays the lion's share. Employing Richard Wollheim's 'see-in' theoretical framework from the visual arts – in painting, one thing is the material surface of the work, which we *see*, and another is the thing that is represented in the painting, which we *see in* it – Biancorosso introduces the 'hear-in' concept: one thing is the musical structure, which can be *heard* mostly with a specialist's attention – 'configurational aspect' – another is what is represented by that music, which does not require a specialist to be *heard in* the music – 'recognitional aspect'.[26] In the case of the shark ostinato, the musical construction and the pairing with the images is so aptly designed and coordinated that it is not so much a matter of *representation* as one of *presentation*. The ostinato does not only translate something into music through a system of signs, but almost unmediatedly materializes it:

> I hear *in* the music. I hear the shark's ominous presence in the combined effect of music and camera movement, just as I read meaning into typographical signs laid out on a page or see landscapes or faces in images.[27]

We can hear the shark *in the music* through the ingenious use that Williams makes of the musical means. We have a musical embodiment of the shark's nature, made possible by music reproducing qualities of extramusical phenomena, what Leonard B. Meyer called 'metaphorical mimicry'.[28] The shark is large and heavy; music employs the 'large and heavy' instruments of the orchestra: double basses and contrabassoons. The shark's aim is only to eat; music presents a straightforward and unyielding course. When approaching the victim the shark gets excited; music gets 'excited' with increasing dynamics and tempo. When the shark grabs its victim, blood makes it frenzied; the string writing gets equally frenzied. The music also mimics the snappy and crashing bite of the shark – through violent *sforzando* rips of the horns.

In terms of what Meyer calls 'cultural metaphors', another function of the overall score is to further separate the two worlds in which the narrative is set: the monster below in the abyss, the humans above on the ground. This is accomplished through the timbres of the orchestra. The monster is a *primordial being* and lives *down*, in the abyss in which *darkness* reigns, while humans are *more complex*, live *up*, in a world *lighted up* by the sun. Accordingly, the shark music has the mechanical *simplicity of an ostinato*, it is *low pitched*, with *dark timbre*, while the human music has the *richness of melodic writing*, it is *higher pitched* and characterized by the *bright timbres* of violins, flutes, trumpets. Yet, the most important mimicry that music performs is that of the shark's movements. More important than the shark that we can *hear in the music* is the shark we can *almost see in the film*.

I have examined the music to *Jaws* elsewhere, from a perspective that is less theoretical and more function based.[29] In my general approach to the formal/stylistic analysis of music in films, I have submitted that music can operate in films by performing three categories of functions, which can overlap. Music fulfils an emotive function (micro or macro), a perceptive function (spatial or temporal) and a cognitive function (denotative or connotative).[30] The shark ostinato has certainly also an emotive function – it is 'scary' music because of its configuration: low-pitched tones, stalking conduct, dark timbres – but above all it has a 'spatial perceptive function', which is when music is designed to attract the viewer's attention to some movement within the film's space or to increase the prominence of a visual event. In a crowded scene a fast descending scale of the strings, played simultaneously to someone falling down a flight of stairs in the background, would point the viewer's attention to that 'isomorphic configuration'[31] and thus isolate an action in the space that might otherwise have gone unnoticed in that visually packed shot. In horror films, the sudden appearance of the monster is typically coupled with a 'stinger', a sudden *sforzando* dissonant chord that has the function not only of 'scaring' the viewer (emotive function) but also of boosting the 'startle response',[32] by adding to the sudden violent movement in the visuals an isomorphic sudden violent movement in the music. Williams's intuition with *Jaws* was precisely to give the shark's music a pre-eminently spatial perceptive function, to use music to indicate the presence and movements of the shark in the film's space. Being an *ostinato*, the shark motif can be easily shortened, extended or reiterated in loops, played louder or softer, and accelerated or slowed down so as to act as the aural equivalent of the shark's movements, which are traced musically on both spatial axes, horizontal and vertical. Horizontal trajectories are visualized through variations of dynamics and tempo: when the music slows down and the volume decreases, we know that the shark is slowing its pace; when the music speeds up or the volume increases we know that the shark is attacking. Movements on the vertical axis are visualized through variations of orchestral texture: when the writing gets thicker, we know that the shark is appearing to the surface; when the writing thins down to dark timbres only (double basses, cellos, bassoons, contrabassoon, bass clarinet) we know that the beast is disappearing into the dark abyss. An example is the pier scene. The plan of two islanders is to catch the shark with a meat bait, but the outcome is the pier being torn away by the beast and them falling into the water. When the shark bites the bait and points off-shore, dragging along the torn pier to which the bait was attached, the shark ostinato begins, played by double basses and cellos. The ostinato keeps playing at the same level and speed during the tearing off of the pier and the falling into the water of the two men, one of whom is pulled off-shore along with the pier. At one point, the pier stops and suddenly reverses, indicating that the shark is now pointing to the swimming islander. Violins and violas abruptly join the cellos and double basses in playing the ostinato, followed by the horns menacingly presenting the shark motto. The music's speed and volume increase as the shark chases the man who is frantically trying to reach the shore. The man gets out of the water, and the shark has to retreat. The music deflates, gradually decelerating and turning into a single sustained bass note that closes the scene. We do not see the shark in this scene – only one of its many signposts, the towed pier – but the music makes us almost visualize the beast's movements and intentions.

Biancorosso, as he states clearly from the outset, is interested in the shark ostinato more than in the whole score and focuses his attention on Chrissie's death sequence that opens the film. Yet, his closing remarks sound rather too dismissive of the rest of the film:

> When, later in the film, the threatening creature is feared to be approaching from afar or is shown explicitly, the shark is deprived of its own gaze, and the increasingly familiar music is reduced to a signal or code: effective as a conveyor of information, to be sure, but far less rich for it, the entirety of its message conveyed with its first instant of sound. By then we will have entered disappointingly familiar Spielberg territory, and in this new, ruthlessly plot-driven space, the Great White will be moving just like a bundle of special effects.[33]

If the first half of the film clearly sees the shark ostinato and violent or eerie non-tonal musical writing as the predominant musical presence, the score also presents other motifs and themes, with particular variety in the second half – the one Biancorosso labels as 'disappointingly familiar Spielberg territory'. We find meditative moments in the score, and even some in which Williams pokes fun at the characters. The first case can be seen in the kitchen table scene between Brody and his youngest son. The police captain is worried about the shark that menaces his community, and his face shows it, with frowns of concern and a sullen look. His little boy sits next to him and observes his father's expressions, which apparently seem comic to the little kid, and he starts mimicking them. Brody soon takes notice, and he momentarily puts his preoccupations aside and abandons himself to a father/son game of grimaces and face impressions. Williams's music is sweet and tender, communicates all the warmth of home and family, with a restrained and sparse harp, piano and vibraphone minimalist writing, a temporary musical solace from the other furiously dense and non-tonal sections of the score. Yet, even if put in the background for this little parental digression, the father and son moment still has the shark menace looming over, and the music communicates this too, having as a background a sustained ominous note by the double basses. When Quint's boat, the *Orca*, prepares to leave for the shark hunt, the aged mariner shows an immodest (and excessive) self-confidence and a fastidious insolence. To further show off his familiarity with all things maritime, he sings an old sea shanty, 'Spanish Ladies'. Later in the film, Quint – too reliant on his own skills and on his boat's resilience and incapable of accepting that the shark has outwitted him – ignores Brody and Hooper's advice to slow the boat down. He pushes the throttle to the maximum, angrily singing 'Spanish Ladies' while doing so. Quint's stubbornness and arrogance cause the breakdown of the engine. The group is thus stranded in the open sea, and the boat is slowly sinking. As a beaten Quint goes below deck to look at the irreparable damage and massive leaking, Williams introduces an impudent flute to ironically cite the same sea shanty that had previously signified Quint's self-assurance and supposed mastery of the seafaring matters; music seems to taunt him.

Though not the thematically richest score in the Williams canon, nevertheless *Jaws* presents other motifs and themes besides the shark's two musical signifiers. There is a broad melody, which can be heard when the shark hunters' boat *Orca* is seen leaving the harbour, then across the whole second half of the film and over the end credits in a serene rendition for strings. This is the principal 'human' melody that contrasts the primitive pulse of the shark motif. It can be associated with the man-versus-beast struggle. Another theme is a buoyant hornpipe-like nautical tune, which can be heard again when the *Orca* leaves. It is associated with sea life and punctuates the humorous and bright moments of the shark hunt. There is even an austere fugato to accompany the assembly of the shark cage in the final act, which infuses what is our heroes' last resort with proper gravitas and seriousness, and 'both indicated the complexity of the job and the urgency of the moment', as noted by Jon Burlingame.[34] Another theme that can be heard during the shark hunt is a heroic fanfare, which conveys the excitement and adventurousness of the expedition. This latter theme, in particular, clarifies how *Jaws* is actually a film with two spirits: the thriller/horror and the adventure. The first one is dominant in the first two acts: discovery of the shark and attempts to solve the problems from the land. Then, as the *Orca* boat leaves the harbour for the shark hunt, the second part begins, with the third act being about the tracking down of the shark and the gradual development of a bound between the hunters, and the final act being the climactic showdown. Williams had perfectly grasped the adventurous spirit of this second part of the film; there are two macro stories, the shark is the protagonist of the first, the group of hunters are of the second. 'When I first showed *Jaws* to John,' says Spielberg, 'I remember [John] said: "This is like a pirate movie! I think we need pirate music for this, because there's something primal about it – but it's also fun and entertaining!" '[35] Williams clarified that intuition: 'When I first saw *Jaws*, it was clear to me that it would require an action/adventure score. ... For *Jaws*, I imagined something big and operatic, something very theatrical.'[36] Clearly, by 'pirate music' Williams meant the old Warner Bros. swashbucklers graced by Erich Wolfgang Korngold's operatic scores. The music for the barrel chase sequence is a perfect example of this: 'It suddenly becomes very Korngoldian, ... you expect to see Errol Flynn at the helm of this thing. It gave us a laugh,' says Williams.[37]

The combination of Spielberg's directorial resourcefulness and Williams's musico-dramatic intuition made it possible for the film to be a hit despite the 'uncooperativeness' of its principal star, the shark animatronic. And when the animatronic appears in the second half of the film, we believe it is a monstrous shark and not a 'rubber ducky' because we have been prepared by music for the entire first half to see the shark as a grave menace, a serious threat, a veritable monster. As Spielberg admitted himself, it was Williams's score that made the puppet credible and truly frightening: 'I think that his score was clearly responsible for half the success of the film.'[38]

A landmark 'neoclassical' score

Besides its merits as a fundamental device within the film system, the score to *Jaws* should also be singled out for its merits as a historic landmark in Hollywood cinema. As I have argued elsewhere, Williams is the founder, single-handedly, of a 'neoclassical' trend in film scoring. By 'neoclassical' I mean that Williams brought back into films, in a revised form, the musical style and scoring approach that were in use in the Golden Age of Hollywood (1930s–1950s), the 'classical' Hollywood music style. This style was characterized by an almost continuous musical flow that accompanied the film's narrative. The language was inspired by the European late-Romantic music of the second half of the nineteenth century – Richard Wagner, Gustav Mahler, Giacomo Puccini, Piotr Tchaikovsky, Sergei Rachmaninov and Richard Strauss being the most prominent models – and the so-called non-diegetic score consisted of instrumental music played by a symphony orchestra, while songs and popular music were presented as diegetic music.[39] Kathryn Kalinak remarks that the fundamental characteristic of the classical Hollywood music was the 'musical illustration of narrative content, especially the direct synchronization between music and narrative action',[40] which was known as 'Mickey-Mousing', because music would closely replicate the visual actions – as in cartoons, when a character tiptoes and a strings *pizzicato* punctuates each step. Particularly in the 1930s, this close music/action adherence – which gives music a preponderant spatial perceptive function – was extensively adopted for dramatic purposes, while today, with an ironic eye, we tend to perceive classical Mickey-Mousing – e.g. as used by Max Steiner in his score to *The Informer* (1935) – as exaggerated and almost comical. The other main technique was the leitmotiv – adapted from Richard Wagner's own – which consisted of a network of very recognizable musical themes or motifs clearly associated with the film's characters or narrative themes, and reprised intensively throughout the film whenever the related character/situation appeared or was mentioned. The Classical Hollywood music style as such lasted from 1933 – the release year of *King Kong*, whose Max Steiner score was seminal in launching and shaping that style – to 1958, when new contractual agreements led to the dismissal of the in-house studio symphony orchestras and ushered in the use of alternate ensembles, such as chamber orchestras, solo players, jazz combos, etc.[41]

After 1958, classical-styled symphonic scores became progressively less and were increasingly perceived as out of fashion. In particular, 'Mickey-Mousing' and the extensive use of a spatial perceptive function for the music definitely sounded stale and old school. The shift from the classical style to what can be called 'modern style' had many reasons. In the 1960s Hollywood cinema was weakened by a severe crisis and it tried to renovate its image by looking at the *Nouvelle Vague* and the European art cinema.[42] European film music had always been less pervasive and less inclined to musical illustration (spatial perceptive function) than Hollywood music. This was accentuated in the 1960s modern cinema: some *auteurs* were openly hostile to film music, such as Éric Rohmer: 'Music is cinema's falsest friend, as it deprives film time of its peculiar exclusivity and objectivity.'[43] Besides up-to-date poetics imported from European cinema, Hollywood revised its musical style mostly for a market-oriented motive. Abandoning the old-fashioned symphonic sound and shifting to the contemporary pop sound was a tactic to attract young audiences, which were the basis of cinema attendance now.[44] The first consequence was the growing importance of pop songs as core elements of the music track, to the point that in the second half of the 1960s a typical musical approach was the 'compilation score', namely having a music track built out of repertoire pop songs.[45] Showcasing pop music and songs in films was a way not only to entice younger viewers but also to complement the box office revenues with those from the Hollywood-controlled record industry.[46] Song writers and pop musicians became film composers – to name one, Burt Bacharach – while conservatory-trained 'classical' composers, like John Williams, who started his film career in the late 1950s, were a minority.

Williams was the one who brought back the classical-styled symphonic music in the late 1970s, namely with *Star Wars* (1977). Yet he had already shown his penchant and flair for the classical-styled symphonic music much earlier, already in his 1960s scores,[47] and *Jaws* should be considered the most important 'neoclassical' score before *Star Wars*. The first notable element is a historical parallel. As Williams's score was fundamental in giving credibility and an aura of invincible power to the rubber shark, the same had happened with the score for *King Kong*. *King Kong* was a similarly challenging film for the special effects of the time, and similarly its main star was an animated puppet that was supposed to be perceived as threatening and scary. The producers feared that the stop-motion puppet would cause laughter instead of fear. It was Max Steiner's score that saved the day by making the puppet credible, and it was not only a major factor in the film's success but also instrumental in demonstrating that music could be a powerful narrative tool. The classical Hollywood music style could be said to begin with *King Kong*. I have already mentioned such 'neoclassical' elements in *Jaws* as the Korngoldian fanfares, or the use of the fugato – a choice that 'classical' film composers Franz Waxman and Miklós Rózsa would have made. And the use of the shark ostinato can be considered one of the finest and subtlest modern use of 'Mickey-Mousing'. One sequence in the film is strongly against the pop fad of the time: the montage of the tourists arriving on the island for the Fourth of July celebrations. This ninety-second sequence would have been the ideal spot to showcase a marketable surf-music song, a choice that would have been clever from a commercial point of view but would have also been interestingly motivated by the contrast between the cheerful tone of the music and the deadly danger looming on the tourists. Instead, the montage is accompanied by a Baroque-ish piece for strings, solo trumpet and harpsichord. Underneath the serene and formal surface of the piece, echoes of the shark ostinato can be heard, offering a kind of black-humoured comment on the pending menace – 'Tourists on the Menu', that's the cue's title. Among the early 1970s films set in the present time and designed to become box office hits, *Jaws* was the first one without any theme songs or pop music.

As Max Steiner had done at the time of *King Kong* for the classical cinema, with *Jaws* Williams demonstrated the contribution that traditional symphonic music could offer to the contemporary cinema. In 1975, a review of *Jaws* took notice of this revival:

> Williams has been highly instrumental in trying to bring back to the movies the full symphonic score, with all its potential for pleasurable manipulation and its intimations of life larger than life. This was an important part of what we got from the movies once, and there are many signs that many of us want it back again.[48]

After years of market-oriented music, Williams's narrative-oriented scores brought back to the general attention the importance of music in films and the fundamental narrative help that symphonic music in particular can give. This revival was completed with *Star Wars*, *Superman the Movie* (1978), the subsequent episodes of the first *Star Wars* trilogy, *E.T.: The Extraterrestrial* (1982) and *Raiders of the Lost Ark* (1981) – a truly Max Steiner-like score. But *Jaws* gave it the first bite.

Notes

1 Ian Freer, *The Complete Spielberg* (London: Virgin, 2001), 47.
2 Carl Gottlieb, *The Jaws Log* (New York: Newmarket Press, 2005), 41.
3 See the documentary *Jaws. The Inside Story*, A&E Television, distributed by Go Entertainment, 2009, DVD, GOHC5587.
4 Gottlieb, *The Jaws Log*, 198.
5 Freer, *The Complete Spielberg*, 50.
6 The analysis was made on the DVD *Jaws. 30th Anniversary*, Universal 2005, 823 527 4.
7 Rudolf Arnheim, *Film as Art* (Berkeley: University of California Press, [1957] 2007), 44.
8 See the documentary *The Shark Is Still Working*, Finatic Productions, 2007, https://youtube/OdtnHBsLcWs (accessed 28 August 2018).
9 *The Big Bang Theory*, Season 4, Episode 6, 'The Irish Pub Formulation', aired 21 December 2010.
10 7 Steven Spielberg in 'Steven Spielberg & John Williams Talk Music', video interview, 1982, https://youtube/uw4Ngb5F3Hk (accessed 8 August 2018).
11 Steven Spielberg, liner notes to *The Spielberg/Williams Collaboration*, CD, Sony Classical, 1991, SK 45997.
12 Derek Elley, 'The Film Composer: 3. John Williams, part I', *Films and Filming*, 24, no. 10 (July 1978): 23. Other composers, like Ennio Morricone, whose approach is more oriented towards rendering the general mood of a situation rather than following the action moment by moment, instead work from scripts.
13 William Booth, 'Shark Attack?! John Williams Liked the Sound of That', *The Washington Post*, 5 December 2004, N04.

14 Jon Burlingame, 'John Williams Recalls *Jaws*', *Film Music Society*, http://www.filmmusicsociety.org/news_events/features/2012/081412.html?isArchive=081412 (accessed 28 August 2018).

15 Derek Taylor, *The Making of 'Raiders of the Lost Ark'* (New York: Ballantine Books, 1981), 166.

16 Jack Sullivan, *Hitchcock's Music* (New Haven, CT: Yale University Press, 2006), 274–50.

17 Steven Spielberg in Laurent Bouzereau, *Jaws*, CD booklet (Decca 2000, 467 045-2), 8.

18 Steven Spielberg in Rebecca Keegan, 'John Williams and Steven Spielberg Mark 40 years of collaboration', *Los Angeles Times*, 8 January 2012, http://articles.latimes.com/2012/jan/08/entertainment/la-ca-john-williams-20120108/3 (accessed 28 August 2018).

19 Giorgio Biancorosso, 'The Shark in the Music', *Music Analysis*, 29 (2010): 306–33 (320), doi:10.1111/j.1468-2249.2011.00331.x (accessed 28 August 2018). Biancorosso further discusses the music's representation of the heartbeat: is this Chrissie's heartbeat, a consequence of her fear? Apparently not, she is not aware of the shark's presence, so she has no reason to be scared. Is this a simulation/trigger of the audience's fear, with the music alerting them that something terrible is about to happen? In this case Biancorosso cites Ben Winters's 'Corporeality, Musical Heartbeats, and Cinematic Emotion', *Music, Sound, and the Moving Image*, 2, no. 1 (2008): 3–25. Is this the shark's heartbeat? Since Biancorosso eventually analyses the opening sequence as having 'nothing less than an interest in representing a moment in the life of the shark's consciousness' (323), this seems to be his explanation.

20 John Williams in Keegan, 'John Williams and Steven Spielberg Mark 40 Years of Collaboration', online.

21 John Williams in Bouzereau, *Jaws*, 8–10.

22 K. J. Donnelly, *The Spectre of Sound. Music in Film and Television* (London: BFI, 2005), 93.

23 Jerrold Levinson, 'Film Music and Narrative Agency', in David Bordwell and Noël Carroll, eds, *Post-Theory: Reconstructing Film Studies* (Madison: University of Wisconsin Press, 1996), 248–82.

24 On 'suspense' vis-à-vis 'surprise', see François Truffaut, *Hitchcock/Truffaut*, revised edn, Helen G. Scott, trans. (New York: Simon and Schuster, 1985), 235–85. On 'suspense' see also David Bordwell, *Narration in the Fiction Film* (Madison: University of Wisconsin Press, 1985), 37.

25 In this sense, the shark motto reminds of another perhaps less famous but equally effective motto of horror cinema, James Bernard's Dracula motto for Hammer's *Dracula* (1958), equally based on the tritone. On the tritone in general, see F. J. Smith, 'Some Aspects of the Tritone and the Semitritone in the *Speculum Musicae*: The Non-Emergence of the *Diabolus in Musica*', *Journal of Musicological Research*, 3, nos 1–2 (1979): 63–74; on its use in film music, see Janet Halfyard, 'Mischief Afoot: Supernatural Horror-comedies and the Diabolus in Musica', in Neil Lerner, ed., *Music in the Horror Film* (New York: Routledge, 2009), 21–37.

26 Biancorosso, 'The Shark in the Music', 315.

27 Ibid.

28 Leonard B. Meyer, *Style and Music. Theory, History, and Ideology* (Chicago: University of Chicago Press, [1989] 1996), 128–9.

29 Emilio Audissino, *Film/Music Analysis. A Film Studies Approach* (Basingstoke: Palgrave Macmillan, 2017).

30 Ibid., 130–51.

31 I use the term 'configuration' as an English translation of the word 'Gestalt' and, drawing from gestalt theory, I see the music/image combination as a fusion between elements that creates a new audiovisual configuration. See Emilio Audissino, 'A Gestalt Approach to the Analysis of Music in Films', *Musicology Research*, 2 (Spring 2017): 69–88. http://www.musicologyresearch.co.uk/publications/emilioaudissino-age staltapproachtotheanalysisofmusicinfilm (accessed 28 August 2018).

32 On the startle response (or reflex), see M. Koch, 'The Neurobiology of Startle', *Progress in Neurobiology* 59, no. 2 (October 1999): 107–28.

33 Biancorosso, 'The Shark in the Music', 324–5.

34 Burlingame, 'John Williams Recalls *Jaws*', online.

35 Steven Spielberg in Bouzereau, *Jaws*, 7.

36 John Williams in ibid., 8.

37 John Williams in Burlingame, 'John Williams Recalls *Jaws*', online.

38 Steven Spielberg in Bouzereau, *Jaws*, 8.

39 Diegetic music is the ambiance music that comes from some source within the narrative world and can be heard by the characters – for example, we see a dance orchestra play and we hear a waltz, to which the characters dance. Non-diegetic music is the 'comment/accompaniment' music that is external to the film's world and cannot be heard by the characters – for example, the shark ostinato, otherwise Chrissie would have fled out of the water as soon as she had heard the first notes.

40 Kathryn Kalinak, *Settling the Score: Music and the Classical Hollywood Film* (Madison: University of Wisconsin Press, 1992), 187.

41 James Wierzbicki, *Film Music: A History* (New York: Routledge, 2009), 186.

42 Kristin Thompson and David Bordwell, *Film History. An Introduction*, 3rd International edn (New York: McGraw-Hill, 2010), 470–6; Tino Balio, 'Diffusione e mercato del cinema europeo dal 1948 a oggi', in Gian Piero Brunetta, ed., *Storia del cinema mondiale, Gli Stati Uniti*, II** (Turin: Einaudi, 1999), 1463–82.

43 Éric Rohmer in Roberto Calabretto, *Lo schermo sonoro. La musica per film* (Venice: Marsilio, 2010), 155n, my translation.

44 Thompson and Bordwell, *Film History*, 472–93.

45 Jeff Smith, *The Sound of Commerce. Marketing Popular Film Music* (New York: Columbia University Press, 1998), 163–72.

46 Ibid., 40.

47 Emilio Audissino, *John Williams's Film Music. 'Jaws,' 'Star Wars,' 'Raiders of the Lost Ark,' and the Return of the Classical Hollywood Music Style* (Madison: University of Wisconsin Press, 2014), 87–103.

48 Quoted in Wierzbicki, *Film Music*, 204.

5

In the teeth of criticism: Forty-five years of *Jaws*

Nigel Morris

The remarkable profitability of *Jaws* and Spielberg's subsequent child-friendly output has been, for many critics, both symbols and causes of the decline of the New American Cinema or 'Hollywood Renaissance'. Spielberg and *Jaws* became hostages in a culture war. Serious-minded critics and scholars condemned Spielberg relentlessly, accusing him of sentimentalizing even solemn subjects with happy endings and being inveterately emotionally manipulative.[1] Spielberg, along with George Lucas, is frequently blamed for terminating the radical 'New Hollywood' of the Nixon era and ushering in the post-classical family-oriented blockbusters that would dominate the industry in the 1980s. By 1975, J. Hoberman laments, the 'Hollywood Renaissance', an 'extraordinary … indigenous avant-garde', was finished,[2] and it was *Jaws*, as Peter Biskind claims in *Easy Riders, Raging Bulls*, that 'changed the business forever'.[3] Critics have recognized the importance of *Jaws*, but typically either as a case study in audience manipulation or as a key 'high-concept film' that 'reflected' such issues as Watergate, masculinity and feminism-induced anxieties within a 'striking, easily reducible narrative'.[4]

Yet forty-five years on, *Jaws* is widely acclaimed as a masterpiece and among the top 100 films according to *Rotten Tomatoes*' amalgamated ratings. This source, hardly scientific but refreshingly open and eclectic – positioning *Star Wars: The Last Jedi* (2017) between *Selma* (2014) and *La Grande Illusion* (1937) – acknowledges the 'compelling, well-crafted storytelling and a judicious sense of terror' that make *Jaws* 'a benchmark in the art of delivering modern blockbuster thrills'.[5] The film has sustained its appeal and profitability through VHS, laser disc, DVD rentals, Blu-ray releases, digital streaming and cinematic re-releases, most recently in 2015 (for its fortieth anniversary) and 2019. Clearly, more is going on than can be explained by audiences being duped by advertising, following herd instincts or responding subconsciously to the film's Vietnam-era sociopolitical parallels. Meanwhile, Spielberg rebranded himself after *Schindler's List* (1993) as a classical film-maker, elder statesman, public figure and popular educator, while more sympathetic academic reappraisals of his work revealed complexities, ambiguities and allusions equal to those of any 'art' film or 'independent' movie.[6] The momentum of shift appears in the difference between Les Friedman stating, in 2006, that a colleague told him that authoring a book about 'the antichrist' Spielberg – academically equivalent to 'appearing in a porn movie' – would destroy his 'scholarly legitimacy'[7] and my invitation, received in 2012, to commission an academic collection on Spielberg for a series that then covered only Haneke, Hitchcock, Fassbinder and Herzog.[8]

This chapter traces the evolution of taste judgements and interpretations in the critical response to *Jaws* over the last forty-five years. Surveying press reviews alongside readings of *Jaws* within the politicized world of Film Studies confirms that emergent middlebrow and Establishment consensus over Spielberg as a quality film-maker has contrasted, until only fairly recently, with consistent academic denigration of both the film and its director.

Reception

Initial reviews were often positive, lauding *Jaws'* technical skill, excitement, humour and central performances. The film's storytelling was praised, for example, for jettisoning the sexual and criminal subplots that padded out Peter Benchley's novel. '*Jaws* aims for the gut, but it doesn't insult the intelligence on the few occasions when it is required', noted *Boston* magazine's Michael Sragow, who admired 'Spielberg's constitutional incapability of cheating his audience' (August 1975). Gary Arnold in *The Washington Post* likened the panic on the beach to Eisenstein's Odessa Steps sequence in *Battleship Potemkin* (1925) and, as did many others, compared the 27-year-old director with Hitchcock. 'I don't think there's a more exciting talent at work right now', Arnold concluded: 'an authentic moviemaking prodigy' whose 'worst problem ... will be preventing success from making a nervous or artistic wreck of him' (15 June 1975).

Jaws was nevertheless also decried as evidence of commerce displacing aesthetic considerations. While *Time's* top 1975 films included *Jaws*,[9] a number of leading reviewers considered it shallow, soulless, gratuitous, crammed with 'clichés and one-dimensional characters'.[10] Vincent Canby (*New York Times*) judged it 'noisy, busy', with 'less on its mind than any child at the beach': 'foolishly entertaining ... nonsense'. The 'best films', he claimed, are 'character-driven' and eschew special effects, whereas *Jaws* subordinates characters to 'action' (27 June 1975). *The New Yorker's* Pauline Kael concurred, deeming *Jaws* a 'cheerfully perverse scare movie' (8 November 1976), while Molly Haskell felt like 'a rat' undergoing 'shock treatment' (*Village Voice*, 23 June 1975), anticipating Spielberg's 1977 admission that *Jaws* resembled 'directing the audience with a cattle prod'.[11] Stephen Farber (*New York Times*) similarly lamented the risk-averse, publicity-driven readiness to treat moviegoers 'like laboratory animals wired to twitch' and deemed the film's success a 'disease': '"Jaws" fever" ' was 'epidemic' (24 August 1975). (Such metaphors conflate enduring traditions in American writing about media: hyperbole about alleged effects on defenceless individuals and – a residual reduction of Frankfurt School concerns – fears of the dehumanization of indoctrinated, gullible masses.) Farber put the high revenues down to aggressive advertising: 'Pitifully naïve' audiences lacked 'free choice' because they had 'been conditioned to' see *Jaws* and liked it only because they were 'too intimidated to resist'. Dismissing *Jaws* as 'shock therapy', Farber substituted snobbery for analysis and set the default tone for Spielberg criticism by predicting that 'the lowest common denominator' would replace 'modest meaningful films'. *Jaws* would get the blame when supporters and makers of New American Cinema found that funding and distribution for that formerly lucrative market sector suddenly evaporated.

Reviewers nevertheless understood that *Jaws*, for all its visceral effectiveness, global impact and B-movie credentials, addressed deep cultural concerns: it was released six weeks after Saigon fell and its cover-up plot seemed to allegorize Watergate. Biskind, writing in a 1975 issue of the left-wing film magazine *Jump Cut*, immediately established the agenda for reading *Jaws* ideologically and responded more positively and perceptively than in his influential later book. Issues of gender politics that he identified are still debated, such as whether Chrissie's death symbolically punishes sexual freedom. Brody, Biskind averred, survives because, as a conventional husband and father, he upholds patriarchy under attack from feminism, Civil Rights and the counterculture which flourished during the Vietnam War (and which supplied audiences for the New American Cinema that Biskind later championed and chronicled). Brody's conservatism nevertheless opposes Mayor Vaughn's, whose business-as-usual attitude evokes 'the public interest' much as Nixon cited 'national security' to justify his excesses. However, Biskind crucially, given his later criticisms, contrasts *Jaws* with the unreconstructed gender politics of 'right wing populist fantasy' films: Quint is punished for his excessive masculinity; Hooper, conversely, tenders 'admiration' and 'love' to the shark but lacks sufficient manliness himself to master it.[12] Nevertheless, as Roger Ebert perceptively observed, while 'there are no doubt supposed to be all sorts of levels of meanings in such an archetypal story, … Spielberg wisely decides not to underline any of them. … [N]one of the characters has to wade through speeches expounding on the significance of it all'.[13]

Jaws divided critics and alienated cineastes who, influenced by auteurism, sought enduring truths from visionary directors with distinctive themes and styles. As an unprecedented commercial and cultural phenomenon *Jaws* was impossible to ignore, even if it was meretricious trash, cynical exploitation or a craze that would eventually go away. Critics feverishly speculated about what its popularity revealed about audiences and ideology, film industry developments and real-life socio-historical parallels. As Raymond J. Haberski, Jr. has shown, opponents blamed Spielberg for rendering criticism redundant and substituting market forces for aesthetic judgement, while *Jaws* raised questions about gratifications that demanded textual analysis and theory. Spielberg personified 'developments that defined debates about the role of film criticism'.[14] After *Jaws* and then *Star Wars* (1977) films increasingly became critic proof as popular taste began deviating radically from authoritative reviewers. *Jaws*' release campaign effectively undermined reviewers' authority, which had been considerable in the early 1970s when critical approval and box office success were remarkably aligned.

Academic criticism

As Haberski states, *Jaws* prompted 'interpretation by the first truly substantial generation of film scholars'.[15] Marxist and psychoanalytically inflected theory – or rather

'Theory' – dominated 1970s academic film criticism and *Jaws*' popularity promised insights into audiences and the ideological machinations of culture. Academic writing about American films, as Paul Kerr contends, typically equated '(economic) profitability' with satisfying '(ideological) expectations'.[16] 'Everyone' undergoes 'the same experience', David Cook claimed – *Jaws* was 'calculated' to 'have all the predictability of a Big Mac'.[17] Analyses aimed to see through films to their ideological core and too often, especially in the 1970s and 1980s, this involved dismissing filmgoers as cultural dupes and making assertions based on subjective impressions or, worse, prejudices, rather than on textual evidence. This is hardly surprising as, before VHS, critics, responding quickly to films, relied on memories or, at best, notes made during theatrical screenings. Moreover, ideological criticism was often insensitive to the diversity of audiences in such terms as class, gender, race, ethnicity, sexuality or (dis)ability. Even so, the best academic criticism of the *Screen* Theory era prompted rigorous debate, reflection on methodology, purposeful and revealing application of theory, textual examination to support meanings and identify codes and conventions that enabled them, recognition of commercial and political contexts, and eventually a turn towards empirical audience research.

Theory generally showed less interest in contemporary popular output than with the avant-garde or mainstream aberrations. Two important commentators, Stephen Heath in 1976 and Fredric Jameson in 1979, nevertheless explored *Jaws*' symptomatic significance.[18] For Heath, '*Jaws* is a Watergate film',[19] simultaneous with the end of the Vietnam War, as well as 'a white male film' that is shot through with castration anxieties and functions to eliminate women.[20] Heath's approach, rooted in relatively abstract but crucial developments such as feminism, embraced connections earlier criticism typically overlooked and, he insisted, superseded 'traditional "content analysis"'.[21] This quantitative method, then common in media studies, entailed systematically counting identified elements in textual form or content. Its weakness is that measurable recurrence does not necessarily prove significance, as the ideological import of structured *absences* shows. Heath's analysis observes, for instance, that there is 'not a single black'[22] in the film, although, by overlooking holidaymakers and Brody's support officer, he ironically and inadvertently perpetuates the invisibility his mode of ideological criticism challenges.

Jameson meanwhile claims that Amity represents Cuba; the shark, 'Northamerican imperialism'.[23] Furthermore the film eliminates Brody and Hooper's class conflict, which Benchley stressed.[24] Jameson adopts a mythological reading that constructs them, along with Quint, as three ages of man. However, Jameson considers why Quint, tradition's representative, perishes while, in the movie, the survivor-hero becomes two characters. He surmises that Quint embodies small businesses' decline, Yankee individualism, the New Deal and nostalgic patriotism. Against such anachronisms Brody and Hooper unite contemporary 'law-and-order' with 'technocracy'. Utopianism, displacing antagonisms, masks emergent discourses that herald 'a whole – very alarming – political and social program',[25] by which Jameson appears to mean alliance between state authorities and multinational capital.

Jaws, released weeks before Laura Mulvey's seminal article on visual pleasure, seemed perfectly to illustrate the 'male gaze' and complement Film Studies' psychoanalytic turn.[26] Academic criticism was quick to highlight the film's supposedly regressive sexual politics as well as its defence of the family. Dan Rubey, for example, also writing in *Jump Cut* in 1976, argued that the shark simultaneously symbolizes misogyny, 'sadistic sexuality', 'predatory' commerce and the fear of 'retribution' for Hiroshima, and that the film's action-fantasy precludes 'social action, excludes women as weak and ineffectual, and erases' historical guilt.[27] Quint 'portrays women as whores', abandoned for 'the serious' manly 'business of war and death'.[28] Removing the novel's affair between Hooper and Ellen externalizes such dangers to family values as sexuality, greed, Vietnam, nuclear war: sharks 'cannot threaten anyone who chooses to stay away from the water'. The attack on Chrissie, punishing her liberal transgression of traditional constraints, communicates the film's sadistic misogyny. Alex's death necessitates characters' affirmation of 'civic responsibility and male protectiveness' towards children whereby patriarchy reasserts itself. Blame shifts to profit-motivation as Vaughn personifies villainy, displaced from the unseen monster. That, Rubey contends, expressed worries about criticism of corporations for creating oil shortages and influencing politics; but these are capitalist abuses, not free-market logic itself, which *Jaws'* conservatism leaves unchallenged.[29]

Scopic alignment with the shark, beginning with the title sequence's point-of-view shot, implies audience complicity in consuming spectacularized female sexuality. For Jane Caputi, treating *Jaws* anthropologically in 1978, 'patriarchal myth' recurrently requires 'vanquishment' – sublimated rape – of monsters symbolizing femaleness. *Jaws'* 'purpose' is 'to instill dread and loathing'.[30] The sea is a 'uterus and the shark's teeth the ferocious mouth of that womb', embodying a castration 'nightmare'.[31] Although psychoanalysis might consider that universal, Caputi particularizes 'fear of abortion':[32] the setting, 'primal womb and source of life', contains 'blood, gore, danger and death'.[33] Caputi figures the shark as the archetypal 'birthing Terrible Mother',[34] while Brody and Hooper are 'puerile'.[35] The ending represents an 'initiatory ritual of matricidal rebirth': the monster 'torn apart (and Daddy rid of in the bargain), the two boys, now men, emerge from the waters'.[36]

Especially problematic to *Screen* theory and feminist and gay criticism in the 1980s was Spielberg's focus on the family – supporting a Reaganite backlash, critics averred, against progressive advances. What Andrew Britton called in 1986 the 'utopianism of the new radical right', supposedly expressed through Spielberg's films, sought to recover a 'golden age in which the nation was great and the patriarchal family flourished in happy ignorance of the scourges of abortion and a soaring divorce rate, gay rights and the women's movement'.[37] Britton psychoanalyses the phallic and territorial struggle between the shark's 'destructive lawlessness' and the authority of 'the policeman's rifle'.[38] The terms of the film's conflict valorize the family, which the institution of marriage reproduces.[39] Brody and Hooper's bonding – a 'classical American … "marriage"' between men, symbolism recurrent in numerous literary works identified by critics such as Leslie Fiedler[40] – is, Britton believes, hypocritically 'conservative' because, he assumes, they return home,[41] although nothing in Spielberg's film indicates whether Brody's marriage to Ellen survives.

Britton helped establish a scholarly agenda that presented *Jaws* and Spielberg as reactionary. Horror abjects female sexuality and so the phallic monster punishes Chrissie for her forwardness; yet, by attacking children and jeopardizing the economy, it also undermines patriarchy and conservatism it supposedly represents. The shark is phallic yet also maternal: it devours and incorporates the male, castrating and emasculating. The film's poster, Griselda Pollock argued in 1976, manifests this dualism: the fish's head, 'aimed at the girl's genitals', is phallic; 'its triangular shape with the central gaping jaws' represents 'female genitalia': 'the vagina dentata' – an interpretation Derek Malcolm's *Guardian* review (22 December 1975) mentioned before the film's British release – 'is mastered' through 'symbolic ejaculation of the canister inside the mouth'.[42] This apparent conflict of meanings is permitted by the Great White's semiotic ambiguity and because it, frankly, represents whatever critics project on to it.

Such readings persisted through the first wave of (mostly psychoanalytic) horror film criticism. Particularly influential was Robin Wood's application in 1979 of Freud's theory of 'the return of the repressed'. Horror's 'true subject', Wood averred, is everything 'civilisation *re*presses or *op*presses'.[43] The 'basic formula' is: 'normality' – conformity, rather than 'health' – 'is threatened by the Monster'.[44] Repressed sexual energy, Wood argues, returns in distorted form as a creature that represents the Other – what culture regards as evil, abnormal, unnatural, perverse and to be repressed. In modern American capitalist patriarchy, the Other includes female sexuality, bisexuality, the working class, black people and so forth, all of which threaten dominant values predicated on the monogamous family. The ideological project of the horror film is therefore to dramatize the return and repression of the Other, thereby legitimizing the social order. Happy endings repress, rather than solve, underlying conflicts.

Wood differentiated between two kinds of horror films, however, and argued that they are not simply reactionary cautionary tales. They can be conservative or radical, either sustaining the social order or criticizing its repression of unconscious desires. It all depends on the film's sympathy for and explanation of the monster. 'Progressive' or radical horror films such as *Last House on the Left* (1972) and *It's Alive* (1974) show monsters to be products of social repression, even of the family and normality itself; they are made rather than born evil. 'Reactionary' horror movies, like *Halloween* (1978), have 'non-human' or purely evil monsters. In Wood's formulation, *Jaws* was reactionary: it celebrated the defeat not only of the shark's threat to bourgeois normality and the family but also of the proletarian Otherness of Quint.[45]

Wood was unremittingly hostile to Spielberg, citing the 'Lucas-Spielberg Syndrome' as evidence of dumbing-down and infantilization in the 1980s. *Hollywood from Vietnam to Reagan* (1986), which developed his theory of horror, said little about *Jaws* specifically, beyond Brody's family situation being 'tense and precarious'.[46] The film is, he claims, an 'attempt to separate the American family from "bad" capitalism, to pretend the two are without connection' by positing them against each other instead of acknowledging their interdependence.[47] One might reasonably object that Wood, from a radically combined position within Marxist and emerging sexual politics, explicitly states neither the connection nor why it matters, appealing instead to assumed consensus.

Jaws featured in exploratory articles by Barbara Creed and Carol Clover preceding their landmark books on gender and horror.[48] Creed redefines the 'archaic mother' the shark symbolizes, as 'its *own point of reference*'.[49] Rather than opposing masculinity, it defines binary logic. It represents death, not the pre-Oedipal Imaginary. A 'primeval "black hole"', self-sufficient, surpassing 'lack',[50] it terrifies because a blank cipher, largely unseen, defies illusory control through categorization by patriarchal logic yet through otherness is aligned with femininity. For Clover, *Jaws*, although 'marginal' to slasher movies, affirms how 'closeness and tactility' characterize that genre's violence, predicated on mastering through presence and confrontation the feared Other: 'fascination with flesh or meat itself', contained or masked by clothing or skin – protective surfaces like the concealing waves in *Jaws* – motivates the killer, enacting spectators' fetishist desire, to penetrate and reveal through sublimated rape.[51] *Jaws* conforms with the 'reactionary' slasher cycle, which includes *Halloween* and *Friday the 13th* (1980). Indeed, Janet Staiger maintains, the 'slasher formula' derives as much from *Jaws* as *Psycho* (1960) or *The Texas Chain Saw Massacre* (1974).[52] Quoting Bruce Kawin,[53] Adam Rockoff restates, following Clover[54] and others, that *Jaws* institutionalized the use of the 'subjective camera' for the predator's perspective. 'Emphasis on the isolated female' replaced the victim's view.[55] *Jaws* anticipates slasher films' dispatching of 'good' and 'bad' girls 'with equal gusto'. That said, death typically follows 'sex' – less condemnation than 'simple exploitation', as titillating, 'liberal … nudity'[56] cashed in on permissiveness following the Production Code's abandonment.

Unanimity thus emerged that *Jaws* was conservative, a backlash against feminism and a comforting reassertion of male authority and middle-class values. The film's supposed ideological project implicitly explained its commercial success. Michael Ryan and Douglas Kellner's 1986 analysis of contemporary Hollywood, *Camera Politica*, summed up the case for the prosecution: *Jaws* evaded 'real' anxieties by opposing countercultural rebellion against 'social authority', 'paternalist power' and 'business and civic leadership'.[57] The 'Patriarchal saviour', Brody, bridging the body politic as both lawman and the individual body as potential shark bait, finally 'restores order'.[58] Ryan and Kellner's *Screen* Theory conflation of Marxism, feminism and psychoanalysis would, however, be less problematic without the residual misogyny in their diagnosis that Brody's main problem is 'cloying intimacy and domesticity associated with his wife' (thereby laying blame at Ellen's feet)[59] or their reduction of popularity to contradictions Reaganism would address, confounding ideological function with intention. They condemn the film's '*use of* one category' as metaphor for another – their example is 'family patriarchy for community leadership' – which, they insist, '*is designed* to' idealize family.[60] Their rhetoric obscures that this comparison is their tendentious reading, not unquestionably a proposition by the text.

Such interpretations, unsupported by audience research or archival work, ascribed agency to a film-maker who lacked control over both the making[61] and the meaning. They facilitated 'vitriolic',[62] even 'vicious',[63] personal attacks that still haunt Spielberg criticism. Misreadings further confuse literal and figurative interpretations. Ryan and Kellner, for example, insist Brody 'peer[s] down into his pants, looking for his own [scar] and not finding one'[64] – metonymizing shark injury with masculinity. Brody in fact is contemplating his unheroic appendectomy; yet the critics fantasize that 'Brody's literal glance into his pants' is 'in search of the missing phallus'.[65] Furthermore, particularly disturbing is the assertion that 'Not surprisingly, many [contemporary horror] films were targeted at low-income, less educated, and less articulate audiences in rural and urban underclass areas'.[66] This assumption, tarnishing *Jaws* by association while seemingly disdaining the people the writers ostensibly profess to care about, sits uneasily with Sheldon Hall and Steve Neale's factual statement that 'large numbers of predominantly young, working-class and black spectators flooded' into 'upmarket residential districts' where the film opened.[67]

Notwithstanding general hostility to Spielberg as a cultural phenomenon, more arresting readings of *Jaws* emerged in the 1990s that saw the film as curative political allegory. Robert Torry in 1993 thinks *Jaws* 'seeks' – intention again – 'to diagnose' and 'remedy' traumatic 'social and political malaise that darkened' bicentennial America.[68] Quint, personifying an 'irreversible, nightmarish recurrence', is 'burnt out'.[69] Brody and Hooper annihilate an unseen, efficient, 'murderous, devious, and implacable enemy': the Vietcong.[70] 'Their mission' provides 'satisfaction' that reality withheld. As the United States sacrificed working-class men, so Quint is scapegoated for military failure.[71] Torry also evokes 'conservative opinion' that politicians restrained soldiering in Vietnam[72] – in *Jaws*, Brody supplants Vaughn as a figure of authority, recruits professionals and wins.

Arguing from a Jungian and ideological perspective, Thomas Frentz and Janice Hocker Rushing (1993) offer a 'moral evaluation' to improve America's 'psycho-political health'. Their analysis of *Jaws* sees femininity 'scapegoated' for capitalism and masculinity 'fragmented' by it.[73] *Jaws* parallels American settlers' 'adaptation of the Indian *hunter* myth': wilderness, although feminine, needs conquering 'for white women and civilization'.[74] Unlike Jameson, for whom *Moby-Dick* (America's commonest allusion in Vietnam narratives[75]) is peripheral, Frentz and Rushing view Melville's epic as a 'tragic commentary' on 'The White Hunter Myth' and *Jaws* as a 'victorious celebration' of it; the respective monsters figure the 'blank continent' luring hunters yet resisting domination.[76]

The shark embodies anxieties about capitalism 'devouring its own'.[77] Its 'horrific power', from consubstantiality with the 'Terrible Mother'[78] as Caputi suggested, fuses opposites. (Monsters, defying binary conventions, typically do this. Consider Dracula's conflation of living and dead, human and animal, and association with the full moon, when night resembles day.) Displacing disruption of masculine capitalism by feminine sexuality, the shark's threat nevertheless opposes Ellen's 'nurturing docility'.[79] Quint's 'dangerous' machismo rejects 'social order', his necessary death paralleling the shark's.[80] Frentz and Rushing figure Hooper not as multinational capital (Jameson's suggestion) but, although he works for 'The Oceanographic Institute', privileged leisure environmentalism. Together, high-tech (Hooper's canister) and the hunting tradition (Quint's rifle) plus courage and initiative triumph, reinstating and re-enforcing masculinity. Whereas Caputi interpreted hunting as initiation into regressive manhood, Frentz and Rushing believe Brody's success redeems him. American founding myths propose the frontiersman's marriage with the Other; Brody, however, 'safe' with a ' "civilized" good wife', lacks 'relationship' to the wilderness 'spirit'.[81] Quint overtly hates bad woman/nature; Hooper loves it; Brody, fearing it, nevertheless is the central protagonist because contemporary ideology serves to preserve class structure, not 'extend the frontier'. Quint, unable to embody the frontier, inhabits the disregarded bottom of America's hierarchy, not the advancing edge represented either by the conservative American Dream or by countercultural ideals.[82] He pursues the hunt to assert his identity, not preserve 'social order'.[83]

With symptomatic interpretations the shark, as 'floating signifier', permits so many readings that murky symbolism obscures surface clarity.[84] One risk is that such interpretations undervalue real audiences, which, if acknowledged at all, are imagined either as objects of indoctrination or as undifferentiated consumers subject to psychosexual regression.

Redemption

In 2007 an academic conference considered Spielberg more seriously than had generally been the case.[85] Scholarly work on *Jaws* now evidences respect for Spielberg as an artist rather than symptom of malaise. Besides analysing his films' formal qualities, investigations often consider the industrial context, in which Spielberg is contemporary Hollywood's 'most visible' and recognized representative 'other than on-screen stars'.[86] He is 'inseparable from the aesthetic, financial, technical and cultural developments his image personifies', as cause or beneficiary.[87]

Journalist Antonia Quirke's 2002 *Jaws* book in the BFI Modern Classics series was significant: an august cultural body with academic connections endorsed the movie as a canonical masterwork. Aesthetic judgements had not overtly concerned Film Studies since the 1970s, but Quirke supposedly eschews 'political and psychosexual' complexities and critical objections to 'infantile and sensational' aspects; both 'obscure', she contends, the movie's accomplishment 'simply' as art.[88] Quirke corroborates Jungian imagery of the sea as abyss and acknowledges Oedipal implications, but it is effectiveness, she believes, that summarizes Spielberg's vision. She notes his humour, declaring it undervalued against New American Cinema's earnestness. Like other critics, she detects misanthropy, underlining humanism: Spielberg fears '*us*' (not, like his fiercest critics, *them*).[89] Amusement intensifies the darker elements, making *Jaws* 'tonally comprehensive'.[90]

Tom Shone, another journalist, contrasts epic heroics against 'downsizing': 'ordinary men' battle 'a single shark, which kills only four'.[91] Humour and humanism underscore a 'dramatic technique' that recalls art movies.[92] Acknowledging highbrow disparagement, related to earlier blockbusters' biblical or classical themes, Shone concludes: 'If you're going to remodel the entire industry on a single movie', *Jaws* is suitable; its entertainment and artistry exceed clever media manipulation.[93] As Mark

Cousins opines, 'a good and nuanced film, *Jaws* would probably have performed very well under the old system of releasing'.[94]

More recently Spielberg's fame and cultural influence encourage academics and popular writers increasingly to discuss *Jaws* along with the rest of his work. There are essentially two camps: those who treat his films seriously and with due consideration, and those (fewer now) who hold them in contempt and find them significant insofar as they illustrate social, technological or commercial trends.[95] Spielberg makes two types of film, Peter Krämer contends: lucrative family adventures and 'adult-oriented drama about important historical issues'.[96] These imply different audiences, strategies, cultural status (partly reflected in awards) and accordingly criteria for criticism. In line with *Jaws*' reputation for destroying adult, inquisitive, innovative, challenging New American Cinema, and despite its violence and adult themes, it was grouped with a set of Spielberg's films that labelled him a children's director. This image, cultivated by branding and promotion, became constricting when he sought recognition for weightier fare. Rather than evidencing maturation, however, 'fantasy adventures and serious dramas', Krämer believes, demonstrate continuity between Spielberg's post-1985 'adult' films and earlier work. Most 'complex and fully realized' are 'his biggest hits, the fantasy adventures *E.T.* [1982] and *Jaws*'.[97] Connections, comparisons and contrasts across films arguably confirm a singular world view. Rather than diverse realization of disparate projects, a creative vision, expressed through the work itself rather than marketing and publicity, bestows artistic status.

Warren Buckland offers precise analyses that 'suspend aesthetic judgements'.[98] Spielberg exploits off-screen presence, Buckland argues, and his painstaking technique achieves 'added value'. *Jaws*, Spielberg's first 'well-made film', possesses that desirable Platonic quality, 'organic unity'.[99] Buckland's formalism reconsiders *Jaws* in relation to successful aspects of Spielberg's other output. Details transcend 'pedestrian filmmaking',[100] enabling Spielberg to embrace 'new tradition (the contemporary blockbuster)' while innovating.[101] Classical principles – creative solutions motivated beyond gratuitous style – persuasively support consideration of *Jaws* as art.

Likewise, Lester Friedman demonstrates how textual analysis, supplanting the received wisdom of Spielbergian 'legend' and Hollywood 'lore', confirms *Jaws*' intricacies.[102] 'To censure' success, he insists, 'is hypocritical and disingenuous'.[103] Friedman likens Quint's *Indianapolis* experience to Coleridge's Ancient Mariner who, surrounded by dying comrades, survived to share his tale.[104] This and other literary parallels, technical mastery and classical Hollywood allusions challenge 'cherished beliefs' to belie, or rather complement, the film's 'popcorn flick' qualities. Such judgement defies Biskind and others who, Friedman protests, 'routinely' practice '*Jaws*/Spielberg bashing'.[105]

My own monograph considers how, alongside production, marketing, promotion and publicity, 'a seemingly impersonal studio film – a cultural rather than individual expression that nevertheless depends on its director's passion for cinema – neatly encapsulates auteurism's contradictions'.[106] Point-of-view and image structures parallel humans with the fish – filmgoers, besides characters – 'deconstructing any facile notion, implicit in mythical resonances, of Good against Evil'. Rather than shark's-eye perspective consolidating ideology, Brody's (admittedly white, masculine, middle class, conformist) 'decency and professionalism' unseat 'intolerant, inhumane judgments the movie opens with'.[107] Ambivalence and complexity contradict 'selective' interpretations, supporting my thesis that Spielberg communicates dialogically. The shark's invisibility for most of the film enables it to embody a wide variety of projected meanings and thereby to symbolize multifarious fears. It also guarantees that these will survive after the shark's destruction. In the end, I insist, after Brody blows it out of the water its final 'exorcism' – to appropriate Britton's terminology and overturn his insistence that *Jaws* screenings were rallies or communion rituals celebrating conservative values – is 'merely formal'.[108]

Arguing that other movies' hype resembled or exceeded that surrounding *Jaws*, Frederick Wasser concludes that *Jaws* consolidated 'an audience that wanted to' attend movies, as *The Godfather* (1972) and *The Exorcist* (1973) proved while already increasing 'supposedly low genres'' budgets.[109] *Jaws*, Wasser contends, discarded New Hollywood's 'discredited establishment' and 'brooding characters', embraced sympathetic protagonists and replaced overt politics with 'new hipness';[110] Spielberg 'emulate[d] Hitchcock while competing with his contemporaries'.[111] Wasser implicitly illustrates the notion of 'high concept', comparing *Jaws*' poster with the cluttered graphics advertising *The Poseidon Adventure* (1972). Moreover, 'Out-of-shape middle-aged fishermen as ineffective stumblers' flattered younger moviegoers, while a policeman hero appealed to older audience members.[112]

Wasser insists that the film's cinematic qualities determined its impact. He utilizes 'Buckland's skillful analysis' to understand how adaptation 'eroded' Benchley's 'moralism': the script moved 'inside the action', maximizing tension with 'immediate "startle effect."'[113] The intensity of *Jaws* surpassed previous disaster films' detachment whereby 'the bad' suffered retribution and, 'while innocent and good people died, they typically had an ethical lesson in sacrifice to impart'.[114] Disaster movies favoured longer shots over close ups and psychologically motivated point of view, maximizing the stars concurrently on-screen.[115] *Jaws*, contrastingly, conveys experience of 'anticipated and actual attacks'. Discounting Benchley's mature relationships, 'Spielberg hooks young adults effortlessly', with the 'open embrace of a hedonistic nighttime beach party' and Hooper's 'subsequent buildup'.[116] Nevertheless, even 'flawed characters' elicit sympathy. Judgement – for example, that 'cooperation or collective spirit' is lacking – is left to the audiences.[117] Wasser in a subsequent publication notes 'the paucity' of 'communal groups in *Jaws*': the opening gathering shows 'lack of communication and exchange', and audiences must observe for themselves that protagonists 'fail to work effectively together even after they ostensibly bond in a drunken evening of telling shark stories'.[118]

Wasser also evokes Howard Hawks, with whom several earlier critics had compared Spielberg negatively. Hawks's characters unite through 'mutual support'; *Jaws*' 'simulation of bonding', contrastingly, 'falls apart'. This can be read equally as a realist take on the difficulties of a divided society confronting existential threat, progressive demonstration of the need for cooperation and collaboration, and as yearning for more authoritarian organization that some critics inadvertently betrayed even as *Jaws*' alleged conservatism was attacked. Spielberg's maritime adventurers, as Jameson argued, exemplify America's changing workforce. Quint 'undermines the working man's dignity', incites 'puerile confrontations' and becomes Hooper's 'generational foil'.[119] The *Orca* team's ineffectiveness causes Hooper's loss and Quint's death. Brody's triumphant rifle shot is fortuitous. Unlike 'Hawks' formulas and disaster movie moralism', Spielberg, caring not 'how we would act' if faced with the characters' difficulties, makes us 'react'.[120] Such comparisons nevertheless assume Spielberg's place in the pantheon – as, paradoxically, did those derogating him (which would not occur if hostile critics had not detected something significant to respond to). That Spielberg's conscious aims and the film's ideology, in a different era, differ from those detectable in Hawks is not in itself a question of quality.

Criticism perceiving Spielberg's tendency towards saccharine entertainment often eclipses the darker aspects of his work, James Kendrick argues, and 'embraceable humanism' is 'mistaken for the whole'.[121] Discrimination between his 'commercial' and 'serious' films overlooks ' "interesting, contradictory, and disturbing work" ' that Andrew Britton argued was being run out of Hollywood … primarily by Spielberg':[122] films that were 'more cynical, and less congruent' than acknowledged.[123] *Jaws* illustrates the recurrent Spielbergian theme of 'childhood victimization'.[124] Kendrick nevertheless identifies humour – 'small, ironic doses'[125] – largely misread or ignored since initial reviews.

'Clichés' about Spielberg's influence falsify film history, argues Stephen Prince. *Jaws* nowadays seems 'staid, classical'. While it remains thrilling, extended shots choreograph 'action with dynamic depth-of-field', shifting between foreground and background. Enhancing 'actors' abilities to contribute', this 'slows the action', permitting subtle characterization and emotion incompatible with a supposed 'voracious machine' calibrated for 'narrative propulsion'.[126] Although violence is central, withholding specifics stimulates imagination. Dread lingers, Prince observes, 'with gory inserts prodding the audience to scream':[127] 'Complexity and ambivalence are the rule'.[128]

Steven Rybin notes how, moving beyond familial 'dissatisfactions', *Jaws* targets failed 'collective social action': officials shirk responsibilities; profit motivates 'fragmented' shark-catching.[129] Highlighting performance choreography, Rybin demonstrates how Scheider's gestures construct Brody 'as anxious, self-contained, and lacking social agency'.[130] Spielberg eschews 'actor-driven' continuity editing; instead, 'fragmented diegetic space moment-by-moment' discloses 'the place of one figure' while camerawork 'suggests evolving emotional relationships to surrounding events'.[131]

'Absolute masterpieces', Roche declares, rank Spielberg among 'the most important filmmakers'.[132] Roche theorizes shifts, involving characterization and themes, between awe, fear, disgust, terror, anxiety, the sublime, dread and horror. *Jaws*, the 'quintessential horror movie', flows 'from dread to terror to horror' through causally motivated metonymy.[133] Roche analyses point of view, variation, repetition, off-screen and 'hidden onscreen' space, music, extra-filmic expectations, manipulated internal norms, even false alarms reaffirming 'the rules'[134] – subtle, rather than formulaic, provocations of reactions. Spielberg's 'aesthetics of suggestion' (off-screen) 'and confrontation' (on-screen)[135] confirm how off-screen space, not inherently threatening, is paratextually, visually and aurally 'charged'.[136]

Conclusion

Critics and academics, Timothy Corrigan says, 'mythologized' *Jaws*' impact.[137] Later studies demonstrate that it 'did not invent the blockbuster',[138] nor originate the marketing, funding, test-screening, advertising and release patterns blamed for destroying innovative, director-driven cinema. Change was inevitable: spiralling costs demanded huge, rapid turnovers,[139] while audiences had continued declining. If 1975 was 'a watershed', as Biskind claims, and leading directors 'went down in flames',[140] causality is not proved by the fact that the top 20 'film rental champs', as Thomas Schatz notes, came after *Jaws* 'recalibrated' success.[141]

Envy, hypocrisy and prejudice taint *Jaws*' and Spielberg's reputations. 'Financial success', Haskell writes, was an 'off-putting ... critical liability'.[142] The film's visceral appeal discomfited many. To master reactions their aesthetics precluded, critics denigrated audiences, director and industry, equating the product with the symbolism that disturbed them. Political commentators affected superior detachment, instead of admitting nostalgia for old Hollywood, New Hollywood or simpler US values, ironically propagating individualist ideology. Spielberg, Hollywood's 'most patronized' film-maker, '*is* contemporary American cinema, for good or ill', I. Q. Hunter claims, and its ' "bad object" ', yet central to 'debate on crucial moments of American identity'.[143]

Disparagement of Spielberg and mainstream entertainment played into how Hollywood niche marketed so-called 'independent' cinema and taste-forming journalists complied. That academic commentators were likewise susceptible until their successors, competent in textual analysis and semiotic theory, became dissatisfied with dismissal of complex and compelling films is a reminder of how entrenched values persist and the need to foster genuine discrimination.

The website *Digital Spy* described *Jaws*, rereleased, as 'a tense, exciting thriller that redefined contemporary cinema', concluding: 'They don't make them like this anymore' (15 June 2012) – nor did they back then of course. Rehabilitated critically and increasingly free from preconceptions and ignorance surrounding Hollywood, Spielberg and the tumultuous milieu it emerged from, *Jaws* retains sufficient clout to have been rereleased in 2019 in several hundred UK screens.

Researchers and pundits will debate its lasting appeal for as long as universal narratives are sought and specific historical circumstances explored.

Notes

1   See Raymond J. Haberski, Jr., 'Sharks, Aliens, and Nazis: The Crisis of Film Criticism and the Rise of Steven Spielberg', in Nigel Morris, ed., *A Companion to Steven Spielberg* (Boston: Wiley-Blackwell, 2017), 435–51.

2   J. Hoberman, '1975–1985: Ten Years that Shook the World', *American Film* (June 1985), 52.

3   Peter Biskind, *Easy Riders, Raging Bulls: How the Sex 'n' Drugs 'n' Rock 'n' Roll Generation Saved Hollywood* (London: Bloomsbury, 1998), 278.

4 Justin Wyatt, *High Concept: Movies and Marketing in Hollywood* (Austin: University of Texas Press, 1994), 115; 12.

5 https://www.rottentomatoes.com/m/jaws#contentReviews (accessed 18 September 2019).

6 See, e.g., Nigel Morris, *The Cinema of Steven Spielberg: Empire of Light* (London: Wallflower Press, 2007).

7 Lester D. Friedman, *Citizen Spielberg* (Urbana: University of Illinois Press, 2006), 2–3.

8 Morris, ed., *Companion*, in the Wiley Blackwell Companions to Film Directors series.

9 Cobbett Steinberg, *Film Facts* (New York: Facts on File, 1980), 178.

10 Peter Cowie, *Eighty Years of Cinema* (South Brunswick: A.S. Barnes, 1977), 312.

11 Joseph McBride, *Steven Spielberg: A Biography* (London: Faber, 1997), 246.

12 Peter Biskind, '*Jaws*: Between the Teeth', *Jump Cut* 9 (October–December 1975): 26.

13 https://www.rogerebert.com/reviews/jaws-1975 (accessed 18 September 2019). The website anachronistically dates the review as 1 January 1975.

14 Haberski, 'Sharks, Aliens, and Nazis', 435.

15 Ibid., 437.

16 Paul Kerr, ed., *The Hollywood Film Industry* (London: Routledge and Kegan Paul, 1986), 185.

17 David A. Cook, *A History of Narrative Film*, 4th edn (New York: W.W. Norton, 2004), 861.

18 Stephen Heath, '*Jaws*, Ideology and Film Theory', *Times Higher Education Supplement* (26 March 1976); reprinted in Bill Nichols, ed., *Movies and Methods*, vol. 2 (Berkeley: University of California Press, 1985). Stephen Heath, 'Narrative Space', *Screen* 17, no. 3 (Autumn 1976): 68–112. Fredric Jameson, 'Reification and Utopia in Mass Culture', *Social Text*, 1 (Fall 1979); reprinted in Jameson, *Signatures of the Visible* (New York: Routledge, 1992).

19 Heath, '*Jaws*', 510.

20 Ibid., 513.

21 Heath, '*Jaws*', 510.

22 Ibid., 510.

23 Jameson, 'Reification', 47, n.12.

24 Ibid., 36.

25 Ibid., 38.

26 Laura Mulvey, 'Visual Pleasure and Narrative Cinema', *Screen* 16, no. 3 (Autumn 1975): 6–18.

27 Dan Rubey, 'The Jaws in the Mirror', *Jump Cut*, no. 10/11 (1976): 20.

28 Ibid., 21.

29 Ibid., 23.

30 Jane E. Caputi, 'Jaws as Patriarchal Myth', *Journal of Popular Film* 6, no. 4 (1978): 305.

31 Ibid., 313–14.

32 Ibid., 312.

33 Ibid., 315.

34 Ibid., 317.

35 Ibid., 315.

36 Ibid., 317.

37 Andrew Britton, 'Blissing Out: The Politics of Reaganite Entertainment', *Movie*, no. 31/32 (1986): 9.

38 Andrew Britton, '*Jaws*', *Movie*, no. 23 (1976–77): 27.

39 Ibid., 29.
40 Leslie A. Fiedler, *Love and Death in the American Novel* (New York: Criterion, 1960).
41 Britton, '*Jaws*', 27; 31.
42 Griselda Pollock, *Jaws* film review, *Spare Rib* (April 1976): 42.
43 Robin Wood, 'An Introduction to the American Horror Film', in Robin Wood and Richard Lippe, eds, *The American Nightmare* (Toronto: Festival of Festivals, 1979), 10.
44 Ibid., 14.
45 Ibid., 11.
46 Robin Wood, *Hollywood from Vietnam to Reagan ... and Beyond* (New York: Columbia University Press, 2003), 156.
47 Ibid., 160.
48 *The Monstrous Feminine: Film, Feminism, Psychoanalysis* (London: Routledge, 1993); *Men, Women and Chain Saws: Gender in Modern Horror Film* (Princeton, NJ: Princeton University Press, 1993).
49 Barbara Creed, 'Horror and the Monstrous-Feminine: An Imaginary Abjection', in James Donald, ed., *Fantasy and the Cinema* (London: British Film Institute, 1989), 81.
50 Ibid., 80–1.
51 Carol J. Clover, 'Her Body, Himself: Gender in the Slasher Film', in Donald, ed., *Fantasy*, 103; Clover, *Men, Women*, 32.
52 Janet Staiger, 'The Slasher, the Final Girl and the Anti-Denouement', in Wickham Clayton, ed., *Style and Form in the Hollywood Slasher Film* (Houndmills: Palgrave Macmillan, 2015), 223.
53 Bruce Kawin, review of *The Funhouse* and *The Howling* in *Film Quarterly*, reprinted in Gregory A. Waller, ed., *American Horrors: Essays on the Modern American Horror Film* (Urbana: University of Illinois Press, 1987).
54 Clover, 'Her Body', 113.
55 Adam Rockoff, *Going to Pieces: The Rise and Fall of the Slasher Film, 1978–1986* (Jefferson, NC: McFarland, 2002), 15.
56 Ibid., 14.
57 Michael Ryan and Douglas Kellner, *Camera Politica: The Politics and Ideology of Contemporary Hollywood Film* (Bloomington: Indiana University Press, 1988), 51.
58 Ibid., 57.
59 Ibid., 60.
60 Ibid., 63–4 (emphasis added).
61 Peter Krämer, 'Dealing with Emotional Trauma in and through *E.T.*', in Adrian Schober and Debbie Olson, eds, *Children in Spielberg* (Lanham, MD: Lexington Books, 2016), 97.
62 Morris, *The Cinema of Steven Spielberg*, 5, 216.
63 Philip M. Taylor, *Steven Spielberg* (London: B.T. Batsford, 1992), 16.
64 Ryan and Kellner, *Camera Politica*, 61.
65 Ibid., 64.
66 Ibid., 169.
67 Sheldon Hall and Steve Neale, *Epics, Spectacles and Blockbusters: A Hollywood History* (Detroit: Wayne State University Press, 2010), 209.
68 Robert Torry, 'Therapeutic Narrative: *The Wild Bunch*, *Jaws* and *Vietnam*', *The Velvet Light Trap*, 31 (Spring 1993): 27, 32.
69 Ibid., 34.
70 Ibid., 27.

71 Ibid., 33.

72 Ibid.

73 Thomas S. Frentz and Janice Hocker Rushing, 'Integrating Ideology and Archetype in Rhetorical Criticism, Part II: A Case Study of *Jaws*', *Quarterly Journal of Speech* 79, no. 1 (1993): 62. Also revised version in Frentz and Rushing, *Projecting the Shadow: The Cyborg Hero in American Film* (Chicago: University of Chicago Press, 1995).

74 Ibid., 63.

75 Frederick Wasser, *Steven Spielberg's America* (Cambridge: Polity Press, 2010), 71.

76 Frentz and Rushing, 'Integrating', 65.

77 Ibid., 67.

78 Ibid., 69.

79 Ibid., 68.

80 Ibid., 70; 76. Brent Askari quotes the script on Quint/shark parallels: '*Jaws*: Beyond Action', *Creative Screenwriting* 3, no. 1 (1996): 32.

81 Frentz and Rushing, 'Integrating', 73.

82 Ibid., 78.

83 Ibid., 72.

84 Ibid., 73.

85 'Spielberg at Sixty', conference at University of Lincoln, UK, November 2007.

86 Nigel Morris, 'Introduction', in Morris, ed., *Companion*, 4.

87 Ibid.

88 Antonia Quirke, *Jaws* (London: British Film Institute, 2002), back cover.

89 Ibid., 50.

90 Ibid., 69.

91 Tom Shone, *Blockbuster: How the Jaws and Jedi Generation Turned Hollywood into a Boom-Town* (London: Scribner, 2004), 32.

92 Ibid., 33.

93 Ibid., 35.

94 Mark Cousins, *The Story of Film* (London: Pavilion Books, 2004), 382.

95 See Morris, *The Cinema of Steven Spielberg*, 47.

96 Peter Krämer, 'Steven Spielberg', in Yvonne Tasker, ed., *Fifty Contemporary Filmmakers* (London: Routledge, 2002), 319.

97 Ibid., 320, 321.

98 Warren Buckland, 'A Close Encounter with *Raiders of the Lost Ark*: Notes on Narrative Aspects of the New Hollywood Blockbuster', in Steve Neale and Murray Smith, eds, *Contemporary Hollywood Cinema* (London: Routledge, 1998), 167.

99 Warren Buckland, *Directed by Steven Spielberg: Poetics of the Contemporary Hollywood Blockbuster* (New York: Continuum, 2006), 4.

100 Ibid., 87.

101 Ibid., 84.

102 Friedman, *Citizen Spielberg*, 178; 162.

103 Ibid., 178.

104 Ibid., 167.

105 Ibid., 176.

106 Morris, *The Cinema of Steven Spielberg*, 46.

107 Ibid., 51.

108 Ibid., 56.

109 Wasser, *Spielberg's America*, 75.

110 Ibid., 64.

111 Ibid., 67.

112 Ibid., 71, 72.

113 Frederick Wasser, 'The Cultural Context of *Jaws* (Foreword)', *Cinergie, il Cinema e le Altre Arti*, Special Edition: Spielberg's *Jaws* and the Disaster Film, No. 7 (March 2015): 46. See also David Roche, 'Spielberg's Poetics of Horror', in David Roche, ed., *Steven Spielberg: Hollywood Wunderkind and Humanist* (Montpellier: Presses Universitaires de la Méditerranée, 2018).

114 Ibid., 46.

115 Ibid., 47.

116 Ibid., 48.

117 Ibid., 49.

118 Frederick Wasser, 'Spielberg and Rockwell: Realism and the Liberal Imagination', in Morris, ed. *Companion*, 289, n6.

119 Wasser, 'Cultural Context', 49.

120 Ibid., 50.

121 James Kendrick, *Darkness in the Bliss-Out: A Reconsideration of the Films of Steven Spielberg* (New York: Bloomsbury, 2014), 5.

122 Ibid., 8.

123 Ibid., 76.

124 Ibid., 64.

125 Ibid., 71.

126 Stephen Prince, 'Too Brave for Foolish Pride: Violence in the Films of Steven Spielberg', in Morris, ed., *Companion*, 292.

127 Ibid., 294.

128 Ibid., 295.

129 Steven Rybin, 'The Spielberg Gesture: Performance and Intensified Continuity', in Morris, ed. *Companion*, 165.

130 Ibid., 166.

131 Ibid., 167.

132 Roche, 'Introduction', in Roche, ed., *Steven Spielberg*, 11.

133 Roche, 'Poetics', in Roche, ed., *Steven Spielberg*, 92, 93.

134 Ibid., 103.

135 Ibid., 102.

136 Ibid., 105.

137 Timothy Corrigan, *A Cinema without Walls: Movies and Culture after Vietnam* (New Brunswick, NJ: Rutgers University Press, 1991), 11.

138 Linda Ruth Williams and Michael Hammond, 'The Seventies: Introduction', in Linda Ruth Williams and Michael Hammond, eds, *Contemporary American Cinema* (London: McGraw-Hill, 2006), 117.

139 Corrigan, *Without Walls*, 20.

140 Biskind, *Easy Riders*, 281.

141 Thomas Schatz, 'The New Hollywood', in Jim Collins, Hilary Radner and Ava Preacher Collins, eds, *Film Theory Goes to the Movies* (New York: Routledge, 1993), 9.

142 Molly Haskell, *Steven Spielberg: A Life in Films* (New Haven, CT: Yale University Press, 2017), ix.

143 I. Q. Hunter, 'Spielberg and Adaptation', in Morris, ed., *Companion*, 225.

6

Jaws, in theory

Murray Pomerance

Here follows an unorthodox foray into Steven Spielberg's *Jaws*, with Kurt Weill's lyrics perhaps haunting the mind –

> Oh, the shark has pretty teeth, dear
> And he shows them pearly white ...

(Trans. Marc Blitzstein)

– and keeping to the view that the film's precious moment, its residue, is the gaping shark maw as the beast emerges unbidden and unannounced from the sea. All of the film anticipates, circles around, is resolved through and is remembered in terms of this mouth, this mouth as an indicator of what the viewer may take as a central proposition in the film's argument, in remembrance of what Kenneth Burke wrote on the subject: '[Men] must develop vocabularies that are selections of reality. And any selection of reality must, in certain circumstances, function as a deflection of reality.'[1] This chapter is a review and clarification of what Spielberg's film is – and was – for me, not a tactic for fabricating something other than what *Jaws* has joyfully and fearfully become for its numerous critics and fans over more than forty years. Perhaps to some degree I contrive to use Spielberg and this young work of his as vehicles for transporting my more general theorizing about film, a burden which could as well apply to other films but which, at the same time – I hope I can show – reverberates with an experience of *Jaws* that if it is mine is not mine alone.

It must briefly be stressed, at the outset, what I am not trying to do. I am not trying to re-examine the by now thoroughly accepted, but certainly questionable, appraisal that *Jaws* is single-finnedly responsible for having changed the nature of cinematic exhibition in our culture (because of its originary blockbuster status). Neither am I commenting upon or taking issue with the many observations and approaches to understanding the film that have been provided by legion scholars, including Nigel Morris, who notes that the film, 'a product of troubled times, embodies contradictions among its discourses, visible in oppositions and image-structures. These, rather than unreflecting conservatism, produce ambiguity and thus appeal to various audiences';[2] Joseph McBride, who claims that 'As a result [of *Jaws*], studios began opening films more and more widely, and eventually it was not unusual for a potential blockbuster to open simultaneously on two thousand or even three thousand screens, backed by advertising expenditures of commensurately gargantuan proportions';[3] or Lester Friedman, who warns that critics 'fail to see that [Spielberg's] films repeatedly demonstrate that apparent safety is the most dangerous illusion of all, since one can never be protected from disaster anywhere or at any time'.[4] Finally, I am not trying to suggest an overriding, unimpeachable, supreme and 'true' decoding that explains everything about the film. But I do want to think about and gaze upon that spectacular mouth and what it implies.

What may seem (but is not) a detour:

Jaws and futurity

In June of 2004 – as he reports in his autobiography *Little Did I Know*[5] – Stanley Cavell, who had written that cinema has not received from philosophy the measure of attention that it calls out for,[6] came to a stark realization about a condition of claustrophobia from which he had suffered, to some degree, most of his life. The triggering event was his being subjected at the time to an MRI, an inconveniencing experience for anyone terrified of being locked in – as I can attest, having been scrutinized in the mid-1970s because of a case of Bell's palsy – and his ruefully noting, as a voice on a speaker informed him that the procedure was complete, that not one person was stepping forward to relieve him from the machine's cocoon. To quote Cavell's deliciously Proustian recollection from that suspending point of the story:

> Within seconds ... I began imagining that the attendant had either forgotten me or had dropped into a faint or some catastrophe had visited the world; and left me strapped in place, neither able to move nor make my cries heard from within this hard cocoon. Recapturing traces – fragments I would rather say – of these feelings as I write this, I realize only now that this sense of absolute abandonment by life replicates, calls back, my experience of bereftness when my mother was two or three minutes late (that is, later than my uninformed expectation assigned for her) in coming to my bedside when I awoke, when I was five or six, in the hospital the morning after I had been struck by the automobile.[7]

Let me emphasize here what I believe Cavell was emphasizing there: that his terror, his sense of absolute 'bereftness of the world', was inspired not by the, for him rather general, incarceration inside the MRI device and consequent passivity in the power of unfamiliar or unconcerned attendants, but by only one tiny moment, lasting, say, a few seconds or a minute, when instead of rushing immediately to his side the agents of medicine busied themselves in other ways, that he could neither imagine nor predict. A very small temporal fragment expanded exponentially for him; a moment became an eternity – a temporal universe.

I addressed an issue similar to this – the very small become very large – but framed in spatial not temporal terms, when in *An Eye for Hitchcock* I discussed vertiginous sensation and its relation to height.[8] *Vertigo* (1958) has intensively spatial elements of construction, for both the central character and the viewer. With his anecdote, however, Cavell swims in time not in space, and he resolves his emotional block, to my mind with incomparable brilliance – or rather, because, again, we are talking of temporal matters, incomparable metre – with a resonant suggestion: 'The role of temporal intervals, let's say of rhythm, in ordering the depth and the fragility of human hopes, say, one's conviction in futurity, must be a basis for the profundity of our need for music.'[9] One could say, with Cavell, moments are essentially musical.

We must wonder how *Jaws* works in terms of our conviction in futurity, the profundity of our need for music, meaning by 'music', of course, tonality (emotion) extended in time. Charles Warren has found this underlying tendency or proclivity towards the extension of feeling in Chantal Akerman's reaction to Bresson's *L'Argent* (1983):

> A sympathetic young man, an outcast, ultimately goes berserk and kills people. [Akerman] remarked on how amazingly tense she found the film, each image filled with a tension ready to explode into the next, which goes on moment by moment all the way through the film. Such tension does not sound like Akerman, and yet she has her tension, as does all valid film, as does all poetry, all that is made – a tension compounded of extension and intension, an attunement to the physical world as it is, in its extension, and an imbuing of the world with meaning … Disclosure of the everyday is much of what she is about, and the emergence of a peculiar tension is at the heart of this disclosure. Tension, in the sense of restlessness, or energy moving more than one way, or the physical held in balance with overtones of meaning, is in the everyday, something to be revealed that we might ordinarily overlook, something for documentation with an intelligent and probing eye.[10]

Jaws fanatics may have guessed where I am headed, namely, to a discussion of the film in terms of the shark's appearances as an important musical element, formed from the extension of apprehension and its resolution in event. My attention here is not for John Williams's music – somewhere between Bartok, Stravinsky and John Phillip Sousa – but for Spielberg's: his production of a constantly developing, modulated rhythm of expectation and fulfilment through which one is offered, in an agony of bloody bleakness, a conviction in futurity (Figure 6.1).

This doesn't mean a futurity in which things turn out nicely, nor one that offers itself plainly to understanding. But we can eclipse both the present and the trap of nostalgia for the past by means of the forward-looking gaze, a gaze upon which, for all its worth, cinema depends. What is coming, *Jaws* suggests outright, will spring from what is waiting to come, what is already there and outside our ken. But, to echo the spirit of Cavell's account, how long, and through what horror, will we have to wait?

A central approach to the issue of impending event and anticipation is opened by Spielberg's portrait of the three fearful boy-men who go a-hunting for the shark. For each of these, as one of the film's stars and therefore a focus of our attention, there is

Figure 6.1 A very classic horror composition, since Chrissie's identifying features are visible above the water's surface but what we cannot see is the source of the agony – ours and hers.

outlaid an aggravating torment that begs for release. Each man sounds his characteristic musical phrase.

Chief Brody (Roy Scheider), he is quick to inform anyone he meets, lives in terror of the water, a landlubber par excellence. Yet because for gainful employment he operates as the principal law officer in an oceanside territory, where at least two young people have been slaughtered at sea, he has no dignified option but to undertake a marine voyage. Here, then, is a man who does not want to get wet finding himself beyond sight of land on a surface that can be penetrated at any moment by monstrosity and death. Futurity sharpens his experiential horizon. Is it death he fears, or the oceanic? Oddly, once he is aboard Quint's craft, the water all around seems more frightening than even any quasi-mythical creature that might emerge from it (we can note the way his fingers tightly grasp at the wooden mouldings of the boat when he moves around); but at the same time, given the early scenes we have seen of watery carnage and devastated bodies, the water can be nothing but metonymous with the beast it contains, and every vast seascape shown as Brody gazes out works to expand the nature and potential of the imaginary force of whatever moves beneath.

Quint (Robert Shaw) is a radically antithetical type. For all his glaze-eyed bluster and tough expertise, for all his curt language which signals again and again that he has forsaken speech and culture, for all the armour his younger companions would like to find a way to strip off him, Quint reveals with his Second World War story, recounted in the envelope of night and after much imbibing, that he has long carried, without the slightest amelioration, a deep and irremediable fear of sharks. He lives in a retrospective interval, every thought of his current prey bringing him back to the Pacific in which he bobbed all night – all through a night like this night – as the sharks went at the crew around him with an intent immeasurable and an endless hunger. It is Quint's primordial fear allied with his toughness and dedication that turn him into the Ahab replica so many viewers have found in the film; but he is no Ahab, and this Great White is no Moby Dick, that whale having set its sights on one sole victim but this shark ready and willing to go for anyone it pleases. Quint might like to imagine himself to be Ahab, might think this enemy is his alone. In such narcissism he would be reduced to a puppet reflection of himself – and all this quite properly, dramaturgically speaking, so that in the moment of his demise we are less crestfallen than we might otherwise be.

Hooper (Richard Dreyfuss) is a fledgling scientist, a rational young fellow who when faced with the directness of experience relies religiously on information. He has inputted, memorized, catalogued and rationalized shark lore, and brings to the encounter with sea life an only slightly arrogant sagacity. Hooper fears fear itself, since fear springs from the forbidden zone of the irrational: the two disparate fears he senses in Brody and Quint are especially perplexing and repugnant to him. An inheritor of Enlightenment wisdom, Hooper sees factuality, not myth, in any marauding shark he believes he can explain. But he shifts into panic when it becomes clear to his rationality that the target of this sailing is a shark Beyond Theory. This is also a shark beyond narrative, since while its continuity motors the plot its appearances are all, musically speaking, ad lib, all outside the tight rhythmic structure the film-maker uses for containing his protagonists (Ridley Scott reprised this structure for *Alien* [1979]). Given that once the boat sails the climate of fear (prepared brilliantly by the civilian killing sequences earlier) surrounds and dominates the characters in a progressive way, like an accumulating fog, it is mostly through the 'music' of editing, performance shaping and varying emphasis that one is brought to sense the darkness and offered reason to yearn for the cadential sunrise that might follow. For Hooper, at any rate, the futurity and musical phrase of the experience lie in an abrupt transformation of consciousness, through which his rational and calculating life suddenly dissolves in the revelation that the world is without order, without reason, without the kind of shape his mind can imagine.

Brody, Quint and Hooper are thus, not unlike Beckett's Vladimir and Estragon, waiting. Waiting for redemption when the sea manifests something out of its grand potentiality; waiting for redemption when the nightmares of history are finally sweetened by the completion of natural justice; waiting for redemption when the haunting metaphysical dream can shine again with the illuminating sunlight of rationality, the darkness becoming the light. The wait will be terminated with the appearance of the shark, and so it is a torture they do not particularly wish to see ended yet one of which they must come to the end, in order that civilization be saved. They wait without knowing for how long, and with what exact consequence, to what exact purpose and with what personally compelling reason.

The moments in *Jaws* most articulately designed to be terrifying one must consider as successive culminations of temporal intervals, indeed intervals of entrapment, when along with the protagonists we are caught in horror, bereft of the salvation of the world. The opening scene off the beach by moonlight, with the buoy wailing; the July 4 beach horror, prefaced by an inconsiderate prank then capped by the attack upon little Alex Kintner (Jeffrey Voorhees); Hooper's nightmare dive to examine the boat wreck; the shark's visit to the stern of Quint's craft and, later, dining on Quint – all of these expand a breath of 'bereftness'. With each interval is introduced a problem that portends – but does not foreclose – a resolution involving the shark. The question of how long we will have to wait until the marauding presence makes itself known and felt thus becomes, in the case of each event, mountingly urgent and real, and a structural chain of growing urgencies is constructed. This question of rhythmic extension is continually on Spielberg's mind, and he knows (one may suspect from studying Hitchcock) that as the film wears on, the intervals may get longer, but also that no interval early or late in the story can be so lengthy as to render the audience effectively catatonic.

Since in their idiosyncratic ways the three protagonists are scripted to endure temporal extension, it makes sense to wonder what, extradiegetically, could have made Brody, Quint and Hooper the way they are. That is, what could have opened the longer interval in the midst of which we find them? (Cavell, for instance, realizes that the piquancy of his fear in the hospital emerged from something earlier and greater, involving his mother.) Quint's horror story of the torpedoing of the USS *Indianapolis* and his confrontation in the south Pacific with a gang of marauding sharks reveals him to have been on that ship because he was in the Navy and implies that he was in the Navy because he was drafted or signed up to avoid civilian engagement of another kind. Social pressure put him there – the pressure to be a proper male in that arena, which is to say, the openly declared willingness towards brutality in the national interest while demonstrating that he could use his maritime strengths. For Quint the *Indianapolis* no more represented a pleasure outing than does this present trip to sea. Quint's socially dictated male dominance, one could say his cultural victimization, is therefore one of the three negative images of the shark produced in the film: much as Quint may try to dominate him, the shark is the dominating brutality that both reflects and diminishes Quint.

Hooper, also a product of his culture but a full generation younger, finds Quint absurd in many ways and espouses countercultural values and a prep school aesthetic. He grew up in the 1960s, a baby boomer trained to believe that education – not hard-driving experience – was the golden key. For him, the ocean is a conceptual space bounded, defined and limited by oceanography: the monster by maritime biology. He can plot no route to resolution except by way of the scientific method: measurement, weighing, inspection, the work of the eye. Under all this is a conviction in the value of reasonable proportion, an eighteenth-century belief that the human mind can encompass Nature and the universe. Hence the necessity and centrality of those eyeglasses – taking them off to clean them, letting the sea spray wash upon them as he pilots the boat, hiding his fallible eyes behind their concupiscent glare – which can be counted upon to bring sharp and relieving focus to a world that is essentially imperceptible, unmeasurable, unknowable, unfathomable. The shark's enshadowed motive, indeterminate trajectory, doubtful origins and visceral capacity constitute the principal negativity for Hooper. In a world of facts and probabilities, formulae and tendencies, algorithms and light beams, the shark constitutes nothing but a question.

As to Brody, he was – and is – Alex Kintner's unrecognized brother, a boy overprotected and oversheltered by parents, perhaps by only a mother, convinced that the outside world, the world beyond his reach, an ocean beyond the lip of experience, lies on the far side of a shielding boundary (the warm sands of the beach) in an unknown and unfathomable zone one should never dare to enter. For Brody the ocean is essentially, inherently frightening, not as an aggregation of qualities but as a forbidden space. The sea voyage for him leads into his own repressions, into the inner chamber of the Temple and thus through the veil of sacred edict.

Jaws and doubt

When the shark rises out of its depths, showing the sailors not merely its size but also a face, it brings emphasis to their extreme vulnerability but in a way that is quintessentially filmic: animal eruptions remorselessly bobbing on a precious, permeable surface, an essence of cinema. When we go to the movies, we are confronted by what Siegfried Kracauer called a 'visual and acoustic kaleidoscope'.[11] There is rapid and repetitive sensory stimulation, echoed in *Jaws* by the use of the characters scanning the horizon line and the ocean's surface for any sign of the rupture by which their future will become their present. Yet, so many are the sensations, writes Kracauer, 'that there is no room left between them for even the slightest contemplation. Like *life buoys,* the refractions of the spotlights and the musical accompaniment [in the theatre] *keep the spectator above water*' (my emphasis).[12] Above water is where our sailors would hope to remain, of course, but the aesthetic event threatens to engulf them (as *Jaws* engulfs its audience). If that threat of being overwhelmed and pulled under is implicit through cinema's nature, it becomes explicit here, in the shark's uninvited face, a face that now occupies the same territory that is home to Quint, Hooper and Brody's faces. Black uncaring eyes. A protruding snout that can smell blood miles away. A mouth of blinding proportion. And no ears to hear one cry. It is with the shark's emergence that the film develops its true form, a scape of a 'sea of amorphousness and unpredictability' (Figure 6.2).[13]

Shall we consider this emergence a bursting forth of natural impulse? Kracauer reflects Hugo von Hofmannsthal's note that 'the spectator's dreams revive those of

Figure 6.2 The audience is gonna need a bigger imagination. Brody's first meeting with the shark.

his childhood days which have sunk into his unconscious. "This whole subterranean vegetation," [Von Hofmannsthal] remarks, "trembles down to its darkest roots, while the eyes elicit the thousandfold image of life from the glittering screen".[14] The shark's appearance points to the sudden and spectacular emergence of unbridled vitality from a zone that lay, as it were, 'within'. In this context let us briefly consider the record of a second personal observation, von Hofmannsthal's astonished account of a show of Vincent van Gogh paintings into which he unexpectedly stumbled. 'Shall I tell you about the colours?', he writes, 26 May 1901:

> There is an incredible blue, most powerful of blues, which constantly reappears, a green like that of molten emeralds, a yellow that deepens into orange. But what are colours if the innermost life of objects doesn't break through them! And this innermost life was there, tree and stone and wall and gorge gave of themselves their innermost, almost casting it at me How can I make it clear to you that here each Being – the Being of each tree, each strip of yellow or greenish field, each fence, each gorge cut into the stony hill, the Being of the pewter jug, the earthenware bowl, the table, the clumsy armchair – lifted itself toward me as though newly born *from the frightful chaos of Non-Living, from the abyss of Non-Being*, so that I felt – nay, so that I knew – how each of these objects, these creatures, was born from a terrible doubting of the world and how with its existence it now covered over forever *the dreadful chasm of yawning nothingness!* (emphases mine)[15]

My interest at the moment is to focus on the seeming 'emergence', even eruption, of van Gogh's colours, as Hofmannsthal experienced them (rather than on the painfully moving, almost chthonic resonances that the colours suggested to him – and may again suggest to us – abided beneath). His 'dreadful chasm' is of course the topos that Hooper does not – will not – imagine; that Quint knows only too well; that Brody suspects, intuits, imagines is out there and fears to encounter or even see. Brody and the fully engaged Roy Scheider incarnating him fixate on Quint's boat as their 'home' territory. Reflect on Scheider's marvellous, spontaneously invented one-liner – 'You're gonna need a bigger boat!' – when first, and from far too proximal a vantage, he sees the shark's face. *Boat*, as in extension of the land. *Boat*, a production from shaved forests. *Boat*, the source therefore of all protection and civility. He prays that the controllable world, the *boat*, should be bigger, the sea more limited. Then recall von Hofmannsthal's stunned reaction to van Gogh's colours, their manifest incredibleness; their ineffable aspect that he doubts whether he can make clear; their rising up shockingly towards the self; thus the sense of a new optical experience immediately born, as though no natural process or imaginable temporal interval could produce so startling an effect. Hofmannsthal's is an acute perception of a deeply hidden 'terrible doubting of the world'. Three-quarters of a century after van Gogh, and with a blunt and incomprehensible presence, Spielberg's shark – that shark's face – would 'cover over forever the dreadful chasm of yawning nothingness'.[16]

The shark is the principal attraction of the film, the reprising motif and major point of concentration. Because of its centrality, there is established a peculiar condition in which, as with Harry H. Hamilton's 'Original and Delightful Excursions to the Continent' of 1860 as described by Erkki Huhtamo, the story can rely 'on visual extravagance rather than on coherent information'.[17] There is no moment in which we vacation from anticipating, experiencing or recollecting this extravagant creature, nor yet a moment in which the thing seems entirely, unequivocally real, which is perhaps its most stunning appeal. If it analogizes cinema itself, by its continual forward movement, it also summons to memory brother monsters whose presence – anticipated and finally embodied – gelled the stories in which they floated: Godzilla in 1954 and King Kong twenty-one years before him. Emerging each from a dark and hidden zone, these icons in their vicious but also playful aggression upon the human world showed it, however organized and civil, empty and – as we see dramatized by the conflict of physical proportions that all these films employ – pathetic. With Godzilla I have in mind the moments in which he steals across Tokyo, stomping on buildings, picking up an elevated train and devouring a car with all its passengers (industrial sushi). With Kong the elaborate and gigantic trestle upon which Fay Wray is pinioned for him to grasp on his first appearance, or the scene with her standing trepidaciously in the palm of his hand. As to the gigantic shark, it almost exactly recomposes a medieval form 'which dwarfs a fragile ship'.[18] As it 'stands' in the water next to Quint's relatively toyish boat the thing is outlandish, exactly as we see in Olaus Magnus's 1538 *Carta Marina* with its representation of the 'Prister' or toothed whale.[19]

Spielberg seems blithely unconcerned as to whether viewers might doubt the authenticity of his shark – he knows it is not the veracity of the creature but the shock of its manifestation that counts. The unmistakable artificiality speaks in many voices at once, both reassuring and aggravating the panic of viewers variously informed and ignorant about oceanic life. Well known (in the wake of copious post-production news releases) is the fact that the shark was an animatronic construction built for the purposes of filming, and real only as such; yet also completely real as such, and in this way as real as anything else in filmic fiction. In their day, Kong and Godzilla were also constructions, palpably false yet wholly and sharply comprehensible in terms of the narratives they inhabited. The artifice of the monster thus invokes a crisis of comprehension and belief, not unlike but perhaps more emphatic than other elements of cinematic construction.

By the complications of Spielberg's story, the film posits about this shark a hyperrational aggressiveness: that it has been lurking, until the commencement of the narrative, in silence and obscurity in order to camouflage itself tactically from the innocents who will be its victims; that it has a mind bent on planning and producing a particular kind of victimization: sudden, remorseless and ravenous; that for effecting carnage it is so horrendously equipped – the pretty teeth, dear, the uncaring black eyes, the muscular torso enabling destructive thrusts. We must wonder through what concatenation of forces such a Being could have been made, extradiegetically, in terms of the magic of creative effects, and diegetically, in terms of the Gods of the undersea, the forces of nature or whatever vast cosmological Entity one might humbly invoke. Did this shark emerge from *within* nature or has it rent the natural fabric as an invading outsider? The uncivilized, unrecuperable, alien quality of the shark's movement and motive – a quality of unrelenting, even insentient hunger – not only seems to have been always already present as given to us here but was already actually present in the 'personality' of the truck driver in Spielberg's first film, *Duel* (1971); and bridges forward, ameliorated and softened, to the peaceable aliens he would design later for *Close Encounters of the Third Kind* (1977), *E.T.: The Extra-Terrestrial* (1982) and even *A.I. Artificial Intelligence* (2001). But even in these more beneficent attractions, contrivances of the plot energize the audience's worry as a form of attentive engagement. On some level, then, to watch is to fear.

The aggression in *Jaws* is structural. Reprising motifs from the submarine films of Spielberg's youth – *Destination Tokyo* (1943), *The Enemy Below* (1957), *Run Silent Run Deep* (1958) – the hunt sequences in the film rely on our understanding of the shark as an invisible military agent, a foe whose proximity invokes navy-style engagement and whose actions are understood not as random or preconscious but pointedly malevolent. The target of the monster's wrath is civilization taken very broadly, but in situational fact American youth, the children of the bourgeoisie who inhabit a gay seaside summer resort, a class whose adult members are primary agents of capitalism in a profit-seeking rampage as relentless as the shark's. Spielberg's shark seems to have a 'mind', at any rate, and to be 'plotting' its moves: the three hunters think of and refer to it this way, in a deliciously ironic reflection upon narrative process (because like sharks no characters in any dramatized story really think about what they will do next).

Jaws is a kind of military tale (we must keep in mind Spielberg's emotional, sometimes stressed, connection to a father who had fought in the Second World War), one of its fundamental claims being the power of hardware and its relation to the ultimate destructibility of the enemy. For all its uncanny and unmeasurable ken, its horrific origins, its brutal and excessive desire, the shark is finally only an enemy, flesh that can be sundered and fragmented; a formation of the sea that can be returned to the sea, if only the right weapon is used in just the right way (as happened against both Kong and Godzilla). Thus, it can only be Sheriff Brody, legally empowered to employ gunpower, who can dispatch it. The huge negativity of the monster sets up, legitimizes and clarifies the technical know-how of the hero, and this in traditional generic fashion; Brody here is finally a recapitulation of John Wayne's sharpshooting Tom Doniphon in *The Man Who Shot Liberty Valance* (1962). And what is painfully – and for fans wonderfully – doubtful about the shark's destruction is that in perfect Aristotelian harmony it returns the scene in the film's very final moment to the placidity with which it started, a primordial moment that – as we learned at the beginning but perhaps in narcotized relief have forgotten by the end – contained within its beautiful peacefulness all the seeds necessary for catastrophe.

A curious paranoiac quality attaches to much reflection about *Jaws*. Watching this bucolic town, the sparkling sunshine, the giggling children, the aesthetic purity of the beach and the charming sweetness of Sheriff Brody at home, then seeing it all ripped apart by the shark's apparently sudden presence, one easily begins to think that perhaps evil has manifested itself not *unbidden* but in response to some unknown, as yet undetected invitation. The shark is here because it was *summoned*. The invoking agency: man's hubris, typified by Amity's trepidatious mayor (Murray Hamilton) and craven businessmen; man's ignorance and unpreparedness, typified by Brody and his wife innocently examining books about shark attacks over their Scotch; man's insatiable and provocative hunger; society's general moral complacency; America's unsophisticated arrogance. Yet the more disfiguring and riddling possibility is the one easiest to neglect: that the shark's appetite and actions are responses to nothing, in short, *not responses*. That there is no explanation for the attacks.

Because it is eruptive, and shockingly so, with each appearance the shark seems to enunciate colour, to exist as blaze, in precisely the sense invoked by von Hofmannsthal, who found it so stunning. While he openly pointed to the exact colours van Gogh had used, Hofmannsthal's true sensibility was for colour itself, in its depth and richness, and this is the stratum of experience he identifies when he suspects a hidden world beneath. Of the shark, too, we may ask, what world is hidden beneath his manifestations? Is he one of a kind or a member of a large tribe, a virtual army? Is this curious sense we have of his motive perhaps an index of our fears about more manifold, more broadly frightening things, down, down, down below the point where swimmers' feet tread and half-devoured bodies hover in wrecks? Hofmannsthal does not mention the teeth of van Gogh's colours, but he seems to sense their presence, quite in the way that Scheider's Brody seems to sense ahead of time the shark that at the back of the boat has come surprisingly to visit him.

And this discomforting possibility brings up two considerations vital, I think, for a thorough appreciation of *Jaws*.

Tool

The first marker: cinema must always and inevitably make its drama visible, and because the visible is played out through compositions upon a surface – the twitching rectangle of the screen – *Jaws* for all its plotting, science, social science and generic fixation engages audiences through depicted action. To the extent that we wish to concentrate on the action of the shark, we must see the beast as not only motile but also rhythmic, colourful and promising. And also *simply here*. Were we to plumb the picture through an ontological scheme – reason preceding event – we would estimate the shark propelled by some *vis a tergo*, a 'motive' pushing towards revelation, transformation, then ultimate decline. (Dining follows hunger.) But here it is precisely this 'causative' moment that is elided, the creature opening its maw without excuse, without a display of hunger, uncoordinated with surrounding affairs. The passionate interior space is too suddenly all present before our eyes – indeed a raw space that organizes the construction of our vision. In the scene where the shark devours Quint and most of his boat, the jerky processional of the action is a pronounced aesthetic effect-without-cause, a springing forward that has its roots in the unpenetrated, uncharted, unassimilable and incomprehensible depths of the sea, a zone of complete indeterminateness. This indeterminateness was foreshadowed in the Fourth of July picnic sequence by Brody's *obstructed* point of view, adopted by the camera. Because of the passers-by happily camped out or marching up and down the beach in front of him he could not get a clear line of sight to the water, where he thought he *might have seen* a fin. The catastrophe of the shark's presence came unbidden. Another foreshadowing was Quint's inebriation as he slurred out his story of the *Indianapolis*, his mental state apparently a vortex of swirling memory fragments and diluted present sensations. A third was Hooper's shocked, dismayed inability to account for the size and power of the predator in terms of the well-remembered, well-articulated, well-filed but totally inadequate data of his experience studying sharks. Inevitably, the shark is the film-maker's tool, ironically his bait – appearing or being expected to appear – for hooking the expectation of the viewer.

But if the shark is Spielberg's utensil, the film that contains it is a utensil, too, aimed to rededicate and reimagine the filmgoing audience in the age of New Hollywood. The beach at Amity, full of holidaygoers who have flocked to the sea and sun, is a reflection of the broad consumerist multitude flocking to theatres to see this film, after all. The idea of *Jaws* as a tool is fundamental to thinking about its historical importance since, as so many critics have claimed, the film initiated the age of the summer blockbuster and latterly of blockbuster cinema in general. But there is a more chilling sense in which Spielberg's shark is a tool, and its gestures through the film a kind of tooling around, or tooling with, the given world. As André Leroi-Gourhan notes:

> The concept 'tool' itself needs to be reviewed with reference to the animal world, for technical action is found in invertebrates as much as in human beings and should not be limited exclusively to the artifacts that are our privilege. In animals, tool and gesture merge into a single organ with the motor part and the active part forming an undivided whole. The crab's claws and jaws are all of a piece with the operating program through which the animal's food acquisition behavior is expressed. The fact that human tools are movable and that their characteristics are not species related but ethnic is basically unimportant.[20]

The shark's starring performance, enacted through gestures, is identical, isomorphic with the shark's utility and capacity to utilize. It moves through the diegetic universe devouring objects in its path, much as the film itself, unspooling, devours the attention and consideration of its viewers without regard for their personal concerns or predispositions. For all its attention to features of contemporary life, *Jaws* is not *about* voracious capitalism or contemporary America, or the family, or the adventure of a hunt on the sea, but about this beast as an unknown, a monster, a mouth that moves forward in unending and insatiable hunger. The shark is Spielberg's device for indicating and achieving narrative thrust, and as such it is the site where tool and gesture are merged into a single organ – his single organ, cinema's single organ (Figure 6.3).

Hitchcockian

My second marker is *Jaws'* relation to Spielberg's happenstantial mentoring by Alfred Hitchcock, since this artful little story of a seaside community and its inexplicable

Figure 6.3 Amity main beach on the Fourth of July. Note Spielberg's framing to show the wide expanse of unmarked ocean and also the very realistic magnitude of the crowd. This would be the beginning of the summer season for many visitors.

manifest infestation by a monstrous animal force is clearly derived, more than from *Moby-Dick, or The Whale* (1851), from *The Birds* (1963). So much cinematic work is deemed 'Hitchcockian' without owing more than a surface debt to Hitchcock's films – some of Brian De Palma's films come to mind – but *Jaws* is genuinely Hitchcockian in its reprising the deep philosophical concern with the moral implication of natural catastrophe. Also in *The Birds* we see the constitution of a natural force as punishing Nemesis, icon of Evil, and, more practically, target of warfare. As in *The Birds*, *Jaws* explicitly displays animal interiority: instead of the opened beaks and startling movement of the gulls attacking Melanie Daniels (Tippi Hedren) in the telephone booth (where she is as frozen as Spielberg's underwater corpse) we see the teeth and dull uncaring thrust of the shark. As in *The Birds*, the fleeing, panicking civilians, notably children; the scientist initially debunking fearmongering (the ornithologist vis-à-vis Hooper); the narratively significant use of boats. And the rational but also intensely feelingful male protagonist: in Hitchcock, the lawyer Mitch Brenner (Rod Taylor), in *Jaws* devoted Brody. In both films a terrified character in the most curious way seems like a savant. Both Lydia Brenner (Jessica Tandy) and Brody display a strange cognition, a notably interiorized awareness of the perturbation in the field of sensation and knowledge being stimulated by the animal presence, the animal presence, I should add, as metonymy, since in both films a principal dynamic mechanism is the presentation on-screen of parts that are generalized, by diegetic protagonists and viewing audiences alike, as malevolent wholes. I would not work to argue that Spielberg was intentionally, or even consciously, borrowing from, imitating or paying homage to Hitchcock, only that given his age he would have to have seen and digested *The Birds* and as a growing film-maker would have to have been deeply affected by its effects. In both films nature is overturned or turned inside-out with enormous consequence, but when we look for motive we find a vacuum (Figure 6.4).

Figure 6.4 One filmic prototype for the shark/villain: Hitchcock's peacefully assembling crows in *The Birds*.

Conclusion

To conclude, a metaphor of self-reflection. I sometimes think of the critical project itself as a kind of shark, growing all the time as it munches on its object and perhaps even become monstrous, relentless, in its search for digestible material; and masterful in its reign over an ocean of artistic possibilities. This certainly does not always happen, any more than Great Whites always show up on our beaches, but it is always possible. As a narrative, *Jaws* can be seen as a lone structure bobbing in a broader space, a craft riding over – or a secure cage resting beneath – the waves of cinema, and locked inside of which is the trifold spirit of its creator, terrified still (like Quint) by films of his childhood; rational (like Hooper) in his process; relatively untried (like Brody) as he sails early in an as yet unassured career (Spielberg hadn't yet reached his thirtieth birthday). So much critical attention has refused to openly revel in this film – couching it in social observation instead, or reviling it as pop cultural trash, or demeaning the film-maker's audacious brashness and – as Spielberg admits he was criticized for during production – profligacy. The challenge of discovering matters of philosophical import in *Jaws* has been largely avoided. And even when writers have admired or raved about the film, praising it rather than burying it, the theme has been a circumlocutionary focus on horror, fear, excitement and violence, the elements one could deduce straightforwardly from any account of a shark attack, any written narrative, without actually looking at Spielberg's screen and the way he has organized images there.

More generally, I often fear, the critic's attention can be aggrandized to the point where no work of art is safe from its marauding. We must remember that critics have their own motives, and that making a meal of a film can be nutritious for reputations. Criticism can swell and dominate to such a degree that the artist himself is evacuated from the scene and the armature he built as a way of saying his piece is rent, disassembled, made into scrap (as we see happening with the shark cage in which Hooper descends for protected investigation). This film, we mustn't forget, not only heralded the age of the blockbuster; it in many ways signalled the age of what critics do in looking at films the critical way: Thomas Schatz's work dates from the early 1980s, Noël Burch's from the late 1970s, Bill Nichols's from the mid-1970s, Robin Wood's from the late 1960s. The critical journey moves forward relentlessly, begetting new and younger voices, and perhaps more and more successfully finding strategies whereby the love of, and meditation upon, cinema can smartly be hidden. Watching *Jaws* might thus become a way not to appreciate film but to attack it, savage it, leave it empty. I deeply believe that all of us, lay viewers and critics alike, can find a better experience than that.

For Stanley Cavell,
in cherished memory

Notes

1 Kenneth Burke, *A Grammar of Motives* (Berkeley: University of California Press, 1969), 59.
2 Nigel Morris, *The Cinema of Steven Spielberg: Empire of Light* (London: Wallflower Press, 2007), 54–5.
3 Joseph McBride, *Steven Spielberg: A Biography*, 2nd edn (Lexington: University Press of Mississippi, 2011), 258.
4 Lester D. Friedman, *Citizen Spielberg* (Urbana: University of Illinois Press, 2006), 175–6.
5 Stanley Cavell, *Little Did I Know: Excerpts from Memory* (Stanford: Stanford University Press, 2010).
6 William Rothman, ed., *Cavell on Film* (Albany: SUNY Press, 2005), 295.
7 Cavell, *Little Did I Know*, 400.
8 Murray Pomerance, *An Eye for Hitchcock* (New Brunswick, NJ: Rutgers University Press, 2004), 217–23.
9 Cavell, *Little Did I Know*, 400.
10 Charles Warren, 'Fiction and Nonfiction in Chantal Akerman's Films', in David LaRocca, ed., *The Philosophy of Documentary Film* (Lanham, MD: Lexington Books of Rowman & Littlefield, 2016), forthcoming.
11 Siegfried Kracauer, *The Mass Ornament: Weimar Essays*, Thomas Y. Levin, trans. (Cambridge, MA: Harvard University Press, 1995), 324.
12 Ibid., 326.
13 Ibid., 102.
14 Siegfried Kracauer, *Theory of Film: The Redemption of Physical Reality* (Princeton, NJ: Princeton University Press, 1997), 171.
15 Hugo von Hofmannsthal, *Selected Prose*, trans. Mary Hottinger and Tania and James Stern (New York: Pantheon, 1952), 147–8.

16 It may delight fans of *Jaws* to peek at Walt Disney's *Bee at the Beach* (1950), in which a relatively gigantic shark leaps vertically out of the water to have a snap at the beleaguered Donald Duck. Spielberg, who was 4 when this was released in theatres, may well have had an impressionable experience.

17 Erkki Huhtamo, *Illusions in Motion: Media Archaeology of the Moving Panorama and Related Spectacles* (Cambridge, MA: MIT Press, 2013), 293.

18 Joseph Nigg, *Sea Monsters: A Voyage Around the World's Most Beguiling Map* (Chicago: University of Chicago Press, 2013), 70.

19 Nigg notes that 'whale', 'shark' and 'sea monster' have common etymological roots in Latin. Tom Conley and Joe Garver graciously assisted me in examining a size-as copy of the *Carta Marina*.

20 André Leroi-Gourhan, *Gesture and Speech*, trans. Anna Bostock Berger (Cambridge, MA: MIT Press, 1993), 237.

Part Two

Interpretation

7

Jaws as Jewish

Nathan Abrams

Introduction

Acknowledgement of the influence of Steven Spielberg's Jewishness has only come belatedly. His great coming out was reckoned to be his Holocaust film *Schindler's List* (1993) followed by his film about the aftermath of the 1972 Munich Olympics massacre, *Munich* (2005). Added to those are his earlier and more overtly Jewish-themed films, *Raiders of the Lost Ark* (1981) and, as producer, *An American Tail* (1986). But it is surely possible that like the shark lurking beneath the waters of *Jaws*, Jewishness lurks beneath the surface of all of Spielberg's films, regardless of the explicit subject matter. Building upon research into Spielberg's ethnic background, but drawing upon a range of other sources, this chapter will argue that *Jaws* can be read as Jewish.

Approach

The conventional dogma on Steven Spielberg was that while he was born a Jew he is not a Jewish director. Indeed, according to David Desser and Lester D. Friedman, his cinema can be characterized by a 'retreat from Jewishness': 'Spielberg's cinema seems to demonstrate his unwillingness to focus overtly on Jewish characters.'[1] Furthermore, his characteristic refusal to address Jewish issues bore an 'eerie similarity to the first generation of Jewish directors in America, those European émigrés studio moguls [who] essentially forbade to tackle Jewish issues'.[2] Nevertheless, they did consider him Jewish enough to devote several pages to him in their book *American Jewish Filmmakers*.[3]

Spielberg was born to two Jewish parents, Arnold Meyer Spielberg and Leah Posner. His paternal grandparents, Samuel (anglicized from the Hebrew Shmuel) Spielberg and Rebecca Chechik, hailed from Kamenets-Podolsk, in Russia. His maternal grandfather, Philip (anglicized from the Yiddish Fievel) Posner, was an immigrant from Odessa in Russia and his wife, Jennie Fridman, was born in America. Spielberg's mother, Leah, was raised among relatives who were involved with Yiddish theatre and vaudeville. Her uncle, Boris, was a Shakespearean actor in the Yiddish theatre. Leah grew up in a devoutly orthodox Jewish household. Fievel Posner fit the image of a *haredi* in his yarmulke, long white beard and traditional black garb who was always praying. As a child, Spielberg was embarrassed by him and tried to keep his non-Jewish friends away from the house when he was visiting. Spielberg's childhood home was only intermittently kosher, and the family attended conservative synagogues.[4] Despite this Jewish background, or maybe because of it, Spielberg didn't practice any religion at the time he made *Jaws*. Nonetheless, despite his embarrassment, Spielberg didn't change his Jewish last name in an industry when Jews were often anglicizing them to make them sound more gentile.

It will be argued here that Spielberg 'directed Jewish', that is, whether consciously or unconsciously, he inserted what Ella Shohat called 'a hidden Jewish substratum' – despite the absence of any such explicit 'ethnic' designation – beneath the surface of the film.[5] As Henry Bial, inter alia, has argued, minority ethnic cultural texts are frequently marked by specialist knowledge unavailable to majority audiences.[6] Such an approach relies on the director, the writer (of source material and/or the screenplay) and often the actors placing, both consciously and unconsciously, characteristics, behaviours, beliefs and other tics, all of which require a prerequisite and prior knowledge of Jewishness and of Jewish culture. In this way, directors (and actors/actresses) encode clues that can be read in terms of Jewish specificity, producing what Jon Stratton has called 'Jewish moments' but which a general audience decodes as universal.[7] This requires a strategy employing a 'complex of codes that cross-check each other' of which the Jewish identities of actors/actresses is a key, but by no means the only, part.[8] Other important clues include historical, traditional and cultural references; appearance; intellect; behaviour; profession; names; physiognomy; foods; verbal and body language; phenotype; aural, visual or emotional/genre signs; speech patterns and accents; hairstyles; anxieties; neuroses and conflicts. This strategy of 'directing' or 'acting Jewish' relies on the viewer to locate, identify and decode those clues which can be both textual and extra-textual. Consequently, the individual viewer is given the possibility of '*reading Jewish*' but not with certainty, and with positing varying degrees of pertinence, in such a reading, to the film's overall meaning.[9] Spielberg's films can also be explored in a process of textual analysis akin to Midrashic study, a kind of formal or informal elaboration on Jewish scripture, to elucidate and elaborate upon their deeper or hidden meanings beneath the surface, that is, the literal reading or representation in his films. This approach invites us to look deeper, to embark on a journey of interpretation that takes us beyond the story, revealing a distinctly Jewish understanding of the universe, especially in the film-maker's use of imagery drawn from the Hebrew Scriptures, Talmud, liturgy and Kabbalah. This approach will be applied to *Jaws* to argue that Spielberg allowed us the possibility, albeit not the certainty, of reading Jewishness in *Jaws*.

Semitizing the screenplay

Jaws was adapted from Peter Benchley's 1974 novel of the same name. There were no extant Jews or Jewishness in the novel apart from one brief reference. Amity's only delicatessen owner, Paul Loeffler, is supposed to hire two delivery boys for the summer but can only afford one. However, one is white, and one is black. When questioned which one he will hire, he responds, 'The black one. I figure he needs the money more. I just thank God the white one isn't Jewish.'[10] Incidentally, the name of the delicatessen owner is a German surname and was the name of the head of the Jewish Affairs department of the Gestapo in Cologne, Germany, during the 1930s and 1940s.

What is more, Benchley's novel was bitter, cynical and pessimistic. Antonia Quirke describes the book as being pervaded by 'a general tone of nastiness' and 'an infernal atmosphere of blood and guts. Sharks eat each other in a hackneyed metaphor for the islanders. One even describes another as a loan shark!'.[11] Quint (played by Robert Shaw in the film) keeps a baby porpoise – a protected species – that he has cut out of its mother, as chum, to lure the shark. In addition, I. Q. Hunter points out how the book is 'haunted by sex, or more precisely rape'.[12] Early on, as context, Benchley describes how a black gardener had raped seven rich white women.[13] He then goes on to describe Matt Hooper's 'obvious, violent climax' with Ellen Brody:

> He was oblivious of the being beneath him, and when, perhaps a full minute after his climax, Hooper still did not relax, Ellen had become afraid – of what, she wasn't sure, but the ferocity and intensity of his assault seemed to her a pursuit in which she was only a vehicle.[14]

Hunter glosses that this 'not only suggests rape but aligns Hooper's angry primal appetites with those of the hyper-phallic shark'.[15]

By contrast, Quirke avers, 'None of this tone is retained by the film.'[16] When adapting the novel, Spielberg removed these nastier elements and, in so doing, infused it with a Jewish sensibility. Jewish writer Howard Sackler was asked to contribute to the screenplay because of his experience as a scuba diver. He did not receive a screen credit, though, as he felt that he didn't work long enough on the film. Sackler, who hailed from the Bronx, was a classmate of the great Jewish director Stanley Kubrick and co-wrote the screenplays for Kubrick's first two films *Fear and Desire* (1953) and *Killer's Kiss* (1955), both of which contained conceptually Jewish characters and sensibilities.[17] Spielberg openly admired Kubrick from whom he took many cues, one of which was how to submerge Jewish issues beneath the surface of the work. Spielberg then asked Jewish actor Carl Gottlieb – whom he had originally hired to play Harry Meadows, the toadying editor of the local newspaper – to redraft the script, adding more dimensions to the characters, particularly (Jewish) humour. John Milius, a Jewish Second World War expert, also had a hand in writing some of the script. These contributions helped to bath *Jaws* in a subsurface Jewishness, resulting in a more hopeful, innocent and optimistic film.

Jewish *Jaws*

The shark can be read as a floating – or swimming – polysemic signifier onto which contradictory imagery can be projected, some of which can be read as Jewish. The image of Jews as being predatory and diabolical like sharks has been around for a long time. An internet search for the terms 'Jews' and '*Jaws*' will encounter any number of images that have replaced the shark with a stereotypically Jewish caricature will come up (see Figure 7.1).

In this context, consider also the idea of Jewish loan sharks raising the 'vig' or Shylock desiring his pound of flesh. But whereas Shylock only demanded a single pound, *Jaws* feasts on multiple pounds of flesh in the film. Indeed, Spielberg named the mechanical shark 'Bruce' after his lawyer, Bruce Ramer, a powerful and influential Los Angeles attorney specializing in entertainment law. So not only is *Jaws* Jewish, he is also an attorney! Ramer later became national president of the defence organization, the American Jewish Committee from 1998 to 2001.

In the movie, the shark is depicted as an outsider who does not belong even though the ocean is his home. A wandering, nomadic predator, *Jaws* is an unwanted presence in the small American coastal resort of Amity. Meaning 'friendship', Amity was most likely the type of place that was probably restricted to Jews in the past subject to

Figure 7.1 *Jaws as Jews.*

that Gentleman's Agreement type of anti-Semitism that denied entry to anyone with ethnically dubious surnames (like 'Abrams'). As I have pointed out above, the novel contains no obviously Jewish characters. The film makes much of the town's close-knit nature and its clapboard houses and white picket fences. Amity is populated by people with such wholesome gentile names as Quint, Meadows and Gardner. *Jaws'* invasion disrupts the equilibrium of this quintessential all-American idyll, as if he were a metaphor for non-white immigration thematically matching the images of the seasonal visitors from New York, disgorged from the shark-like maw of the ferry, including an African American woman, a nun and a man in a yarmulke (see Figure 7.2). This seasonal multiculturalism highlights the town's mono-culturalism.

The very idea of having a Jewish shark as a protagonist raises the ugly head of the historic blood libel. It taps into age-old fears of the Jew as predatory, lusting after gentile women and the blood of young Christian children. This Jew was the product of Christian theology, medieval anti-Jewish polemics, religious art and latterly anti-Semitic propaganda. In medieval and pre-modern times, for example, the Jew was

Figure 7.2 A seasonal visitor to Amity: A man in a yarmulke.

viewed as a primitive, sexually rapacious monster who was a debased lecher yearning for Christian girls (preferably virgins).[18] Shylock in Shakespeare's *Merchant of Venice* and his supposedly sadistic demand for a pound of Christian flesh can be understood in this light.

Matt Hooper (Richard Dreyfuss) seeks to dispel such notions when he states, 'It wasn't Jack the Ripper, it was a shark', but his allusion implicitly compares *Jaws* to the infamous Victorian serial killer who was also alleged to be Jewish. During the fin de siècle in England, a heady brew of xenophobia and anti-Semitism led to the spread of stories that Jack the Ripper was Jewish. The public's knowledge that Jews required ritual slaughterers for their kosher meat, coupled with the setting of the murders in the East End, where the majority of London's Jewish community lived, led to the conclusion by many at the time, as early as 1888, that the murders might be the handiwork of a skilled Jewish butcher. Jack's alleged description, printed in the newspapers, sketched him in a vague but stereotypically Jewish fashion: dark beard and moustache, dark jacket and trousers, black felt hat, foreign accent and hooked nose.[19] Consequently, a significant proportion of the suspects interrogated by police were Jews given the largeness and proximity of the Jewish community in Whitechapel. It was almost irrelevant whether Jack the Ripper really was Jewish or not because the figure of Jack the Ripper played into long-held stereotypes in England during the nineteenth century of the criminality and sexual deviancy of the Jew of which he was only one incarnation. Svengali, Dracula and other stereotypes of English literature in particular also fit into this characterization and would have spoken to their nineteenth-century audiences whether explicitly named as Jewish or not.[20]

This stereotype found its way into Victorian English literature of the nineteenth century. Mr. Isaacs, the cruelly caricatured Jewish theatre manager in Oscar Wilde's 1891 novel *The Picture of Dorian Grey*, was a sexual predator who controls the fate of the Christian heroine, Sibyl Vane. Earlier in Charles Dickens's 1838 *Oliver Twist*, the implied sexual deviancy towards children of Fagin, who was explicitly named as Jewish, also paralleled Ripper's perversions. Svengali, the explicitly Jewish antagonist of George du Maurier's *Trilby* (1895), was a dirty, sinister and predatory figure, selfishly manipulating the innocent heroine of the novel through mesmerism or hypnotism. Bram Stoker's *Dracula* (1897) would have been understood by contemporary audiences, as Jewish, whether explicitly revealed or otherwise. As an immortal yearning for the life force of the pure, virtuous Christian women he took under his spell, he embodied the Christian blood libel.

Surely, then, it is no coincidence that the first victims in the film are a (presumably) non-Jewish blonde and a young boy. Indeed, the poster for the film plays on these fears in its depiction of a blonde female swimmer being menaced by the huge (read: phallic) shark. Certainly, the terms in which Benchley's novel describes its potential victims paint them in terms of a superior, Aryan, racial elite:

> Privilege had been bred into them with genetic certainty. As their eyes were blue or brown, so their tastes and consciences were determined by other generations. They had no vitamin deficiencies, no sickle-cell anaemia. Their teeth – thanks to

either breeding or to orthodontia – were straight and white and even. Their bodies were lean, their muscles toned by boxing lessons at age nine, riding lessons at twelve, and tennis lessons ever since. They had no body odor.[21]

Further linking the shark with Jack the Ripper was Spielberg's decision to shoot the killings from the shark's point of view. This was, as I. Q. Hunter points out, a cinematic device borrowed from *A Study in Terror* (1965) that depicted Jack the Ripper's killings through point-of-view shots.[22]

Even the throwaway parallel between *Deep Throat* (1972) and the dead shark's agape maw taps into this discourse. The male star of *Deep Throat*, Dr. Young, was played by Harry Reems, born Herbert Streicher, and elements of the film operate within a Jewish humoristic idiom. Only Linda Williams has pointed out how

[j]ust as a golf pro might instruct a golfer to relax into the swing, so the doctor instructs Linda to relax her throat to make possible the deep penetration that will scratch her itch. At one point he adopts the accent of a Yiddish grandfather in imitation of a familiar Alka-Seltzer commercial: 'Try it, you'll like it!'.[23]

And 'patient' Jacob Maltz (Bill Harrison), in name, phenotype and accent, is clearly represented as Jewish, particularly for those who recognize the codes. Jacob is a biblical name and, in a perhaps unintentionally Oedipal manoeuvre, his wife in the film was called Sarah (in the Bible Sarah is Jacob's mother). Like Dr. Young's Yiddish grandfather, Jacob's accent is recognizably and heavily accented Eastern European English. He also manifests other very stereotypical Jewish traits. He is very hirsute. He boasts about having plenty of cash ('Money is no object'). The close of the sequence confirms the ethnic delineation in the utilization of the familiar trope of Jewish financial acumen when he invites Debbie to return on a regular basis to administer the same treatment. She responds that it will be rather expensive to which he ripostes, 'Don't worry, my dear. I have Blue Cross.' This closing line shows that Maltz has a sense of humour, another quality ascribed to Jews who tend to appear in comedic genres. Turning back to *Jaws*, recall how Carl Gottlieb had been hired to inject more Jewish humour into the film.

Another historical marker of Jewishness, the colour yellow, is omnipresent in *Jaws* – the yellow lilo; the blonde girl; Mrs. Kintner's (Lee Fierro) yellow hat; the yellow blanket, the yellow sand; the yellow sun; the yellow jumper; the yellow oilskin; Brody's yellow car; the yellow billboard. Quirke describes the story as 'in official yellow'.[24] Whenever Jaws appears yellow is prominent in the background. Indeed, in an ingenious cost- and time-saving device, Spielberg substituted the mechanical shark with yellow barrels. For centuries, yellow has historically connoted Jewishness. Jews were ordered to wear distinguishing yellow badges in the medieval period. A variety of sumptuary laws in fifteenth-century Italy established various markers as Jewish signs, including a circle cut out of yellow cloth for men and a yellow veil for women. A Jewish woman discovered in the street without her distinguishing yellow veil could be publicly stripped (incidentally, this was the sign used elsewhere to mark prostitutes who suffered the same punishment). Rebecca the Jewess in Walter Scott's *Ivanhoe* (1819), adapted into a 1952 film, wears a yellow turban, signifying her Jewish difference. These signs morphed into the yellow badge of the Nazi period, culminating in the yellow triangle for Jewish camp inmates. In this light, the yellow barrel becomes emblematic of *Jaws'* symbolic Jewishness.

Made only a couple of years after the Yom Kippur War, *Jaws* can also stand in as the tough Israeli Jew. A ruthless and efficient killer, he anticipates Spielberg's *Munich*. If this seems to be a stretch, in December 2010, following several shark attacks that occurred off the coast of the southern Sinai resort of Sharm el-Sheikh in Egypt, the Egyptian media and authorities accused those tourist-killing sharks of being Mossad-trained spies. It was alleged that a GPS tracking device had been found on a dolphin and had been planted by Israeli agents. In a television interview, the governor of South Sinai, Mohammad Abdul Fadhil Shousha, seemed to confirm this. In response, the Israeli foreign ministry suggested that Shousha had seen '*Jaws* one time too many'.[25]

Certainly, Spielberg seems to identify with the shark. He said that when he first read the novel, he found himself rooting for the shark, because the human characters were so unlikeable. This explains the high number of point-of-view shots in the film, where we see things from Bruce's subjective perspective, that is, of the shark (this was also dictated by pragmatic concerns as the mechanical shark kept breaking down). We can also interpret this as a projection of Spielberg's own sense of childhood otherness among a largely gentile population in which there were few other Jews:

> 'I never felt comfortable with myself,' he confessed, 'because I was never part of the majority … I felt like an alien … I wanted to be like everybody else … I wanted to be a gentile with the same intensity that I wanted to be a filmmaker'.[26]

Spielberg recalled being physically bullied and subject to anti-Semitic comments as a child. In 1988 Spielberg told *American Film* magazine about why he undertook to adapt Alice Walker's seminal novel, *The Color Purple*, in 1988: 'I had some anti-Semitic experiences when I was growing up,' he recalled, 'including prejudice and everything else I had to go through at one particular high school'.[27] David Desser and Lester D. Friedman write,

> Spielberg's mother confirms his exposure to anti-Semitism as a youth and has wondered if she was mistaken in moving her family from Cincinnati to Scotsdale, Arizona, where they were bothered by neighborhood children who stood outside their home and yelled 'The Spielbergs are dirty Jews. The Spielbergs are dirty Jews'.[28]

'He wasn't like the normal kids in the neighbourhood. He wasn't the muscle guy. He got bullied a lot. That was tough', Spielberg's sister recounted.[29] 'I was just a lonely guy', Spielberg himself said.[30] His earlier film *Duel* (1971) had explored these experiences:

> My early themes always had the underdog being pursued by indomitable forces of both nature and natural enemies and that person has to rise to the occasion to

survive and a lot of that comes just from the insecurities I felt as a kid and how that bled over into the work. I was always the kid with the big bully and *Duel* was my life in the schoolyard. The truck was the bully and the car was me.[31]

Jooper

Another Jew is drafted in to help hunt down *Jaws*, possibly along the lines that it takes one to know one. The young Jewish actor, Richard Dreyfuss, whom Spielberg called his 'alter ego', plays Matt Hooper, the young ichthyologist and oceanographer.[32] Dreyfuss had previously played the intellectual in *American Graffiti* (1973) and the lead role in *The Apprenticeship of Duddy Kravitz* (1974), 'a kind of Canadian *Catcher in the Rye*'.[33] Peter Krämer refers to Dreyfuss's 'distinctly non-WASPish looks',[34] but, as Joseph McBride points out, Spielberg did not direct attention to his characters' ethnic backgrounds.[35] Like Spielberg, Dreyfuss was small in stature and full of what Spielberg called 'kinetic energy' and Gottlieb referred to Dreyfuss's 'fast moving mouth'.[36]

The casting of Dreyfuss as Hooper significantly changes the character and the tone of the film. In the novel, Hooper is young, rich and virile. He has an affair with Ellen Brody – the violence of his lovemaking has been described above – and ultimately dies. Gottlieb recalls how when offered the role, Dreyfuss was 'unhappy with the superficiality of the character. He would rather see this movie than be in it'.[37] Together, Dreyfuss, Gottlieb and Spielberg fleshed out Hooper's part, making him much more sympathetic than in the novel. To this end, Spielberg et al. removed the affair between him and Ellen Brody. It was out of these changes that one of the film's most illustrative sequences emerges: Quint and Hooper face each other across the deck and Quint drains and crushes a beer can, throwing it over the side in one strong move, and Hooper counters by crushing a Styrofoam cup with a silly plop and putting it in the trash container on board.

Hooper, whose surname can be considered a Jewish name, fits the stereotype of what Michael Rogin has called 'Jew is mouth as nervous brain'.[38] Antonia Quirke describes him as a 'compulsive talker';[39] 'Hooper talks and reacts quicker than anyone else in *Jaws*, with speedier details.'[40] Thus, one of the first things that we understand about him is that he is defined by intellectual activity rather than his physical properties, manifesting what is known as *Yiddishe kopf* or 'Jewish brains', tapping into a trend, predating the invention of motion pictures, whereby the Jew is defined by his mind. Spielberg would later cast Jeff Goldblum in just such a role in *Jurassic Park* (1993) – a film with a similarly suggestive homophonous name to *Jaws* – as in Jew-rassic. Hooper, like the shark, is a loner. And like the shark and a stereotypical Jew, he is obsessed with food. When he first lands on the island, he enquires about a good restaurant. He arrives at Brody's house with two bottles of wine and inquires after the unwanted food, which he then proceeds to ravenously attack: 'Hooper eats the untouched meal Ellen made for Brody with his fork moving fast from plate to mouth.'[41] He is the only one eating. He talks with food in his mouth and out on the water offers Brody a pretzel. Hooper is always eating just like the shark which Hooper calls an 'eating machine'. The shark has no table manners and lacks decorum, more stereotypically Jewish traits. And Hooper uses culinary terms when discussing the shark: humans are a 'smorgasbord' of 'food' for the shark.

When Hooper takes to the seas with police chief Brody and grizzled seaman Quint, Jackie Mason's quip, 'Is there a bigger schmuck on this earth than a Jew with a boat?', immediately comes to mind. Stereotypically, Diaspora Jews are not seen as a seafaring people and when we see Hooper initially neither are we convinced. He seems more like a student rabbi who has inadvertently taken a wrong turn. Indeed, when he is aboard the boat hard-boiled Quint gives him loads of stick, reflecting their public off-screen relationship in which they did not get on at all. Shaw accused Dreyfuss of cowardice and suggested that Dreyfuss would only have a career 'if there's room for another Jewish character man like Paul Muni'.[42] Born Frederich Meshilem Meier Weisenfreund, Muni had begun his acting career in the Yiddish theatre.

'In casting the young actor he came to view as "my alter ego", Spielberg was reshaping the character and the film to reflect his own sensibilities,' McBride argues.[43] According to Spielberg, Dreyfuss 'represents the underdog in all of us'.[44] Benchley, however, was less than impressed and described Hooper as 'an insufferable, pedantic little schmuck'.[45] Hooper is marked by his thirst for knowledge and eagerness to question the status quo. Carl Gottlieb explains how he 'represents civilization and education and modern science'.[46] In stereotypical fashion, Hooper is the rationalist, sceptical intellectual, whose knowledge is invaluable in the shark hunt. Hooper wears glasses, a stereotypical Jewish trait, in the past connoting spiritual blindness but more recently suggesting scholarliness. When Brody, marvelling at his boat, asks, 'Are you rich?', 'Yeah', replies Hooper with no sense of shame. Quint inspects Hooper's 'city hands' and denigrates them: 'You've been counting money all your life', he growls, buying into anti-Jewish canards. Hooper rejects such 'working-class hero crap'.

Hooper's oceanographic expertise taps into a long history of Hebrew fishing knowledge dating back at least to when they were slaves in Egypt as recounted in Numbers 11:5. The Bible and Talmud are littered with references to fish and how to catch them. Arguably, Jews have been fascinated with sharks since the Hebrew prophet of Jonah. When Jonah is cast into the sea he is swallowed by a 'huge fish' (Jon. 2.1). Given that the Bible explicitly refers only to a fish and never calls it a whale, and this fish is big enough to hold the body of a man, a great white shark is a distinct possibility. The Bible refers to a legendary sea monster, the Leviathan, and one of Benchley's original titles was 'Leviathan Rising'. Only a brief reference remains in the novel. Sharks are *treyf*, that is, they are not fit for Jewish consumption because they lack proper scales and for a fish to be truly kosher it must possess both fins and scales. In a Talmudic discussion of nautical matters found in tractate Bava Batra (73–4), Rabbi Yochanan related:

> Once we were traveling on board a ship and we saw in the ocean a chest set with precious stones and pearls which was guarded by a shark. A diver went down to retrieve the chest, but the shark noticed him and was about to wrench his thigh. Quickly, the diver poured a bottle of vinegar on it and the shark sank into the sea.

Fast-forwarding a few hundred years in to the modern age, contemporary Jewish thinker, Woody Allen, in his *Annie Hall* (1977), released not long after *Jaws*, uses marine metaphors to reflect on companionship when his character Alvy Singer famously opines, 'A relationship, I think, is like a shark. You know? It has to constantly move forward, or it dies.'

Another persistent stereotype is that of the Western Jew of the Diaspora as unnatural, that he does not belong in nature. Jews are today considered to be an extraordinarily urban people and the city, the prototypical Jewish space. Furthermore, media representations of Jews are overwhelmingly urban, urbane and metropolitan. As David Desser has pointed out:

> a variety of forces have contributed to an ongoing media stereotyping of Jewish men as, on the one hand, physically small, weak, urban dwellers ill at ease on the farm and in the country; or, on the other, clever cunning, fast-talking city slickers. These images of frail urbanites, more verbal than physical, more devious than brave, in short, more brainy than brawny, have adhered to Jewish men ever since the encounter of the *Ostjuden* [lit. 'Eastern Jews'] with modernity, the shtetl or city-dwelling Eastern European Jews butting up against the forces of the Enlightenment and their Western European brethren.[47]

Thus, the natural landscape and environment, in particular the ocean, is constructed as a place which is alien to the Jew and in which the Jew is (an) alien from which he is excluded. Yet, equally, there is also a growing trend 'placing characters equipped with one set of skills (wit) into situations where the other (brawn) is required'.[48] As McBride points out,

> Dreyfuss's Hooper, a bearded, bespectacled, deceptively nerdy-looking intellectual, uses brains (and technology) more than brawn to hunt the shark, but summons up the courage to descend in an underwater cage with a poison-dart gun when there seems no other alternative. The offbeat, sarcastic Hooper serves as a Spielbergian foil for the traditional hero figure, Shaw's swaggeringly macho, Ahab-like Quint.[49]

As Pauline Kael observed,

> When the three protagonists are in their tiny boat, you feel that Robert Shaw, the malevolent old shark hunter, is so manly that he wants to get them all killed; he's so manly he's homicidal ... The director, identifying with the Dreyfuss character, sets up bare-chested heroism as a joke and scores of it all through the movie.[50]

Brody also reads as a (Jewish) fish out of water. In the novel, he is a native islander. But in the film, he hails from New York City and is afraid of boats and the water. While Benchley came up with the name, it is a surname of Jewish origin, associated with the Ukrainian city of Brody. Brody looks petrified for most of the movie and kibitzes and fusses of the welfare of his children – both his own and those in his charge in Amity. He feels genuine remorse and real guilt over the death of Alex Kintner (Jeffrey Voorhees) (unlike the town's mayor) and yearns to do the right thing. He, like Hooper, wears glasses but his are oversized. And he smokes – another signifier of Jewish Otherness.[51] Spielberg was determined to, in his own words,

> take the edge of Roy Scheider as the hotshot masculine leading man ... and let him have all the problems, all the faults of a human being. And let him have fears and phobias, and bring all these fears and phobias out in the picture, and then not resolve all of them. Because you can't. that's why a person spends all his life learning about himself.[52]

As Quirke explains,

> he wears a neat cagoule. This is Ellen's work, you're sure. He couldn't be less masculine than he is now, telling Hooper that he left New York because of the danger to schoolchildren, telling him that in Amity where there is no crime, one man can make a difference.[53]

Finally, adding another layer of implicit Jewishness is the presence of Lorraine Gary (née Gottfried), who played Ellen, Brody's wife; she was the girlfriend of Jewish producer Sid Sheinberg.

Menschlikayt versus *goyim naches*

Peter Biskind suggests that in *Jaws*, Spielberg 'deftly uses the Us/Them formula deployed by films like *Bonnie and Clyde* [1967], *Easy Rider* [1969], and *M*A*S*H* [1970]'.[54] He continues to say ' "Us" is no longer narrowly and tendentiously defined as the hip counterculture, but is expansive an inclusive, a new community comprised of just about everyone – all food, so far as the shark is concerned'.[55] There is another way that Spielberg deployed the Us/Them formula, but one missed by Biskind, in its injection of a clearly Jewish sensibility.

Together Spielberg and Gottlieb used Hooper as a mouthpiece to voice a social perspective. As 'an American Jew with clearly defined ethnic roots', Dreyfuss embodied what Gottlieb defined as 'a tradition of intellectual inquiry, respect for learning, and intense involvement with morality and law'.[56] Brody wishes to close the beaches but is prevented from doing so by the mayor and the town council because Amity needs the business. The mayor puts commerce before human life. In a shift from Benchley's novel where the pressure to keep the beaches open comes from shadowy pseudo-Mafia figures in the background, Spielberg placed the blame firmly on Amity's merchants and civic representatives, the latter represented by one particularly 'strident and humourless' motel owner, 'concerned only with the money she stands to lose if the beaches are closed'.[57] Thus, as Dan Rubey points out, '[T]he greed and wilful blindness of the business community causes the death of a young boy, Alex Kintner, and of an unidentified man on the July Fourth weekend.'[58] Against them stands Hooper:

> Those qualities are abundantly present in the film's Matt Hooper, the voice of scientific reason and civic responsibility against a town who leaders initially are more concerned with tourist dollars than with protecting their citizens against harm. In taking a principled stand against official hypocrisy, Hooper helps awaken the conscience of Roy Scheider's police chief Martin Brody. After an initial display of cowardice, Brody risks his career to defy the venal mayor (Murray Hamilton), the toadying newspaper editor (Gottlieb), and the town's short-sighted merchants.[59]

In this way, Hooper exemplifies best the uniquely Jewish code of *menschlikayt*. It is the Yiddish expression referring to ethical responsibility, social justice and decency for others expressed in kindness. The Yiddish writer Leo Rosten described a *mensch* as

> 1. A human being. 'After all, he is a *mensh*, not an animal.' 2. An upright, honorable, decent person. 'Come on, act like a *mensh*!' 3. Someone of consequence; someone to admire and emulate: someone of noble character. 'Now, there is a real *mensch*!'.[60]

In the words of Rebecca Alpert, a *mensch* is 'an ethical human being who displays his virtues through gentility and kindness'.[61] *Menschlikayt* rejected '*goyim naches*', a phrase that 'broadly describes non-Jewish activities and pursuits supposedly antithetical to a Jewish sensibility and temperament'.[62] Literally meaning 'pleasure for/of the gentiles', its root is the Hebrew word *goy* (singular of *goyim*, meaning gentiles) but which also derives from the word for 'body' (*geviyah*). It can therefore also be interpreted to mean, as Jeffrey T. Sammons points out, a 'preoccupation with the body, sensuality, rashness, and ruthless force', as manifested in such physical activities as bearing arms, horse riding, duelling, jousting, archery, wrestling, hunting, orgies and sports in general.[63] Denied the right to participate in such activities, Jews instead denigrated them, consequently also disparaging those very characteristics that in European culture defined a man as *manly*: physical strength, martial activity, competitive drive and aggression. *Goyim naches*, therefore, in Daniel Boyarin's words, was 'the contemptuous Jewish term for the prevailing ideology of "manliness" dominant in Europe'.[64] Since toughness was downgraded in normative rabbinic culture, physical, martial and bodily virtues, which flowered in natural surroundings, were rejected in favour of a scholarliness that thrived indoors.

If Hooper represents *menschlikayt*, then Quint is the embodiment of *goyim naches*. Indeed, the film expands the rivalry between Quint and Hooper, contrasting the former's goyishness with the latter's *menschlikayt*. Quint is a sexist, misogynistic, macho drunk. When he sings about Spanish ladies he's not only suggesting prostitution but also Hopper's femininity. He tells Hooper to stop playing with himself. When Shaw squeezes an empty beer can flat, Dreyfuss satirizes him by crumpling a Styrofoam cup – Styrofoam is urban and urbane, the domain of the office worker and feminizing. Where Hooper carries temperature gauges and spear guns, Quint is armed with ropes and a rifle. Quint demeans Hooper's sailing experience as 'pleasure boatin''. As the two men compare scars at night on the boat, Quint shows the one he got arm wrestling in a bar celebrating his 'third wife's demise'. In return, Hooper shows his own woman-related mark, an invisible scar on his chest placed there by 'Mary Ellen Moffett: she broke my heart'. Ironically, though, Quint's great speech about the 1945 sinking of the *USS Indianapolis* in shark-infested waters (explaining his visceral hatred for the creatures) was written by two Jews. Sackler began it and it was, according to some accounts, expanded by John Milius.

For Jews, fish had to be netted. Typically, Jews have not killed animals for sport and in the medieval period they were denied opportunities to hunt. In his book, *Fishing from the Earliest Times*, William Radcliffe blamed Jews for lacking a competitive and sporting spirit since they caught fish by the net and not with a rod.[65] Indeed, Jews equated the hook with cruelty or as an instrument used by foreigners – note the close up of the large hook that Quint produces – a sign of his inherent cruelty. In the rabbinic period, the hook, which entered the mouth of the fish, typified cruelty and was hence compared to the disease of croup which attacks and chokes infants.[66]

By contrast, Gottlieb described Quint as 'the eccentric, complex professional sharker who kills the beasts for pleasure as well as gain, and provides the brute, animal cunning that first snags the monster in the story'.[67] A sign of his character was that Gottlieb felt that Sterling Hayden was the perfect choice to play him in part not only because of his seafaring knowledge ('seawater ran in his veins') but also because of the role he had played as the psychotic General Jack D. Ripper in Stanley Kubrick's *Dr. Strangelove, Or How I Learned to Stop Worrying and Love the Bomb* (1964).

But Hooper proves himself to be tougher than that. When he faces off against *Jaws*, it is the Diaspora Jew versus the tough shark and the former wins. Hooper is thus the brave Jewish outsider coming to the rescue of the gentiles. He ultimately disputes Jackie Mason's quip about Jews on boats so much so that, Peter Biskind argues, a nascent homosexual bond develops between Quint and Hooper which the shark destroys.[68] In fact, Hooper outlives Quint who becomes the shark's fifth victim (hence his name, Latin for five or fifth). In an act of possible retribution for his harsh treatment of Hooper, Spielberg stages Quint's death as particularly gruesome.

The Holocaust

Can we, in some way, consider *Jaws* a post-Holocaust film? After all, in additions to the film that did not appear in the novel, the ghost of the Second World War haunts the film (in the novel it is the Vietnam War). Furthermore, if, as I. Q. Hunter suggests, 'the first shark attack intricately re-imagines' the shower scene in *Psycho* (1960), is there some way we can consider *Jaws* as a Holocaust film?[69] After all, there is a body of work to suggest that *Psycho* itself, in particular the shower sequence, was influenced by Alfred Hitchcock's work on editing documentary death camp footage as *German Concentration Camps Factual Survey* (1945).[70] On this note, it is significant that John Williams's score draws on Stravinsky's 'The Rite of Spring' (1913), something which, Hunter points out, 'filmgoers of Spielberg's generation might recognise as the soundtrack to the dinosaur sequence in *Fantasia* (1940) – an entirely appropriate reference point for *Jaws*' invocation of ancient primeval terror'.[71] While Hunter here is presumably referring to dinosaurs, the date of *Fantasia* also points to a more contemporaneous horror. What is more, the allusion in the film to the Second World War and the atomic bomb – Quint survived the sinking of the USS *Indianapolis*, which delivered the Hiroshima bomb to the island of Tinian in 1945 – in some ways serves to obliquely conflate the Holocaust with nuclear holocaust in the way *Dr Strangelove* did back in 1964. Dan Rubey writes how *Jaws* reflects 'a fear of retribution for the atomic bombing of Hiroshima'.[72] But perhaps *Jaws* actually mirrors a revenge fantasy for the Holocaust – a foreshadowing of *Munich*.

Conclusion

In his adaptation of Peter Benchley's novel, Spielberg inter alia infused a subsurface Jewish sensibility through the constant juxtaposition of a set of binary opposites. City slickers and urbane urbanism is contrasted with the rough working-class rustic on the one hand and small-term meanness on the other. As conceptual Jews, both Brody and Hooper represent an unmanly metropolitan masculinity versus Quint's rustic ruggedness. Yet, they work together to defeat another conceptually Jewish character: the shark. Successful in their quest, the wild is tamed and becomes a place in which *menschlikayt* triumphs over the values of *goyim naches*. Both Brody and Hooper survive, swimming home, replicating the endings of two other conceptually Jewish films: *Casablanca* (1942) and *Some Like It Hot* (1959).

Notes

1   David Desser and Lester D. Friedman, *American Jewish Filmmakers*, 2nd edn (Urbana: University of Illinois Press, 2004), 303.
2   Ibid.
3   Ibid., 302–9.
4   Joseph McBride, *Steven Spielberg: A Biography* (London: Faber & Faber, 1997), 19–26.
5   Ella Shohat, 'Ethnicities-in-Relation: Toward a Multicultural Reading of American Cinema', in Lester D. Friedman, ed., *Unspeakable Images: Ethnicity and the American Cinema* (Urbana: University of Illinois Press, 1991), 220.
6   See Henry Bial, *Acting Jewish: Negotiating Ethnicity on the American Stage and Screen* (Ann Arbor: University of Michigan Press, 2005); and Nathan Abrams, *The New Jew in Film: Exploring Jewishness and Judaism in Contemporary Cinema* (New Brunswick, NJ: Rutgers University Press, 2012).
7   Jon Stratton, *Coming Out Jewish* (London: Routledge, 2000), 300.
8   Bial, *Acting Jewish*, 70. See also Joel Rosenberg, 'Jewish Experience on Film – An American Overview', in *American Jewish Year Book, 1996* (New York: American Jewish Committee, 1996), 26.

9 Bial, *Acting Jewish*, 70.

10 Peter Benchley, *Jaws* (London: Pan, 1975), 200.

11 Antonia Quirke, *Jaws* (London: British Film Institute, 2002), 49.

12 I. Q. Hunter, *Cult Film as a Guide to Life: Adaptation, Fandom and Identity* (New York: Bloomsbury, 2016), 122.

13 Benchley, *Jaws*, 13.

14 Ibid., 180–1.

15 Hunter, *Cult Film*, 122.

16 Quirke, *Jaws*, 49.

17 See Nathan Abrams, *Stanley Kubrick: New York Jewish Intellectual* (New Brunswick, NJ: Rutgers University Press, 2018).

18 See Joshua Trachtenberg, *The Devil and the Jews: The Medieval Conception of the Jew and Its Relation to Modern Antisemitism* (New Haven, CT: Yale University Press, 1943).

19 See Judith R. Walkowitz, 'Jack the Ripper and the Myth of Male Violence', *Feminist Studies*, 8, no. 3 (Autumn 1982), 542–74.

20 See Jules Zanger, 'A Sympathetic Vibration: Dracula and the Jews', *English Literature in Transition, 1880–1920*, 34, no. 1 (1991): 33–44.

21 Benchley, *Jaws*, 52.

22 Hunter, *Cult Film*, 183, n. 43.

23 Linda Williams, *Hard Core: Power, Pleasure, and the 'Frenzy of the Visible'* (Berkeley: University of California Press, 2008), 133.

24 Quirke, *Jaws*, 47.

25 Nina Strochlic, 'Hamas Arrests "Israeli Spy" Dolphin', *The Daily Beast*, 20 August 2015, https://www.realcleardefense.com/2015/08/20/hamas_arrests_039israeli_spy039_dolphin_27 3300.html (accessed 3 June 2019).

26 McBride, *Steven Spielberg*, 18.

27 Anon, 'Dialogue on Film: Steven Spielberg', *American Film* 13 (June) 1988: 14.

28 Desser and Friedman, *American Jewish Filmmakers*, 303.

29 *Spielberg* (dir. Susan Lacy, 2017).

30 Ibid.

31 Ibid.

32 McBride, *Steven Spielberg*, 236.

33 Carl Gottlieb, *The Jaws Log*, expanded edition (New York: Dey St., 2001), 65.

34 Peter Krämer, ' "He's Very Good at Work Not Involving Little Creatures, You Know": *Schindler's List, E.T.*, and the Shape of Steven Spielberg's Career', *New Review of Film and Television Studies* 7, no. 1 (2009): 26.

35 McBride, *Steven Spielberg*, 19.

36 Ibid., 236.

37 Gottlieb, *The Jaws Log*, 67.

38 Michael Rogin, *Independence Day* (London: British Film Institute, 1988), 49.

39 Quirke, *Jaws*, 44.

40 Ibid., 33.

41 Quirke, *Jaws*, 39.

42 'Trivia: *Jaws* (1975)', IMDb, https://www.imdb.com/title/tt0073195/trivia (accessed 3 June 2019).

43 McBride, *Steven Spielberg*, 236.

44 Ibid.

45 Qtd. in ibid., 239.

46 Gottlieb, *The Jaws Log*, 64.
47 David Desser, 'Jews in Space: The "Ordeal of Masculinity" in Contemporary American Film and Television', in Murray Pomerance, ed., *Ladies and Gentlemen, Boys and Girls: Gender in Film at the End of the Twentieth Century* (Albany: State University of New York Press, 2001), 269.
48 Andrea Most, ' "Big Chief Izzy Horowitz": Theatricality and Jewish Identity in the Wild West', *American Jewish History* 87, no. 4 (1999): 315.
49 McBride, *Steven Spielberg*, 247–8.
50 Qtd. in ibid., 248.
51 Sander Gilman, *Jewish Frontiers: Essays on Bodies, Histories, and Identities* (Basingstoke: Palgrave Macmillan, 2003), 96–100.
52 Qtd. in McBride, *Steven Spielberg*, 248.
53 Quirke, *Jaws*, 41.
54 Peter Biskind, *Easy Riders, Raging Bulls: How the Sex 'n' Drugs 'n' Rock 'n' Roll Generation Saved Hollywood* (London: Bloomsbury, 1999), 279.
55 Ibid.
56 Gottlieb, qtd. in McBride, *Steven Spielberg*, 236.
57 Dan Rubey, 'The *Jaws* in the Mirror', *Jump Cut*, 10–11 (1976): 20–3, available at https://www.ejumpcut.org/archive/onlinessays/JC10-11folder/JawsRubey.html (accessed 3 June 2019).
58 Ibid.
59 McBride, *Steven Spielberg*, 236.
60 Leo Rosten, *The Joys of Yiddish* (London: Penguin, 1972), 240.
61 Rebecca Alpert, 'The Macho-Mensch: Modeling American Jewish Masculinity and the Heroes of Baseball', in Raanan Rein and David M. K. Sheinin, eds, *Muscling in on New Worlds: Jews, Sport, and the Making of the Americas* (Leiden: Brill, 2014), 109.
62 Ibid.
63 Jeffrey T. Sammons, *Beyond the Ring: The Role of Boxing in American Society* (Urbana: University of Illinois Press, 1990), 91. See also Laurence Roth, *Inspecting Jews: American Jewish Detective Stories* (New Brunswick, NJ: Rutgers University Press, 2004), 31.
64 Daniel Boyarin, *Unheroic Conduct: The Rise of Heterosexuality and the Invention of the Jewish Man* (Berkeley: University of California Press, 1997), 23, 78.
65 William Radcliffe, *Fishing from Earliest Times* (London: J. Murray, 1921).
66 C. Montefiore and H. Loewe, *A Rabbinic Anthology* (Philadelphia: Jewish Publication Society, 1960), xcii.
67 Gottlieb, *The Jaws Log*, 64.
68 Peter Biskind, '*Jaws*, between the Teeth', *Jump Cut* (February 1976): 26, https://www.ejumpcut.org/archive/onlinessays/JC09folder/Jaws.html (accessed 3 June 2019).
69 Hunter, *Cult Film*, 81.
70 See I. Q. Hunter, 'Spielberg and Adaptation', in Nigel Morris, ed., *A Companion to Steven Spielberg* (Chichester: Wiley Blackwell, 2017), 221; Nigel Morris, *The Cinema of Steven Spielberg: Empire of Light* (London: Wallflower, 2007), 236–7; Caroline Joan S. Picart, 'The Documentary Impulse and Reel/Real Horror', in Harry M. Benshoff, ed., *A Companion to the Horror Film* (Chichester: Wiley Blackwell, 2014), 536–53.
71 Hunter, *Cult Film*, 81.
72 Rubey, 'The *Jaws* in the Mirror'.

8

Children as bait

Linda Ruth Williams

Steven Spielberg is an acutely visceral film-maker, exuberantly deploying exploitation techniques, even as he co-invents New Hollywood's all-audience-encompassing adventure films. Despite his family-friendly appeal, he does not shrink from representing bodies radically transformed through violence, whether to stir up drive-in thrills (people as meat in *Jurassic Park* [1993] and *The Lost World: Jurassic Park* [1997]) or to reinforce historical veracity (the amputated limbs and limbless torsos of the Normandy beach sequence in *Saving Private Ryan* [1998]). Of course, images of violence to children's bodies is one of the strongest taboos in mainstream Hollywood cinema, and children are seldom the focus of extreme corporeal disturbances: Spielberg is undoubtedly better known for idealizing children than dramatizing their dismemberment (though adolescents and young adults are fairer game). Across his work children more regularly witness and share screen space with adult bodily violence, transferring risk from the spectacle of physical to the presumption of psychological damage. Though frequently imperiled in all sorts of dramatically juicy ways, Spielberg's children usually survive – but not always. If children's bodies are generally sacrosanct in the family adventure film, they are, of course, central to the historical horror of *Schindler's List* (1993). But in *Jaws*, their treatment is – at times – altogether more exploitatively brutal. This chapter investigates the uneasy line the director walks in articulating *Jaws*' cavalier relationship to children's bodies, before thinking about the way in which press around the release of the film in the UK responded to the interrelationship between violated children on-screen and the protection/exploitation of the child in the audience. It finds children as both pleasurably and painfully suffering, both in the story and in the auditorium.

A wicked streak of callousness towards children worries its way through Spielberg's first blockbuster hit, animated by a film-maker who was at that point publicly identified primarily in two ways: as himself a preposterously youthful helmer and – distinct from the earnest auteurs of the American renaissance generation he helped to move Hollywood away from – as ringmaster of cinematic thrills. David A. Cook shows the continuation of Tom Gunning's cinema of attractions mode running through the history of horror into the 1970s, citing Stephen Farber's observation, a year before *Jaws*' release, that 'Movies were a form of circus spectacle long before they began to tell stories – and long before they were considered an art [A]nd that is the backwards direction they seem to be taking in the seventies.'[1] The entertainment spectacle of

New Hollywood, which Thomas Schatz has argued was inaugurated by *Jaws*,[2] has much in common with circus entertainment of a pre-cinema age, perhaps even of the original Circus Maximus itself, with all its human and animal carnage. Spielberg's child-biography (of his childhood self and of his profile as a playful directorial Peter Pan) runs through the history of the marketing and reception of his films (though most particularly after *Jaws*) and the circus story is one such thread. One of Spielberg's foundational autobiographical memories which has become public myth is of being taken to see a 'circus movie' by his father when he was a very young child – his first ever cinema experience. Young Steven thought he was going to an actual circus and felt acute disappointment that Cecil B. DeMille's *The Greatest Show on Earth* (1952) was *just* a film, with no live elephants: 'For a while I kept thinking, Gee, that's not fair I was disappointed by everything after that. I didn't trust anybody I never felt life was good enough, so I had to embellish it.'[3] *The Sugarland Express* (1974, in post-production as *Jaws* was in pre-production) followed the road movie thriller precedent of *Duel* (1971) in honing Spielberg's ringmaster skills, orchestrating ambitious pursuit sequences across diverse locations. *Jaws* is the first of Spielberg's celebrated circus-thrill films – notwithstanding the argument that *Jaws* simply replays *Duel* with an organic monster. This is not because of its central animal act, Bruce the animatronic shark, the film's shocking spectacle and driver of risk. It is not the shark that forms the film's primary attraction. Instead it is its endangered children, dangled through the narrative as fresh (and, considering Spielberg's later legacy, surprising) bait, and sometimes even as its consumed, consummate victims.

The imperiled child

It is no secret that *Jaws* hijacked the terrain of the Corman-esque exploitation film and gave it a bigger budget. What Spielberg then continues to do is make exploitation fodder ever more family-friendly through systematic focus on the child. In the midst of a remarkably violent horror-action milieu, he places on his child performers the mantle worn otherwise by female imperiled victims. The scream-teen performances of 13-year-old Ariana Richards and 10-year-old Joseph Mazzello in *Jurassic Park*, 10-year-old Dakota Fanning in *War of the Worlds* (2005) or 13-year-old Vanessa Lee Chester in *The Lost World*, as well as the less nuanced performances of smaller-role children in *Jaws* cement the development of horror-for-families. However here I want to focus on something rather darker, 'rendered' – in all senses of the word – even more precisely. *Jaws* dares to propose children as meat. Though never actually showing a child being actively dismembered by a dinosaur or a shark, this highly taboo notion haunts these hugely popular films. While adults are very visible meat for lower organisms in *Jaws* and both Spielberg-directed *Jurassic Park* films, children are still – albeit less visibly – pursued and even consumed. Part of the power of these films for family audiences is the creatures' indiscrimination – they do not respect age or minority, gender or race, strength or weakness (though conventions of censorship and taste which constrain Hollywood family productions do). As Martin Brody (Roy Scheider) says in *Jaws*, opening the beaches is 'like ringing the dinner bell'. The Spielberg we think of as supremely child-friendly is then not above using the imperiled child to turn the screw of affect – as he also does in other horror-tinged and action-animated blockbusters. James Kendrick has more generally spot-lit this darker Spielberg in his fine 2014 study,[4] but the specific exploitation of the child in *Jaws* merits further investigation.

The closest Spielberg gets to displaying a child's dismemberment is the foaming scarlet and shredded lilo of Alex Kintner's demise. Both are metonyms for the shredded child, a taboo notion which is the dark energy driving Spielberg's creature-features. But it is particularly acute in the first two acts of *Jaws*, when this ostensibly family-friendly director seems to relish the peril of the child's vulnerable body as much as he sentimentalizes their precarious rescue. While Spielberg may not be a body-horror director like Cronenberg, Tsukamoto or Romero, *Jaws* presents a meditation on mortality via the body's fragility. Even in his less visceral moments, he is always a corporeal sensationalist, pushing the audience's physical response buttons (weeping or disgust) as the child's body is endangered on-screen. But equally physical endangerment is also a strategy for raising the stakes of suspense, and this is ever more effective when children are in line. He is not the only film-maker to understand that the younger or more vulnerable the performer, the more acute will be the resulting affect, but his child-focus – as someone who regularly directs children and orchestrates child-point-of-view stories, and as a dominant architect of cinematic childhood – means that these moments when he puts children on the rack are particularly shocking. Spielberg deploys a familiar syndrome of sympathy: as Karen Lury puts it in *The Child in Film: Tears, Fears and Fairy Tales*,

> We are feeling sorry for those who cannot care for themselves and for those we believe should be cared for as some kind of universal right. The innocence ascribed to children and animals often makes them an object, if not the subject, of films about war, in a strategy designed to provoke emotion and moral satisfaction.[5]

Of course, Spielberg deploys all forms of vulnerable bodies, and not just in his war stories: he even uses animals as metonyms for children, or to pre-empt their fate. Pippet the dog's demise on Amity's beach in *Jaws*, confirmed by the supremely economical shot of his abandoned stick, prefigures Alex's death, confirmed by the lilo remains. *The Lost World* follows this metonymic cue, with the suburban San Diegan family apparently next in line after the T. Rex is seen waving their dog's empty kennel aloft, an image which recalls the tethered goat followed by the goatless leg which confronts the children of *Jurassic Park*. Dead dogs ultimately mean dead children, when dead children would be too extreme an image to dish up. Indeed, dead dogs are also too extreme for family entertainment, so can only be referenced via their cherished objects (Pippet's stick, the San Diegan dog's kennel). All of these suggest that while W. C. Fields warned adults against acting with children or animals, children or animals should be very afraid of acting with Spielberg.

Jaws foregrounds the particular vulnerability of young people from the start. While the participants of the opening beach party are not small children (though the extras here may be actual minors – the age of majority only changed in Massachusetts from 21 to 18 in 1974, when *Jaws* was shot), the scene nevertheless conforms to the code of moral horror which deems that the stronger a young victim's culpability (drugs, drink, sexual availability) the more deserving is their demise. This has certainly inflected readings of the skinny-dipping Chrissie (Susan Backlinie), the shark's first victim (who as a character is not a minor – the death report tells us she is 24). However the film soon shifts its focus of concern to younger (and presumed more innocent) figures. In the very next scene the worried police chief Brody, awake early and surveying the sea from the window, is asked by his wife Ellen (Lorraine Gary), who is still in bed, 'Can you see the kids?'. Peril therefore envelops children from the start: eldest son Michael (Chris Rebello)[6] is already injured when he first appears on-screen, presenting his bloodied hand to his parents. It is an injury borne of adult neglect: his father has not yet fixed the 'dangerous' play-swings in the garden, so from the start the adult's failure to protect children is bound to the shark's opportunity. Ellen cleans the wound, fielding questions about whether Michael can go swimming with his bleeding hand (the film has not yet revealed information about the attractiveness of blood and movement to the roving shark). At the same time Brody's attention strays, hijacked by a phone call he takes in the foreground of the shot, reporting the now-missing Chrissie. Child injury and casualty report are then all framed together in one kitchen-set family tableau, the actuality of the first death and the future potential of many more, bound to and within the everydayness of the domestic. As Brody departs the house for work we see Ellen and younger child Sean playing again on those dangerous swings, apparently risking further injury. Then at the police station, while Brody files his report about Chrissie's death, his secretary, discussing small-town minutiae by way of fleshing out the image of Amity as a 'regular' place, tells of a group of 9-year-old martial artists karate chopping picket fences, a detail evidencing Amity's more customary everyday perils: hooligan children, up to mischief. But children are soon fixed as potential victims rather than perpetrators. Before Brody can put up 'Beach Closed' signs we hear of boy scouts already in the water competing for their Merit Badges and are then shown already far out in the bay. They splash around in a group, trailing behind their coach's boat, apparently beyond phone contact, beyond a speedy rescue. McBride reports that throughout the film Spielberg wanted the blood to seem ever more stark by the absence of the colour red in design or costume (though there is still plenty of it). Here there is red: the boat is an alarming red, rendering it a loud-and-clear target. In keeping with the ambivalence about children as threat or as threatened which pervades early 1970s cinema, this first 62 minutes of *Jaws* has efficiently set both paedophobic *and* child-protective alarm bells ringing.

And then comes the first beach scene proper, replete with numerous playful children, including doomed Alex Kintner in his red swimming shorts. The scene does indeed lay out a 'smorgasbord' (to use Brody's term) of vulnerability, allowing us (like Brody) to wonder who will succumb. A frolicking young woman screams as if in pain, but it turns out to be only the pleasure of romantic-play. An overweight person seems to be singled out by an approaching fin, but it is only old man Harry's swimming hat. A crowd of children run into the water in a group; Pippet the dog disappears. We then follow the shark's underwater point of view as it weaves through kicking limbs. Spielberg told the press that he wanted to highlight the vulnerability we all feel about what we can't see of ourselves beneath the surface,[7] but – though we know there are also adults in the water – the travelling camera only picks out children's legs, before closing in on Alex on his lilo. The ghastly medium shot which follows, confirming the attack, is from the perspective of the other nearby children: all that is visible is shark and children and Alex, though it is all horribly confusing. Nigel Andrews calls this a 'windmilling flurry of dark movement':[8]

> You can see *Jaws* again and again and still not work out the components of that abstract ballet. What exactly is revolving: the mattress, the shark, the boy's limbs? It doesn't matter – uncertainty compounds terror. It's a perfect nightmare collage, a Catherine wheel of the scene's previous hoaxing shapes. We see in it the dog's stick, the killer-fish's fin, the youngster's upraised silhouette, all twirling until the gush of red.[9]

With the fountain of blood the upper half of Alex's body is flung upwards, and then – close by again – we watch from below as he fails and falls, disappearing into red. Then, from the surface, it appears that only children are left in the water, by now themselves swimming in red. Brody shouts for everyone to get out of the water, but in the panic this has the opposite effect: instead, the adults run towards it, as protectiveness becomes stupidity. In a manoeuvre that Spielberg will repeat across his work, the child's vulnerability endangers the adults. Children are perilous when themselves imperiled because adults must protect them. Or, as Tom Hanks's Captain Miller says in *Saving Private Ryan*, when the rescue of a refugee French girl results in the death of an American combatant, 'That's why we can't take children'. The next evening, Michael's proximity to the water even stops Brody and his wife from 'get[ting] drunk and fool[ing] around' – Brody panics when he realizes that Michael is sitting in a tied-up boat with little brother Sean sweetly guarding from the jetty above (and, as the subsequent scene shows all too well, jetties are hardly safe places).

Of course adults actively endanger children too, even beyond the riskiness of failing to secure garden swings, and the later Fourth of July beach scene only intensifies these child-focused anxieties. When an Amity official is ordered into the water to set an example to frightened tourists, he is revealed as even more venal by herding his young children in with him. These are then unceremoniously tipped from their lilo into the water when panic ensues around the (prank) shark fin appearance. As Mayor Vaughn (Murray Hamilton) later says, 'My kids were on that beach too.' He is, of course, one of the few people in the story as yet fully aware of the danger, but he still sends his children to the front line. And in the midst of the panic there is no 'women and children first' etiquette: numerous children are seen being brutally pushed aside by adults desperate to get back to the safety of the sands first. At least the shark is motivated by hunger; here the stronger will sacrifice the weaker through callous self-preservation (Kendrick reads this as *Jaws*' darkest moment).[10] When it turns out that this is not a real shark attack but a hoax perpetrated by children themselves with a model shark fin, they become the focus of military might as the misdirected protection services step up to attack. By distracting these guards the prankster children ensure that other children, boating in the adjacent estuary, are vulnerable to be attacked for real, with no help on hand. But still the film knows where it wants to apportion blame: while the hoaxing children with their home-made fins are pulling off an effectively scandalous spectacle not unlike that of Spielberg himself (deploying a hokey rubber shark to provoke a national sensation), it is the capital-protecting adults whom the film ultimately condemns. As Fidel Castro said, *Jaws* shows just how far capitalism will go to protect its investment.[11]

The estuary sequence is particularly important for the ghoulish visual trick it plays on its audience and the moral quandaries raised by Spielberg and Verna Fields's editing, which plays horribly with the viewer's expectations. The shark glides up to two isolated boats, one containing a nameless man fishing, while the other is Michael Brody's new birthday-present boat, manned by Michael and his friends. We already know that – as Ben Gardner has discovered – boats are no safer than jetties. Ichthyologist Matt Hooper (Richard Dreyfuss)'s backstory includes his own childhood near-miss: his first encounter with a shark was when it dismembered his boat when he was 12. The estuary sequence shows both the fisherman's and Michael Brody's boats being swiftly overturned; the shark then overcomes the man, and a severed leg drops to the seabed. Intercutting with the scene's resounding image – Michael's stricken face looking to camera, which takes the position of the shark – the narrative deliberately (sadistically) compounds the question of whose leg it was. Clearly Michael is a character we know, and the fisherman is the expendable unknown – so briefly the film makes us entertain the ghastly 'hope' that the leg belongs to the latter rather than the former. Finally when the adults arrive Michael is dragged from the water, and Spielberg's camera lingers a little too uncomfortably on a 'reveal' moment, which does indeed confirm that he still has both legs (improbably, he emerges from the experience just suffering from, as the hospital doctors put it, 'mild shock'). The spectre of child-dismemberment is suggested and then expunged; what remains is relief not that violence didn't happen but that it happened to someone else.

Still the awful possibility that a family's cherished child has value in death only as meat is kept off-screen and, in the excitement of these sequences, to the sidelines of consciousness. In his article on hunger and the interiority of eating in Spielberg, Murray Pomerance highlights the off-screen destruction of the live steer after it is dropped into the velociraptor enclosure in *Jurassic Park*: 'we do not see monstrosity (and therefore we do not see monstrous hunger or its satiation), and our excitement is spurred by this invisibility'.[12] By *The Lost World* Spielberg still refused to display this head-on: while opening his film with a scene of a small girl being attacked by some compsognathuses, he keeps the consumption off-screen (and the girl survives) and suggests a wicked boredom with the spectacle by cross-cutting the girl's screaming mother with Jeff Goldblum yawning. But *Jaws* had already flirted with breaking open the interiority of digestion – the 'proper' hiddenness of animals eating each other, which might not remain so hidden. It dares to threaten us with something worse than the drama of children being eaten, suggesting also the spectacle of their eaten remains. When Hooper proposes performing an autopsy on the Tiger Shark on the quayside to see what it ingested in the last 24 hours, Mayor Vaughn is left to spell out the hazard: 'I am not going to stand here and see that thing cut open, and see that little Kintner boy spill out all over the dock.' The falling leg, Ben Gardner's head and the small amount of Chrissie which can fit into the coroner's drawer are all body parts which the shark left behind. Corpses are 'remains'; these parts are what literally remain, undigested, in the aftermath of an attack. The 'spilling' Kintner boy is one of the most appalling ideas in *Jaws* because it is evidence of incorporation and digestion – remains that weren't even supposed to remain. Nevertheless, while all of these tense moments of peril contribute to *Jaws*' thrills, they position the threatened child as significant because of the impact on that child's related, affected adults. Horrifying as Alex Kintner's death is in its froth of bloody brine, there are no visible body parts. Though we see him fall and fail, death is confirmed not by a corpse but by his mother's grief. Michael's near-miss is most acute because he is Brody's son. And what would be ghastly about the public shark autopsy is the possibility that everyone might have to confront the child as digested meat.

The imperiled viewer

This all seems to be a long way from the image of Spielberg as child-friendly and child-focused, and indeed he was rarely so cavalier about child-death in entertainment cinema after this. By the time of *The Lost World*'s release, child endangerment was so rare in Spielberg's work that, despite the compsognathus sequence being arguably legitimized by the victim-girl's family being too colonial, too posh and too English, it would still be contained by the later off-hand report of the child's precarious survival. But the mid-1970s '*Jaws* moment' was only just becoming a 'Spielberg moment'; as Carl Gottlieb writes, 'He wasn't STEVEN SPIELBERG yet. He was just Steven,'[13] and *Jaws* attracted its celebrity and notoriety from Peter Benchley's bestseller rather than the director's reputation. Indeed, contemporary press around the release of the film largely fails to focus on it as 'A Steven Spielberg picture' in the manner that would become universal from the late 1970s onwards. Those reviews which do consider the director as a galvanizing force hardly mention what we think of now as indelibly Spielbergian auteurial features. Some link the suspense strategies of *Jaws* to those of *Duel* and the chase-motif of *The Sugarland Express*. As I argue in *Steven Spielberg's Children*, by the early 1980s, Spielberg's star had been firmly hitched to childhood and to children as central actors and protagonists of his films, but the '*Jaws* moment' precedes this. However one element related to this which did begin to come to the fore is a dawning discourse positing the director as child, articulated as a form of boy-wonderhood and, with the astonishing success of *Jaws*, uncommon precocity. Preternatural youth, relative to success in helming the (then) most commercially successful film of all time, is highlighted in numerous reviews and profile pieces, but it isn't (as yet) identified with the 'sentimentalizing' impact of identification with the child.[14] The director as child-identified and as a strong employer of child actors only really begins to appear as a distinct element of his profile with the intensifying child-focus of *Close Encounters of the Third Kind* (1977) and later with *Empire of the Sun* (1987) and *A.I.: Artificial*

Intelligence (2001). The developing auteurial branding of a man-child director obsessed with the figure of Peter Pan perhaps reached its apotheosis in *E.T.: The Extra-Terrestrial* (1982), but this was a full six years after the release of *Jaws*.

The darkness of some of the images in *Jaws* is confirmed and augmented by quotes from the director in press materials around the release of the film, which suggest that he also wanted the attack sequences to leap from the screen and into the auditorium. In this promotional moment he articulates an active desire for the viewer to feel under attack too. This is clearly Spielberg in the guise of the circus ringmaster, but with the hindsight of our knowledge of him as the exemplary family-friendly director, his *Jaws*-era statements of intent are nevertheless surprising. 'I wanted to do *Jaws* for hostile reasons' he said in 1975, adopting a more sensational tone than he would ever use again in publicity: 'I read it [the novel upon which the film is based] and felt that I had been attacked. It terrified me, and I wanted to strike back.'[15] Here then there is a chain of affect, rearticulated as a chain of hostility running from novelist Benchley to director Spielberg to any audience member 'struck' by the film. In another interview he also said that he 'wanted to make a horror movie. I wanted to give people backaches from sitting forward so long'.[16] This realization that orchestrating a spectacular form of narrative sadism could enforce an edge-of-the-seat pleasure-panic on the part of the audience is crystallized in (what would later become uncharacteristically) unguarded statements throughout the publicity campaign. By 1977, the traces of this shock still reverberated through press anticipation of his next major film. No-one yet knew how life-affirming *Close Encounters* was to be; Spielberg was still marked by a sadism of affect. *Time* magazine called *Jaws* 'a merciless attack on the audience's nerves' which had quickly 'established its creator as the reigning boy genius of American cinema'.[17] Spielberg himself told *Sight and Sound* in 1977 that through the direction of *Jaws* he had also been 'directing the audience with an electric cattle prod'.[18] This is a small step away from the circus ringmaster's whip, both overt agents of audience manipulation and sensational exploitation thrills. Nor were contemporary reviewers particularly concerned about the child-death-count in *Jaws* – critics found nothing particularly shocking about the foaming blood of Alex's death, no more than the deaths of adults or teens. The shark isn't picky, and neither were the critics, though there was a marked relish in the violence of the film. Celebrated visual culture theorist Griselda Pollock, then early in her career and writing for the feminist journal *Spare Rib*, read it as 'a "vagina dentata" movie, symbolizing the psychological violence of the devouring vagina and the threatened male'.[19] Margaret Hinxman's article in the *Daily Mail* was headlined 'Jaws – an open and shut case for making the most of a horrible thought'.[20]

If children featured at all in press around the film, the primary focus of anxiety in Britain was its impact on child viewers. One British newspaper concluded a sensational report with 'So all a parent has to do now is to decide: How young is very young?'[21] In the United States *Jaws* was given a PG-rating, leading Charles Champlin in the *Los Angeles Times* to worry that 'The PG rating is grievously wrong and misleading ... Jaws is too gruesome for children and likely to turn the stomach of the impressionable at any age.' The original (highly negative) review was republished by the *LA Times* on *Jaws*' fortieth anniversary, with something of an air of chagrin considering the subsequent success of the film.[22] In the UK its A certificate meant that all children could see it as long as they could attest that they had their parent or guardian's permission; in the United States children needed to be accompanied by an adult, but could still see it at any age.[23] In both the United States and the UK, warnings were added to the publicized ratings stating that the material would be too strong for young children, but in neither territory were higher age-ratings imposed that would significantly limit audience and box office. Champlin's focus on child harm does cite a British source (though he fails to understand the nature of this source):

> Careful studies by the Children's Film Foundation in England have confirmed what common sense suggests: Children identify most strongly with what happens to children on screen, are most impressed and terrified by the violence done to or endangering other children. 'Jaws' is nightmare time for the young.

However the British chief censor James Ferman, responsible for endorsing the A certificate and therefore a target in the furore about whether young children should be allowed to see the film, was bullish. Having consulted child psychologists on the question of potential harm he even claimed that *Jaws* could be good for child viewers: 'It is generally assumed by the media that all frightening experiences are harmful, but this is not so. They are part of growing up and maturing.'[24]

Then followed a newspaper tabloid frenzy which focused not only on the film but also on the film in relation to its young audiences. The coverage by the *Daily Express* begins 'At 13, Jenny slipped back into being a little girl again as she left the cinema. "Oh" she said, "it was awful" "But I liked it"', while 5-year-old Richard is reported as saying 'I hid behind the seat sometimes', and a Harley Street psychiatrist, Dr Christopher Woodard, consulted for an expert opinion worried: 'I sometimes wonder if we know what we are doing to our children. What they must dream about after seeing a film like "Jaws" is nobody's business.'[25] Rival British newspaper *The Sun* mounted its own poll of child-viewers leaving the Plaza cinema in London after the first UK screening and found that fear-responses were part of an experience of entertainment pleasure, from 'It's the best film I've ever seen … not as scary as Dracula' to 'Sure, there was a lot of blood, but I wouldn't have missed a minute of it' to 'It certainly beat anything on TV this Christmas, I can tell you.' One child does report that 'Most of the time I had my coat over my head', though even she says 'The bits I saw I really enjoyed.'[26] *Jaws* did not become a case-study for effects theorists, and its legacy – while industry changing – was not that of child harm, even given the child risk portrayed on-screen.

The redemptive child

Two other smaller moments in this film point to where Spielberg is going next, focused around some unaffected physical acting by little Jay Mello playing Brody's youngest child Sean. I may even have started on my research into Spielberg and children courtesy of these singular images. The 'Spielberg shot' in this film for me is simply that of little

Sean playing sandcastles on the beach, singing to himself as a still moment prior to the kinetic and chaotic 'Kintner-boy' death scene, and then again in its midst as chaos swirls around. Spielberg is known for eliciting skilful and nuanced performances from his young leads (e.g. Henry Thomas as Elliott in *E.T.*; Christian Bale as Jim in *Empire of the Sun*; Haley Joel Osment as David in *A.I.: Artificial Intelligence*). But he also sprinkles children in strongly signifying small roles and as featured extras throughout his films, to suggest a complex panoply of child's-eye views and images of childhood. These are customarily read by journalists and academic interpreters alike as idealizations or sentimentalized views of childhood, which I find in my wider work on Spielberg to be neither fair nor accurate, and do not represent the full range of distinct and different views of childhood across Spielberg's work. Little Sean Brody is framed here not primarily as a child who signifies because of the adults he is related to, but simply as a self-contained toddler caught within the bubble of his own subjectivity. His mother and father, sitting a little way off on the beach, can see where he is, so he is liberated to be by himself in the crowd and is 'good' enough to be able to amuse himself. The view is fleeting – we briefly dip into his world, and then out again – but it is powerful. It is also easily overlooked in the midst of the scene's flashy 'Hitchcock shot', the dolly zoom which dramatizes Brody's shocked realization so brilliantly; this, combined with the insinuation of John Williams's 'shark voice' and the sheer catastrophe of Alex's spilled blood, eclipses anything more subtle. But this brief child-glimpse begins to tell a more complex story about Spielberg as interrogator of cinematic childhood. It also, of course, sets up the untouched child as only safe while the adults around him remain vigilant and does not risk him in the choppy waters of too-early, too-rash independent action. Sean's present safety also bespeaks his vulnerability.

Later, Sean focuses another 'moment' – a dinner table scene which poignantly and comically prefigures the mashed-potato scene in *Close Encounters of the Third Kind* (as well as countless other dinner table scenes across Spielberg's work where children are bemused or tormented by adults, or display their radical difference from them). Here then Brody broods, unsettled by the mounting death count and his own inability to make a difference in the face of the monstrous beast and the monstrosity of the town's power-brokers. Sean begins a brilliant sequence of physical acting, copying his father's disturbed movements. Through a touching mimed performance the small child shows imitative empathy: both hold their heads; both drink their drinks in the same way; both cross their fingers. Then the two pull faces at each other, and finally Brody asks for a kiss. Mimicry can be parody, but here it is not so. This is the child as healer of the adult, an idealized form who would become a central auteurial motif, though not one which goes unquestioned.

As *Jaws* proceeds it becomes more of an adult – indeed, a men-only – affair, culminating in its 'three men in a boat' final act. The first 62 (primarily land-based) minutes are driven by child-anxiety and anxiety for the child which is both exploited and sought-out. The final 56 (sea-focused) minutes are driven by adult men. In *Steven Spielberg's Children* I argue that in the absence of actual children adults take up child-to-adult, parent-to-offspring positions relative to each other (here as father figures and rookies: Quint calls Hooper a 'squirt' and accuses Brody of being on a 'boy scout's picnic'). In this final act actual children are left behind as adult men mimic a war-story scenario in fighting to protect the women and children back home. It is a brilliant and iconic endgame, in which the imperiled child mantle is taken on by boy-men who become men in the process of conquering the circus beast. Spielberg was of course to return to the child, and exploit its vulnerability, on numerous occasions, but it is through conceiving of, and then drawing back from, the horror of the child as meat that he cuts his exploitation teeth.

Notes

1 David A. Cook, *Lost Illusions: American Cinema in the Shadow of Watergate and Vietnam 1970–1979* (Berkeley: University of California Press, 2000), 44.

2 See Thomas Schatz, 'The New Hollywood', in Jim Collins, Hilary Radner and Ava Preacher Collins, eds, *Film Theory Goes to the Movies* (New York: Routledge, 1993), 8–37.

3 Joseph McBride, *Steven Spielberg: A Biography*, 3rd edn (London: Faber & Faber, 2012), 51.

4 See James Kendrick, *Darkness in the Bliss-Out: A Reconsideration of the Films of Steven Spielberg* (London: Bloomsbury, 2014). This does discuss *Jaws* as a sporadically 'dark' film, but does not focus on its treatment of children.

5 Karen Lury, *The Child in Film: Tears, Fears and Fairy Tales* (London: I.B. Tauris, 2010), 105–6.

6 Both actors playing Brody's children – Chris Rebello (Michael) and Jay Mello (Sean), as well as Jeffrey Voorhees who plays Alex Kintner, were local children cast as part of the Boston Screen Actor's Guild determination that a proportion of actors from the Boston area be given speaking parts in the film (Carl Gottlieb, *The Jaws Log* [New York: HarperCollins, 2012], 65). Gottlieb reports that Rebello 'calculated he made more than $100,000 in the last twenty-five years, thanks to Screen Actors Guild residual payments based on the constant revenue stream generated by *Jaws*' (202).

7 Monte Stettin, 'From Television to Features ... Steven Spielberg', *Millimeter* 3, no. 3 (March 1975): 24.

8 Nigel Andrews, *Jaws* (London: Bloomsbury, 2000), 69.

9 Ibid.

10 The elderly fare no better than the children – Kendrick writes, 'one of the film's most disturbing images is not of a shark attack, but rather a low-angle shot in the surf of an apparently lifeless elderly man who has been trampled by fellow swimmers and is being dragged out of the water' (*Darkness*, 145).

11 Quoted by Quentin Curtis in '*Jaws* Still Bites', *Daily Telegraph*, Arts & Books section, 17 June 2000, 1.

12 Murray Pomerance, 'Digesting Steven Spielberg', *Film International* 6, no. 2 (2008): 35.

13 Gottlieb, *The Jaws Log*, 196.

14 I tell the story of Spielberg's developing auteur profile as 'boy wonder' and 'child genius' through the ups and downs of the 1970s and 1980s in chapter one of *Steven Spielberg's Children* (New Brunswick, NJ: Rutgers University Press, forthcoming). For contemporary reviews of *Jaws* which note the director's youth, see David Helpbern, 'At Sea with Steven Spielberg', *Take One* 4, no. 10 (March/April 1977): 8–22; Barbra

Paskin, 'How Do You Follow a Smash Like Jaws?', *Film Review* 26, no. 2 (February 1976): 6–7; David Robinson, 'The Shark Has Pretty Teeth', *The Times*, 24 December 1975 (accessed through BFI Clippings service; no pagination given). Gottlieb reports that, to assuage the boredom of waiting at sea for the animatronic shark to be ready, Spielberg suggested a lunchtime skeet shoot, but the crew could not countenance loaded guns on board: 'They will grant him his phenomenal professionalism as a director; he is the youngest they've ever worked with. But when it comes to guns he's still a kid, the crew thinks, and no kids with guns on the cramped decks of the picture boat' (*The Jaws Log*, 151).

15   TIME Magazine, 'Summer of the shark', *Time*, 23 June 1975, 34.

16   Stettin, 'From Television to Features', 24.

17   Frank Rich, 'The Aliens Are Coming!', *Time*, 7 November 1977, 34–6.

18   Quoted by McBride, *Steven Spielberg*, 246.

19   Griselda Pollock, 'Review of *Jaws*', *Spare Rib*, 4 (April 1976) (accessed through BFI Clippings service; no pagination given).

20   *Daily Mail*, 22 December 1975. Article sourced in BFI Clippings service; no pagination given.

21   James Davies, 'Jaws', *Daily Express*, 27 December 1975. Article sourced in BFI Library clippings file; no pagination given.

22   See Meredith Woerner, 'L.A. Times' Original 1975 Review of "Jaws" Unearthed: We Hated It', *Los Angeles Times*, 20 June 2015, archived at https://www.latimes.com/entertainment/herocomplex/la-et-hc-jaws-original-review- 20150619-story.html. This contains Champlin's original review, which was published on 20 June 1975.

23   This is discussed in George Gordon, 'How One U.S. Family Reacted', *Daily Mail*, 7 November 1975, sourced in BFI Library clippings file; no pagination given.

24   Quoted in Roderick Gilchrist, 'Children Can Watch Jaws', *Daily Mail*, 7 November 1975; see also James Davies, 'Jaws', *Daily Express*, 27 December 1975. Articles sourced in BFI Library clippings file; no pagination given.

25   Davies, 'Jaws'.

26   Michael Gay and George Lynn, 'They Were the First – and They Loved It!', *The Sun*, 27 December 1975. In the same *Sun* newspaper coverage (strapline: 'As Jaws-mania strikes, the kids vote it a hit') an accompanying sidebar suggests that a more significant focus of harm could be women, who – a Harley Street psychologist said – could be 'turned frigid' by the film which is a 'classic sex-attack symbol' (Leslie Toulson, 'It Could Shock Women Frigid', *The Sun*, 27 December 1975). Both articles sourced in BFI Library clippings file; no pagination given.

9

Reflexive epistemology in *Jaws* and *Jurassic Park*

Robert Geal

Jaws is useful to scholarship not only because of its interesting narrative, aesthetic style, performances and production history, but also because it is amenable to academic interpretations from a number of different, potentially contradictory theoretical paradigms. These divergent analyses, in addition to offering their own accounts of how *Jaws* functions, also suggest that certain films relate to contested theoretical premises in inconsistent, ambiguous and overlapping ways. If rival academic paradigms are really so irreconcilable, as they so frequently claim, then a film which can be convincingly analysed by more than one rival approach suggests either some fundamental flaw in one of the paradigms or that significant elements of the film respond to the competing paradigms' very different conceptualizations of how film operates. Proponents of competing theories typically take the former approach, making the case that certain methodological errors invalidate the rival account. This chapter, however, is an exploration of the latter possibility. I argue that the film-making and spectatorial motivations over which competing theories claim an explanatory monopoly can be manipulated in intersecting and symbiotic ways in films like *Jaws* and another Spielberg film that stages horrific non-human violence against a backdrop of human duplicity, *Jurassic Park* (1993).

The chapter outlines how existing scholarship conceptualizes film-making and spectatorship, discussing rival claims about how Spielberg attempts to engender certain different spectatorial responses to *Jaws*. I then analyse the ways that the film manipulates ostensibly contradictory dramas associated with these rival scholarly theories, suggesting that Spielberg intuits diverse forms of spectatorial pleasure and is able to create films which elicit multiple spectatorial responses. I finish by briefly comparing *Jaws* to *Jurassic Park*, in order to establish how Spielberg's multiple dramas relate to potential technological determinants.

Competing theoretical approaches to *Jaws*

For the sake of brevity, and because certain scholarly theories have focused more attention on *Jaws* than others, I will focus on two leading paradigms, poststructuralism and cognitivism, both of which claim to reveal why film-makers construct films in certain ways, and the kind of activities spectators engage in while watching films. Both poststructuralism and cognitivism conceptualize theoretical enterprise and film-making as distinct activities.[1] The scholar does not think of the film-maker as working in explicitly theoretical terms.

I shall argue that theorizing and film-making are not as distinct as is normally assumed. Any film theory claims – with caveats about various historical, socio-cultural and/or industrial conditions – that film-makers attempt to engender a certain range of audience responses. Rival paradigms disagree about the nature of those film-making motivations and spectatorial responses (which may be thought of as either conscious or unconscious), but each theory offers a different explanation for the activities of everyone involved in making or watching a film. My suggestion here is that the non-scholarly film-making and spectatorial activities relevant to any particular film need not necessarily be only those advocated by a single academic paradigm, with alternate theoretical interpretations a diametrically opposed refutation of those other interpretations. So, it need not necessarily be the case that a film is either evidence of the film-makers' and spectators' unconscious desires or conversely evidence of the film-makers' and spectators' rational cognition. Instead, film-making in films like *Jaws* and *Jurassic Park* can attempt to activate diverse audience responses that film theories have hitherto claimed are mutually exclusive.

The two principal paradigms that have been applied to *Jaws* are, first, a hybrid of semiotics, (neo-)Marxism and psychoanalysis, which, for the sake of simplicity can be termed poststructuralism,[2] and, second, a form of Post-Theory that is most frequently called cognitivism.[3] The ostensible irreconcilability of these approaches is demonstrated by the extent to which proponents of these theories characterize them as epistemologies – that is, as complete philosophical models for understanding what can be known about human consciousness and what light can be shed on film.[4] It is this epistemological dimension that makes poststructuralism and cognitivism irreconcilable, because they make diametrically opposed claims about how consciousness works, and about how this consciousness then makes and interprets films.

For poststructuralism, consciousness is determined by factors outside its direct control. Socio-cultural and economic conditions create what the French psychoanalyst, Jacques Lacan, calls the 'Symbolic Order' which human subjects assent to enter and which constructs their consciousness (at least in part).[5] One of the defining features of the Symbolic Order is René Descartes's characterization of humanity as the *res cogitans* ('thinking thing') at the centre of meaning and being.[6] Cartesian subjectivity generates aesthetics which replicate the centrality of the *res cogitans*, so that art imitates a certain illusion about life. Renaissance perspective painting was the pioneering form of this aesthetic, constructing an impression of reality which seems to flow out from the perfectly positioned and centralized observer. Film, too, constructs imagery which fixes the spectating subject as the locus of action and meaning. Film, however, consists of moving images and so the perspectival stability of the spectating *res cogitans* subject is constantly in flux. Like the famous oblique skull in Hans Holbein's painting *The Ambassadors* (1533), film's perspectival vision is incomplete, and therefore potentially threatening to the stability of the Cartesian subject. For cognitivism, on the other hand, the human mind is rational rather than irrational. Humans consciously determine their ways of thinking and behaving (and seeing), rather than being unconsciously determined by an internalized Symbolic Order.[7]

Jaws has been understood as an exemplar of both of these key epistemological claims. Stephen Heath's poststructuralist analysis, for example, stresses how realist films like *Jaws* inevitably attempt to compensate for the incomplete nature of both perspectival vision and the Symbolic Order that structures the Cartesian illusion of geometric perspective.[8] Realist films compensate for this incompletion through a visual regime that repeatedly recentres the inevitably decentred spectator. The cathartic nature of this recentring is so powerful that film repeats the psychological mechanism at the level of narrative. As Heath puts it, cinema is fundamentally

> the organization of a point of view through the image-flow, the laying out of an intelligibility, the conversion of seen into scene as the direction of the viewing subject. ... [B]ut film, in its flux, can also produce discontinuities, disruptions, 'shocks'. Hence, from the start, there is a need to reconstruct the truth of vision, to establish ways of holding a film's relations as the coherence of the subject-eye – continuity techniques, matches, 30-degree and 180-degree rules, codes of framing, and so on. Indeed, the drama of vision becomes a constant reflexive fascination *in* films. ... *Jaws* is ... relevant with its play on the unseen and the unforeseeable, the hidden shark and the moments of violent irruption. ... Film is the constant process of a phasing-in of vision, the pleasure of that process – movement and fixity and movement again, from fragment (actually thematised in *Jaws* as dismemberment) to totality (the jubilation of the final image).[9]

What Heath calls the 'drama of vision', then, is an oscillation between a perspectival stability structured around conventionalized film grammar, and reflexive metaphorical film-making commentaries about the limitations of this perspectival stability.[10] *Jaws* has a drama of vision which reflexively renders film's inevitable perspectival instability into the shark's ambiguously shown movements, brief violent shocks and fragments of bodies representing the fragmentary nature of cinematic framing, editing and of the Symbolic Order.

In contrast, from a cognitive perspective, Noël Carroll approaches *Jaws* in relation to what he calls 'erotetic narration'.[11] This is an almost ubiquitous narrative structure, present in many films, in which

> scenes, situations, and events that appear earlier in the order of exposition in a story are related to later scenes, situations, and events in the story, as questions are related to answers. ... Such narration, which is at the core of popular narration, proceeds by generating a series of questions that the plot then goes on to answer.[12]

Carroll states that erotetic narration in *Jaws* and many other films

> is driven explicitly by curiosity. It engages its audience by being involved in processes of disclosure, discovery, proof, explanation, hypothesis, and confirmation. Doubt,

skepticism, ... are predictable foils to the revelation (to the audience or to the characters or both) of the existence of the monster.[13]

Carroll therefore explains film-making motivations and spectatorial engagement very differently from Heath. For Heath, the spectator gains unconscious pleasure from threats to perspectival security which are quickly and repeatedly resolved. Film-making in *Jaws* unconsciously manipulates this spectatorial pleasure by generating and resolving ambiguity about the shark's movements, by including brief shocks and by reflexively turning fragments of imagery into fragments of limbs: both film-makers and spectators are motivated by unconscious forces outside their full control. For Carroll, the spectator gains pleasure by consciously decoding information, speculating about how characters might respond to that information, and having these speculations confirmed or refuted. *Jaws* – or rather the film-makers – consciously manipulates spectatorial pleasure by providing ambiguous information, encouraging speculation about how characters might respond to this information and by confirming or refuting these speculations. Film-makers, as the leading cognitivist, David Bordwell, puts it, 'solicit story-constructing and story-comprehending activities from spectators'.[14] Although Carroll does not use the following precise terminology, it makes sense to define the film-making motivations and spectatorial pleasures associated with erotetic narration as the 'drama of knowledge',[15] in contradistinction to Heath's 'drama of vision' since both of these theoretical accounts claim that film-makers attempt to elicit certain dramatic responses from audiences.[16]

Jaws' multiple dramas

Jaws' opening scene demonstrates how film-making motivations seem to encourage audiences to respond to both of these dramas. In terms of the drama of vision, the opening sequence establishes the film's distinction between ambiguous imagery that threatens to decentre the spectator – the 'violent underwater movement tied to no human point of view'[17] – and the catharsis of the cut to the perspectival and grammatical coherence of the beach party – 'the cut is heavily marked by changes in colour, ... in music, ... and in rhythm'.[18] The oscillation between these juxtaposed image systems can then play out over the course of the film. These 'knot together as figures over the film. ... [T]he underwater shot is then used ... to signify the imminence of attack'.[19]

In terms of the drama of knowledge this scene sets up the first element of what Carroll identifies as a

plot structure [which] has four essential movements or functions. They are: onset, discovery, confirmation, and confrontation. The first function ... is *onset*. Here the monster's presence is established for the audience. For example, in the film *Jaws*, we see the shark attack. We know the monster is abroad.[20]

Carroll is principally concerned with the presentation of a diegetic threat to characters rather than with how that diegetic threat might alternately/also function as a threat to spectatorial subjectivity. The shark's underwater point-of-view shot establishes a particular form of visual representation which can then be repeated to prompt spectators to speculate about another imminent attack. In erotetic terms, it is entirely appropriate for this visual sign of an impending attack to consist of an underwater shot which has a different colour palette, musical accompaniment and form of camera movement. These alterations to the rest of the film's more geometrically and grammatically ordered compositions are elements of *conscious* film-making attempts to set up spectatorial expectations which can then signal the subsequent repeated monstrous '*onsets*' to audiences consciously decoding such cues.

Both of these competing epistemological perspectives thereby explain the same filmic elements – tonal differences related to colour, music and camera movement – in very different terms, with each assigning film-makers and spectators very different motivations. However, a film scholar can only decide which explanation (s)he finds convincing enough to invalidate the other explanation based on a priori decisions about how human consciousness relates to film generally. The film text itself can bear the burden of both of these epistemological claims, and the film-making may therefore attempt to elicit both the drama of vision and the drama of knowledge.

The two different paradigms certainly stress, however, the importance of two different elements of the film-making. Carroll states that, in addition to establishing a visual regime that will mark the reappearance of the shark's threat, the monstrous presence invites audience speculation about how such a threat will be countered. Thus, what Heath interprets as a threat to the security of spectatorial vision, Carroll interprets as cues about how the narrative will develop:

> The onset of the creature, attended by mayhem or other disturbing effects, raises the question of whether the human characters in the story will be able to uncover the source, the identity and nature of these untoward and perplexing happenings. This question is answered in the second movement or function in the kind of plot we are discussing; I call it *discovery*.[21]

The drama of vision's oscillating grammatical inconsistency/consistency is therefore also the drama of knowledge's movement from unknowing to knowing.

This element of the relationship between the two dramas actually begins to point towards some kind of divergence, with one theory offering a more convincing account of certain scenes than the other theory and vice versa. Heath's focus on the oscillations from grammatical/geometric stability to a disruptive instability, and Carroll's plot function '*discovery*', both have the potential to explain how audiences might experience suspense in terms of how these dramas play out as the film develops, but these are quite different kinds of suspense. The drama of knowledge exploits suspense about which characters have access to what information – for Carroll, '[s]uspense in fictional narratives is generated as an emotional concomitant of a narrative question that has been raised by earlier scenes and events in a story'.[22] The drama of vision exploits suspense about how film might suddenly shift from stability to instability at any moment – the 'play on the unseen and the unforeseeable, the hidden shark and the moments of violent irruption'.[23]

In the opening scene, and subsequent repetitions of the underwater point of view signalling an attack, these two forms of suspense closely overlap. The spectator can simultaneously experience both the drama of knowledge (asking whether another attack is imminent, who will be the victim and whether the attack will be successful or averted) and the drama of vision (unconsciously experiencing a momentary decentring that will quickly be cathartically resolved). Indeed, both of these dramas can also be experienced when the film manipulates and subverts the connection between the underwater attack and the shark. Heath writes that '[o]nce systematized, [this connection] can be used to cheat: it occurs to confirm the second daytime beach attack, but this is only two boys with an imitation fin'[24] so that the drama of vision can threaten spectatorial security without directly threatening the diegetic characters. This cheat can fit into an erotetic context by subverting established expectations, manipulating the spectator's involvement in 'processes of disclosure, discovery, proof, explanation, hypothesis, and confirmation'.[25] However, other scenes in *Jaws* seem more conducive to one dramatic form of suspense than the other.

For example, the scene that introduces Brody (Roy Scheider) and his family engenders the suspense associated with the drama of knowledge but not the suspense associated with the drama of vision. The scene does not immediately establish that Brody is Chief of Police, but an erotetic suggestion is made that he might be some kind of authority figure, since he answers a phone and takes part in a conversation about the events shown in the first scene, though their deadly nature is not hinted at in the half of the phone conversation that the spectator can hear. Just before Brody answers the phone his young son Michael (Chris Rebello) enters the house showing a bleeding hand cut in a minor accident. As Brody picks up the phone, Michael asks his mother, Ellen (Lorraine Gary), if he can go swimming. She replies that he can after she has washed his hand. A clear locational connection to the opening scene has already been established via a match between a night-time long shot of the sea from the shore and a daytime shot of the sea from the shore into which Brody emerges from off-screen. The spectator therefore knows that a fatal shark attack has recently taken place near to the Brody house. Suspense is created because the spectator is aware that swimming with a bleeding wound in such waters might be dangerous. Suspense here operates within the context of what Carroll calls

> phasing in the development of [the] onset movement. That is, the audience may put together what is going on in advance of the characters in the story; the identification of the monsters by the characters is phased in after the prior realizations of the audience. That the audience possesses this knowledge, of course, quickens its anticipation.[26]

The erotetic nature of this suspense is heightened by Brody's phone conversation and the dramatic irony of Michael preparing to swim with a bleeding wound.

However, the erotetic suspense generated here does not overlap with the kind of suspense associated with the drama of vision. While Brody is on the phone the spectator is unlikely to suspect that a shark is going to burst through the windows. The probability of Heath's 'violent irruption'[27] at this precise moment is practicably zero. (Only in the *Sharknado* franchise (2013–18) are such 'violent irruptions' possible in this type of inappropriate location.) This scene therefore exploits the drama of knowledge but not the drama of vision. Nevertheless, the drama of knowledge does point temporally forwards to subsequent dramas of vision. Even if the spectator does not expect a shark attack on Michael at that moment, he or she may speculate that one will occur later in the film. The scene's erotetic drama of knowledge points towards a later potential drama of vision, so that even when the film does not directly combine these dramas together, it does construct a temporal landscape in which they can interact.

In other scenes, the kind of suspense generated by the drama of vision takes precedence. The famous scare of Gardner's (Craig Kingsbury) bloated head (or possibly whole corpse) bobbing into the hole in his boat's hull is a clear example of Heath's 'play on the unseen and the unforeseeable, the hidden [corpse] and the moments of violent irruption'.[28] Warren Buckland states that Spielberg achieves a

> strong audience reaction [because] the head appears almost 'too soon'; that is, it appears unexpectedly, rather than after a long period of suspense. Spielberg could have delayed the appearance of the head, but this would have created the expectation that something was going to happen.[29]

Hooper (Richard Dreyfuss) only enters the frame to investigate the hole a moment before the head emerges. The 'violent irruption' is therefore part of the logic of a form of suspense in which a shock may suddenly create temporary spectatorial instability at any moment, rather than a form of suspense which invites specific speculations about specific threats.

The traumatic nature of this threat to perspectival stability is demonstrated by the image that Spielberg associates with the visual drama – a lifeless head, somewhat like Holbein's skull, representing the annihilation of subjectivity inherent in the temporary collapse of the Symbolic Order's unity. Gardner's dead head, moreover, allegorizes the drama of vision's threat to the spectator's otherwise unthreatened security of *seeing*, with one of the dead eyes eaten away to reveal the tendrils of the brain's optic nerve, the other fully open but incapable of sight (Figure 9.1).

The close up of the head, moreover, follows a close-up of Hooper staring directly at the camera so that the spectator is offered Hooper's traumatized point of view after seeing him from what turns out to be the dead eye's impossible point of view (Figure 9.2).

Here, the mechanisms of shot/reverse shot, which conventionally play such an important role in re-centring the decentred spectator, become a traumatic interrogation of filmic Cartesian subjectivity. This form of film-making does not just diegetically

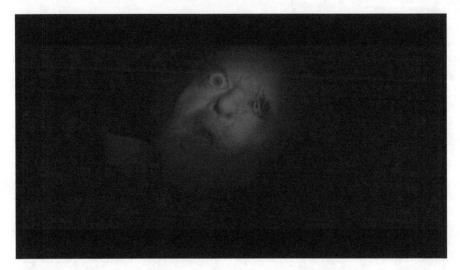

Figure 9.1 Gardner's unseeing eyes as reflexive allegory for the limitations of seeing.

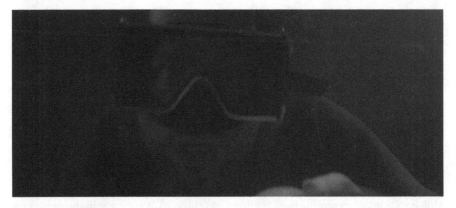

Figure 9.2 Hooper's traumatized reaction, from the dead unseeing Gardner's point of view.

threaten a character but also cinematically threatens the spectator's subjectivity, briefly demonstrating that vision and subjectivity, so centrally linked in Descartes' *res cogitans*, are not necessarily the same thing.

The 'violent irruption' of Gardner's head also relates to Heath's claim about how film's constant movement from 'fragment … to totality' is 'thematised in *Jaws* as dismemberment'.[30] Close inspection of the scene suggests that the head is still attached to (at least part of) the body. Gardner's head is shown in two shots. In the first it bobs into the hole in the hull on the left side of the frame, with Hooper peering into the hole from the right. The intact part of the hull conceals almost all of the body below the neck, and it is the head which appears first. In the second shot, Hooper's torch picks out the head from the surrounding darkness (see Figure 9.1). Thus, if the head is not diegetically fragmented, then it is cinematically fragmented – Buckland refers to a head rather than a corpse, confirming that the scene suggests fragmentation even if it does not show it directly.[31] Hooper, too, collects a fragment of the shark, in the form of a large tooth imbedded in the hull.

This particular moment of suspense is associated with the drama of vision's 'play on … the hidden shark and the moments of violent irruption'.[32] Because the head appears 'too soon' it prevents a direct erotetic question-and-answer drama – the answer appears before the audience has had time to ask the question. It is also the case, though, that this scene overall creates a form of suspense more consistent with the drama of knowledge. Hooper and Brody, after all, have just discovered that the other shark has not eaten the 'Kintner boy' (Jeffrey Voorhees). They set out on their night-time boat trip to find answers to questions, and these multiply as the scene goes on: Is there a shark or any evidence of its behaviour out here? What does Hooper's underwater tracking technology uncover? What is that object floating in the darkness? What caused the damage to the boat? What will Hooper find underwater? What is the object he pulls out of the hull?

Some of these questions are answered quickly – the object is Gardner's boat, Hooper's torch reveals a shark's tooth – but some are answered ambiguously and some of the answers are deferred. The technology finds 'probably [but not definitively] just a school of mackerel', and Hooper's boat's searchlight pans across a silhouette of Gardner's boat's hull to show a large hole above water that might have been caused by a shark attack or by an accidental boat collision. This erotetic structure invites the drama of knowledge's suspense about the exact nature of the threat. The spectator is invited to speculate that Gardner's boat might have been attacked by the shark and that the shark could still be nearby and attack again. The reintroduction, when Hooper goes overboard, of both underwater camerawork and John Williams's menacing music reinforces this suspense.

There are, in fact, two holes in the hull below water. Hooper picks the tooth out of the first, and Gardner's head bobs into the second. The suspenseful threat of the shark spreads across the entire scene, but the tooth explicitly links the threat to the holes in the hull. Erotetic suspense invites speculation that the water around the boat generally, and the holes in the hull specifically, contain a diegetic threat to Hooper associated with the shark. Thus, when the head bobs into the second hole, although it comes 'too fast' to elicit a direct question about what threat will emerge from the hole, the broader contours of that question have been generated erotetically. The precise effect eliciting the drama of vision has been facilitated and enhanced by the scene's symbiotic drama of knowledge. The drama of vision can occur whenever a film 'play[s] on the unseen and the unforeseeable, the hidden … and the moments of violent irruption'.[33] However, the power of these elements in this scene is derived from a set-up inherent in a form of suspense that provokes spectators to erotetically speculate about the unseen and the unforeseeable. The moment of 'violent irruption' can therefore be somewhat prepared for, but it is also a shock.

I mentioned above that the shock element of the suspense associated with the drama of vision can occur at any time, in the sense that this suspense does not require a specific erotetic set-up. If the camera lingered longer over the hole in the hull, then an erotetic form of suspense would generate a definitive question – what is in the hole? The drama of vision's suspense is built on a temporally longer scale because a shocking 'violent irruption' might occur at any moment. But such 'violent irruptions' require not only appropriate settings but also an appropriate erotetic backdrop. The shock of the head's irruption might be an answer to a direct question that hasn't been posed, but the shock occurs as part of a broader erotetic landscape, in which the more general suspenseful questions about what happened to Gardner and his boat *have* been posed. The drama of vision's 'violent irruptions' cannot, then, occur at any moment, but only at moments sanctioned and foreshadowed by the drama of knowledge.

The film-making here, then, seems to intuit reflexively both of these potential forms of spectatorial pleasure. This reflexivity consists of not only an intuition about how audiences respond to dramas but also a close link between the narrative and cinematic elements of these dramas. I mentioned above how Gardner's head links together the drama of vision's cinematic fragments (compositional framing, lighting to pick out the head, shot/reverse shot between the points of view of a traumatized character's head and a dead head) with narrative fragments (body parts, tooth, eaten eye and unseeing eye). The drama of knowledge also has certain reflexive links between narrative and cinematic style. Hooper's searchlight panning over Gardner's boat is simultaneously a narrative element of the drama of knowledge – providing characters and spectators with information – and a reflexive element of the drama of knowledge. The beam of searchlight both resembles the light from a film projector and also reveals and partly conceals information in the same way as the film projection does at this moment. Spielberg seems to not only intuit the dramatic potential of film-making and spectatorial motivations associated with two different academic epistemologies, but he also seems to recognize the potential of inscribing these motivations into intrinsically cinematic metaphors.[34]

The film's other principal 'violent irruption' occurs in the last act, when the shark lurches out of the water behind Brody as he throws chum overboard. In this instance the erotetic element is downplayed. Yes, Brody, Hooper and Quint (Robert Shaw) are out searching for the shark, prompting questions about how and when they will find it. It is also the case that the chum Brody is shovelling in the water is narratively associated with the shark because it is a means to attract it as well as being visually associated with the shark: When the *Orca* leaves harbour the film dissolves to a blood-red sea. This has been seen before, during the shark's second and third attacks, but on this occasion the camera moves up to show that the blood comes from the chum. These associations function as part of what Carroll calls the drama of knowledge's 'processes of disclosure, discovery, proof, explanation, hypothesis, and confirmation', making narrative and visual connections between the chum and the shark.[35]

Nevertheless, the suddenness with which the shark rears up, even more than when Gardner's head appears, prevents a direct question about the shark's appearance from arising. The first erotetic signs of the shark's appearance have already been suspended – these were small movements that Quint notices on his fishing line, which neatly synthesize a drama of vision about the unseen with a drama of knowledge about what information these small movements might reveal. The spectator's expectations about this first bundling of dramas have been subverted, as the shark escaped unseen. A dissolve then signals that time has passed. Hooper is playing solitaire with cards, while Brody is complaining about Quint telling him to resume chumming. Brody continues to complain while his face is turned away from the water, so that he does not immediately see the shark's 'violent irruption'. These elements combine to downplay the erotetic element. Although there is an overall question concerning the shark's whereabouts, it makes its appearance precisely when the urgency of the question is temporarily suspended. (This is different from the moment when the shark interrupts the crew's drunken singing, because on that occasion the unseen presence of the shark is signalled to the spectator first, via a shot of the attached barrel rising to the surface of the sea).

The extent to which the erotetic element of the shark rearing up behind Brody is downplayed is demonstrated by the famous ad-libbed statement that he utters in response – 'You're gonna need a bigger boat.' A few moments later this statement will be repeated as a question, 'You're gonna need a bigger boat, right?', once the erotetic drama of knowledge returns to precedence. 'How do we handle this?' Brody asks, twice, as the crew scrambles into action, a close up of slipping feet on the side of the boat inviting the spectator to ask whether one of them will plummet overboard. But prior to this resumption of erotetic drama, Brody's statement is definitive rather than interrogative, just as the shark lurch is a movement from unseeability to a 'violent irruption' rather than a clearly cued outcome of an erotetic set-up – the emergence of the shark is not an answer to the direct question 'what is behind Brody?', even if the broader question about the shark's whereabouts motivates the scene overall. Here again Spielberg temporarily separates the dramas of vision and of knowledge, better to exploit their potential effects on audiences.

The question about technological determinism – How the dramas of vision and knowledge in *Jurassic Park* compare to *Jaws*

I want to finish up by making a quick comparison with how Spielberg exploits these dramas in *Jurassic Park*. Keeping the shark off-screen in *Jaws* has often been explained as a solution to technical difficulties with the pneumatic prop shark nicknamed 'Bruce'. The coincidentally named Bruce Isaacs states that the

> shark remains [predominantly] unseen, incrementally swelling in the mind of the spectator. ... The shark had been storyboarded into all of the attack sequences, and would have been used extensively in production had it not broken down prior to shooting; the absent image is, ironically, a function of technological failure.[36]

There may be some merit to this claim, and to Isaacs's analysis of how, by the time of *Jurassic Park*, 'Spielberg ... had recognized the primal desire of the spectator to encounter images of excess, technologies of exhibition, and mass cinema's orientation toward spectacle'.[37]

Jurassic Park certainly delivers this form of excessive spectacle in a way that Bruce's technological limitations made impossible. Geoff King claims that even though the dinosaurs are sometimes offered as a 'contemplative spectacle'[38] to be gazed at in technological awe, their spectacular nature always has specific narrative purposes. Thus, the first lingering spectacle of a dinosaur is presented

> as an object for our contemplation, but it is not bracketed off from the narrative space for the precise reason that our contemplative gaze is motivated by that of the protagonists, getting their first stunned sight of the recreated dinosaurs.[39]

This combination of narrative and spectacle can activate both the drama of vision and the drama of knowledge. In terms of the former, the first dinosaur, an enormous herbivore, poses no threat, to either the characters or the spectator's security, as it ambles sideways rather than lurches forwards. Indeed, at this point the drama focuses on the pleasures of looking. The spectator is shown the dinosaur only after seeing palaeontologist Grant (Sam Neill) looking with wonder. His vision is a form of pleasure beyond words – he reaches out to turn the head of Ellie (Laura Dern) so that she can share his gaze. The camera repeats an upwards movement as both characters stand incredulously. At the same time, in terms of the drama of knowledge, the spectator is invited to speculate about how these miraculous events came about and what their consequences might be.

The full extent of these dramas, however, can only be experienced when the spectacle of the dinosaurs become threatening (both diegetically and spectatorially). These threats, moreover, frequently downplay excessive spectacle in a manner that is reminiscent of *Jaws*' barely seen monster. *Jurassic Park* begins, for example, with a shot reminiscent of the scene with Gardner's boat. In a darkness backlit with shafts of white light, something menacing approaches. This approach, however, is shown through movements in trees which eventually reveal a forklift carrying a crate, rather than through the CGI spectacle of a dinosaur. The attack of the velociraptor in the crate is also mostly unseen, with only the effects on the human worker shown. (The unseen attacks of the velociraptors are repeated a little later when a cow is lowered into their enclosure.) The only part of the velociraptor seen in this scene is its menacing eye, intercut with the desperate Muldoon's (Bob Peck) eye. Here, vision is neither safe nor stable. The scene also has a clear erotetic component: What is emerging from the trees? What is in the crate? Will the events transpiring end in a tragedy, as is suggested by the ominous lighting and music? Will the worker be rescued or killed?

The eye of the T-Rex, too, is part of what makes the drama of vision's mostly unseen monstrosity just as menacing as the full CGI spectacle. The T-Rex is introduced by absence: cars pull up at its enclosure to see only a sign of its non-presence in the form of a tied-up goat. After the power outage, the approach of the T-Rex is seen indirectly. Indeed, the first sign of its approach is a sound rather than a sight, with its footsteps causing ominous audible rumbles. These rumbles then translate into vicariously monstrous visual images – the water in a cup vibrating (later repeated as vibrating water in a giant footprint), a point-of-view shot through night-vision goggles of the post and tether without the goat, the goat's severed limb falling onto the car's glass roof (dismemberment, again). The first actual glimpse of the T-Rex is little more spectacular than Bruce's fin, merely a claw scraping at the powerless electric fence.

The T-Rex, here, like *Jaws*' shark, is mostly unseen and capable of 'violent irruptions' like the falling goat leg or its later *deus ex machina* attack on the velociraptors at the end of the film. The protagonists' first response to the T-Rex, moreover, allegorizes the dangers and incompleteness of vision. The young girl Lex (Ariana Richards) panics, waving a torch's shaft of white light (similar to those in the film's opening scene and in the scene in *Jaws* with Gardner's head). She thereby puts herself in danger through the projection-like beams of light, the dinosaur's huge eye dilating menacingly through the car's window. The T-Rex can also be deceived by light. Grant saves the children by waving a flare, so that the scene sets up vision as both dangerous and deceptive, and renders this in a reflexive metaphor for cinematic vision.

The scene also encourages a spectatorial drama of knowledge. Just as the unseen suggestion of the approaching dinosaur facilitates the drama of vision, it also functions erotetically. Genarro (Martin Ferrero) tries to explain the vibrations by saying, 'Maybe it's the power trying to come back on', encouraging ambiguity about the potential threat. The alternative to Genarro's hypothesis is also shown and articulated – Lex asks, 'Where's the goat?' Most important, the dramas function closely together here – the answer to Lex's erotetic question is the 'violent irruption' of a fragmented body part landing on the glass roof, frightening and shocking both her and the spectator.

The velociraptors, too, will not remain unseen throughout the film, but their spectacularity can still be marked by 'violent irruptions', such as when one lurches through the cables behind Ellie in the bunker towards the end of the film, just when her guard is down after restoring the electricity.[40] Even when the full CGI spectacle of the velociraptors is shown, such as in the scene where they stalk the children in the kitchen, Spielberg can still develop reflexive ways to demonstrate the incomplete nature of vision. When Lex hides inside a metal cupboard, desperately trying to close the entrance before a velociraptor reaches her, the camera rapidly dollies forwards towards her, just behind the dinosaur's feet. The cut to the shot of the leaping velociraptor shows it crash into the side of a different cupboard – the image of the child was a reflection. Here Spielberg tricks the spectator as well as the dinosaur, with the incomplete nature of vision rendered in reflexive narrative and cinematic terms. The velociraptors' attacks, however, can also be more erotetically coded in a manner that is facilitated by the technological developments achieved between the making of *Jaws* and *Jurassic Park*. When Muldoon tracks them, and thinks he has one in his sights, he is outflanked by another which appears from out of the jungle canopy beside him. This could have been filmed as a 'violent irruption', moving swiftly from unseen to the attack. In this instance, however, Spielberg decides to stress the drama of knowledge. This drama begins by establishing that Muldoon has seen one of the velociraptors – they are first shown by unseen movements in the foliage, and then not by a 'violent irruption' but by a slow realization, as the camera moves slowly over Muldoon quietly extending the handle of his gun. When the trap is finally sprung, the flanking dinosaur pauses long enough for Muldoon to compliment it by saying 'clever girl', so that the audience can note a character's understanding of events rather than a character's shock at events. It is also the case that this scene is the answer to an erotetic question established near the start of the film. When a sceptical brat of a boy (Whit Hertford) tells Grant that a velociraptor sounds like a 'six foot turkey', the palaeontologist frightens the child by explaining the flank attack tactic. Carroll's 'processes of disclosure, discovery, proof, explanation, hypothesis, and confirmation', therefore, cue audiences to expect to see an outflanking attack at some point, and Spielberg does not use a 'violent irruption' to disrupt this erotetic pleasure.[41]

However, this separation of the dramas of knowledge and vision is more the exception that proves the rule than it is evidence that Spielberg only employed a largely unseen menace in *Jaws* because of technological constraints. Or, in an approximate middle ground between these positions, as Buckland has it, Spielberg 'turned the production limitation into a stylistic feature of his filmmaking'.[42] Whatever the precise circumstances by which he developed this film-making style, Spielberg uses both dramas in these two films, most frequently intertwining them completely, and at points emphasizing one drama over the other, with his motivations predominantly determined by dramatic rather than technological considerations. As demonstrated above, even when Spielberg utilized technological advances which allowed him to show the details of dinosaurs in a way that he was never able to show Bruce the shark, he continued to use the same reflexive oscillation between the unseen and the seen which I have associated with both the drama of vision and the drama of knowledge. Technological changes allowed Spielberg to extend these dramas, but did not encourage him to dispense with them, so that his intuitions about how spectators respond to these dramas was consistent in both *Jaws* and *Jurassic Park*, even if he had additional techniques available to manipulate these spectatorial responses.

Scholarship, then, generally delimits the various ways that film operates. Competing paradigms criticize rival interpretations in epistemological terms – Carroll's cognitivism claims that 'once the reigning psychoanalytic-marxist theory is assessed according to canons of rational enquiry and compared to alternative cognitive theories, it appears baroque and vacuous, indeed, altogether an intellectual disaster',[43] while Heath's poststructuralism maintains that ' "to remain at the level of a content analysis ... is to fail to engage with the fact of film" '.[44] *Jaws* and *Jurassic Park*, however, suggest that both of these theories provide appropriate tools to analyse different aspects of film because film-makers, with Spielberg a clear example, can exploit the very different motivations associated with paradigms that are ostensibly irreconcilable at the purely epistemological level, and can do this in sophisticated reflexive terms.

Notes

1 There are, of course, a small number of films that explicitly engage with issues relating to film theory, such as *Le Vent D'Est* (1969), *Riddles of the Sphinx* (1977) and *News from Home* (1977).

2 Stephen Heath, 'Jaws', Ideology and Film Theory', in Bill Nichols, ed., *Movies and Methods Volume II* (Berkeley: University of California Press, 1985), 509–14.

3 Noël Carroll, *The Philosophy of Horror, or, Paradoxes of the Heart* (London: Routledge, 1990).

4 For examples of scholarship addressing the epistemological irreconcilability of these paradigms, see David Bordwell, 'Contemporary Film Studies and the Vicissitudes of Grand Theory', in David Bordwell and Noël Carroll, eds, *Post-Theory: Reconstructing Film Studies* (Madison: University of Wisconsin Press, 1996), 3–36; and Warren Buckland, 'Critique of Poor Reason', *Screen* 30, no. 4 (1989): 80–103.

5 Jacques Lacan, 'Freud's Papers on Technique 1953–1954', in trans. John Forrester, ed. Jacques-Alain Miller, *The Seminar of Jacques Lacan, Book 1* (New York: Norton, 1991).

6 René Descartes, *Principles of Philosophy*, trans. Valentine Roger Miller and Reese P. Miller (London: Kluwer, [1644] 1982).

7 Carroll, Noël, *Mystifying Movies: Fads and Fallacies in Contemporary Film Theory* (New York: Columbia University Press, 1988).

8 Heath, '"Jaws"'.

9 Ibid., 513–14, original emphasis.

10 Ibid., 514.

11 Carroll, *Philosophy*, 130.

12 Ibid., 130.

13 Ibid., 182.

14 David Bordwell, *Narration in the Fiction Film* (London: Methuen, 1985), 335.

15 Carroll does not use the term 'drama of knowledge' to discuss the overall pleasures of erotetic narration, but he does use similar terminology in his discussion of the more specific 'drama of proof' (*Philosophy*, 102–7, 119, 126–8, 157, 182–90) and 'drama of disclosure' (*Philosophy*, 144, 182, 186–7).

16 Heath, '"Jaws"', 514.

17 Ibid., 512.

18 Ibid.

19 Ibid., 512–13.

20 Carroll, *Philosophy*, 99, original emphasis.

21 Ibid., 100, original emphasis.

22 Ibid., 137.

23 Heath, '"Jaws"', 514.

24 Ibid., 513.

25 Carroll, *Philosophy*, 182.

26 Ibid., 100.

27 Heath, '"Jaws"', 514.

28 Ibid., 514.

29 Warren Buckland, *Directed by Steven Spielberg: Poetics of the Contemporary Hollywood Blockbuster* (New York: Continuum, 2006), 103.

30 Heath, '"Jaws"', 514.

31 Buckland, *Directed by Steven Spielberg*, 103.

32 Heath, '"Jaws"', 514.

33 Ibid., 514.

34 Other than Heath's account of reflexivity in *Jaws*, most existing scholarship tends to link Spielberg's reflexivity with an *auteur*-like cinephilia and postmodernism. See

Nigel Morris, *The Cinema of Steven Spielberg: Empire of Light* (London: Wallflower, 2007), 136.

35 Carroll, *Philosophy*, 182.

36 Bruce Isaacs, *The Orientation of Future Cinema: Technology, Aesthetics, Spectacle* (London: Bloomsbury, 2013), 190.

37 Ibid., 190.

38 Geoff King, *Spectacular Narratives: Hollywood in the Age of the Blockbuster* (London: I.B. Tauris, 2000), 74.

39 Ibid., 48.

40 This scene also includes another example of a reflexive fragmented limb – Arnold's (Samuel L. Jackson) arm rests reassuringly on Ellie's shoulder, but when she puts her hand on the arm it swings over her, dismembered at the shoulder.

41 Carroll, *Philosophy*, 182.

42 Buckland, *Directed by Steven Spielberg*, 104.

43 Noël Carroll, 'Cognitivism, Contemporary Film Theory and Method: A Response to Warren Buckland', *Journal of Dramatic Theory and Criticism* 6, no. 2 (1992): 200.

44 Heath, 'Jaws', 511.

10

'We delivered the bomb': On *Jaws*, guilt and the atomic myth

Matthew Leggatt

Walking around the National Atomic Testing Museum in Las Vegas, Nevada, located less than a hundred miles from the site of nearly a thousand nuclear tests during the early years of the Cold War, one finds plenty of information about atomic weapons and yet little by way of reference to the approximately 200,000 people killed in Hiroshima and Nagasaki. That these nuclear tests would become commercial events and consumed as spectacle by those out of town, who flocked to local bars and sat on rooftops to watch the mushroom cloud, tells a story in of itself about America's relationship with the atomic bomb.[1] But this story is reaffirmed by the museum exhibits more broadly which serve as a celebration of nuclear weaponry and its impact on world history. Indeed, on its website the National Atomic Testing Museum announces that visitors will 'reflect on the history of atomic testing and its relevance to national security and international stability', already framing the debate about the weapon's destructive potential: the Bomb, and its detonation, is credited with producing a global landscape no longer at risk of major multi-theatre war.[2] The story behind President Harry S. Truman's decision to drop the Bomb is neither short nor simple, but one of that story's most remarkable footnotes has a deep connection with Steven Spielberg's 1975 blockbuster, *Jaws*, a film about the heroic triumph of Amity Island police chief, Martin Brody (Roy Scheider), over a dreaded sea monster that comes from the abysmal depths to terrorize a small coastal town. And, as testament to the power of the movie moment, I can tell you that, walking around that museum, I couldn't stop thinking about Quint's (Robert Shaw) near four-minute-long *Indianapolis* monologue, the moment in the film that Spielberg himself labelled as his favourite.[3]

The USS *Indianapolis*, a US Navy heavy cruiser departed, on 16 July 1945 from San Francisco on its way to Tinian carrying essential components (primarily the Uranium-235 and the trigger mechanism) for 'Little Boy', the atomic bomb which B-29 bomber *Enola Gay* would drop on Hiroshima on 6 August. But after delivering its payload, the *Indianapolis* was torpedoed and sunk by a Japanese submarine on its return voyage across the Philippine Sea. Of the 1,197 men on board only 317 were left alive when they were rescued more than four days later. While some 300 died in the initial explosion, the rest were either taken by sharks or killed by exposure.[4] Still, as

Quint offers in a mocking toast at the close of his monologue about that fateful trip, they 'delivered the Bomb ...'.

Quint's speech in *Jaws* immortalized the *Indianapolis* disaster. Indeed, according to Olson, Johns and Doescher, 'many people become aware of [the disaster] through [the] memorable scene in Steven Spielberg's ... film'.[5] In this way, *Jaws* not only mediates history but also serves to preserve accounts of the *Indianapolis*. The film is both informed by history and has also become an instructive account of history which through careful analysis can help reveal more about the importance of the *Indianapolis* story within the context of America's use of the atomic bomb.

Like many in the audience, Brody is also introduced to the story of the *Indianapolis* by Quint's speech. While in the final cut of the movie Brody's ignorance of the story is less explicit, in Benchley and Gottlieb's initial script Brody asks Quint, 'what's that, a ship?' when he sees the scar of his tattoo, since removed, commemorating his service aboard the *Indianapolis*.[6] While the name '*Indianapolis*' is unfamiliar to Brody, Hooper's (Richard Dreyfuss) deep knowledge of sharks has made him acutely aware of the story. When Quint says, at the end of the speech, 'we delivered the Bomb', we should think of this on a number of levels. In the context of the film it is, indeed, Quint who has delivered the Bomb or at least the 'bombshell'. We see this in Hooper's reaction to Quint's opening gambit. 'You were on the *Indianapolis*?' Hooper says, dumbfounded. For a moment, the film seems to stand still, even as the boat rocks gently back and forth. The characters' laughter peters out to be replaced by Hooper's wheezing as Quint's incredible tale unfolds. Indeed, it is easy to get swept away by such a powerful narrative, made all the more arresting by Shaw's grimly sardonic delivery, but one minor detail of the speech has always, for me at least, held the key to understanding its place in the story of *Jaws* and the Bomb.

The important question is why did Quint cover up the tattoo? After all, there are a number of other ways by which the speech could have been introduced. Would it not have been simpler, for instance, for the tattoo to have been on display? Here a timeline for the tattoo is instructive. Copes and Forsyth argue that, 'until the 1960s tattooing remained a practice of certain subcultures rather than a trait of the entire population' and before this 'tattoos in the United States were first displayed by merchant seamen to advertise their travels'.[7] This history helps make sense of Quint's tattoo, which he would have surely had inked while still serving aboard the *Indianapolis*. In fact, in Benchley and Gottlieb's draft of the speech, Quint states this explicitly by telling Hooper that the tattoo read 'U.S.S. Indianapolis, 1944', the inclusion of the date clearly telling the audience that Quint got the tattoo *before* the Hiroshima mission.[8] It is also worth noting that it wasn't until the 1980s that laser removal treatments for tattoos were first developed. Prior to this, tattoo removal was a much more difficult and painful experience and likely to leave a great deal of scar tissue. It was not something one would undertake lightly. Assuming that the tattoo was symbolic of Quint's comradeship with his fellow sailors, removing it after their deaths might seem callous unless, perhaps, the tattoo has come to represent, for Quint, a deeper level of guilt and shame about his role in the delivery of the Bomb.

Indeed, Antonia Quirke intimates this in her book on *Jaws*. Discussing the post-war rise in living standards and radical transformation of American society that followed the dropping of the Bomb, she suggests that Quint's recounting of the *Indianapolis* story is bittersweet. Its telling becomes an acknowledgement of the role Quint, himself a Luddite still clinging wistfully to the old ways of doing things, played in the creation of a world of his own obsolescence:

> It was never possible for the Eisenhower era to be free of the suspicion that the scarcely believable rewards, all the electric toothbrushes and cars and fridge-freezers and twin ovens, all the mod cons of the baby-boomers, had been parented by the atomic bomb. And so there's a double meaning in Quint's ironic toast, as he raises a mug of something clear and bitter to his shipmates. It is he who delivered the world he so dislikes.[9]

This resentment is spelled out in Quint's relationship with Hooper. At first, hunting the shark gives Quint a new sense of purpose because youths like Hooper don't seem tough enough to confront this most ancient of perils. But finally, with the *Orca*'s engine blown and the ship sinking, Quint admits defeat and asks Hooper for help: 'Hooper, what exactly can you do with these things of yours?' It is noticeable too that it is specifically Hooper's 'things' from which Quint hopes to draw inspiration. For, as the *Indianapolis* speech seems to declare, *men* like Quint on the frontline are the victims of *boys and their toys* (Figure 10.1).[10]

In *The Jaws Log* Carl Gottlieb, co-writer of the film's screenplay, devotes a full two pages to his memories of the collaborative writing effort that went into the creation of the *Indianapolis* speech, noting that the speech 'made everyone nervous' primarily it would seem because of its length.[11] Yet the speech served a greater purpose than to fill time in a movie notoriously besieged by production difficulties and to show fewer shots of a shark

Figure 10.1 Quint hands the baton to Hooper: 'What exactly can you do with these things of yours?'

whose mechanical stunt doubles were proving especially unreliable. By any standards the monologue is long but there are other reasons for the writers' 'nerves', for according to Gottlieb, the speech was 'absolutely essential to understanding Quint's character'.[12] This statement certainly suggests that the content of the speech was very carefully considered. Indeed, Gottlieb recounts that a handful of contributors, including John Milius, tried their hand with writing it until Robert Shaw himself penned the version that appears in the film. Acting as more than just a revelation to the audience about Quint's character, however, I would argue that the speech becomes emblematic of the issues surrounding guilt, shame and responsibility that circulate in the film more widely.

Guilt

In considering the radical changes Spielberg and his team of writers made to Peter Benchley's novel, it is striking how many relate to transference of guilt. Benchley's novel is also a text about guilt, primarily Ellen Brody's guilty affair with Hooper, but Spielberg replaces this with a narrative about *men's* guilt, particularly men who have to pull the trigger. Brody is an awkward hero figure. He is, after all, the one with the burden of this responsibility, the one who must eventually pull the trigger on the 'bomb' that will destroy the great fish. But he is also culpable for the death of Alex Kintner (Jeffrey Voorhees), which plays a key role in Brody's later moments of indecision. Brody's more cavalier attitude in the novel is replaced by this indecisiveness as emphasized in, for example, the combined dolly and zoom of Brody on the beach which reveals his horror as he realizes the consequences of bowing to Mayor Vaughn (Murray Hamilton) and keeping the beaches open. Thus, while the film treats him with some sympathy, he is, after all, much less deserving of his guilt than the Mayor, we see him continually struggle with his guilt throughout.

This comes to a head in Brody's confrontation with the grieving Mrs. Kintner (Lee Fierro) on the dock as, moments after delivering a sharp slap to his face, she accuses him of negligence:

> You knew there was a shark out there. You knew it was dangerous. But you let the people go swimming anyway. You knew all those things. But still my boy is dead now. ... I wanted you to know that.

Mrs. Kintner's understanding of knowledge here obscures the complexity of the situation in which Brody finds himself. For Kintner, knowledge is objective and should lead to action. Hers is a fairly typical understanding of the role authority figures, particularly those meant to protect us, play in the social hierarchy. But far from knowing, Brody's initial inaction stems precisely from his uncertainty, all the more evident because of the blithe certainty of the other central characters who browbeat him: The Mayor is certain that the closure of the beach will be a disaster for the town; Hooper is a shark expert whose knowledge of sharks is proven when he cuts open the tiger shark; and Quint is an experienced shark fisherman who knows exactly what to do. For Brody, who is dealing with these three competing perspectives, knowledge is very much subjective.

Despite Brody's confident assertion over dinner with Hooper and Ellen Brody (Lorraine Gary), that 'I can do anything, I'm the chief of police', the film is, in fact, punctuated with moments of insecurity. Brody is described by Hooper as the only rational person on Amity island, other than himself of course, but this certainly does not make up for his lack of knowledge. We see this explicitly as the exasperated Brody pores over books about sharks only to find that even the experts don't know all that much: 'People don't even know how old sharks are? And I mean that they live two, three thousand years? They don't know!' he tells Ellen, expressing both his frustration and with it providing a rather desperate excuse for his own ineptitude. By the time we reach the extended sequence aboard the *Orca*, we know Brody as a man who, while equipped for leadership in terms of his innate sense of responsibility, is horribly out of his depth. The scene in which Hooper and Quint compare scars only serves to highlight Brody's isolation. His own appendix scar is too insignificant to share with the others whose scars are evidence of hard-earned knowledge from lusty bar brawls and encounters with big fish. Indeed, as Brody glances down at *his* scar one senses his guilt. He is the man from the city, saddled with the job of protecting his town, but he lacks knowledge and conviction.

For me, the lingering question mark over *Jaws* remains, however, what to make of Quint's speech. Like the National Atomic Testing Museum *Jaws seems* to engage in a similar cathartic re-narrativization, mythologizing America's history with the Bomb. After all, it replaces a story in which Japanese civilians are the victims with one in which the American armed forces are mourned and a historic technological triumph is celebrated. Indeed, Rubey argues that

> when Quint is killed by the shark, he takes with him the history he represents. History, the bomb, and the Cold War are all erased, just as Quint himself erased the U.S.S. Indianapolis tattoo from his arm. Quint and the shark die together, leaving Brody and Hooper to kick for shore.[13]

But this reading feels limiting. Why bring the history into the story simply to cover it over? Is the fact that the film covers it over not, itself, the point? The speech seems to make considerably more sense, however, in the context of a film about men's guilt. It might be Brody with whom we sympathize, but really his guilt and insecurity, the revelation of *his* scar, is all just a kind of bait leading to the real revelation of the scene: the unspoken narrative of Japanese destruction that lingers under Quint's tale of death by shark. After all, it is not the scar tissue that means much at all, but rather what is underneath that Quint reveals, making himself vulnerable for the first time. His final perspective on the *USS Indianapolis*'s mission crystallizes the film's message that knowledge is both painful and subjective because all it can bring with it is the guilt of *actions*, some taken, some not.

A nuclear context

As this book attests, there are many rich and varied ways to engage with *Jaws*. I. Q. Hunter writes that, 'in spite of its basic simplicity, *Jaws* was wildly over-determined by metaphorical and symbolic contexts, cannily solicited in the film'.[14] He cites 'Watergate, paranoia, styles of masculinity, the myth of the hunter, allegories of class, misogyny, guilt over Hiroshima and Vietnam' as forming the locus of common readings of the movie both by cultural commentators or journalists in the 1970s and by academics since.[15] Picking up particularly on one of these readings, Dan Rubey argued shortly after its initial screening that the movie articulated, among other things, 'a fear of retribution for the atomic bombing of Hiroshima'.[16] Noting that the film's release in the summer of 1975 marked 30 years since the Hiroshima Bomb, or as he describes it, 'the anniversary of the atomic age',[17] Rubey went on to suggest that the shark is not just a representation of a fear of atomic weaponry – as in the monster movies of the 1950s like *The Thing from Another World* (1951), *It Came from Outer Space* (1953), *Godzilla* (1954) and *Them!* (1954) – but also a manifestation of 'feelings of guilt and doubts about the justifiability of our actions'.[18] He continued, 'here it is not a question of being punished for our actions by some superhuman agency. Rather, it is that we have somehow made ourselves vulnerable to the savagery of nature by our own participation in that savagery'.[19] It is, perhaps, for this reason (a display of pure savagery) that Spielberg must have the impossible: a shark that leaps out of the water and onto the boat in order to devour its victim.

What Rubey's reading of *Jaws* doesn't take into account, however, is America's fascination with nuclear weaponry, as well as the naturalization of such weaponry in the general discourse since the end of the war in the Pacific. It is worth remembering, for example, that many members of the movie's audience would have been schooled in the 'duck-and-cover' method of protecting oneself in case of a nuclear strike with drills that ran throughout the 1950s and into the early 1960s. Equally, movies had played a crucial role in this, particularly the monster flicks noted above. As Cyndy Hendershot suggests, 'Sf films of the 1950s attempted to represent the nuclear threat by utilising metaphors that helped American audiences to concretise and tame the unthinkable threat of nuclear war'.[20] For Hendershot such films prepared the psychic space for coping with the threat by 'express[ing] both the deepest fear (the nuclear is everywhere, inescapable) and reassuring comfort (the nuclear is a recognisable fear in the form of such things as giant insects, uncanny doubles, and aliens from outer space)'.[21] To at least some extent, *Jaws* is also inspired by these atomic age movies since, as Biskind highlights, early in Spielberg's career he made no secret of his 'nostalgia for '50s science fiction films' and it is no coincidence that his next film, *Close Encounters of the Third Kind* (1977) which had been in the works before the director had become involved in *Jaws*, would be a homage to those movies.[22]

Jaws appeared in cinemas with America in the midst of an energy crisis now often referred to as the first oil shock.[23] In October 1973 OAPEC (Organization of Arab Petroleum Exporting Countries) cut off its oil supply to a number of countries including the United States, Canada and the UK, for their support of Israel during the

Yom Kippur War, forcing the price of crude oil from around $3 per barrel in 1973 to as much as $11 by 1974. The impact of the crisis was widely felt and precipitated the depression of the mid-1970s, with the US economy confronting a two-year period of recession between 1973 and 1975 that seemed to signal the end of the post-Second World War boom in living standards. This was also a pivotal moment in the history of atomic proliferation. In 1974, despite the Nuclear Non-Proliferation Treaty being in force, India became the first nation other than the permanent members of the UN Security Council (the United States, the UK, the Soviet Union, China and France) to successfully detonate a nuclear weapon.[24] Codenamed 'Smiling Buddha', this was widely condemned and the United States reacted with understandable anxiety. While the Nixon administration's response was fairly muted as a result of its long-standing ties with India, Jarrod Hayes notes that shortly afterwards a spokesman for the State Department 'did attempt to link India's nuclear blast to a threat to world stability'.[25] While on the official level, then, as a result of political circumstances, attempts were made to play down the impact of the detonation, from the point of view of public perception the proliferation of nuclear arms beyond the core group of Security Council members can only have caused concern.

Where the energy crisis brought more squarely into public focus debates around the use of nuclear power, revivifying interest in the use of nuclear power as an alternative energy source,[26] and also putting American livelihoods at the mercy of a newly emerging global economic system, the spread of nuclear capabilities to other nations suggested new threats and eroded confidence in America's global stature. *Jaws* might not be explicitly about these two contexts – though the barrels harpooned into the shark can be read as metaphors for oil barrels – but, as Barbara Flueckiger suggests, the 'powerlessness' experienced by Brody 'directly reflects the emotions of a majority of Americans at the time of the Vietnam debacle and the oil crisis'.[27] While *Jaws* has been read as a film about the war in Vietnam – in this instance the shark's attacks can be interpreted as representative of the guerrilla warfare tactics of the Vietcong – such a reading rather neatly ignores that Martha's Vineyard is on the Atlantic rather than the Pacific coast of the United States and that the young Spielberg, having avoided the draft, promptly, according to Peter Biskind, 'lost whatever concern he had over the Vietnam War'.[28] Indeed, when we dig into Spielberg's history and catalogue his concern – understandable given his Jewish heritage – it is with the Second World War and the Holocaust rather than with Vietnam.

Against this historical backdrop it is easy enough to see the powerlessness of Chief Brody, who, as the representative of law and order, is surely *supposed* to symbolize moral certitude and decisive action, as reflecting contemporary anxieties about America's position in the world. Frederick Wasser has suggested that 'as *Jaws* eroded the moralism of the underlying story, the script lost interest in judging characters'.[29] The movie, he argues, broke with a 'disaster film formula of didactic lessons and moral retribution', dispensing with 'an older aesthetic that asked the audience to judge characters and to measure the fictional response to disaster'.[30] Wasser's comments chime with the general desire to read *Jaws* as the prototypical big summer blockbuster because it reduces the movie to a sophisticated exercise in spectacle creation at the expense of narrative and character development. However, I should argue that *Jaws* is very much a film concerned with how one responds in the face of disaster.

On 25 July 1945, less than a fortnight before the Hiroshima Bomb was dropped, Truman wrote in his diary: 'We have discovered the most terrible bomb in the history of the world.'[31] Similarly, Truman's secretary of war, Henry L. Stimson, stated in a memorandum to the President during the lead-up to the first atomic test that 'within four months we shall in all probability have completed the most terrible weapon ever known in human history, one bomb of which could destroy a whole city'.[32] These critical observations, however, were not enough to prevent Truman and his advisors from deploying the weapon as soon as it was available. Records state that none of Truman's close advisors opposed the decision. They all saw it as preferable to the immense death toll on both sides if the United States invaded Japan. This certainty continued to fuel support for Truman's call long after the dust of Hiroshima had settled. Even today, according to polling, it is only America's youngest generation who are beginning to question its necessity.[33]

The lack of controversy about Truman's world-changing decision is startling, though doubtless it is partly because bombing Hiroshima and Nagasaki did force Japanese surrender and end the war in the Pacific. However, the secrecy of the *Indianapolis*'s mission, which is hinted at in Quint's speech, also played its part. It is unclear how much Captain Charles B. McVay knew about his ship's mission, though according to Dan Kurzman, 'long after the war, McVay would claim that he *was* told. He was given a sealed letter with the information ... and he read it when the ship had left San Francisco'.[34] It is nonetheless highly unlikely that the crew would have been aware of the sensitive cargo they were carrying or of its significance. In fact, in an earlier draft of the *Indianapolis* speech Quint mentions that only the captain knew the true nature of their cargo and one has to doubt whether the mass destruction of civilians was the kind of mission all the sailors aboard the *Indianapolis* would have signed up for willingly.[35]

Indeed, Truman himself only learnt of the existence of the Manhattan project upon entering office because of the secrecy surrounding the atomic bomb. As David Nye notes, 'the atomic bomb had come into being not as a result of open debate but as the result of a secret project that was never subjected to the normal controls of a democratic process'.[36] It is, perhaps, this very lack of debate which encouraged such widespread support for the use of the Bomb. Little was known by the general public at the time about just how terrifying a weapon this would prove to be. Walker points to a number of polls taken in the immediate aftermath of the dropping of the bombs in 1945 which suggested somewhere in the region of 85 per cent supported the atomic attacks.[37] However, he also highlights that scholarship on the events developed and improved over time with additional documentation becoming available:

By the mid-1970s scholars concluded that the primary motivation for dropping the bomb was to end the war with Japan but that diplomatic considerations played a significant, if secondary, role in the Truman administration's view of the new weapon's value.[38]

Thus, around the time that *Jaws* was being made the decision to use the nuclear bomb was coming under increasing scrutiny in academic circles, not least of all given Truman's death in December of 1972.

Wilson D. Miscamble notes that, while 'Truman ... hardly became a nuclear pacifist', his 'experience in August of 1945 deeply colored his whole attitude to nuclear weapons'.[39] Miscamble writes of his 'serious moral qualms' over the decision and his distaste for the mass deaths of civilians: 'In a post-Hiroshima world Truman understood what he had not completely grasped in 1945. In his farewell address in January 1953 the president held that "starting an atomic war is totally unthinkable for rational men"'.[40] The statement seems indicative of an underlying sense of guilt and unease felt by the outgoing president. Much like Quint's *Indianapolis* tattoo, it seems as though the real story behind the president's decision has been covered up, or at least re-narrativized, in an effort to purge the guilt from the collective conscience. What stands in its place is a mythical account in which the complexities of the political decision to use the most terrifying weapon in history have been expunged.

Conclusion: Destroying a beast

Rather than seeing in the *Indianapolis* story another way to skirt the real story of the thousands of dead Japanese civilians, Quint's guilt and his subsequent attempt to erase his part in that history serve to highlight the unspoken horror at the heart of Spielberg's film. This is crystallized in one of the most significant elements over which Benchley and Spielberg disagreed: the ending. In the documentary, *From Page to Screen: Jaws*, Benchley articulates his disagreement with Spielberg over the film's ending, which Benchley felt would simply be difficult to believe.[41] The decision to blow the shark up is important. Surely Spielberg and his team wanted a more spectacular ending than the novel's, in which the shark merely dies from its wounds before it can eat the helpless Brody. And what could be more spectacular and more Hollywood than an exploding shark? Not just any explosion, but one so powerful that there can be no question of the shark's evisceration; a release of tension so great that audiences actually cheered in the cinema (Figure 10.2). The beast, in short, cannot return. Indeed, Richard Jackson asserts that, 'after ordering the use of atomic bombs on Japan, President Truman opined, "When you have to deal with a beast you have to treat him as a beast"'.[42] In order to justify the use of ultimate force, it seems, one must reduce the enemy to the other, the unknowable. Is this not akin to what Quint does in the *Indianapolis* speech? Whereas Hooper spends much of the film insisting vainly on the beauty of the shark, Quint exercises the most effective form of othering in order to justify his hatred of the beast:

> You know the thing about a shark, he's got lifeless eyes, black eyes, like a doll's eyes. When he comes at you, he doesn't seem to be livin'. Until he bites you, and those black eyes roll over white and then, and then you hear that terrible high pitched

Figure 10.2 And the shark explodes ... Spielberg's rewritten ending.

screamin', the ocean turns red and despite all the poundin' and the hollerin', they all come in and rip you to pieces.

In this key speech, not only do we learn something vital about Quint's character, but the final and definitive understanding of the shark is revealed. It is nothing but a terrible beast. It is neither beautiful, as Hooper asserts, nor intelligent as its actions at moments lead us to believe. It is a beast, and as such it must die like a beast – not just killed but obliterated; wiped from the face of the earth.

And yet there is something unsatisfying about this ending. Not at all in the explosion itself – that's certainly what the audience wants. But a lingering doubt hangs over the closing credits: what happens in those moments after the elation of the shark's destruction? As Brody and Hooper swim for shore, the audience is left to wonder what else might be out there in the unfathomable depths. In the film's final moments, we see the two in extreme longshot against a vast ocean of threat. Now that the painful knowledge of what lies out in those waters has been earned, we are left no longer with the fear of the unknown, but rather the pain of knowledge and guilt. Brody has, like Quint, delivered the Bomb but there will surely be other beasts that will return to Amity and what options are left when the last recourse has already been resorted to? In a film about a deadly shark, what is lurking beneath the surface is undoubtedly what one fears and, yet, as Benchley makes his cameo appearance in the film as a TV reporter he asserts that the dread comes not from below, but from what is overhead:

> Amity Island has long been known for its clean air, clean water, and beautiful white sand beaches. But in recent days a cloud has appeared on the horizon of this beautiful resort community, a cloud in the shape of a killer shark.

Maybe this rather cheesy line is just a cheap shot at the media, a moment of light relief for the terrified audience, but for me it has resonance, for me the cloud that looms over this film is not in the shape of a shark but rather in the shape of a mushroom.

Notes

1　For more detail on how atomic tests in Nevada were used as tourist attractions, see David E. Nye, *American Technological Sublime* (Cambridge, MA: MIT Press, 1994), 233.

2　National Atomic Testing Museum, 'About the Museum', http://nationalatomictestingmuseum.org/about/about-the-museum/ (accessed 22 May 2018).

3　Rob Goldberg, *Jaws: The Inside Story* (USA: History Channel, 2010).

4　Donald Olson, Brandon Johns and Russell Doescher, ' "Ill Met by Moonlight": The Sinking of the USS Indianapolis', *Sky & Telescope*, July 2002: 31.

5　Ibid.

6　Carl Gottlieb and Peter Benchley, 'Stillness in the Water, AKA: Jaws', 1975, http://www.imsdb.com/scripts/Jaws.html (accessed 17 July 2018).

7　John H. Copes and Craig J. Forsyth, The Tattoo: A Social Psychological Explanation" ', *International Review of Modern Sociology*, 23 (1993): 83.

8　Gottlieb and Benchley, 'Stillness in the Water'.

9　Antonia Quirke, *Jaws* (London: BFI, 2002), 73–4.

10　It is rather appropriate then that, in his piece 'The Man-Boys of Steven Spielberg', Murray Pomerance refers to Hooper as one of the director's archetypal 'man-boys' (Murray Pomerance and Frances K. Gateward, eds, *Where the Boys Are: Cinemas of Masculinity and Youth* [Detroit: Wayne State University Press, 2005], 139).

11　Carl Gottlieb, *The Jaws Log: 25th Anniversary Edition* (London: Faber & Faber, 2001), 207.

12　Ibid.

13　Dan Rubey, 'The *Jaws* in the Mirror', *Jump Cut: A Review of Contemporary Media* (1976): 41, https://www.ejumpcut.org/archive/onlinessays/JC10-11folder/JawsRubey.html (accessed 26 May 2018).

14　I. Q. Hunter, *Cult Film as a Guide to Life: Fandom, Adaptation and Identity* (London: Bloomsbury, 2016), 93.

15　Ibid.

16　Rubey, 'The *Jaws* in the Mirror', 10–11.

17　Ibid.

18　Ibid.

19　Ibid.

20　Cyndy Hendershot, *Paranoia, the Bomb and 1950s Science Fiction Films* (Bowling Green, OH: Bowling Green State University Popular Press, 1999), 127.

21　Ibid.

22　Peter Biskind, *Easy Riders, Raging Bulls: How the Sex-Drugs-and Rock 'n' Roll Generation Saved Hollywood* (New York: Simon & Schuster Paperbacks, 1998), 262.

23　The second 'oil shock' in 1979 saw the price of oil more than double from its already historic high point.

24　Although it must be noted that India had refused to sign the Treaty.

25　Jarrod Hayes, *Constructing National Security: U.S. Relations with India and China* (New York: Cambridge University Press, 2013), 82.

26　Bertrand Goldschmidt, *The Atomic Complex: A Worldwide Political History of Nuclear Energy* (La Grange Park, IL: American Nuclear Society, 1982), 331–2.

27　Barbara Flueckiger, 'USO: The Unidentified Sound Object', Marcy Goldberg, trans., http://www.zauberklang.ch/uso_flueckiger.pdf, 4 (accessed 20 June 2018).

28 Biskind, *Easy Riders, Raging Bulls*, 257.
29 Fredrick Wasser, 'Spielberg's *Jaws* and the Disaster Film, *Cinergie*, 7 (2015): 46.
30 Ibid., 46–7.
31 Pages from President Truman's diary, 17, 18 and 25 July 1945, Harry S. Truman Presidential Library, https://www.trumanlibrary.org/whistlestop/study_collections/bomb/large/documents/fulltext. php?fulltextid=15 (accessed 15 July 2018).
32 J. Samuel Walker, *Prompt and Utter Destruction: Truman and the Use of Atomic Bombs against Japan* (Chapel Hill: University of North Carolina Press, 2016), 13.
33 Ibid., 4–5.
34 Dan Kurzman, *Fatal Voyage: The Sinking of the USS Indianapolis* (New York: Broadway Books, 2001), 19–20.
35 Gottlieb and Benchley, 'Stillness in the Water'.
36 David E. Nye, *American Technological Sublime* (Cambridge, MA: MIT Press, 1994), 231.
37 Walker, *Prompt and Utter Destruction*, 98.
38 Ibid., 103.
39 Wilson D. Miscamble, *The Most Controversial Decision: Truman, the Atomic Bombs, and the Defeat of Japan* (New York: Cambridge University Press, 2011), 117.
40 Ibid.
41 *From Page to Screen: Jaws* (2002).
42 Richard Jackson, *Writing the War on Terrorism* (Manchester: Manchester University Press, 2005), 75.

11

The way home: Shifting perspectives in *Jaws*

Daniel Varndell

The modern condition

While seafaring has been associated with suffering, pain, separation and loss since the ancient Greeks, it was reimagined by the Romantics as desirable for all men of 'sensibility and honour', and, as W. H. Auden put it, it emerged as 'the real situation and the voyage ... the true condition of man'.[1] From the late 1800s on, however, seafaring has given way to pleasure cruising, the sense of the 'voyage' corporatized by a glib, postmodern 'shrinking-world' mentality so characteristic of the inexorable expansion of capitalism into all senses of what constitutes the modern (western) condition. This chapter is about that condition as it appears in Steven Spielberg's *Jaws* (1975), particularly in the contradictions, tensions and ambivalences that threaten to undermine the fictional Long Island coastal town of 'Amity', such as the contradictory logic of local 'islanders' keen to defend their way of life (traditions) against tidal waves of city tourists, who, at the same time, drive their economy.

Into this unstable environment strides a reluctant and thoroughly ambivalent hero, Martin Brody (Roy Scheider), who, despite being the police chief of a coastal town, is a self-professed landlubber phobic of water. It is not for nothing that critics have often drawn intertextual connections between *Jaws* and Henrik Ibsen's *Enemy of the People* (1882), along with Herman Melville's *Moby-Dick* (1851).[2] However, Brody's struggle with corrupt coastal politics (as in *Enemy*) and his confrontation with extreme fishing (as in *Moby-Dick*) do not quite reflect the full complexity of his character. This chapter will argue that Brody reflects the tensions of a *modern* condition particular to an increasingly globalized world, tensions exacerbated by the context of the 'New Hollywood' period in which *Jaws* was made (described by David A. Cook as one of 'great expectations and lost illusions'), a period the film arguably had a hand in dismantling.[3] Brody is out of his depth wherever he finds himself – in the city or at the coast, on the beach or out to sea – and Spielberg's updating of the age-old seafaring voyage of self-discovery emerges as a comment on and dramatization of the antinomies at the heart of the modern condition.

Amity folks

In the mid-1800s, the beaches of Coney Island were so sparsely populated that Walt Whitman wrote of sun bathing in the nude and running along the 'long, bare, unfrequented shore, which I had all to myself', following which he would 'declaim Homer or Shakespeare to the surf and the seagulls by the hour'.[4] By the early 1880s, however, over a million and a half people travelling by steamboat were arriving to take advantage of the scenery. The period saw an immense shift in the perception of the beach as a place of leisure and relaxation. Paintings from the time, such as Samuel S. Carr's *Children on the Beach* (1879–81) and William Merritt Chase's *At the Seaside* (c.1892), depicted scenes of families playing blissfully on spacious beaches dressed in their city clothes, with the waves lapping at the children's feet as they sloshed about in the shallows, their parents gazing out at the ocean. It was a scene that astonished (and horrified) José Martí in 1881, when he wrote of 'that superficial, vulgar, and boisterous intimacy' of the wealthy vacationers hitting the beaches of Coney Island;[5] a scene not so much poetic as 'queer', as William Dean Howells wrote shortly after he bought a summer house in Far Rockaway in 1896, pointing out that the ocean had been rendered 'modest' by the 'restaurants and bathhouses and switch-backs and shops that border it'.[6]

Jean-Didier Urbain notes that it is odd that in our time we cease to be astonished by the beach, by its existence.[7] Far from astonishing, the beach began to 'str[ike] a chord with the teenage psyche' from the late 1950s, even spawning a short-lived but hugely popular 'Beach Party' subgenre in Hollywood film.[8] These were 'fantasies exporting the glamorous myth' of beach culture as 'escape from reality', as one of the stars of *Beach Ball* (1965) put it.[9] What these breezy, politically neutral and – given the promise of sex and rebellion – somewhat innocent films did not explore was the impact on local communities of this turn towards 'beach-life', and especially its impact on local fishing and whaling traditions. Indeed, the mass migration of summer visitors flocking into coastal towns has been documented by local Long Island historiographer Jeannette Edwards Rattray, who observed that city folks 'were a different breed of cat altogether. It took two World Wars to make the Eastern Long Islanders realize that foreigners were people, and it took a depression to make the City Folks folksy and the Natives less stand-offish'.[10]

New England coastal towns were stubbornly unwilling to accept outsiders, and while the Beach Party subgenre was powered by youth opposition to orthodoxy and (what they saw as) parental responsibility, part of the richness of *Jaws* derives from its tapping into the long-standing antagonism between the 'city folks', whose numbers especially swelled during the summer months, and the 'islanders', who are famous for their 'territoriality'.[11] Hence, it is a key element of the film that, in moving beyond the youths playing on the beach (with whom Spielberg – who famously belonged more to the establishment than to the counterculture generation – would scarcely have identified), the film introduces Brody who is neither a tourist nor, despite being police chief and standing at its civic core, an 'islander'. As with the fantasy of the beach, Jonathan Lemkin emphasizes that such coastal towns as Amity no longer exist (if they ever did). Rather, Amity serves as an archetype in opposition to the setting of so many

formula monster movies located in New York, itself substituting for any metropolis –
even when King Kong scaled the iconic Empire State Building in *King Kong* (1933)
or the 'beast' terrorized Coney Island in *The Beast from 20,000 Fathoms* (1953). Here,
Amity *is* 'America',

> [P]erhaps an America that does not exist and never did, but one the audience
> recognizes nonetheless. … Spielberg distills elements from a variety of American
> landscapes into one ideal, mythic landscape. In the process lies the power of the
> film to evoke a place that everyone in the audience recognizes as 'America'.[12]

As 'archetypal coastal town', Amity stands for the founding myth at the root of the
American imagination, preceding both the rural settlements (inland) and the western
frontier. After all, it was on the beaches that the very first immigrants landed and from
the East that the frontier pushed West both geographically and in the imaginations
of the American people. This 'symbolic landscape', Lemkin writes (quoting D. W.
Meinig), is 'part of the shared set of ideas and memories and feeling that bind a people
together'.[13] In a modern context, the Eastern shore thus comes to represent as complex
a nexus of feeling as the West: on the one hand, a reversal/regression back to the
bloated excesses of the old (and by now exhausted) European masters, via the *fons et
origo* of the ocean from which all civilization ultimately sprang; on the other, the East
Coast is, as Rattray puts it, a place 'deeply rooted in a community … where every house
is rich with associations'.[14]

But one can point to various Long Island coastal towns, like Amagansett or
Montauk, as possible analogues which did and very much do exist. While the film
was shot on location at Martha's Vineyard, and Mayor Vaughn (Murray Hamilton)
mentions a series of rivals competing for Amity's 'summer dollars' (including Cape
Cod, the Hamptons and East Island), Amagansett and neighbouring Montauk were
perhaps foremost in the minds of the film's creators: Frank Mundas, the colourful
shark hunter on whom Quint (Robert Shaw) was reportedly based, was a local legend
in Montauk, a place with which Peter Benchley, author of the novel, was familiar.[15]
Spielberg was so taken with the area that he moved there following the success of *Jaws*,
around which time the area began to be known as 'The Hamptons'.[16] The rising stock
of these coastal towns exemplifies the problem of globalization: tourism equals money,
and tourists come for the 'sights', but the local history and traditions that underpin the
richness of the town's historical roots are eroded by the steady march of the 'summer
folks', their parasols eclipsing the light of the town's past. In such modern societies,
local legends like Quint cease to play a part, except, as Pierre Daninos put it, to be
'used by summer residents as barometers; frequently asked to predict the weather'.[17]
The shark is ironic, then, since his own 'territoriality' threatens to devour the summer
trade and reignites the whaling traditions on which such coastal towns used to rely. (In
a further irony, as Peter Biskind and Nigel Morris have pointed out, *Jaws*' budget sky-
rocketed because the shoot overran into the summer season, during which time the
local rates trebled and continuity issues arose with background crowds with the arrival
of *real* holidaying tourists.[18])

Tourists, then, serve different (at times contradictory) purposes. The islanders depend on them as a necessary evil bringing in revenue, replacing the traditional whalers and fisherman (true Bonacs) of the past. They also function, however, as a means to distinguish 'true' islanders from those who moved in and (especially) those who visit to get a tan. Furthermore, Amity seems precariously positioned in the market for summer dollars. While those dollars might be there for the taking, the town is only ever one shark attack away from economic disaster ('If you want to stay alive, then ante up', warns Quint, before adding: 'If you want to play it cheap, be on welfare the whole winter'). However, Spielberg, building on the work of screenwriters Benchley, Howard Sackler and Carl Gottlieb, uses the shark to counterpoise, rather than undermine these tensions: first, through nuances in the dialogue; second, in the way dialogue and frame composition are punctuated by key visual cues; and third, in Scheider's performance.

First, when the mayor Vaughn effectively bullies Brody into changing his report on the cause of death for the first victim, Chrissie (Susan Backlinie), from 'shark attack' to 'boat propeller', his real motive is clear: 'You yell "shark," and we've got a panic on our hands on the Fourth of July' (the situation is perfectly clear to Brody, who, not a fool, looks to cover his back). However, there is a telling detail in the dialogue when the Mayor spins a little yarn to convince the suspicious chief: 'A summer girl goes swimming, swims out a little far, she tires, fishing boat comes along ....' For 'summer girl' one can read 'outsider', that is, *not* an islander. The comment suggests that for the Mayor at least, Chrissie is (regretfully) considered to be within the margins of what constitutes an 'acceptable loss' in business terms. When one considers, as J. Hoberman has noted, that it was on the island of Chappaquiddick that an automobile accident in 1969 involving Senator Edward Kennedy resulted in a young campaign worker, Mary Jo Kopechne, being drowned and left for dead, this dialogue is even more chilling.[19]

Second, in the following scene, Brody is scanning the horizon for any sign of the shark as Ellen Brody (Lorraine Gary) asks a local friend (Fritzi Jane Courtney) when she gets to become an 'islander' herself. She receives a sharp reply: 'Ellen, never, *never!* You're not born here, you're not an islander, that's it!' While humorously delivered, the response nonetheless smacks of a desperate provincialism, but our eye is drawn to little Alex Kintner (Jeffrey Voorhees), wearing red (a colour scarcely seen in the movie except to signify imminent threat/death) who is shortly savaged by the shark.

Third, earlier in the film, as Brody searches the beach for Chrissie with the teen (Jonathan Filley) she ran off with, their conversation quickly shifts as Brody asks him if he is an islander. When the teen reveals he is, but that he lives in Cambridge and studies at Hartford, Brody's face suddenly brightens; the rapport they have, coupled with Brody's animation upon learning that this kid is in college, suggests Brody sees himself as something of an intellectual. When the teen responds by asking if Brody is an islander himself, the Chief replies with a firm 'No, I'm from New York' (meaning *City*). Their discussion is interrupted by the grim discovery of Chrissie's savaged body, to which both men react with disgust and horror.

In these three examples, Brody's contradictory nature is laid bare: while he struggles to 'get' coastal politics he quickly squares it morally with himself; while denied (never to be granted!) status as an islander, he is also – somewhat paradoxically, given his contempt for the city – *disdainful* of that islander identity. The shark deaths do not simply frame Brody's cognitive dissonance, they aggravate it, dredge it to the surface as something increasingly difficult to ignore.

Compare the relaxed, easy conversational tone Brody uses to converse with Chrissie's pursuer as they search the beach, with the way he dismissively handles the islanders (who are not, in his eyes, educated). He scarcely feigns interest in reports of karate-chopped white picket fences and parking violations and is outright condescending to his deputy and colleagues at the police station. Perhaps the worst of Brody's sneering attitude emerges when Alex Kintner's mother (Lee Fierro) places a sizeable bounty on the shark that killed her boy, drawing scores of islanders to set off on precarious vessels to claim the prize. Brody implores the would-be Ahabs to listen to him, but eventually retreats to the harbourmaster's cabin, exasperated at his lack of authority. As the furrows in his brow deepen, he demands his deputy (Jeffrey Kramer) take action: 'These are *your* people. Go talk to them', and, later, 'You know their first names, go talk to these clowns.' From the 'summer girl' only good for her 'summer dollars' to the perception of Brody as non-islander (like Chrissie, hence second class) and his disavowal of the 'clowns' he won't count among his own 'people'; in such moments as these culminating in the tumult of the town meeting, it is the native islanders of Amity, who, like sharks, take to eating each other.

A fish out of Brooklyn

One must balance this attitude with the other side of Brody as a man who, for all his flaws, clearly does seem to care. According to Lester D. Friedman, if Hooper (Richard Dreyfuss) is the archetype in Spielberg for what Murray Pomerance has coined the 'man-boy', then Brody is one of many 'flawed men' in the director's filmography, men who never seem sure in their interactions with loved ones (whether parents, children, wives or lovers).[20] Their 'macho aggressiveness', Friedman writes, 'is balanced with awkward uncertainty'.[21] For such men, it is *only* when faced by insurmountable challenges, or else forced into action by events beyond their control, that they establish their authority in a positive way (cf. Robin Williams's lapsed Peter Pan in *Hook* [1991] or Sam Neill's sceptical father-figure in *Jurassic Park* [1993], both of whom, like Brody, are shown betraying the confidence of children). In this sense it is perhaps no coincidence that Spielberg wanted Brody to cut an indecisive, if not outright ambivalent figure, who might have the 'stuff' of a hero, but whose heroic potential has a dark quality. Brody over-thinks things and even feels out of place in his own home (where the sunshine persecutes him). But more than this, he is a man utterly terrified of failure.[22]

Prior to *Jaws*, Roy Scheider was known to audiences as a tough, intelligent (and occasionally ruthless and unorthodox) New York cop (*The French Connection* [1971], *The Seven-Ups* [1973]), hence it is not only Brody but *Scheider* too who is 'no longer' a New Yorker. The film breaks with a number of New Hollywood movies featuring tough urban men in NYC, from Gene Hackman as 'Popeye' Doyle in *The French Connection* to

Clint Eastwood's *Dirty Harry* (1973). Brody calls up the masculine 'outsider' stereotype, but unlike a western hero like Alan Ladd's Shane in *Shane* (1953), whose outsider status is belied by his dazzling gunplay, or even Clint Eastwood's Coogan in *Coogan's Bluff* (1968), who eventually thrives in the city, Brody remains a foreigner in these parts. In this, he is closer to Gene Hackman's 'Popeye' Doyle in *French Connection II* (1975) who neither speaks nor makes any effort to learn French as he ill-fatedly swaps the streets of his native New York for the markets of Marseille. Outside the big city he fears (a place of 'violence, rip-offs, muggings'), Brody is deprived of an ability to 'map' his environment, which, as Kevin Lynch pointed out, affects one's capacity to think and act.[23] By setting Brody up as a fish out of water the film places a New Hollywood actor in an unfamiliar environment, aligning Scheider more with an older generation of actors, like Humphrey Bogart in *To Have and Have Not* (1944) and Spencer Tracy in *The Old Man and the Sea* (1958), more comfortable with traditional masculinity.[24]

In *Jaws*, Scheider magnifies the hesitations and uncertainties he brought to his NYC roles to emphasize Brody as a thinker and a doer who has, perhaps, lost that single-minded resolve and clarity of vision we imagine him having in the streets of the big city (he notably wears glasses in this movie, losing them when he discovers his sea-legs, and hence his bearings, later in the film). Brody's irascibility denotes a man not simply struggling to save the town he loves from its own weakness or incapacity (as in *High Noon* [1952]) nor is he too embattled by corruption to effectively discharge his duties (*Serpico* [1973]). The problem with Brody's attitude is akin to his fumbling awkwardness around town – knocking things over at the general store, tripping on the harbour boards, ineptness at tying a basic sheepshank (which *any* islander could tie!) – which is rooted in the fact that he doesn't (yet) love Amity or respect its people and traditions enough to adapt to it.

As a city person, Brody does not feel the need for or doesn't *understand* the communal bonds so intrinsic to coastal living. As Yi-Fu Tuan puts it, city people 'are freer to move about geographically and socially, freer to be themselves, freer to think – indeed, *forced* to think, if only because they are constantly encountering other groups that hold different values and viewpoints'.[25] When Brody moves to Amity, it is this 'city thinking', the need to hold different values and viewpoints, which is his undoing. It is telling that Brody's eventual initiation into the shark hunting group revolves around his focusing on skills that demand undivided attention, like tying a basic sheepshank knot, engaging in small talk and communal singing ('Show Me the Way to Go Home'). It takes a voyage on to the ocean to achieve such clarity and sense of belonging. Terra firma simply won't do, since, as Byron put it in *Childe Harold's Pilgrimage*, while

> Man marks the earth with ruin – his control
> Stops with the shore.[26]

When Brody finally goes out to sea, giving up on his self-deluding refusal to acknowledge and accept Amity as an island (he earlier pointed out that it is 'only an island if you look at it from the water'), it is against the context of a potentially ruined shore. Visiting his traumatized son in the hospital, a visibly shaken Mayor cedes control to him by signing the order to contract the services of Quint. When Brody tells his wife to take their younger son home, she checks: 'Home, New York?' 'No', he replies, 'Home *here*.'

Sea change

The new attitude to beaches in the late nineteenth century gave rise to 'an entirely new rhetoric of gestures and ways of looking'.[27] Visually, the way Spielberg shoots the ocean is quite unlike many of the more romantic visions of the sea, which often compare the horizontality of the ocean's surface with that of the desert[28] or with landscapes such as the prairies depicted by Fenimore Cooper.[29] However, Brody quickly reorientates his perspective in the famous scene in which, distracted while chumming, the shark silently breaks up through the waves to remind him that, when fishing, it is the depths one must watch for.[30] The moment is one of several shots that seem inspired by C. F. Tunnicliffe and Raymond Sheppard's illustrations for the special edition of Ernest Hemingway's *The Old Man and the Sea* (1952): 'when he had seen the fish come out of the water and hang motionless in the sky before he fell, he was sure there was some great strangeness and could not believe it.'[31] This shift to the verticality associated with the depths is linked by a slow zoom shot as the *Orca* chugs out of the harbour carrying its crew, framed by the gaping jaws of one of Quint's boiled shark bones, drawn through the jaws of death.[32] The depths to which Brody is exposed in this moment of disbelief (yielding his famous request for a 'bigger boat') do not, however, simply connote death. For if, on Amity, Brody's failure to map his identity as an islander is signified by the appearance of bodies washing up on the beach, then his association with the sea is signified by this image of the gaping maw of the shark.

Brody identifies with Amity by departing from it through the jaws of the dragon he must slay, pointing to one of the great myths explored by Mircea Eliade: that of 'swallowing by a monster',[33] specifically a sea monster, as a moment of initiatory suffering. It is in the belly of the beast, wrote Eliade, that biblical figures like Jonah learned the secrets of nature, hence the jaws no longer connote *cessation* but *rite of passage*.[34] In this sense, an unintentional truth can be read into Hooper's joking suggestion in the drunken camaraderie scene that the tattoo Quint has removed must have been: 'Mother.' After all, Quint is the film's shaman figure, the 'savant' who returned from that orgiastic death by sharks in the doomed *USS Indianapolis* incident. He and to a much lesser extent Hooper are already 'initiated'; Brody, thinking better of showing off his appendectomy scar, is not. The revelations and confessions in this scene mark the point when Quint finally acknowledges Hooper and especially Brody as fellow seafarers.

But Brody is not just initiated as a seafarer. By slaying the shark (dragon) he is initiated into Amity life, also. It is telling that the line which concludes his odyssey, 'Smile, you son of a bitch', a line memorably snarled at the shark before blowing up the gas tank lodged in its teeth, asks for those jaws to open once more, except this time it is in the spirit of the hunter waiting patiently for the precise moment prey and rifle become aligned. It is little wonder that Brody's reaction is to smile himself. He has gone through a fairly conventional character arc for the Everyman out of his depths, who, by confronting his fears, returns revivified with new knowledge. As Thomas Frentz and Janice Hocker Rushing wonder what kind of a leader Brody will be 'after his moment in the sun' they ask: 'can he translate his hard-earned *heroism* into *leadership*?'[35] While they answer 'no' (citing the western hero's inability to return or remain in society to become a civic leader – John Wayne's Ethan remaining on the porch at the end of *The Searchers* [1956]), J. Hoberman observes that (quoting Susan Sontag), while the 'imagery of disaster in science fiction is above all the emblem of an inadequate response', this is 'scarcely the case with *Jaws*. Brody is born again – literally, baptised in the sea – to be precisely the Adequate Response'.[36] He has earned his status as an islander by protecting the summer dollars by defeating the shark *and* reigniting traditions undermined in modernity. After all, Louise Maunsell Field notes that tradition dictates '[a] young man in Amagansett had not won his spurs until after he'd gone on his first whale-chase and had come back, literally from the shadow of death, covered with the blood of the dying whale'.[37]

As Brody swims to shore with Hooper, quipping that he 'used to hate the water', and with the memory of that haunting shot of the exploded shark carcass descending once more to the murky depths from which it came, Brody not only has won his spurs but also desires to wear them. (In addition to no longer hating the water, might we infer that he now 'loves the island', too?) The film strikes a note that resonates with what Yi-Fu Tuan calls the 'cosmopolitan hearth', which is an attitude that reconciles a highly educated and cosmopolitan outlook with the values and sentiments of small-town living (which coastal towns are a variation of). In such attitudes, 'cosmos' and 'hearth' are reconciled.[38] It is in this sense that I think we must take Brody as a hero in *Jaws*: a character who undergoes a sea change, emerging both rich and strange. It is something of a double irony, then, that just as modern coastal communities thrive off the stories and traditions of a past they are so often credited as ending, and *Jaws* is regarded as heralding the end of experimental New Hollywood and ushering in the era of the blockbuster by using the formal techniques and styles of that period.[39]

However, in reconciling with Amity, Brody recalls John Hall Wheelock's poem, *Noon: Amagansett Beach*, which refers to the coastal landscape as 'my heart's country … my heart's home'. Far from idealizing coastal living, however, Wheelock writes of the sterile sands enveloping bitter, primordial waters ('These winds and waves that roam / Old, desolate ways forever').[40] In such a town, 'one man can make a difference', as Brody puts it, echoing the western hero, but emerging, finally, as a *coastal* hero, a family man who loves the island not in spite of *but because* of its limitations, since those limitations reflect his own. This is what Wheelock means by the 'heart's country': it is a sense of a community fixed by the landscape and charged with tales of the harsh ocean and monstrous beasts, as well as the men who confront them.

Notes

1 W. H. Auden, *The Enchafèd Flood: Or, the Romantic Iconography of the Sea* (London: Forgotten Books, 2015), 12.

2   See Nigel Morris, *The Cinema of Steven Spielberg: Empire of Light* (New York: Columbia University Press, 2007), 48; J. Hoberman, ' "Nashville" Contra "Jaws" or "The Imagination of Disaster Revisited', in Thomas Elsaesser, Alexander Horwath and Noel King, eds, *The Last Great American Picture Show: New Hollywood Cinema in the 1970s* (Amsterdam: Amsterdam University Press, 2004), 212.

3   David A. Cook, *Lost Illusions: American Cinema in the Shadow of Watergate and Vietnam 1970–1979* (London: University of California Press, 2000), 6. See also Peter Biskind, *Easy Riders, Raging Bulls: How the Sex 'n' Drugs 'n' Rock 'n' Roll Generation Saved Hollywood* (London: Bloomsbury, 1999), 278.

4   Quoted in Kenneth W. Maddox and Samuel S. Carr, *Children on the Beach*, www.museothyssen.org/en/collection/artists/children-beach (accessed 16 August 2018).

5   José Martí, *Selected Writings*, ed. and trans. Esther Allen (London: Penguin Books, 2002), 91.

6   William Dean Howells, 'The Beach at Rockaway', in David Widger, ed., *Literature and Life*, 26 October 2006, at http://www.gutenberg.org/files/3389/3389-h/3389-h.htm (accessed 3 July 2019).

7   Jean-Didier Urbain, *At the Beach*, trans. Catherine Porter (London: University of Minnesota Press, 2003), 27.

8   Thomas Lisanti, *Hollywood Surf and Beach Movies: The First Wave, 1959–1969* (Jefferson: McFarland, 2005), 13. The subgenre was spearheaded by American International Pictures (AIP), and its heyday lasted between *Beach Party* (Asher, 1963) and *Thunder Alley* (Rush, 1967).

9   Chris Noel, quoted in Lisanti, *Hollywood Surf*, 15–16.

10   Jeannette Edwards Rattray, *Discovering the Past: Writings of Jeanette Edwards Rattray, 1893–1974* (New York: New Market Press, 2001), 597. Indeed, a joke published in a 1950s edition of *The New Yorker* captured the sentiments of East Islanders perfectly: 'It behooves us to be forgiving and understanding and tolerant toward all of God's children, and that includes the summer people' (qtd in Rattray, *Discovering the Past*, 598).

11   Known locally as 'Bonackers', from Accabonac (meaning 'root place'), referring to the natives who inhabited this part of the island before European settlement.

12   Jonathan Lemkin, 'Archetypal Landscapes and *Jaws*', in Charles L. P. Silet, ed., *The Films of Steven Spielberg: Critical Essays* (Lanham, MD: Scarecrow Press, 2002), 4.

13   Lemkin, 'Archetypal Landscapes', 4.

14   Rattray, *Discovering the Past*, 158.

15   Dennis Hevesi, 'Frank Mundus, 82, Dies; Inspired "Jaws" ', *New York Times*, 16 September 2008, at https://www.nytimes.com/2008/09/16/nyregion/16mundus.html (accessed 5 July 2019).

16   Barbara L. Goldstein, *In the Hamptons 4Ever: Mostly True Tales from the East End* (Albany: State University of New York Press, 2015), xi.

17   Urbain, *At the Beach*, 37.

18   Morris, *Cinema of Steven Spielberg*, 44; Biskind, *Easy Riders*, 266.

19   Indeed, Hoberman quotes a Martha's Vineyard resident who wrote that: 'here perhaps more than anywhere else [Kopechne's death] has remained a live and bitter controversy. On this island – aside from everything else – leaving a body in the water is unforgivable'. Quoted in Hoberman, ' "Nashville" contra "Jaws" ', 201.

20 Murray Pomerance, 'The Man-Boys of Steven Spielberg', in Murray Pomerance and Frances Gateward, eds, *Where the Boys Are: Cinemas of Masculinity and Youth* (Detroit, MI: Wayne State University Press, 2005), 133–56.

21 Lester D. Friedman, *Citizen Spielberg* (Chicago: University of Illinois Press, 2006), 7–8. And as Joseph McBride points out, this description was perhaps most befitting of Spielberg himself, who derived most of his instincts from his troubled childhood, which created in him a drive 'to seek acceptance and approval from the majority'. See Joseph McBride, *Steven Spielberg: A Biography* (New York: Faber & Faber, 1997), 232–3.

22 Might we not see him as a reflection of the film's young director, who, helming his first major Hollywood movie under constant threat of being fired (as both the length and cost of production spiralled), might have felt something of this pressure?

23 Kevin Lynch, *The Image of the City* (Cambridge, MA: MIT Press, 1960), 158.

24 I would like to thank I. Q. Hunter for making this connection.

25 Yi-Fu Tuan, *Cosmos and Hearth: A Cosmopolite's Viewpoint* (London: University of Minnesota Press, 1996), 155.

26 Lord Byron, 'Childe Harold's Pilgrimage', in Les Bowler and David Widger, eds, *The Project Gutenberg*, February 2004, at http://www.gutenberg.org/files/5131/5131-h/5131-h.htm (accessed 5 July 2019). Or, to quote James Russell Lowell, 'And to Our Age's Drowsy Blood / Still Shouts the Inspiring Sea'. James Russell Lowell, *The Vision of Sir Launfal*, Robbins Library Digital Projects, at https://d.lib.rochester.edu/camelot/text/lowell-vision-of-sir-launfal (accessed 4 July 2019).

27 Mottet, 'Toward a Genealogy', 76.

28 Auden, *The Enchafèd Flood*, 15–16.

29 Mottet, 'Toward a Genealogy', 76.

30 Consider the sudden muteness of Chrissie as she is dragged beneath the surface, silenced in the depths – what is described as 'The horror of the half-known life' by Melville in *Moby-Dick*, and as the 'teeming life that lies hidden below the surface which, however dreadful, is grander than the visible' – Auden, *The Enchafèd Flood*, 19.

31 *The Old Man and the Sea* (London: Jonathan Cape, 1971), illustration on 88, quote on 92. See also Sheppard's overhead image of the giant fish 'prowling' around the old man's skiff (page 86) which resembles overhead shots of the shark under the Orca, or Tunnicliffe's magnificent rendering of the shark's attempt to pull the boat down (page 95), which Spielberg captures in the final attack on Quint.

32 The image recalls early-twelfth-century clergyman imagining the Hellmouth as a marine beast devouring the doomed ('Hellmouth, Locked by an Archangel', from the *Winchester Psalter*, c. 1150), as well as the captured imaginations of mid-sixteenth-century fresco painters depicting the last judgement as a Leviathan ('The Last Judgement', by Giacomo Rossignolo, c. 1555). The image is captured in the movie by Quint's grim description of this kind of shark as one that will 'swallow ya whole. Little shakin', little tenderizin', down you go.'

33 Mircea Eliade, *Myths, Dreams and Mysteries: The Encounter between Contemporary Faiths and Archaic Reality* (London: Fontana Library, 1968), 222.

34 See Eliade, *Myths*, 228. Auden noted likewise that the sea is a 'place of purgatorial suffering … It is a pain which must be accepted as cure, the death that leads to rebirth', *The Enchafèd Flood*, 11.

35 Thomas Frentz and Janice Hocker Rushing 'A Case Study of *Jaws*', in Silet, *The Films of Steven Spielberg*, 38.

36 Hoberman, '"Nashville" contra "Jaws"', 218.

37 Louise Maunsell Field, ed., *Amagansett Lore and Legend* (New York: Amagansett Village Improvement Society, 1948), 46, digitized 23 February 2016, at http://longislandgenealogy.com/Amagansett.pdf (accessed 3 July 2019).

38 See Tuan, *Cosmos and Hearth*, 182–3.

39 See Biskind, *Easy Riders*, 278; and Morris, *Cinema of Steven Spielberg*, 59.

40 Quoted in Field, *Amagansett*, vi.

12

Relocating the western in *Jaws*

Matthew Melia

Introduction

During the *Jaws 40th Anniversary Symposium*[1] Carl Gottlieb, the film's screenwriter, refuted the suggestion that *Jaws* was a 'Revisionist' or 'Post' western and claimed that the influence of the western genre had not entered the screenwriting or production processes. Yet the western is such a ubiquitous presence in American visual culture that its narratives, tropes, style and forms can be broadly transposed across a variety of non-western genre films, including *Jaws*. *Star Wars* (1977), for instance, a film with which *Jaws* shares a similar intermedial cultural position between the Hollywood Renaissance and the New Blockbuster, was a 'Western movie set in Outer Space'.[2] Matthew Carter has noted the ubiquitous presence of the frontier mythos in US popular culture and how contemporary 'film scholars have recently taken account of the "migration" of the themes of frontier mythology from the Western into numerous other Hollywood genres'.[3]

This chapter will not claim that *Jaws is* a western, but that the western is a distinct yet largely unrecognized part of its extensive cross-generic hybridity. Gottlieb has admitted the influence of the 'Sensorama' pictures of proto-exploitation auteur William Castle (the shocking appearance of Ben Gardner's head is testament to this) as well as *The Thing from Another World* (1951),[4] while Spielberg suggested that they were simply trying to make a Roger Corman picture.[5] Critical writing on *Jaws* has tended to exclude the western from the film's generic DNA. Frederick Wasser, for example, filters his discussion of the film through the prism of the disaster movie, while Warren Buckland, in his meticulous formal analysis of Spielberg's cinema, suggests that *Jaws* was 'the first film to conform to ... blockbuster qualities'[6] and notes that the film combines elements of the slasher film, the monster movie, the thriller, the buddy-cop movie ('the bonding between three men at the end of the film was a popular subject in the 1970s') and the car chase movie – a sub-genre which gained popularity in the 1970s off the back of *The French Connection* (1971) and in which *Jaws* star Roy Scheider played a supporting role to Gene Hackman's Detective Jimmy 'Popeye' Doyle.[7] Although neither Wasser nor Buckland (nor indeed most writers on *Jaws*) cite the western as a part of the film's generic matrix, *Jaws* appropriates the genre's visual and linguistic grammar and specifically references classic Hollywood westerns such as *High Noon* (1952) and *Rio*

Bravo (1959). Like many other New Hollywood films, *Jaws* takes the western as a point of reference for critiquing a set of heroic male myths that were increasingly under scrutiny during the late 1960s and early 1970s as a result of the trauma of the Vietnam War and the apparent failure of male authority as evidenced by the Watergate scandal. Moreover, through intertextual references to classical westerns, *Jaws* relocates and displaces the genre's frontier landscapes and both interrogates and reaffirms romantic and heroic frontier mythologies.

The revisionist or 'post-western' in the New Hollywood

Matthew Carter has observed the rise and fall of the symbiotic relationship between frontier mythology and cinema in the twentieth century noting that it was through the medium of cinema that 'frontier mythology was popularised'[8] and romanticized. In the second half of the century, Carter notes, however, that 'The grand narrative of the frontier had splintered under the weight of historical revisionism, so too was the cinematic Western understood to be anachronistic, leading to the common appellation of 'post', as in 'post-Western'.[9] The 'Post' or 'Revisionist' western began to emerge in the early 1960s and became increasingly present across the 1960s and 1970s in the work of the young directors who made up the 'New Hollywood'. While these cine-literate 'Movie Brats' still celebrated the once dominant form of the western, it was nevertheless perceived to be culturally dead: a cinematic relic whose reactionary white, male, colonialist frontier mythologies no longer chimed ideologically with the (counter)cultural zeitgeist – especially given the contemporary US political climate and military intervention in Vietnam.[10] Commenting on this shift in perception, Carter observes that the frontier ideologies of

> 'the domestication of the wilderness' and 'Manifest destiny' have been largely discredited. Many analyses of the politics of Westward expansion have interpreted the process of 'Nation building' as nothing short of imperialism motivated by economic forces: imperialism that often resulted in wars of expansion against America's indigenous population.[11]

Thomas Schatz further proposes that by the 1960s the western had run its course as a 'viable Hollywood commodity'[12] and that the importance of its national myth was dwindling as a result of 'market saturation and generic exhaustion'.[13] It was also finding new life within art cinema and as an object of film/genre parody, as in *Blazing Saddles* (1974).

The western myth of the monumental and charismatic, stoic, strong male hero – the kind of hero epitomized by actors like John Wayne, Henry Fonda or Gary Cooper – was deemed increasingly obsolete in the immediate post-studio years (see, e.g., the tragic depiction of obsolescence' and cultural displacement in *Lonely Are The Brave* [1962]). The western frontier mythos had been a utopian and hopeful one, defined by a sense of 'Adventure, optimism for the future, the beauty of the land, and the courage of the individuals who won the land'.[14] But by the end of the 1960s the genre had moved further away from any traditional or romantic representations of male heroism or redemptive narratives. In Italy and Spain, countries with first-hand experience of Fascism, the genre was appropriated and given a nihilistic and existential overhaul – the Italian 'Spaghetti' western popularized by Sergio Leone's 'Dollars' trilogy (1964–6), for instance; *Django* (1966); the array of 'Zapata' westerns which gained popularity during the period or even the surreal nihilism of Alejandro Jodorowsky's avant-garde Mexican 'Western' *El Topo* (1970). US films of the period like *Soldier Blue* (1970) and *A Man Called Horse* (1970) critiqued the treatment of the Native Americans by a racist white (male) military through representations of extreme confrontational, nihilistic violence and brutality. Directors of the 'New Hollywood', such as Robert Altman in *McCabe and Mrs. Miller* (1971), were also preoccupied with updating and displacing the traditions of the western with new locales, landscapes, environments and frontier spaces within which to recontextualize traditional western ideologies. They were also concerned with demythologizing (or at least re-interrogating) the 'heroic' male myth, often borrowing and re-imagining the iconography of the genre within the context of a new frontier: the city where anti-heroic, violent cops replaced the noble cowboy.

Brody

So how does *Jaws* refit and relocate the western?

Richard Torry avoids directly identifying *Jaws* as a western (or indeed 'post western') but he does discuss the film alongside Sam Peckinpah's violent revisionist film, *The Wild Bunch* (1969). He uses the two films as a prism through which to examine the collective trauma of the conflict in Vietnam. *The Wild Bunch,* Torry claims, aims to deconstruct the mythology of romantic heroism which pervades the classical Hollywood western by replacing its heroic protagonists with violent, brutal slayers. Referring to John Cawelti's analysis of *The Wild Bunch*, he notes how the film's deconstruction of ' "the conventional Western's heroic struggle" ' is closer to the truth when he discovers in *The Wild Bunch* a 'coherent example of the deconstruction *and* reaffirmation of myth'.[15] *Jaws* works in a similar way: it both repositions and relocates the western according to the paradigm of the New Hollywood, not only calling into question but also reaffirming traditional approaches to mythic male heroism, for example, in Quint's *USS Indianapolis* monologue and through the character arc of the family-oriented, conflicted, outsider/Everyman persona of Chief Martin Brody.

Brody is a New York City cop who has relocated with his family to the white picket fenced, WASPish New England seaside island town of Amity. Given the preponderance of anti-heroic cops/urban cowboys and sheriffs across the American New Wave ('Popeye' Doyle, 'Dirty' Harry Callaghan [Clint Eastwood]) and the depiction of the tough contemporary crime-ridden urban landscape as the new Wild West, it is possible to read Brody's outsider position here as a meta-textual (and intertextual) repositioning of this new (urban) 'western' cop-hero outside of his 'natural environment' (much like the 'rogue' shark). That Roy Scheider had previously played Detective Buddy 'Cloudy'

Rousso in the urban (anti/post)-western/cop thriller *The French Connection* four years earlier contributes to the intertextual composition of his (post)-western character in *Jaws*. Nevertheless Brody is presented throughout as an Everyman who must rise above his own limitations, and the film questions his 'heroic' status. In the final third of the film Ahab-esque fisherman Quint (Robert Shaw) and wealthy ichthyologist Matt Hooper (Richard Dreyfuss) fraternally compare their scars accrued from various struggles with the sea, in manly tests of endurance (Quint's 'arm wrestling competition in an Okie bar in San Francisco') or romantic interludes ('Mary Anne Moffat – she broke my heart'). Brody, however, has only an appendectomy scar (which he attempts to hide out of embarrassment) and not a hard-earned wound as a signifier of grizzled and authentic masculinity.

Furthermore, setting off to investigate the shark's apparent hunting ground, Brody drunkenly tells Hooper,

> I'm tellin ya, the crime rate in New York will kill ya. There's so many problems, you never feel like you're accomplishing anything. Violence, rip offs, muggings. The kids can't leave the house. You gotta walk 'em to school. But in Amity, one man can make a difference!

This payoff line has echoes of the western, presenting Brody as the lone Sheriff, the heroic individual come from outside to clean up the town. It harks back to the mythos of one man being able to make a difference. This is a clear aspiration for Brody as New York appears to have defeated him. It also gives insight into the less noble or 'charismatic' aspects of his character: he has been unable to 'make a difference' in New York, but in the supposedly genteel, 'civilised' and 'respectable' environment of Amity, where the most pressing problems are karate-chopped picket fences, errant parking of garbage trucks and Harry's 'bad hat', 'making a difference' is a distinct possibility. This quaint representation of Amity contrasts with Peter Benchley's novel where the Mayor is threatened by the presence of the Irish mafia and the townspeople are themselves alarmed by the presence of Polish drug dealers and an alleged black rapist in their midst. Here the 'rogue' shark becomes a cipher for the town's white middle-class anxiety (and racism) over the presence of outsiders and non-Islanders. Brody seems to have given up on New York and opted for what seems like the easier, softer option, perhaps trying to evade his responsibilities (and reality?). The arrival of the shark becomes a 'test' of manhood for Brody, forcing him to overcome the obstacles which face him (his terror of the sea) and confront his professional, family and masculine duties.

If Carl Gottlieb seemed keen to play down the relationship of *Jaws* to the western and its tropes, producers Daryl Zanuck and David Brown offered a contrary perspective, claiming, 'It's a Cowboy myth. For the folk on the beach have to hire the local fisherman, the Sheriff in other words, who is a hard boiled and salty tongued ... maniacal bastard.'[16] This suggests that, at a studio level, the film had been at least partly imagined in terms of the western 'myth' and also that Quint seems to have been viewed in terms of 'The Sheriff', not Brody (as might be imagined). Brody is the 'Chief' (a term by which he is referred to even by his wife Ellen [Lorraine Gary]) – an ambiguous and ironic term which not only connotes the role of 'Sheriff' with all its associations of patriarchal and paternal authority (and authoritativeness – a quality Brody seems to lack given that no one seems to listen to him – least of all his own family) but also Native American-ness – raising questions over land ownership, belonging and marginalization (Brody as the head of a marginalized 'tribe' of non-Islanders). When Ellen asks 'When do I get to become an Islander?' she is cut to the quick by her friend: 'Ellen, never. Never. If you're not born here you're not an Islander. That's it.'

Throughout the film Brody's outsider position is formally suggested by the way he is positioned to either side of the shot, rarely centrally. Brody exists not only on the margins of the town both figuratively (as a non-Islander) and literally but also on the margins of the frame. What is more, throughout the film, this 'Sheriff's' authority is constantly belittled and downgraded – by Hooper who admonishes him for smoking in the morgue and for disturbing the compressed air canisters on board the *Orca*; by Ellen who sends him off like a mother packing a child off on a school trip: 'Did you take your Dramamine? I put an extra pair of glasses in black socks, and the stuff for your nose'; by Quint, who when Brody fails to tie his sheepshank patronizes him: 'Well, nothing's easy, is it Chief?' (as Brody sits at his feet rather like a young child sitting at the feet of his grandfather). This infantilization and diminishment of authority is embellished in the sequence in which Brody and his infant son Sean (Joe Mello) play at copying each other – one becoming a mirror for the other. In the western, romantic masculinity is directly associated with power, law and order, with decisive action, protecting the home and family, and preserving consensus and community. Later, as he and Hooper go off to autopsy the shark the mob has caught, Brody has to reaffirm his own position of authority to Ellen when she questions his authority to make such a split decision: 'I can do anything – I'm the Chief of police!' He has, nevertheless, earlier been powerless to stop young Alex Kintner (Jeffrey Voorhees) being devoured on his watch; his horror, disorientation and confusion at both what is happening and his inability to act in time is signified by the famous dolly/zoom. Here the film draws attention to a moment of historical crisis. The death of Alex Kintner on his inflatable raft anticipates the *USS Indianapolis* speech. Alex's gruesome death may read as a signifier of the brutalization of American male youth in the wake of Vietnam (his mother is left anxiously waiting on the edge of the home front/beach for her lost son). The death is pushed to the back of the frame, almost unnoticed at first by the bathers and, to an extent by the viewer, until we are shocked into gory realization along with Brody. There is an implicit parallel here in the way this formal arrangement of the shot anticipates Quint's later statement about how the *USS Indianapolis* and another generation of expendable young men who went to their deaths were similarly unnoticed until it was too late: 'What we didn't know was our bomb mission was so secret, no distress signal had been sent … They didn't even list us as overdue for a week.'

Brody's seemingly impotent authority is later reinforced by the resounding slap in the face given to him by Alex's mother, Mrs Kintner (Lee Fierro), for not closing the beach, the frontier space between the safety of the home and the savagery of the wilderness ('My son is dead ... I wanted you to know that'). It is a wakeup call to responsibility and duty, and a catalyst in Brody's decision to take action.

Brody's closest cinematic antecedent is Marshall Will Kane (Gary Cooper) in *High Noon*, a film which 'celebrated the nobility of the individual in the face of failed public morality'.[17] Both Kane and Brody are confronted not only with outlaw Frank Miller/ the rogue shark but also with a wave of public and official opposition. Neither is able to preserve the consensus. Kane is blamed for Miller coming back to town, something that will damage the town's reputation and as McGee notes:

> One of the public officials of Hadleyville turns on him and blames him for the inevitable gunfight that must take place and will ruin the reputation of the town ... To justify this view, Henderson explains that 'People up North are thinking about this town ... about sending money down here to put up stores and factories' ... Frank Miller [the film's antagonist] is in alliance with those 'People up North' who have money to invest in the town.[18]

Like Kane, Brody clashes with the community fathers (and mothers), who are unable to maintain a consensus of opinion. There are similarities between the church scene in *High Noon* in which Kane faces down the town elders and the town hall sequence in *Jaws* during which Brody states his intention to close the beaches. He too is met with opposition from the town's captains of industry who think that closing the beaches will ruin their businesses. It is only later when Mayor Vaughn's hand is forced ('My kids where on that beach too') that Brody is able to act. In this instance it is not as a traditional western hero that Brody succeeds, but as an Everyman, like Marshal Kane, willing to take a stand.

Landscape and masculinity

Jaws can be aligned with the western not only in its representation of Brody as a sheriff but also in its reworking of western tropes of the landscape (relocated, obviously, to the ocean); in its treatment of masculinity; and its depiction of Amity as a frontier town. During his professional career Spielberg has never made a western. The only outright western he made was as an aspiring film-maker aged 13: a three-minute, 8mm film titled *The Last Gunfighter* (1959).[19] As an American youth in the immediate post-war years he (and indeed screenwriter Carl Gottlieb) would certainly have been exposed to not only the twilight years of the classical Hollywood western but also the serialized western on the emergent medium of television. Nevertheless, despite the genre's absence in his professional canon, it is iconographically present in a number of his films. Take, for example, *Indiana Jones and the Last Crusade* (1989), during whose opening sequence Young Indy (River Phoenix) attempts to rescue the fabled 'Cross of Coronado' from the clutches of 'Fedora' (Richard Young). The sequence is a genre pastiche bearing the iconographic hallmarks of the western ('yee-hawing' villains; an abandoned mine shaft; a cross-country horse/locomotive chase and so on) and was filmed in Moab, Utah, which had also served as the location for several John Ford westerns including *Rio Grande* (1950), *Wagon Master* (1949) and *Cheyenne Autumn* (1964). *Close Encounters of the Third Kind* (1977) also draws on the western in its landscapes (the Devils Tower National Monument: Wyoming plays a key narrative role and was the backdrop of Ford's *My Darling Clementine* [1949]) and its themes. Lester Friedman observes how *Close Encounters* 'reaffirms America's historical sense of Manifest Destiny, substituting Space for the western frontier'[20] and 'clearly reconnects American culture to the lofty sense of national purpose that characterized, at least in retrospect, the Kennedy era.'[21] In discussing *Jurassic Park* (1993), he observes how the film reworks the classic western opposition of the desert and the garden and how the films' narrative structure calls to mind 'a western more than a conventional monster movie'[22] recalling the clash between 'civilisation and savagery'[23] that typified the Hollywood representation of the American frontier. He notes how '[t]he dinosaurs represent the forces of unrestrained nature, usually embodied by fierce and uncivilized Indians, who oppose the forces of progress; Sattler [Laura Dern] is the civilizing female presence.'[24]

This reaffirmation of 'traditional' and the 'recapitulation' of the 'battle between civilisation and savagery' is anticipated by *Jaws*, which itself also may be viewed as the third part of an early 'trilogy' of films comprising *Duel* (1971) (whose opening point of view shot anticipates that of *Jaws*) and *The Sugarland Express* (1974). Robert Cumbow proposes a thematic overlap across these films: 'the mechanization of the animal' and the role of the machine across these films with *Jaws* as the culmination of Spielberg's exploration of this theme (up to that point).[25] These films establish an obsession with presenting the American landscape and wilderness as a nostalgic and romantic space as well as a disorienting and threatening one. In each, there is a dramatic chase across a natural, monumental terrain (or oceanscape in the case of *Jaws*), a wild no-man's land which recalls the untamed space of Geronimo, in which the passengers of the *Stagecoach* (1939) are impelled to travel through. *Duel* also looks to the frontier tension between civilized and savage, filtering it through the prism of contemporary class politics. Furthermore the rusting, monstrous truck which relentlessly pursues David (Every) Mann (Dennis Weaver) is adorned with plates from Nevada, Wyoming, New Mexico, Arizona, Idaho, Montana and California: all frontier states which had been home to a wide variety of native American tribes (thus, from a western genre perspective, further embellishing its 'savagery').

Spielberg frames the ocean in much the same way as John Ford panoramically frames the monolithic landscape of the West with a prominent horizon line stretching fully across the frame. In the film's third act, Spielberg presents the *Orca* in long shot much like a Fordian 'stagecoach' set against the expansive panoramic landscape.

Moreover, Michael Budd has noted the oppositional nature of the genre which pits 'civilisation and savagery, culture and nature, East and West, settlement and Wilderness'.[26] These binary oppositions (as Budd notes) are the foundations of the genre and 'Every director who has constructed a distinctive Western world in his films has made images with which to visualise and particularize the meanings latent in these abstract elements.'[27] *Jaws*, too, is constructed from binary oppositional narrative, (inter) textual and visual structures. The pond adjacent to the beach, for instance, may be read as 'Garden', a ring-fenced (via a sea wall/barrier) and supposedly tamed wilderness-space. The violent death of the fisherman, devoured coming to young Michael Brody's (Chris Rebello) aid, indicates that *this* (oceanic) wilderness will not be tamed or colonized. Amity itself is a frontier township, an island, which occupies an intermedial space between city (as represented by Brody) and sea (as represented by Quint and to a lesser extent Hooper who is associated with both spaces – 'you got city hands Mr Hooper, you've been counting money all your life'). Spielberg transposes, relocates and rebuilds the western town/settlement in this oceanside locale. In doing so he supplies the viewer with a series of iconographic and recognizable tropes. Mrs Kintner putting a bounty of $3000 on the shark calls to mind the image of the outlaw with a bounty on his head. Furthermore, leading into the Town Hall sequence the viewer is presented with a shot of what amounts to a 'Wanted' sign. This generic western imagery is later compounded by the flotilla of boats/lynch mob that leave the harbour to hunt down the (wrong) shark. The lynching and hanging of the innocent tiger shark ('from Southern Waters') not only has western connotations (here the rule of law is removed from the hands of the Sherriff by the mob) but this 'lynching' carried out by braying white men with metal hooks recalls the end sequence of another Hollywood Renaissance horror film: George Romero's *Night of the Living Dead* (1968).

As with the poetic Golden Age studio westerns of Hawks and Ford in which the untamed and uncivilized landscape of the American west becomes a testing ground for a set of 'natural' (White American) male virtues: heroism, chivalry, stoicism, self-sacrifice, honour, competition and brotherhood, in *Jaws* the ocean plays a similar role. Jim Kitses defines the typical Fordian male protagonist and suggests that Ford's films celebrate 'strong masculine leadership'.[28] The retiring Captain Nathan Cutting Brittles (John Wayne) in *She Wore a Yellow Ribbon* (1949), for instance, embodies this approach to masculinity – his name connoting the duality of strength and fragility typical of the Fordian hero. For Kitses, the Fordian hero is one 'poised between individualism and the community'[29] and who 'acted not for himself but for larger causes – duty, honour, loyalty'.[30]Patrick Brereton develops this analysis stating, 'John Ford embodies the western ideal. In his extensive use of Monument Valley he recognised in nature the true romantic spirit of adventure. Out there, men could "be" themselves and act out their true masculine selves'.[31]

In *Jaws* Spielberg offers both a celebration of this mythic and romantic conception of masculinity as well as a study of contemporary masculinity in crisis. This is established in the opening campfire sequence prior to poor Chrissie Watkins's (Susie Backlinie) violent demise. The camera pans from the harmonica player across a scene of countercultural permissiveness (kids making out, others smoking joints, etc.) and comes to rest on a medium close up of young lothario Tom Cassidy (Jonathan Filley), whose attention is fixed with shark-like predatory attention on someone off-screen. The shot cuts to the object of his attention: Chrissie, and the viewer notes immediately that they are almost an identical match with their long blond hair. This juxtaposition feminizes Cassidy diminishing his masculinity. He is at one extreme end of the film's spectrum of manliness, while the uber-maleness of the working-class John Wayne-esque Quint (a frontiersman) is positioned at the other. Cassidy displays none of the romantic Fordian notions of masculinity, un-chivalrously falling asleep drunk on the beach, too incapacitated to either fulfil his sexual ambitions with his mate and/ or protect her from her impending doom out in the wild ocean-space. Here we see the first example of the wilderness as testing space for the male values – a test that Cassidy fails.

On their run down to the water, Chrissie and Cassidy's route is dictated by ragged fence (whose posts resemble jagged teeth – a 'signpost' towards the fate that is about to befall Chrissie).[32] Fences mark and define space and territory, and later in the film Polly (Peggy Scott) will complain to Brody about the youngsters from the karate school 'karate-ing the picket fences' – such boundaries and territorial demarcation in *Jaws* are continuously contested. This fence also has a visual prominence in the subsequent sequence in which Chrissie's body is discovered (we may also note here that her bag, collected by Brody, is of Native American design), a visual reminder of the tension between the home front and untamed ocean wilderness. Fences also feed into the film's concern with 'territoriality' (also a prominent theme of the western). They demarcate property and indicate ownership and separate neighbours (we see a prominent picket fence around Brody's house). As part of the film's visual language they prompt us to raise questions of ownership and colonization, reminding us of the enclosed nature of 'civilised' space and the uninhibited nature of the wilderness.

In his analysis of *Stagecoach*, Michael Budd also comments on the role of fences in Ford's film: '*Stagecoach* marks the journey from Tonto to Lordsburg with images of gates and fences which spatially separate the relative safety of the towns and way stations from the open desert where the stagecoach is vulnerable to Indian attack.'[33]Furthermore, Budd also comments on the framing of the shot in Ford's films, suggesting that

[s]hots looking through doors, through windows, gates, porches and canopies bring indoors and outdoors into juxtaposition. Such images are sufficiently pervasive to suggest a structuring vision of the nature of the frontier itself. Images using a frame are a central aspect of the visual organization which complements the narrative in every film.[34]

Spielberg consciously adopts this visual language across his film: in the sequence in which Brody and Ellen relax at home and plan to 'get drunk and fool around' as Michael and friends play in the boat outside. The ocean is present throughout the scene, framed in the background through the window of their home, juxtaposing the supposed safety of the 'homestead' and the wilderness outside. We are introduced to Brody as he wakes up, framed in extreme close up from behind looking out through the window to the sea that fills the frame (in this shot even the window frame is eliminated). Later, Deputy Hendricks (Jeffrey C. Kramer) is also viewed through the window of the harbourmaster's cabin wearing a Stetson and smoking a cigarette/cheroot.

This framing device is used as 'the posse' of Brody, Quint and Hooper ride out in the *Orca* to confront the shark. As it departs, the boat is framed through the jawbone of a shark adorning the window of Quint's workshop, and earlier in the film, after the fisherman is devoured in the boating pond, the wilderness of the ocean is framed through the supporting pillars of the pier. All of these shots present the threshold between the wild unknown and the safety of home. These 'safe' domestic spaces, however, are threatened by the rogue shark. We know from films like *The Searchers* that the safety of the home is often illusory, especially when it exists on the frontier with nature. As Budd reminds of the Fordian western:

> The complex of home-wilderness images seems central to the similarities among Ford's Westerns: not only does it bring together the underlying elements of the genre, connecting the dynamics of the Western to the specific concerns of the director, but it also permeates the formal pattern and texture of the films. The meeting of home and Wilderness, the edge of the frontier, is constituted in the design of the images itself.[35]

Budd reminds us that the idea of civilization is encoded through images of family and community (e.g. during the square dance sequence in *My Darling Clementine*) and is associated with the homestead, settlement or cavalry fort; with stagecoaches, or covered wagons, 'Home and Shelter is juxtaposed with its opposite, the desert wilderness, within single images.'[36] Throughout *Jaws* there is an emphasis on such spaces and structures: the cabin of the *Orca* or the Brody's home for instance, a white clapboard house by the water which is situated on the outside of the town rather than in it. Brody has to drive some distance at the start of the film to enter the town. This underlines the Brodys' status as outsiders/non-Islanders as well as the Chief's own marginal position. Spielberg establishes their home as a 'Western homestead' from which he 'rides out' at the start of the film. From the start Brody is associated with paternalism, patriarchy, domesticity and the drive to protect the family. He embodies these normative 'male' virtues, but the ocean, a territory where he is least in his comfort zone, becomes the testing ground for these values.

Three men in a boat

Throughout *Jaws* Spielberg foregrounds a series of fraternal and paternal, familial and platonic male relationships: Quint and Hooper bonding over their scars and drinking to their legs in a moment of friendly, fraternal competition and setting aside their class differences aboard the *Orca*; young Sean Brody calling for his big brother Michael on the beach; Brody and Sean sharing an affectionate moment around the dinner table; Brody sitting at the feet of Quint (in his rocking/fishing chair like a grandfather) trying unsuccessfully to tie a sheepshank. These are moments where the film reaffirms the romantic and mythic idea of masculinity. These are, however, fleeting moments of amicability which are followed by moments of trauma or crisis which textually rupture this romanticism: the revelation of Quint's experience on the USS *Indianapolis*; Michael's narrow escape in the boating pond, where male experience is tested. At the table Brody asks his young Sean to give him a hug; when asked why, he replies 'Because

I need it', immediately bringing into question assumptions about the solid, impregnable and monumental nature of masculinity.

If *High Noon* is one point of reference for *Jaws*, then in its presentation of masculinity and brotherhood, the film looks to Hawks's *Rio Bravo*, a film about both redemption and fraternal male relationships and comradeship. *Jaws* in that sense unites two ideologically opposed westerns:

> Director Fred Zinnemann and star Gary Cooper shared the view that the film celebrated the nobility of the individual in the face of failed public morality. John Wayne, *the* film star and conservative archetype of the period, declared it un-American.[37]

Aboard the *Orca*, in a moment of respite Hooper and Quint attempt to 'man off' against each other comparing scars and, after the pivotal moment of Quint's *USS Indianapolis* speech, join in drinking and the comradely singing of 'Show Me The Way To Go Home'. Here there are clear echoes of *Rio Bravo* in which, waiting for the final standoff, Sheriff John T. Chance (John Wayne) is positioned at one side of the frame with a coffee (like Brody) while Colorado Ryan (Ricky Nelson), Stumpy (Walter Brennan) and Chance's deputy, Dude (Dean Martin) join together in singing the similarly comradely 'My Rifle, My Pony and Me', a wistful tune about companionship. In *Rio Bravo,* drinking and singing play important roles (as they do here) – for Dude, alcoholism is an obstacle, a test, he must overcome with the help of his comrades to earn back his guns and allowing him to overcome Joe Burdette (Claude Atkins), towards the end of the film. Furthermore, Nathan Burdette (John Russell) pays the men in the saloon to play 'The Cutthroat song', a song dating from the Alamo and connoting 'No Quarter' to one's enemies. In *Jaws* 'Show Me the Way to Go Home' signifies here not only a moment of male bonding, a recapitulation of the jailhouse sequence from *Rio Bravo,* but inverts Hawks's sentiment with a song about dislocation and masculinity in crisis (post-Vietnam), all lost at sea. It indicates a desire to go back, to return home and to take comfort in what is familiar and traditional. This song also works on a meta-textual level – when considering the film's recapitulation of the romantic Hollywood western and its male ideals, it is a call to return to this more (culturally) comforting and traditional cinematic zeitgeist. The final third of *Jaws*, which plays out like an aquatic gunfight at the O.K. Corral and here finally, reaffirms and rehabilitates the 'lost' western male virtues it has been seeking to re-establish. It is here on the ocean, at the end of the film, that Brody finally occupies the centre of the frame. Forced to overcome his fear of the water, his individualism and resourcefulness are tested as he confronts the shark alone (like Kane in *High Noon* facing Frank Miller). Leaning against the mast of the sinking *Orca,* he (significantly) uses a rifle to finally dispatch the shark via a well-placed shot to a compressed air canister, which he ineptly knocked over earlier. He has passed the test the film has set him. Leaning against the sinking mast Brody also takes on the shark sightless in the final standoff/shootout – he has lost his glasses in the earlier chaos and the spare pair so carefully packed by Ellen are nowhere to be seen (presumably gone down with the ship). Brody's vanquishing of the shark, the 'outlaw' opponent, is an act of blind faith (a test not unlike that of Odysseus firing an arrow through the axe heads at the end of Homer's *The Odyssey*) in both himself and the true aim of the rifle (returning us to 'my rifle, my pony and me'). Brody is ultimately redeemed as heroic (not unlike Dean Martin's 'Dude' in *Rio Bravo*), emerging from the margins to conquer his enemy. He is the one who ultimately rehabilitates the romantic and heroic male values of the western.

Conclusion

This chapter has attempted to illustrate the rarely discussed presence of the western in *Jaws* and how the film engages iconographically, textually and thematically with the genre. Spielberg's Hollywood Renaissance film engages with both the tenets of the New Hollywood and its approach to genre revisionism as well as nostalgically recalling and reaffirming the classical Hollywood western's romantic approach to masculinity and the landscape. Certainly Spielberg softens Benchley's source material. In the novel, Quint has no *USS Indianapolis* backstory to justify his obsession with the shark; he is a pure sadist, gruesomely eviscerating a Blue Shark, relishing feeding it to itself and gleefully revealing his 'special' shark bait: a foetal porpoise cut from the living belly of its mother. Spielberg, who famously didn't like any of the characters in the novel, aligns them to the more romantic, noble and (in the wake of the trauma of Vietnam) more optimistic mythos espoused by directors like Hawks or Ford. The film concludes with a moment of brotherhood and camaraderie as Hooper and Brody (re-emerged from the depths and the dead) share a moment over their fallen brother, Quint, and swim back to land (they ride off into the sunset). It finally closes as the credits roll on an image of the beach, a reminder of and return to the frontier space with which it opened.

Notes

1   De Montfort University, Leicester, UK, 17 June 2015. See https://www.dmu.ac.uk/about-dmu/news/2015/june/film-academics-mark-40th-anniversary-of-blockbuster-jaws.aspx (accessed 3 December 2019).
2   Michael Kaminski, *The Secret History of Star Wars: The Art of Story Telling and the Making of a Modern Epic* (Kingston, Ontario: Legacy Books, 2008), 17.
3   Matthew Carter, *New Perspectives on Hollywood's Frontier Narrative* (Edinburgh: Edinburgh University Press, 2014), 2.
4   Emilio Audissino, *John Williams's Film Music: Jaws, Star Wars, Raiders of the Lost Ark, and the Return of the Classical Hollywood Music Style* (Wisconsin: University of Wisconsin Press, 2014), 108.
5   Peter Biskind, *East Riders Raging Bulls: How The Sex 'n' Drugs 'n' Rock 'n' Roll Generation Saved the World* (London: Bloomsbury, 1998), 265.
6   Warren Buckland, *Directed by Steven Spielberg, Poetics of the Contemporary Blockbuster* (New York: Continuum International Publishing, 2006), 18.

7   Ibid.

8   Carter, *New Perspectives*, 2.

9   Ibid.

10 Michael Pye and Linda Myles, *The Movie Brats: How the Film Generation Took over Hollywood* (New York: Henry Holt, 1984).

11 Carter, *New Perspectives*, 2.

12 Thomas Schatz, 'Cowboy Business', *New York Times Magazine (Film Issue)*, 10 November 2007, https://www.nytimes.com/2007/11/10/magazine/11schatz.html (accessed 26 June 2019).

13 Ibid.

14 Malgorzata Martynuska, 'The Evolution of the Western Genre Resulting from Social Change in the USA', *International English Studies Journal*, 6 (2009): 66.

15 Richard Torry, 'Therapeutic Narrative: *The Wild Bunch*, *Jaws*, and Vietnam', *The Velvet Light Trap*, 31 (Spring 1993): 27–38.

16 Cited in Nigel Andrew, *Nigel Andrew on Jaws: A Bloomsbury Movie Guide* (New York: Bloomsbury USA, 1999), 21.

17 Matthew Costello, 'Rewriting *High Noon*: Transformations in American Popular Political Culture during the Cold War 1952–1968', in Peter Collins and John E. O'Connor, eds, *Hollywood's West: The American Frontier in Film, Television & History* (Lexington: University of Kentucky Press, 2005), 175.

18 Patrick McGee, *From* Shane *to* Kill Bill: *Rethinking the Western* (Oxford: Blackwell, 2007), 115.

19 Lester D. Friedman and Brent Notbohm, eds, *Steven Spielberg Interviews* (Jackson: University of Mississippi Press, 2000), 66.

20 Lester D. Friedman, *Citizen Spielberg* (Chicago: University of Illinois Press, 2006), 58.

21 Ibid.

22 Ibid., 139.

23 Ibid.

24 Ibid.

25 Robert Cumbow, 'The Great White Eating Machine', *Movietone News*, 52 (October 1976).

26 Michael Budd, 'A Home in the Wilderness: Visual Imagery in John Ford's Westerns', *Cinema Journal* 16, no. 1 (Autumn 1976): 62–75.

27 Ibid.

28 Jim Kitses, *Horizons West: Directing the Western from John Ford to Clint Eastwood* (London: British Film Institute, 2004), 30.

29 Ibid.

30 Ibid.

31 Patrick Brereton, *Hollywood Utopia: Ecology in Contemporary American Cinema* (Bristol: Intellect Books, 2004), 92.

32 There will be a similar 'signpost' shortly, when young Michael enters the Brody residence with a bloody hand.

33 Budd, 'A Home in the Wilderness', 63.

34 Ibid., 62.

35 Ibid., 63.

36 Ibid.

37 Costello, 'Rewriting High Noon', 175.

Part Three

Beyond *Jaws*

13

'Just when you thought it was safe …': The *Jaws* sequels

Kathleen Loock

In *Back to the Future Part II* (1989), Marty McFly (Michael J. Fox) travels forward in time from 1985 to the year 2015 and finds himself in a world of hoverboards, flying cars and self-lacing shoes. Stepping into the Hill Valley town square, Marty marvels at the unfamiliar objects but suddenly stops in his tracks when he hears the menacing two-note musical motif from John Williams's iconic *Jaws* theme. Seconds later, a giant shark is coming at him and he screams in horror as he ducks for cover. The moment the shark snaps at Marty, however, it simply disappears. Having found his cool again, Marty only comments 'Shark still looks fake'. As it turns out, the great white is a hologram promoting the latest sequel of Steven Spielberg's 1975 classic *Jaws* that is running at the local 'Holomax' cinema (Figure 13.1). *Jaws 19* is emblazoned in big red letters on the cinema marquee, with the director's name – Max Spielberg – to the right, and the movie tagline – 'This time it's REALLY, REALLY personal' – to the left.

This short scene presents a vision of the future in which cinema is invested in developing and perfecting new technologies (like 3-D holography) yet clings to an old production trend that Marty is already familiar with from the 1980s: sequelization. That *Jaws 19* hits theatres in 2015 (the year of *Jaws*' fortieth anniversary) is a tongue-in-cheek comment about Hollywood's immediate past, present and future as well. After the formidable rise of the sequel in the 1970s and 1980s, *Back to the Future Part II* predicts that sequels are here to stay and that they will endlessly continue familiar stories.[1] The *Jaws* sequel is readily recognizable for Marty and constitutes one of many cross-generational reference points that help him to make sense of the future with what he knows to be the past (i.e. in this time-bending tale, his own 1980s present). The idea of generational continuity is taken up through the name of the fictitious *Jaws 19* director Max Spielberg. Max is the name of Steven Spielberg's real-life son, who was born in 1985. Here, he is presented as belonging to a Hollywood dynasty and as the rightful heir of the long-running *Jaws* franchise. This is another ironic twist, if one considers that Steven Spielberg (who had his breakthrough with *Jaws* and who co-produced *Back to the Future Part II*) was very much against sequels when *Jaws* was released, calling them a 'cheap carnival trick'[2] in an interview.

Figure 13.1 *Back to the Future, Part II*: Marty McFly discovers that the sequel *Jaws 19* runs at the local cinema in the year 2015.

Apart from these purely fictional implications of the 'Holomax' blockbuster, *Jaws 19*'s 'This time it's REALLY, REALLY personal' is a direct reference to *Jaws: The Revenge* (1987), the fourth and (at least for the time being) last *Jaws* movie with the tagline 'This time it's personal'. The addition of two small extra words to the sentence ridicules *Jaws*' seemingly unlimited potential for self-renewal while also drawing attention to the intensification-oriented principle of repetition and innovation that informs sequel production more generally. The central aim of the sequel is to retell an already familiar story in an enhanced and therefore potentially new way[3] because the sequel is reminiscent of its predecessor but cannot repeat the pleasure of the first viewing experience. To compensate for this disadvantage, it 'amplif[ies] certain recurring elements, delivering more of the same with an emphasis on "more"[4] – more violence, more stars, more special effects ... more jaws'.[5] By following a serial logic of one-upmanship, the sequel promises audiences that it will be at least as good as (if not better than) the original. If the sequel employs excessive intensification strategies in order to compete against its predecessor and other genre films, however, it can easily come across as a parody and reinforce a feeling of disappointment that many viewers associate with the sequel in the first place.[6]

In short, *Back to the Future Part II* addresses the widely accepted view, especially among film critics, that *Jaws* was suffering from a bad case of 'sequelitis' – a creativity-hampering epidemic that had supposedly befallen Hollywood and that was to blame for an avalanche of mediocre follow-ups in the 1970s and 1980s. After all, the box office success of *Jaws* alone had spawned altogether three sequels over more than a decade: *Jaws 2* (1978), *Jaws 3-D* (1983) and *Jaws: The Revenge*. At a time when the sequel was still only an afterthought, 'conceived, created, and released after a self-contained movie, which usually delivered closure without built-in sequel options, had proven popular with audiences'.[7] *Back to the Future* tries to avoid the sequel label altogether by claiming to be different from *Jaws* and more like *The Godfather* (1972) and *Star Wars* (1977), which changed course and conceived of themselves as trilogies in the making once their respective first films had earned commercial and critical acclaim. As a trilogy, *Back to the Future* develops and concludes a narrative arc across three parts. It is committed to a work-bound aesthetic, to creating a self-contained 'whole'[8] with its three instalments standing in opposition to the endless stream of sequels that film critics had come to associate with Hollywood's unstoppable recycling mania. *Part II* playfully evokes this criticism of 'sequelitis' and simultaneously eludes it by renouncing its own sequel status. The press kit for *Part III* (1990) picks up on the *Jaws 19* joke, announcing that 'This time it's really, really over'.[9]

This chapter takes a closer look at the idea of Hollywood 'sequelitis' and examines each of the *Jaws* sequels. First, I will explore the context for sequelization in the 1970s and 1980s and the ways in which popular film critics discussed Hollywood's burgeoning trend for sequels at the time. Why did sequels appeal to audiences? What were their main characteristics and how did they differ from earlier instances of serialization in Hollywood? The second part examines the *Jaws* movies. How did the sequels establish narrative continuity? What were their strategies of competition and one-upmanship? Taking both the more general discussion of Hollywood 'sequelitis' and the analysis of the *Jaws* sequels into consideration, I conclude this chapter with remarks on the emergence of the self-reflexive sequel.

'Would you repeat that, please?': Hollywood 'sequelitis'

In 1985, *Village Voice* film critic Jim Hoberman looked back on the past decade and noticed that *Jaws* had turned out to be a real game changer for Hollywood cinema: 'Its presold property and media-blitz saturation release pattern heralded the rise of marketing men and "high concept".[10] The spectacular box office records of *Jaws* and later *Star Wars*[11] encouraged Hollywood's search for the ultimate success formula and favoured the production of sequels. 'So powerful was the urge to duplicate past triumphs,' Hoberman observed, 'that sequelitis ran rampant during the late seventies and early eighties.'[12] According to an old rule of thumb in Hollywood, 'a successful sequel could be expected to do about two-thirds the business of the original'[13] – still an enormous sum considering the money that blockbusters like *Jaws* and *Star Wars* had made at the box office. Then, in the early 1980s, it became apparent that there were movies to which the old rule of thumb no longer applied: *The Empire Strikes Back* (1980), *Rocky III* (1982) and *The Karate Kid, Part II* (1986) earned even more money than their predecessors, indicating the sequel's unlimited money-making potential.[14]

Many studio bosses considered the sequel to be a relatively safe investment in the face of rising production costs during the 1970s and 1980s. The sequel meant fewer financial risks because it reduced the amount of time and money that went into the development of a movie but also because, in a business that depended on fickle audience tastes, the repetition of a successful formula guaranteed that, even if the next movie did not prove to be another hit, it would at least not tank at the box-office.[15]

To be sure, not every sequel came with a built-in guarantee for success, but there was a broad consensus that 'within certain parameters, you can take a sequel to the bank'.[16] Columbia president Frank Price even found that sequels were an economic necessity. In an interview with *Variety*, he said:

> It would be extremely foolish not to pursue the matter of a sequel after a huge hit – it may be fiscal irresponsibility not to. … If you have a goldmine, your responsibility to the stockholders is to mine that gold![17]

Although *Jaws* producers Richard D. Zanuck and David Brown did not resort to that kind of gold-digger rhetoric, they quickly agreed that (by Hollywood logic) the sensational box office success of *Jaws* called for an 'obligatory sequel'.[18]

While moviegoers seemed to confirm the studios' business model as they flocked to the theatres to watch every new sequel, popular film critics vehemently disliked the production trend. Soon they spoke of 'sequelitis' and 'sequelmania', convinced that the sequel epitomized Hollywood's money-grubbing instincts and utter lack of creativity. The fact that moviegoers bought their tickets as they would buy a bar of soap, a toothpaste or any other mass-produced commodity, that is, 'on the basis of a familiar brand name',[19] devastated film critics and it puzzled them, too. Throughout the 1980s, they published articles and think pieces in newspapers and trade publications in which they tried to come to terms with audiences' almost uncanny enthusiasm for Hollywood's sequels.[20] First and foremost, critics blamed television for the inexplicable appeal of the sequel. An entire generation of viewers, they argued, had been conditioned by episodic TV series and television reruns. They loved to see familiar characters again on the big screen and to watch the same stories over and over. The sequel form was also particularly popular with viewers because it functioned as a form of risk management. As Caryn James explained in the *New York Times*, those who had enjoyed a movie, 'minimize[d] the risk of boredom, of wasting their own time and money, by heading for the sequel'.[21]

Although the role that television played in habitualizing cinema audiences may be exaggerated in these accounts, film critics basically identified what Roger Hagedorn has described as the binding effect of serial narratives. According to Hagedorn, serial narratives function 'to promote continued consumption of later episodes …, product loyalty … [,] [and] the very medium in which they appear'.[22] Seriality, then, is more than a structuring device for television; it also pervades newspapers, radio and cinema. As Hagedorn explains, serial narratives 'have been introduced into every medium precisely at the point at which they are emerging as a mass medium: because they constitute a remarkably effective tool for establishing and then developing a substantial consuming public for that medium'.[23]

In Hollywood, serialization was no exclusive feature of the blockbuster era but had been an important means of attracting and engaging mass audiences since the period of early cinema.[24] What was different in the blockbuster era was that Hollywood sequels combined serial elements with high-concept, big-budget event movies in order to attract and engage audiences over many years and decades. To be sure, the sequel's historical roots were well known among popular film critics, who were eager to get to the bottom of the sequel's appeal in the 1970s and 1980s. Many of them remarked that some form of 'sequelitis' had always been a fixture in the film business: from early silent film serials like *The Perils of Pauline* (1914) and *The Exploits of Elaine* (1914), to *Charlie Chan* (1931–1948), *Tarzan* (1932–1948) and *Sherlock Holmes* (1939–1946), as well as the *Thin Man* (1934–1947) and *Andy Hardy* (1937–1946) series of the 1930s and 1940s, to *Ma and Pa Kettle* (1947–1957) and *The Bowery Boys* (1946–1958), whose instalments appealed to cinemagoers until the late 1950s. Considering such lists, the president of 20th Century-Fox, Alan Ladd Jr., told *Variety* in an interview in 1977:

> I don't think there are any more sequels these days than there have been in the past. In fact, sequels used to be more prevalent. You had the Andy Hardy series, the sequels to *Frankenstein* [1931], including, *The Bride of Frankenstein* [1935], and *The Return of Frankenstein* [sic]. It's hard to say what sequels are. You could say the [Clark] Gable/[Spencer] Tracy and [Bing] Crosby/[Bob] Hope pictures were sequels. They just changed the characters' names and situations, but what they did was exactly the same as what they had done in the past.[25]

Ladd, Jr.'s comment is revealing, if one is looking for answers to the more general question: 'What is a sequel?' On the one hand, this quotation and the lists that film critics compiled to historicize the current sequel trend mark the absence of theoretical discussions in the 1970s; on the other hand, they draw attention to the fact that Hollywood's serial forms are historically evolving. Recent academic studies differentiate the sequel from other formulaic productions like the film series or film cycle, defining it as

> a repetition-based continuation or extension of a closed or partly closed narrative that relies on recurring characters, and which has a chronological relationship to its predecessor (events in the sequel occur after events in the earlier film) as well as narrative continuity (what happened in the earlier film continues to be meaningful in the sequel).[26]

For Ladd, Jr., in contrast, the labels are interchangeable. Jennifer Forrest confirms that even today

> [n]either [film critics] nor the industry executives make a distinction between sequels and series, using 'sequel' as a general term that identifies any production that follows on a tail of a successful earlier release, whether that means through a

film that picks up on a story where a previous film left off (the 'true' sequel) or new adventures for recurring characters (the 'true' series).[27]

Such terminological uncertainties as well as the choice of examples underline the historical evolution of the sequel, even if Ladd, Jr. ignores the shifting nature of Hollywood's serial forms.

Accepting the idea that serialization is a historically variable practice,[28] one can identify four major changes that Hollywood's sequel trend introduces during the 1970s and 1980s: (1) the sequel replaces the star vehicle; (2) B movie material is produced on an A movie budget; (3) Roman numerals triumph in Hollywood; and (4) serialization strategies and open-endedness are increasingly more important than narrative closure.

(1) The sequel replaces the star vehicle. In the past, the stars of a successful movie would usually reteam to make a similar movie rather than a sequel. But in the 1970s, studios start to extend the story of a box office hit onto the next movie instead of re-combining its stars or single elements in innovative ways.[29] In an interview with *Variety* in 1978, Universal producer Jennings Lang said about the trend away from the star vehicle and towards the sequel: 'They used to make Paul Newman movies, because there was always an audience of Paul Newman fans willing to see the picture. The sequel is used more as a star now. It's the event that makes it work.'[30]

(2) B movie material is produced on an A movie budget. Except for MGM's *Andy Hardy* and *The Thin Man* series that were produced as A movies, Hollywood's serial forms 'occupied the film industry's bargain basement'.[31] They were 'cheaply produced B-movies ... meant to bolster the bottom half of double-bills'.[32] This was no longer the case in the blockbuster era, as Gregg Kilday observed in the *Los Angeles Herald-Examiner* in 1982:

> What is *new* about the current generation of sequels is the way they've graduated to the top of the studio's release schedules, winning bigger budgets and prominent ad campaigns – particularly during the summer months – shouldering aside more adventurous, idiosyncratic movies that don't boast established stars in pre-sold roles in retreaded plots.[33]

(3) Roman numerals triumph in Hollywood. The most conspicuous change in the 1970s and 1980s, however, concerned sequel titles: Roman and Arabic numerals replaced the well-tried descriptive titling that echoed the sequel's predecessor. As a result, variations like *Son of (Kong)*, *Return of (The Whistler)* or *(The Lone Ranger) Rides Again* quickly became a thing of the past.[34] Because more and more movies had numbers in their titles, many film critics felt 'as if the industry had been taken over by mathematicians'.[35] Some made Francis Ford Coppola responsible for the trend, claiming that he had set a precedent with *The Godfather, Part II* in 1974.[36] Other movies followed the *Godfather* example, apparently in the hope that adding 'part' and a Roman numeral would automatically bestow cultural value on any sequel by proximity to Coppola's immensely successful and critically acclaimed follow-up and because the number, paired with the word 'part', paradoxically distracted from the film's seriality, promising a work-bound continuation geared towards closure instead. *Rocky* (1976), *Superman* (1978), *Halloween* (1978), *Star Trek* (1979), *The Karate Kid* (1984) and *Back to the Future* (1985) numbered their three, four, five or six parts with Roman numerals, whereas the sequels of other franchises, like *Jaws*, carried Arabic numbers in their titles. The *Jaws* sequels are an interesting case because they were so inconsistent with their numbering. Covering the production and release of the second film, the trade press often printed Roman numerals, although the film was marketed with an Arabic two. The third film carried a *3-D* in the title to mark both its position in the franchise and its signature technological innovation. Yet, it was advertised with the Roman III, which featured prominently in the trailer and in the press kit for the movie. And finally, the trade press referred to the last sequel as *Jaws IV*, simply rejecting the correct title, *Jaws: The Revenge.*

(4) Serialization strategies and open-endedness become more important than narrative closure. Sequel production also affected the ways in which stories were being told on the big screen. Movies no longer strove for narrative closure but combined closed and open plot lines that could easily be taken up in a sequel. Such open endings and built-in options for sequelization were characteristic for movies such as *Psycho II* (1983), *Star Trek II: The Wrath of Khan* (1982) and *Rocky III*. They followed a serial strategy that was invested in the future of the franchise and eager to establish audience loyalty for the next upcoming release. For film critics, this was the essence of sequelitis, pure and simple. Apparently, Hollywood had become completely consumed by the possibility of 'developing characters and film properties that could be manufactured in perpetuity'.[37] Or, as Peter Rainer observed in the *Los Angeles Herald-Examiner*:

> In the days when movies were based predominantly on novels and stage plays, plots usually had a beginning, middle and an end. Especially an end. Nowadays, with sequelmania so rampant, it's the rare film that ends conclusively. Plot threads are left dangling, just in case there's room for one more or two or three.[38]

These four new characteristics of the sequel in the blockbuster era largely apply to the movies of the *Jaws* franchise. There is only one big stumbling block that complicates matters: the shark is killed at the end of the first movie so that there is no open plot line and hence no narrative motivation for a sequel. This was one of the reasons why actor Roy Scheider (who plays Police Chief Martin Brody) was reluctant to get involved in *Jaws 2*. In an interview, he told the *LA Times*: 'Look, any sequel is like doing *Hamlet II*.'[39] The film critic's response to this was, of course: '[I]f *Hamlet* had made the money *Jaws* has made, no doubt a way would be found to make *Hamlet II* even though, like Bruce [as the film crew called the mechanical shark], Hamlet did not survive *I*.'[40] Purely commercial considerations like these were obviously the driving force behind the *Jaws* follow-ups, but they did not change the fact that each of the three *Jaws* sequels had to face unique challenges as far as the logic of narrative continuity and the serial dynamics of one-upmanship were concerned.

Narrative continuity and the dynamics of one-upmanship: *Jaws II–IV*

Only a few weeks after the release of *Jaws*, and at the request of Universal Studios, producers Zanuck and Brown started to make plans for a sequel. They reached out to screenwriter Howard Sackler, who had already worked on the first film, and together they pondered over what *Jaws 2* could look like. At first, Sackler thought of a prequel based on the monologue that Quint (Robert Shaw) delivers in the first film. Aboard the *Orca*, during the shark hunt with Brody and marine biologist Matt Hooper (Richard Dreyfuss), Quint talks about 'the men who survived the sinking of the *USS Indianapolis* in the last weeks of World War II, only to be slowly and horribly killed off by marauding sharks as they [floated in] the water waiting for rescue'.[41] MCA president Sidney Sheinberg disliked the prequel idea and proposed a more conventional sequel that would be set in the seaside resort of Amity Island, just like *Jaws*. Sackler then came up with a story that centred on a group of teenagers who go sailing and are attacked by a shark. Police Chief Brody tries to warn his community that there is another great white and eventually sets out alone to hunt the fish and to rescue the teenagers, among them his two sons Mike (Marc Gruner) and Sean (Marc Gilpin).[42]

Jaws 2 illustrates the sequel's difficulty in finding the perfect balance between repetition and innovation. On the one hand, the movie provides novelty to attract viewers a second time around. It does so by introducing teenagers, sail boats and water skiing to the familiar formula and by intensifying elements from the first movie. Director Jeannot Szwarc was convinced that '[T]his time, there had to be more fear – that is, more shark – because, at least subconsciously, the audience would expect more of that kind of suspense and excitement'.[43] The great white shark audiences had seen only sporadically in *Jaws*, but which was nonetheless ever-present in the underwater footage, and John Williams's memorable score appeared more often in the sequel. And the shark could do more than in the first movie: it even attacks a helicopter in one scene. In *Jaws*, Spielberg had deliberately withheld the fish from audiences for almost an hour, showing mostly underwater views from the shark's perspective, a strategy that increased the movie's suspense but had at least as much to do with the technical problems caused by Bruce, the animatronic shark. Szwarc, by contrast, wanted to show the shark as often as possible, for he was aware that the image of the great white coming out of the water for the first time was already familiar to audiences who had seen *Jaws*. The sequel therefore features a new point-of-view shot that puts viewers behind the shark's dorsal fin (Figure 13.2).

The sequel's insistence on showing the shark more often might explain why some critics charged the fish with 'overacting'[44] while others found it to be 'a bit more obviously a mechanical contraption than the real thing'.[45] Or, as Marty McFly would later put it: 'Shark still looks fake.'

On the one hand, then, the sequel bets on strategies of one-upmanship that are geared towards innovation. On the other hand, *Jaws 2* employs repetition in order to establish continuity with its predecessor. The purpose is, of course, to invoke a direct

Figure 13.2 'Behind the fin' point of view.

relationship with the earlier box office hit and ultimately profit from its past success. This is apparent in the film title and the much advertised fact that members of the original *Jaws* team had returned to make the sequel – among them producers Zanuck and Brown, actors Roy Scheider, Lorraine Gary (who reprised her role as Ellen Brody), Murray Hamilton as the Mayor and Jeffrey Kramer as the Deputy. Screenwriter Carl Gottlieb and film composer John Williams were again on board, as well as production designer Joe Alves and the team responsible for the special effects, stunts, sound and PR.[46] On the textual level, repetition ensures that the direct relationship between *Jaws* and *Jaws 2* remains recognizable for audiences. The sequel returns to the same location, focuses once more on Chief Brody and his family, and – above all – it again revolves around the danger of a great white shark lurking beneath the surface of the water. But did it all make sense? Addressing its own logic of narrative continuity, *Jaws 2* posed a crucial question in its trailer that served to reopen *Jaws'* closure, justify the existence of the sequel and to create new suspense. The trailer asked: 'How could there have been only one?' The movie's promotional campaign framed the sequel in a similar manner, with the provocative tagline 'Now, just when you thought it was safe to go back in the water ...', directly linking it to the phenomenon that became known as 'Jawsmania': the fear of sharks and open waters that accompanied the release of the first movie.[47] Repetition of the well-tried *Jaws* formula proved successful as far as audiences were concerned. Critics, however, pointed out that, even if *Jaws 2* had turned out to be fairly entertaining, it was not plausible *because* it recycled so many elements of the first film. '[O]ne wonders why Amity Island attracts Great Whites like a picknick blanket draws ants,' one of them wrote,[48] and others wondered how it was possible that Brody still had to convince the same mayor, businessmen, tourists and community that there was a shark threatening their lives. Why did no one believe him after everything that had happened in the first movie? These lapses did not prevent *Jaws 2* from turning into one of the commercially most successful sequels of all times, an outcome that paved the way for the next instalment (Figure 13.3).

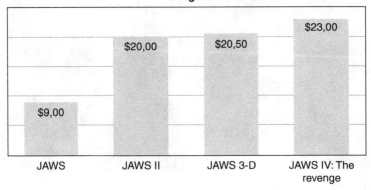

Budget

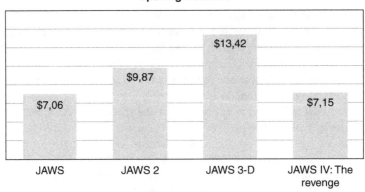

Opening weekend

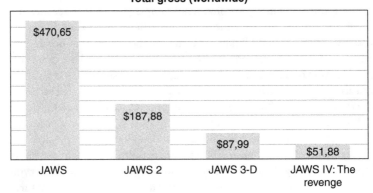

Total gross (worldwide)

Figure 13.3 Overview of the budgets and box office of all four *Jaws* movies (in millions of US dollars).

Jaws 3-D, directed by Joe Alves (the production designer of the first two films), put even more emphasis on innovation than *Jaws 2*. It relied on a new location, new characters and new technology (3-D) to tell the familiar fish-eats-man story as a new story. Even though producer Rupert Hitzig stressed that the sequel would not follow up on the first film,[49] *Jaws 3-D* still clings to familiar elements. This time, the story centres on Mike and Sean, the two grown-up sons of Police Chief Martin Brody. Mike is an engineer at a SeaWorld theme park in Florida that is about to open the 'Undersea Kingdom', a new attraction featuring underwater glass tunnels. The only problem is that not one but two sharks enter SeaWorld's man-made lagoon: a mother and her baby. Trapped inside the theme park, the mother shark attacks several people and destroys the underwater control room, but Mike eventually succeeds in killing the shark with a hand grenade. The all-new cast – Dennis Quaid plays Mike and John Putch his brother Sean – is complete with Mike's love interest Kathryn Morgan (a marine biologist played by Bess Armstrong) and her two trained dolphins Cindy and Sandy, manager Calvin Bouchard (Louis Gossett, Jr.) as well as underwater film-maker and photographer Phillip FitzRoyce (Simon MacCorkindale).

Newsweek critic David Ansen simply asked: 'Does anybody give a flying shark fin about the "plot" of *Jaws 3-D*? We all know what we're in for: the old bite and run.'[50] The major draw (and biggest innovation) of the sequel was not the plot but its use of 3-D technology, which, according to the movie's tagline 'The third dimension is terror', opened up a new, even more terrifying perspective on the *Jaws* formula.[51] The 'immersion effect' *Jaws 3-D* promised to deliver was additionally enhanced by the movie's theme park setting and 'movie ride' aesthetic.[52] The trailer emphasized the new, immersive quality of the latest sequel. It begins with a black screen and the sound of splashing waves, before voice-over narration establishes the connection between all three *Jaws* movies:

> *I* terrified you like nothing you have ever experienced, when it captured your imagination and tapped your fear like no movie before it. Then ... just when you thought it was safe to go back in the water, *II* continued the legend and spread the fear. Next summer, nature's most terrifying creature takes on an all new dimension, in an all new adventure ... and for the first time, the terror of *Jaws* will not stop at the edge of the screen.

With the mention of each movie, Roman numerals appear (first *I*, then *II* and *III*), and as gradually more line segments are added on the black screen, they open the view onto the open sea behind it and, finally, onto the approaching white shark.

Containing its main attraction behind the Roman numerals, the trailer stirs interest by showcasing how the movies build upon, continue and surpass each other. With *Jaws 3-D* the franchise finally reaches a point where the shark is no longer bound to the screen, coming right at the audiences (Figure 13.4). *Newsweek*'s David Ansen quipped that '[b]y the time of *Jaws 4*, no doubt patrons will be required to bring towels',[53] apparently assuming that the franchise would have to continue to reinvent and surpass itself if it wanted to remain profitable in the future. Ansen further remarked that 'the

Figure 13.4 In the trailer for *Jaws 3-D* (1983), the shark is swimming directly towards the audience.

revival of the 3-D phenomenon must have seemed a godsend to the *Jaws* producers, the inevitable bait to lure patrons back into the bloody water for a third go-round'.[54]

Jaws 3-D was probably the most expensive and most eagerly anticipated movie of a short-lived 3-D film cycle that hit cinemas in the early 1980s. The surprise success of the low-budget spaghetti western spoof *Comin' at Ya!* (1981) had set the trend in motion, and after *Friday the 13th Part III* (1982) racked up big box office numbers, 3-D technology became a favourite method for reviving horror and other franchises (for a few years at least). Third parts were perfect because 3-D could replace the Part III, or the Roman or Arabic number in the title. In that respect, *Jaws 3-D* was no exception. If the 3-D instalments of horror franchises like *Friday the 13th* generally featured 'a transgressive use of off-the-screen effects, with implements of destruction and body parts repeatedly thrust out into the audience space',[55] *Jaws 3-D*'s director of photography James Contner claimed to employ the technology 'as enhancement, not a gimmick'.[56]

Critics were still disappointed by the results, even though some of them praised the underwater scenes and a new camera perspective – this time from the point of view of the victim inside the shark's jaws. According to *Variety*, the *Jaws* franchise had 'reached its end and nadir with this surprisingly tepid 3-D version'.[57] *Jaw 3-D* just strayed too far from the original, the review continued, and 'as the bellwether 3-D movie of the year, it doesn't point to much of a future for three dimensional film. If 3-D can't enhance a pic about a devouring shark, what's left except lame novelty?'[58] Despite negative reviews, the sequel made over $13 million on its opening weekend and emerged as one of the commercially most successful movies of 1983.[59] However, the numbers are misleading because if one compares the total gross of each *Jaws* film, it becomes evident that the overall profits decreased significantly with the third part. Worldwide, *Jaws 3-D* earned about $100 million less than *Jaws 2* and almost $400 million less than *Jaws*. This trend continued with the final sequel, *Jaws: The Revenge*, which was released in 1987.

Jaws: The Revenge drew attention to an underlying dilemma of the franchise: by now, the event movies about a man-eating shark were conceived as a multigenerational family saga. This sequel largely ignores its direct predecessor, *Jaws 3-D* (the Brody sons are played by new actors and have different jobs), and initially returns to the location of the first two films: Amity Island. Chief Brody's widow Ellen (who is again played by Lorraine Gary) still lives in the seaside resort, as does her grown-up son Sean (Mitchell Anderson), who works as a police deputy. It is Christmas time and while a children's choir is singing carols, Sean is attacked and killed by yet another shark that is terrorizing the Amity Island coast. After Sean's death, Ellen decides to move in with her other son Mike (Lance Guest), because he works as a marine biologist in the Bahamas, where great white sharks have never been sighted. Ellen meets the pilot Hoagie (Michael Caine) and falls in love with him, yet their young romance is overshadowed by a great white that roams the tropical waters. Ellen is convinced that the fish has followed her to the Bahamas in order to take revenge on her family, and when her little granddaughter Thea (Judith Barsi) barely survives an attack, she steals a boat and heads out to the sea to confront the shark herself. Hoagie, Mike and his colleague Jake (Mario Van Peebles) go after Ellen in Hoagie's plane, everyone is in life-threatening danger and eventually they manage to kill the shark using a complicated electrical contraption (Figure 3.5).

Critics like Roger Ebert have discussed the logical problems of the film in great detail;[60] Caryn James of the *New York Times* simply wondered: 'Why hasn't this family moved to Nebraska?'[61] Apart from its flaws, this fourth part, with the tagline 'This time it's personal,' makes perfect sense as a sequel. All *Jaws* films revolve around the same

Figure 13.5 Attack of the great white in *Jaws: The Revenge* (1987).

family; the Brodys are a constant while the great white shark is a different one each time. Already in *Jaws 2*, police chief Martin Brody thinks that the new 26-foot shark that is attacking his seaside resort wants to avenge the death of the fish he helped to kill in the first movie. And even though, a marine biologist explains, 'Sharks don't take things personally, Mr. Brody', the groundwork for part four is laid in this very scene. Basically, each great white of the franchise was after the Brodys, and the personal vendetta of this sequel's specimen, which literally leaps out of the water and can roar like a lion, involves another gesture of one-upmanship, of taking up and surpassing a familiar plot element from earlier renditions.

Sepia-tinted flashbacks, which Caryn James described as 'a bad case of *Jaws 1* worship',[62] also serve to establish the narrative continuity of the sequel. Flashbacks and picture frames with photos of Chief Brody are attempts to make Roy Scheider a part of this sequel despite his absence, to keep the memory of the original *Jaws* alive and thereby link *Jaws: The Revenge* more closely to the aura of Spielberg's successful blockbuster. The break in continuity with *Jaws 3-D* (which had strayed too far away from the first two movies) and the return to the familiar Amity Island setting work towards the same goal. However, these efforts did not achieve the desired effect: instead of heart-stopping suspense, many scenes in *Jaws: The Revenge* created unintended humour, and the flashbacks and references to *Jaws* just reminded audiences of how much better the original one was.[63] Film critics tore this sequel to pieces, complaining that *Jaws: The Revenge* 'wastes some good performances on an implausible, poorly paced story',[64] that Michael Caine 'manages to provide at least a little suspense [...] by raising the question: Will an Oscar winner be allowed to become fish food?'[65] and that '[t]his special-effects Great White is so transparently a machine that it could well be a shark Terminator'.[66] All efforts to act within the logic of narrative continuity and the serial dynamics of one-upmanship seemed to have reached a dead end with this sequel.

Conclusion: The self-reflexive sequel

The Godfather, Part II is usually considered the best film that Hollywood produced during the 'sequelmania' of the 1970s and 1980s: an aesthetically legitimate sequel that expands and enriches the first part. Todd Berliner associates the movie's tremendous success with its 'inventive approach to sequelisation', namely the brilliant feat of incorporating 'into its plot the very nostalgia, dissatisfaction, and sense of loss that sequels traditionally generate in their viewers'.[67] *The Godfather, Part II* is not only considered to be the best sequel but also an exception to the rule. Film critics normally held little hope for sequels, commenting often and in very different ways on Hollywood's 'sequelitis'. In a humorous piece for example, Alphonse Simonaitis suggested that genre hybrids could solve the problem of endless repetition: 'Instead of sequels with such lame titles like *Jaws XXIII*, it might be more rewarding to combine two films and achieve a totally new concept.'[68] For example: '*The Jaws of the Godfather*: Mafia don "Big Tuna" threatens swimmers in a coastal resort until he is finally reeled in and packed in the Big Can.'[69]

This pitch certainly promises to add an interesting twist to a worn-out formula. At the same time, it illustrates that the sequelization of *Jaws* poses greater challenges than that of *The Godfather* or other franchises simply because there is very little room for variation. Or, as David Ansen put it: 'Let's face it: an enraged shark is not one of your more versatile villains. Compared to a mad slasher with a knife, say, or a demon-driven child, its repertoire is severely limited.'[70] Each sequel relied on a more sophisticated and bigger (but also increasingly artificial looking) mechanical shark in order to compete against its predecessor. But that did not change the fact that the narrative potential of the fish-eats-man story was basically exhausted after the first sequel. 3-D technology eventually extended the lifespan of the franchise and arguably justified the production of another sequel, but that did not change the fact that *Jaws* was theme-driven rather than character-driven, which now roughly translates into sequel-proof vs. sequelizable in Hollywood.[71] Universal had initially planned to produce a parody after *Jaws 2*, as Mike Clark and Bill Cotter reported in the monthly science fiction film magazine *Starlog*.

> [Universal execs] felt comedy was a viable choice, especially since NBC's *Saturday Night Life* had already featured a *Jaws* satire, with a foam-rubber 'land shark' (Chevy Chase) menacing the Not-Ready-For-Primetime Players. This shark did something that beloved 'Bruce' could never attempt: it walked, made telephone calls, delivered candygrams and imitated voices![72]

The proposed title for the parody was *Jaws 3, People 0*, which revolved around a shark that sabotaged the filming of a new *Jaws* sequel. For over two years people worked on the project – until Universal shelved it and focused on a serious alternative instead, namely *Jaws 3-D*.[73]

Unlike other sequels that were becoming 'progressively more coy and self-conscious'[74] since the early 1980s, the *Jaws* franchise takes itself seriously until the very end. There is a scene in *Rocky III*, for instance, in which Rocky (Sylvester Stallone) is in bed with Adrian (Talia Shire) and they sing a few bars of the movie's soundtrack. And then there is John McClane (Bruce Willis), who comments on what is happening to him in *Die Hard 2* (1990), the first sequel of the successful franchise. Stuck in a very similar situation, he wonders, 'Oh man, I can't fucking believe this. Another basement, another elevator. How can the same shit happen to the same guy twice?' Such self-reflexive moments have become much more pronounced (and ironic) in today's blockbusters, sequels and remakes in particular.[75] Yet none of the *Jaws* follow-ups contains instances in which it explicitly reflects on its own status as a sequel, even though each one of them tries very hard to maintain the narrative continuity with its predecessors and to surpass it at the same time. It is only in *Back to the Future Part II* – a sequel that was released two years after *Jaws: The Revenge* – that we find such a comment on *Jaws*.

Notes

This chapter is a translated and slightly revised version of Kathleen Loock, 'Zwischen Jawsmania und Sequelitis: Die Fortsetzungen von *Jaws*', in Wieland Schwanebeck, ed., *Der weiße Hai Revisited: Steven Spielbergs Jaws und die Geburt eines amerikanischen Albtraums* (Berlin: Bertz+Fischer, 2015), 231–44.

1 On the rise of the sequel, see Kathleen Loock, 'The Sequel Paradox: Repetition, Innovation, and Hollywood's Hit Film Formula', *Film Studies*, 17, no. 1 (Autumn 2017): 92–110.

2 Spielberg Spanks Sequels as 'Cheap Carnival Trick', *Variety*, 29 October 1975: 30.

3 Andreas Jahn-Sudmann and Frank Kelleter, 'Die Dynamik serieller Überbietung: Amerikanische Fernsehserien und das Konzept des Quality TV', in Frank Kelleter, ed., *Populäre Serialität: Narration – Evolution – Distinktion. Zum seriellen Erzählen seit dem 19. Jahrhundert* (Bielefeld: Transcript-Verlag, 2012), 207. In their work on US American 'quality TV' series, Andreas Jahn-Sudmann and Frank Kelleter have introduced the concept of one-upmanship to describe 'the repeated intensification of successfully established strategies of distinction'. It is closely tied to television series' need to constantly reinvent themselves in direct competition with themselves (intra-serial distinction) and with other series (inter-serial distinction). This serial logic is not exclusive to the television series; rather, it also informs the production of sequels and remakes. On the remake, see Kathleen Loock, 'The Return of the Pod People: Remaking Cultural Anxieties in *Invasion of the Body Snatchers*', in Kathleen Loock and Constantine Verevis, eds, *Film Remakes, Adaptations and Fan Productions. Remake/Remodel* (Basingstoke: Palgrave Macmillan, 2012), 134. On the sequel: Todd Berliner, 'The Pleasures of Disappointment: Sequels and The Godfather Part II', *Journal of Film and Video*, 53, nos 2–3 (2001): 109; Lianne McLarty, ' "I'll Be Back": Hollywood, Sequelization, and History', in Paul Budra and Betty A. Schellenberg, eds, *Part Two: Reflections on the Sequel* (Toronto: University of Toronto Press, 1998), 204–5.

4 Stuart Henderson, *The Hollywood Sequel: History and Form, 1911–2010* (London: BFI, 2014), 145.

5 Initially, *More Jaws* was proposed as title for the first *Jaws* sequel, but, according to co-producer David Brown, the idea was rejected as being 'rather captious'. Brown quoted in Jeff Melvoin, 'Capping the Teeth of *Jaws II*', *Women's Wear Daily*, 6 October 1978: 13.

6 For most critics and many film scholars, disappointment is a standard reaction to Hollywood sequels, which they view as nothing else but 'exploitative products that cash in on the popularity of earlier blockbusters, invariably inferior to the original films' (Berliner, 'The Pleasures of Disappointment', 107). Some even speak of disappointment as an 'unavoidable consequence' (ibid., 108) of sequelization, a shortcoming that is inherent in the form. Cf. Paul Budra and Betty A. Schellenberg, 'Introduction', in Budra and Schellenberg, *Part Two*, 3–18; Jim Hoberman, 'Ten Years that Shook the World', *American Film* 10 (1985): 34–59. Recent studies contest such ideas, however, seeking instead to understand the aesthetics, narrative structures and cultural work of the sequel. See, e.g., Carolyn Jess-Cooke, *Film Sequels: Theory and Practice from Hollywood to Bollywood* (Edinburgh: Edinburgh University Press, 2009); Carolyn Jess-Cooke and Constantine Verevis, eds, *Second Takes: Critical Approaches*

to the Film Sequel (Albany, NY: SUNY Press, 2010); Henderson, *The Hollywood Sequel*; Loock, 'The Sequel Paradox'.

7 Loock, 'The Sequel Paradox', 93.

8 On how the promise of wholeness or containment runs counter to the broken, multiple nature of serial narratives, see Sean O'Sullivan, 'Serials and Satisfaction', *Romanticism and Victorianism on the Net*, 63, 22 July 2014, https://www.erudit.org/fr/revues/ravon/2013-n63-ravon01450/1025614ar/ (accessed 12 July 2019).

9 'Production Notes', *Back to the Future Part III*, Press Kit (Universal Studios, 1990), 17.

10 Hoberman, 'Ten Years', 36.

11 *Star Wars* surpassed *Jaws* to become the highest grossing film.

12 Hoberman, 'Ten Years', 38.

13 Gregg Kilday, 'Sequels: Will It Play Again in Peoria?' *Los Angeles Herald-Examiner*, 4 June 1982: 6.

14 Ibid., 6; Charles Fleming, 'Try, Try, Try Again: If Your Film Works the First Time – Sequelize', *Los Angeles Herald-Examiner*, 28 May 1988, C1, C5.

15 Loock, 'The Sequel Paradox', 96.

16 Fleming, 'Try, Try, Try Again', C1.

17 Quoted in Lilly Lipton, 'Sequels: Or Trying to Make a Hit Pay off Again', *Variety*, 31 October 1978: 86.

18 Brown quoted in Melvoin, 'Capping the Teeth', 13.

19 David Kehr, 'Once Is Never Enough: Titles, Not Actors, Are the Stars of the Eighties', *Chicago* (September 1983): 138. See also Kilday, 'Sequels', 6.

20 For a detailed analysis of the critics' reactions, see Loock, 'The Sequel Paradox'.

21 Caryn James, 'Twice-Told Tales Can Cast a Spell', *New York Times*, 6 August 1989: 28. See also Aljean Harmetz, 'Boom Summer for Film Sequels', *New York Times*, 3 May 1989, C19; Kilday, 'Sequels', 6; and Leslie Wayne, 'Hollywood Sequels Are Just the Ticket', *New York Times*, 18 July 1982: 1, 17.

22 Roger Hagedorn, 'Doubtless to Be Continued: A Brief History of Serial Narrative', in Robert C. Allen, ed., *To Be Continued … Soap Operas around the World* (London: Routledge, 1995), 28–9.

23 Ibid., 28.

24 Cf. Hagedorn, 'Doubtless to Be Continued'; Christian Junklewitz and Tanja Weber, 'Die Cineserie: Geschichte und Erfolg von Filmserien im postklassischen Kino', in Robert Blanchet et al., eds, *Serielle Formen: Von den frühen Film-Serials zu aktuellen Quality-TV- und Online-Serien* (Marburg: Schüren, 2011), 337–56.

25 Quoted in Lipton, 'Sequels', 86.

26 Loock, 'The Sequel Paradox', 94. See also Budra and Schellenberg, 'Introduction', 7; Jennifer Forrest, 'Introduction', in Jennifer Forrest, ed., *The Legend Returns and Dies Harder Another Day: Essays on Film Series* (Jefferson, NC: McFarland, 2008), 5–7; Jess-Cooke, *Film Sequels*, 3–4. Henderson, *The Hollywood Sequel*, 3–5. On the film series, see Jennifer Forrest, ed., *The Legend Returns and Dies Harder Another Day: Essays on Film Series* (Jefferson, NC: McFarland, 2008); Junklewitz and Weber, 'Die Cineserie'. For a detailed discussion of the film cycle, see Amanda Ann Klein, *American Film Cycles: Reframing Genres, Screening Social Problems, and Defining Subcultures* (Austin: University of Texas Press, 2011).

27 Forrest, 'Introduction', 7.

28 More generally on this idea, see Frank Kelleter and Kathleen Loock, 'Hollywood Remaking as Second-Order Serialization', in Frank Kelleter, ed., *Media of Serial Narrative* (Columbus: Ohio State University Press, 2017).

29 Peter Rainer, 'Sequelmania: Is It Throttling Hollywood?' *Los Angeles Herald-Examiner*, 8 July 1983, D7.

30 Quoted in Lipton, 'Sequels', 86.

31 Kilday, 'Sequels', 6.

32 Ibid.

33 Ibid.

34 Bernard A. Drew, *Motion Picture Series and Sequels: A Reference Guide* (New York: Garland, 1990), 8.

35 Stephen Prince, 'Introduction: Movies and the 1980s', in Stephen Prince, ed., *American Cinema of the 1980s: Themes and Variations* (New Brunswick, NJ: Rutgers University Press, 2007), 2.

36 Charles Champlin, ' "Would You Repeat That Please?": Sequels – A Fresh Deluge', *Los Angeles Times*, 28 May 1989: 3.

37 Ibid.

38 Rainer, 'Sequelmania', D7.

39 Quoted in Michael Dempsey, 'The Return of *Jaws*', *American Film* 3, no. 8 (1978): 31.

40 Ibid.

41 Ray Loynd, *The Jaws 2 Log* (New York: Dell, 1978), 25.

42 Cf. ibid., 23–6.

43 Quoted in *Jaws 2 – Movie Program* (Universal Studios, 1978).

44 David Sterritt, 'Shark Found Guilty of Overacting in Sequel', *Christian Science Monitor*, 5 July 1978: 22.

45 John Azzopardi, 'A Great White Too Many', *East Side Express*, 22 June 1978: 11.

46 *Jaws 2 – Movie Program*; 'Production Notes', in *Jaws 2: Press Information* (Universal Studios, 1978), 1, 5–9.

47 On 28 July 1975, *Newsweek* wrote about the 'Jawsmania' phenomenon: 'Its symptoms are saucered eyes, blanched faces and a certain tingly anxiety about going near the water.' Peter Goldman, 'Jawsmania: The Great Escape', *Newsweek*, 28 July 1975: 16.

48 Azzopardi, 'A Great White Too Many', 11.

49 'Produktionsnotizen', in *Der Weiße Hai–3D* (Werbematerial, Universal Studios, 1983), 4.

50 David Ansen, 'Slack Jawed', *Newsweek*, 25 July 1983: 41.

51 Cf. 'Produktionsnotizen', 4.

52 See Constance Balides, 'Immersion in the Virtual Ornament: Contemporary "Movie Ride" Films', in David Thorburn and Henry Jenkins, eds, *Rethinking Media Change: The Aesthetics of Transition* (Cambridge, MA: MIT Press, 2003), 316–36.

53 Ansen, 'Slack Jawed', 41.

54 Ibid.

55 Ray Zone, *3-D Revolution: The History of Modern Stereoscopic Cinema* (Lexington: University Press of Kentucky, 2012), 115.

56 Quoted in Linda Lovely, '*Jaws 3-D*', *American Cinematographer* 7 (1983): 60.

57 Loyn, '*Jaws 3-D*', *Variety*, 27 July 1983: 21.

58 Ibid.

59 Zone, *3-D Revolution*, 119.

60 Roger Ebert, 'It's Nothing to 'Jaw' about', *New York Post*, 18 July 1987: 18.

61 Caryn James, 'Film: *Jaws the Revenge*, The Fourth in the Series', *New York Times*, 18 July 1987: 15.

62 Ibid.

63 Cf. Juliann Garey, '*Jaws: The Revenge*', *The Village Voice*, 4 August 1987: 60.

64 Camb, '*Jaws: The Revenge*', *Variety*, 22 July 1987.

65 Hal Hinson, '*Jaws* Without the Bite: The Shark Takes Arms against a Sea of Troubles', *Washington Post*, 17 July 1987.

66 Desson Howe, 'Gag Me with a Shark', *Washington Post*, 26 July 1987.

67 Berliner, 'The Pleasures of Disappointment', 108.

68 Alphonse Simonaitis, 'Humor: He Sees Sequels and Asks Why Not', *Los Angeles Times*, 8 April 1979: 58.

69 Ibid.

70 Ansen, 'Slack Jawed', 41.

71 Cf. Hank Gallo, 'Hollywood's Instant Replays', *New York Daily News*, 20 January 1991: 15. See also Loock, 'The Sequel Paradox', 104.

72 Mike Clark and Bill Cotter, 'Shark's Alive!: The Terrors of *Jaws 3-D*', *Starlog* (September 1983): 52.

73 Ibid.

74 Kilday, 'Sequels', 6.

75 I have discussed this phenomenon for the current cycle of remakes that are based on 1980s television shows and films such as *21 Jump Street*, *The A-Team*, *Footloose* and *The Karate Kid*. See Kathleen Loock, 'Retro-Remaking: The 1980s Film Cycle in Contemporary Hollywood Cinema', in Amanda Ann Klein and R. Barton Palmer, eds, *Multiplicities: Cycles, Sequels, Remakes and Reboots in Film & Television* (Austin: University of Texas Press, 2016).

14

Martha's Vineyard revisited: The making-ofs and their narrative strategies

Felix Lempp

Brody, Quint – and Bruce! The making-of as disclosure of the production process?

On its fourteenth day of release following its opening on June 20, 1975, Jaws *turned a profit. Sixty-four days later, on September 5, it surpassed Francis Ford Coppola's* The Godfather *[1972] to become the most successful film in motion picture history to that date.*[1]

It is hard to express the immediate success of Hollywood's first big blockbuster in a more succinct way. But this sober description, based solely on box office takings, does not come close to reflecting the wave of enthusiasm caused by Steven Spielberg's third big-screen feature film after the cinema release of *Duel* (1971) and *The Sugarland Express* (1974). It is highly unlikely that the instant success of *Jaws* came as an enormous surprise to those involved in the production as they later claimed.[2] However, the continuing cultural impact of the 'phenomenon of *Jaws*' today calls for explanation. While many studies stress the timeless character of the conflicts and motifs dealt with in the movie – for example, the fight of heroes against evil, endangered family models or the eerie depth of sexuality[3] – film fans' interest focuses largely on the film-making process. It is by looking at the phenomenon ex post that many viewers wonder if a movie with such an exceptional history of *reception* might have an equally fascinating history of *production*. Indeed, in the case of *Jaws*, such a history exists. In the internet age, colourful legends attributed to the cruel hardships of shooting *Jaws* on Martha's Vineyard have perpetuated to such an extent that interviewers have felt the need to confront the former cast and crew predominantly with questions about the veracity of these anecdotes.[4] Therefore, film expertise in the case of *Jaws* not only consists of knowledge about the diegetic content of the movie but also includes the persistently investigated lore of the production adepts.[5] Therefore, the well-versed fan is not only able to name Brody, Quint and Hooper in his or her sleep, but s/he also knows the off-screen name of the film's actual protagonist – Bruce, the mechanical shark, which members of the cast and crew named after Spielberg's lawyer.

The fan community's curiosity is an indication of the 'ironic inversion [that] the narrative of how a film was created can seem as compelling, as expressive, perhaps as consequential, as the creation that appeared in theaters'.[6] This curiosity has since been fed by an inestimable flood of official, semi-official and non-official making-ofs of *Jaws*,[7] which differ not only in extent and production expense but also in terms of their mediality. Besides the many filmic formats, one also finds an array of written making-ofs, such as interviews with the cast, crew and producers, or production reports in book format.[8] Among the latter, *The Jaws Log* (1975) – written by one of the scriptwriters on *Jaws*, Carl Gottlieb – is arguably the most famous. It is not only Hollywood insiders who have published their retrospective account of the summer of 1974 and its aftermath: Edith Blake's *On Location ... On Martha's Vineyard. The Making of the Movie Jaws* (1975) and Matt Taylor's collected memories, *Jaws: Memories from Martha's Vineyard* (2011), represent the perspective of the inhabitants of Martha's Vineyard within the making-of genre.[9] The reader of these partly anecdotal books learns, among other things, how often Mrs. Kinter (Lee Fierro) had to slap Chief Brody (Roy Scheider) until Spielberg was satisfied (seventeen times) or that the quarrel between crew and locals escalated to such an extent that one morning the crew found a dead fish placed in front of the production office – *The Godfather* sends its regards![10]

The common factor in all these different making-of formats is the promised disclosure of the production process of *Jaws* and, as a consequence, the chance of a glimpse behind the scenes of the dream factory that is Hollywood. This 'utter dependency on a prior text' combined with a 'surprising surfeit of shapes and sizes' leads Paul Arthur to describe making-ofs as 'the perfect postmodern movie genre'.[11] While the history of (filmic) making-of documentaries dates back at least to the beginning of film as an art form,[12] the breakthrough of the genre in its contemporary manifestation is closely linked to the rise of the DVD format in the mid-1990s.[13] With regard to the publishing of movies on DVD, Craig Hight observes a double-tracked strategy:[14] for viewers only interested in watching the movie itself, the distributors offer the standard edition. Additional material, which includes making-of sequences and is published in special editions DVD-sets, addresses aficionados willing to pay for their acquisitions' multimedial paratexts.[15] Particularly the special editions of bigger film productions tend to contain an elaborately produced documentary. However, in the meantime, quite cheaply assembled making-ofs also play a key role in the process of promoting a new blockbuster: 'In the guise of presenting a production narrative, such texts in fact serve as extended trailers,' as Hight puts it.[16] Therefore, the goals of different making-ofs appear to be as diverse as their production expenses. While lavish documentaries often depict difficult development histories in a critical manner,[17] many low-priced and quickly produced making-ofs just capitalize on the 'marketing potential of the medium'.[18] However, whether making-ofs are discerning analysis or largely uncritical promotion of the latest blockbuster, a closer look at making-of practices in the film business greatly undermines the objective disclosure of the production process that the genre so often promises. At times in which the marketing budgets of Hollywood blockbusters are now bigger than the overall budget of *Jaws*, it becomes clear that making-ofs aestheticize and thereby stage the very production processes they pretend to describe objectively – a process quite worthy of the attention of cultural studies.[19]

This chapter will not re-narrate the familiar production history of *Jaws*. Instead, it aims to show that every description of a production process implies the latter's (re)construction by means of narrative strategies. Any *Jaws* making-of is, first and foremost, an attempt to organize one's own or others' memories and legendary memorabilia. Each return to Martha's Vineyard therefore narrates its own history about the coming-into-being of the 'father of blockbuster cinema'. The chapter covers three of these narrations, beginning with Carl Gottlieb's *The Jaws Log*, which was published almost simultaneously with the movie. The chapter will then explore the dramaturgical composition of two filmic making-ofs, which were created a good many years later, when *Jaws* had long become an established cultural phenomenon: *The Making of Steven Spielberg's Jaws* (1995) was released on the movie's 20th anniversary, while *The Shark Is Still Working: The Impact and Legacy of Jaws* (2007) examines the *Jaws* phenomenon a decade later.

The production of *Jaws* as adventure of a sworn comradeship – *The Jaws Log* (1975)

Jaws is a rewarding subject for any making-of documentary not only because of its spectacular success but also because this movie was Spielberg's breakthrough. The director was not an established brand at the beginning of the shooting and therefore the success of *Jaws* was far from guaranteed. Despite this, an integral part of all the production narratives is the claim that everyone involved in the filming sensed that they were participating in something extraordinary from the very beginning. Thus, Peter Benchley, the author of the 1974 novel on which the movie is based, emphasizes in his preface to the 25th anniversary edition of Gottlieb's *Jaws Log*: 'All of us ... knew that we were witnessing something memorable, exciting, probably unprecedented, and, at times, altogether weird.'[20] In just a few words, Benchley here evokes the dramaturgical scheme that Gottlieb then delivers in the following pages. The scriptwriter portrays the emergence of *Jaws* as an exciting, in part highly difficult and memorable piece of cinematic pioneer work. His introduction to the *Log's* anniversary edition of 2001 is of particular interest for the following analysis as it contains specific reflections on the problems of fixing memories by writing – that is, of producing a making-of narrative. For Gottlieb, these problems are caused mainly by the challenge of reconciling objective events and subjective memories.[21] Hence, he starts his making-of narrative with the remarkable admission that the book presents his subjective perspective on the shooting of *Jaws* and he ends his introduction with the sentence: 'This was how I saw it.'[22] Special consideration should be given here to the use of the past tense. Gottlieb states that his narrative presents the all-in-all unchanged text of 1975. Because of this, *The Jaws Log* preserves even in the 2001 edition the perspective of the younger scriptwriter still unaffected by the movie's exceptional later success, a perspective that may not necessarily coincide with Gottlieb's retrospect 25 years later. *This was how*

I saw it – with this remark, Gottlieb witnesses the following *Log* with the authority of the scriptwriter. However, at the same time, he historicizes it as the subjective narration of his younger self – which, in a way, relativizes the making-of narration of *The Jaws Log*.

A closer look at the composition of the actual *Log* reveals that Gottlieb's writing, typical for the making-of genre, reproduces the chronology of the production process. The acquisition of the film rights and the adaption of Peter Benchley's novel are followed by the budgeting process and the casting of the actors. Nine chapters cover the actual shooting on Martha's Vineyard, while the process of post-production and the first previews of the movie are dealt with in one last section. The main part of the narrative (chapters 7 to 15, pp. 71–174) concentrates on the actual shooting of the movie between May and September 1974. One striking aspect here is the fact that Gottlieb follows the dramaturgic composition of his cinematic model. While reporting very little on the onshore shooting, he focuses mainly on the filming of the chronologically last part of the movie on the open seas. The struggle between film crew and nature thereby mirrors Brody's, Quint's and Hooper's fight against the great white. Thus, like Spielberg's movie, *The Jaws Log* is the narrative of a heroic battle whose dramaturgy unfolds by first establishing and then solving a variety of problems faced by cast and crew.

The first problems, which occur at the very beginning of shooting, are caused by the conditions on the island, which is depicted partly as alien and at times even hostile. In Gottlieb's description, cast and crew had to deal with the islanders, the 'stubborn Yankees on the Vineyard',[23] who lived in a 'baroque superstructure' of friendships and enmities – established over many generations and hardly decodable for outsiders.[24] In fact, the various local communities did permit the shooting after long and thorough bureaucratic disputes, '[b]ut dissatisfaction, legal unpleasantness, and plain old sabotage and dirty tricks were never far away'.[25] A picture of the production team's solidarity (which they set against this hostile environment) recurring in Gottlieb's *The Jaws Log* is the almost daily communal dinner of the film team at their residence on Martha's Vineyard.[26] Whenever Gottlieb's narrative mentions the pressure on the production team, it nearly always depicts it as emerging from the high goals of the crew and cast or else from the problems created by the island and its inhabitants.[27] Little does *The Jaws Log* tell of any pressure exerted on Spielberg and his crew from the production management team in Hollywood.[28] When Gottlieb observes a certain kind of 'island fever',[29] it is typical for his narration that cast and crew immediately channel this fever into the progress of the production as the desperate attacks on the shark are staged all the more fiercely and authentically.[30] Accordingly, the rewards are high for this solidarity and loyalty, which enabled the film team to withstand the adverse shooting conditions, as Gottlieb states when he looks back on the production 25 years later: 'Almost everyone connected with *Jaws* in any capacity went on to have a long and successful career, regardless of his or her previous experience.'[31]

The second obstacle the film team faced, especially while shooting on the high seas, is a technological one. Gottlieb comments on the technical uniqueness of the entire undertaking very early in the *Log*: 'In many ways, launching *Jaws* was a film production problem analogous to NASA trying to land men on the moon and bring them back. It just had never been done.'[32] These abstract technical problems experience their anthropomorphization particularly in the shape of Bruce, the mechanical shark. Difficulties are signalled early on when initial considerations about the taming and training of real sharks for the movie are ridiculed and deemed illusionary.[33] Therefore, Bob Mattey, a former special effects specialist at the Disney Studios, was hired to construct three mechanical sharks, but when shooting began the latter did not function, as the time for testing was far too short. Despite these early problems with Bruce, Gottlieb insists on the fact that the inventive talent and persistence of the crew succeeded.[34] So with respect to these technical problems embodied by the mechanical shark it can be concluded that Gottlieb stresses their solution, but also that his narrative demonstrates another dramaturgical accordance with its cinematic model. In both the movie and the making-of narration, the shark turns out to be the main antagonist.

Particularly after the beginning of the shooting on high seas, a third type of problem dominates Gottlieb's making-of narrative: the dangers posed by nature itself. These perils are already touched on with respect to the problems with the mechanical sharks: 'Even Bob Mattey, who would never admit that anything was really wrong … said, later, that they had underestimated the power of the sea.'[35] It is remarkable that although this 'power of the sea' is underlined by examples of specific problems, Gottlieb henceforth intersperses his humorous and ironical narration with abstract personifications of the unpredictable elements, for example, by emphasizing the goodwill of the 'gods of the sea' as crucial for the undertaking of filming *Jaws*.[36] However, besides such literary exaggerations, Gottfried strives to depict the work processes (as dictated by an incalculable sea) in a precise manner. The weather forecast had to be analysed on every shooting day before the cast and crew were transported to the film location, and the mechanical shark had to be put in place and prepared prior to any actual shooting.[37] Once again, it is the team spirit and technical professionalism of everyone involved in the shooting that gains the upper hand in the battle against the ocean. For this hard-won success, Gottlieb conjures an image of maritime heroism which is both highly humorous and typical for his narrative strategy:

> All over, the picture shows signs of going down like the *Titanic*, but calm hands are at the helm, and cool heads are on the bridge. Steven is the Boy who Stood on the Burning Deck; Dick and David [Richard Zanuck and David Brown, the producers of *Jaws*] are like Nelson at Trafalgar, calm, resolute, never showing any outward signs of anguish or despair. The picture is clearly going to cost millions more than budgeted; how much is anyone's guess. But the strength of *Jaws* is greater than the *Titanic*'s – we *are* unsinkable.[38]

It is characteristic that even as the rescue of the production is guaranteed by all those involved in the filming – the ship's crew, to stick to Gottlieb's literary image – the screenwriter puts some naval leaders in prominent positions. One of these heroes within Gottlieb's vivid sea battle imagery, as well as in the entire narration, is Steven Spielberg. *The Jaws Log* introduces Spielberg as an artist who supervises the whole process of the film production from the planning process's very first steps until the final phase of post-production. As an auteur, he therefore vouches for the quality of his artwork – a role many making-ofs attribute to directors, thereby creating 'an updated myth of auteurism'.[39] During the shooting, Spielberg appears as a highly respected member of the film team. However, in some parts of Gottlieb's narration the director is also shown as a lonely genius, for example, in this description of a shooting day's end: 'Steven, sitting morose and alone on the bowsprit …, looks up in time to see the sun setting, losing the light, ending shooting for that day'.[40] But ultimately, Spielberg owes *Jaws* as much as the movie owes him. In Gottlieb's narrative, the tracing of the shooting is also the story of a young director's coming-of-age, the story of his road to uncontested mastership: '[H]e was twenty-six when the picture started shooting and about 101 when it ended'.[41]

In *The Jaws Log*, Gottlieb presents the filming history as an adventure of a sworn comradeship of solidly united moviemakers who overcome a multitude of problems caused by the insular inhabitants, technology and nature. Arranging the story of the shooting in this manner, Gottlieb thereby copies the dramaturgical core concept of the movie: a group of heroes, standing alone against unpredictable problems. This picture is as true for Brody, Hooper and Quint as it is for Spielberg, his cast and his crew – and it links *Jaws* to the genre of popular 1970s disaster movies.[42] Hence, the success of the film is attributed to the loyalty of those involved in the shooting – in particular to the young Steven Spielberg who, through overcoming all the production problems, reaches mastery as director.[43] Summing up, it is conspicuous that Gottlieb's making-of narrative develops a story of the filming process pursuant to a strict and cinematic dramaturgy of tension without getting merely bogged down in anecdotes. On the other hand, we can observe that Gottlieb aims for a precise and comprehensible explanation of the shooting's technical details and requirements.[44]

The production of *Jaws* as creative problem-solving – *The Making of Steven Spielberg's Jaws* (1995)

The first of the two making-of documentaries analysed in this chapter dates back to 1995. To a large extent Laurent Bouzereau's *The Making of Steven Spielberg's Jaws* relies upon interviews with cast and crew members complemented by short excerpts from the original movie, production stills and hitherto unreleased material. Hence, its dramaturgical structure orients itself closely to the production chronology of *Jaws*, a feature Bouzereau's film shares with *The Jaws Log*. However, unlike Carl Gottlieb's book, *The Making of Steven Spielberg's Jaws* does not focus to the same extent on the shooting on Martha's Vineyard and instead pays attention to the movie's pre- and post-production. Interestingly, even though Bouzereau's making-of describes the film production from the distance of two decades, it does not go much further than the date of the movie's first previews, which Gottlieb's account also covered.[45] This chronological limitation identifies the actual process of the filming as the central topic of Bouzereau's documentary. Besides its chronological structure and focus on production, the documentary shares another commonality with *The Jaws Log*. Like most making-ofs, *The Making of Steven Spielberg's Jaws* depicts the film's genesis as a sequence of problems for which the crew and actors find creative solutions. Bouzereau presents Bruce, the mechanical shark, as the exaggeratedly emphasized main concern of the production. His description of Bruce's conception and construction as well as its spectacular malfunctions under real-life conditions takes up a big part of the narrative. The interviews describe the construction of the shark in detail. The process is illustrated by footage from the workshops and sketches made by those responsible. Joyful and optimistic music laid down under the 'shark construction scenes' expresses the crew's optimism. Their optimism is destroyed all too soon as – much to the horror of the production team – the little-tested Bruce drowns during the first technical rehearsal on the high seas, endangering the whole movie. As producer David Brown recalls: 'And we felt that our careers in motion pictures had gone with it.'

Yet Bouzereau's making-of shows a tendency to reinterpret the problems with Bruce that are absent from *The Jaws Log* by presenting the technical calamities as forcing those in charge to create solutions that, in retrospect, contributed *to Jaws'* uniqueness and success. They include, for example, the use of yellow barrels emerging from the depths of the sea, indicating the presence of the otherwise invisible great white.[46] Even Spielberg himself admits, in Bouzereau's documentary: 'I really owe the shark a lot.' At the same time, he emphasizes that the technical problems with Bruce do not account for the shark's absence in every famous scene. According to him, the opening scene, in which a young female swimmer is pulled back and forth before being dragged down by the invisible shark, was planned this way from the very beginning, and the shark was never intended to be shown: while technical problems did have a bearing, the visual absence of the predator, according to Spielberg, is by no means simply a compromise dictated by necessity but much more an artistic decision by the director.

While Gottlieb's book also addresses difficulties connected to the mechanical shark, Bouzereau's film uncovers problematic areas largely undiscussed in *The Jaws Log*. For instance, Spielberg describes the enormous pressure exerted on the team and crew during the shooting. The longer filming went on, the more acutely his team started missing their families and life at home. He himself felt bad because he had to postpone their return to normality: 'I always saw myself in the negative.' Spielberg as a lonely director, troubled by the increasing mental pressure on his cast and crew – such a picture can hardly be found in Gottlieb's narrative of the film-makers' community. Bouzereau's making-of also mentions the pressure exerted on the production from the outside, which is also almost completely ignored in *The Jaws Log*. In *The Making of Steven Spielberg's Jaws*, the producer David Brown recalls that 'The decision to continue filming *Jaws* was a very shaky one.' In fact, the studio's confidence in Spielberg was probably not as infinite as Gottlieb would have his readers believe.[47]

Bouzereau's narrative frames Spielberg as a great director, too.[48] His account, however, differs from Gottlieb's in not identifying the movie so comprehensively with its director. Even though Gottlieb mentions that Spielberg was not the producers' first choice as director,[49] the incident in pre-production recounted in Bouzereau's film, when Spielberg wanted to back out and the producers had to persuade him to continue, is not found in *The Jaws Log*. In Bouzereau's documentary, it is recounted not by Spielberg but by his producer, Zanuck.[50] Perhaps Gottlieb did not know about this back in 1975, but maybe it would also have contradicted his narrative's insistence that Spielberg, as an auteur-director, took responsibility for *Jaws* from beginning to end.

To summarize, *The Making of Steven Spielberg's Jaws* does not follow a dramaturgic story arc that is as strictly composed as Gottlieb's narrative of film-makers' comradeship defying nature, technical problems and stubborn islanders. Nevertheless, the making-of also develops a narrative of problem-solving. Bouzereau emphasizes the technical side of production by interviewing the leading cinematographer and showing technical models and sketches, as well as providing an insight into the studio system by speaking to the screenwriter and the producers. Therefore, Bouzereau's film follows 'a popular [making-of] trope of organization: tell the story of creative ontogeny from inspiration to Oscar ceremony'.[51] There is one significant deviation, however. As mentioned earlier, Bouzereau ends with the previews of *Jaws* and therefore long before Oscar night. Although the end of the documentary indicates *Jaws'* commercial success, the sequels and the film's cultural footprint are not part of Bouzereau's narrative. This is hinted at only when Gottlieb says in the making-of, 'When a movie has the success that *Jaws* had, it becomes more than an entertainment. It becomes part of the popular culture.' The role that *Jaws* plays within this culture is examined in a making-of made yet another decade later.

From the description of the film production to the description of the cultural phenomenon: *The Shark Is Still Working* (2007)

Erik Hollander's *The Shark Is Still Working*, an elaborate production made for *Jaws'* 30th anniversary, has completely different objectives from Laurent Bouzereau's making-of. The producers' aims, stated in a text panel at the very beginning of the film, is 'to chronicle and acknowledge the lasting impact of this groundbreaking movie'. Consequently, only four of the film's ten 'chapters' address the actual filming of *Jaws*,[52] whereas the other six primarily deal with the movie's reception history since 1975.[53]

The first chapter, 'Martha's Vineyard, 1974', underlines the film's perspective on the shooting of *Jaws*. At its beginning, the viewer faces a mash-up of production stills underlaid with alarming music interspersed with occasional radio messages, one of which recurs with special persistence: 'The shark is not working!' This making-of focuses almost exclusively on the shooting on the high seas and relies on its audience's pre-existing knowledge of *Jaws'* troubled production history from the start: 'Stories of the hardships experienced during the filming of *Jaws* are the stuff of Hollywood legend.' Thus, the production is introduced as a by now legendary disturbing endeavour for all involved. Spielberg himself confirms this view with the authority of a star director: 'Making *Jaws*, still looking back 30 years ago [*sic*], was the toughest filmmaking production experience I've ever encountered. Nothing's ever come close to the production difficulties.' Coincidently, the making-of creates a sense of tension – after all, in 2007 everybody knows about the success of the movie – by labelling *Jaws*, at least at the time of its production, as 'one of Hollywood's little movies that *couldn't*'. David Brown, who is also interviewed in *The Shark Is Still Working*, carries this revisionism to extremes, when he states that 'I like to think of [*Jaws*] as a big independent movie masquerading as a big studio movie' – a questionable interpretation given that the novel, which the studio had optioned while it was in galleys, had become a spectacular success while the film was in pre-production.

As to the challenges faced during the shooting, it is striking that even though the documentary touches on the production's well-known difficulties, they all remain vague with one exception. It comes as little surprise that the problem of the malfunctioning mechanical shark (already hinted at in the making-of's title) constitutes the documentary's central calamity. A whole chapter devoted to Bruce comprises a large-scaled reinterpretation of his role in the production. While the narrator recounts how problems with the mechanical shark darkened the team's mood, David Brown, looking back after thirty years, evaluates Bruce's relevance from a new perspective: 'We've complained about the shark not being able to perform, because it couldn't. It was never ready. That was what saved us. That was the artistry of the film.' In Brown's memory, Bruce therefore changes from the production's main problem to its saviour. Spielberg agrees to this assertion and explains it in greater detail when he points out that it was exactly the impossibility of showing the shark that led to the special atmosphere and quality of the movie. It was an atmosphere impossible to achieve with computer-animated monsters, and Spielberg evinces yearning for the era of pre-digital technologies, which he himself terminated with *Jurassic Park* (1993).

It is remarkable that Spielberg revises some of his statements in other making-ofs in favour of the new narrative of the 'shark as saviour'. In *The Making of Steven Spielberg's Jaws*, he had stated that keeping the shark off-screen during the first killing had always been part of his artistic concept. A good ten years later, in 2007, he recalls this differently and admits that the shark should have been visible in this and other scenes. The technical malfunctions roundly cursed by cast and crew thirty years earlier are re-evaluated as a piece of luck: 'I did that [i.e. filming without a visible shark] because the shark kept breaking down! ... So I was saved by the breakdown in technology 30 years ago.'

The handling of Bruce is characteristic of the overall concept of *The Shark Is Still Working*. The narrative aims not so much to reveal and explain the production process, as to contribute to the legend-building surrounding *Jaws*' production. The film's production and shooting no longer constitute the main focus, which is instead the '*Jaws* phenomenon' and the film's impact well beyond cinema itself. Accordingly, the making-of concludes with the statement: '*Jaws* goes on forever.'

'This is how it *was*': Making-of narratives and the prerogatives of interpretation

Comparison of these three making-ofs makes clear that each tells – and thereby constructs – the production process of *Jaws* in its own unique way by employing distinct narrative strategies. The differences between the narratives' depictions range from the choice of diverse perspectives to plain contradictory assertions. Equally different are the objectives of the making-ofs. Over the years, the technical explanation of film-making has been superseded by the exploration of *Jaws* as a cultural phenomenon.

Paradigmatically, the differences between the three making-ofs can be illustrated by their depiction and interpretation of Bruce, the mechanical shark. While Bruce represents one of the shooting's main problems in *The Jaws Log* as well as in *The Making of Steven Spielberg's Jaws*, Erik Hollander's *The Shark Is Still Working* reinterprets the malfunctioning shark as the saviour of the whole movie. Hence, we can identify two reverse tendencies regarding the manner of Bruce's depiction over the decades. Initially, the making-ofs aim to technically explain the functioning of the shark, which in the movie is surrounded by an aura of terror and awe. The heroes' unpredictable and nightmarish antagonist becomes Bruce, the mechanical fish, whose emergence as a hissing and crackling hydraulic monster in *The Making of Steven Spielberg's Jaws* appears almost comical. In *The Shark Is Still Working*, however, Gottlieb and Bouzereau present Bruce as a technically explicable robot while Spielberg and Brown reinterpret him as the saviour of the whole movie, whose technical flaws inspired Spielberg to his greatest directorial ideas. This romanticization of analogue techniques and their purported drawbacks would have been scarcely imaginable in the pre-CGI era. The making-ofs' focus on Bruce is unsurprising, for it is one of the genre's 'recurring tactic[s] ... to seize on an integral trope for the filmmaking process that mirrors the typology of the original narrative'.[54] In the same way the (anti)hero of *Jaws* is the (mostly) non-visible shark, the real hero of the making-ofs is the (mostly) non-deployable Bruce.

Every making-of depicts the production of *Jaws* in its own individual way and with its own individual narrative strategies, making the documentaries as subjective as the memories of those involved.[55] Paul Arthur's hope therefore seems highly doubtful when he understands 'a notable subset' of making-of documentaries as an 'aid in our ongoing quest to demystify' the process of moviemaking.[56] Often it is precisely making-ofs' mystifications that give them that extra something their audiences seek. Whether it is the mystification or explanation of film production, the proliferation of competing narratives must lead to a struggle for the prerogative of interpretation, which becomes even more difficult now that real or self-appointed experts can spread their own narratives online.[57] Therefore, the attempt to impose a certain narrative is an integral component of every making-of. The narratives discussed in this chapter aim to do so by highlighting the authority of those involved in the production itself, whether it is the screenwriter, Gottlieb, in the case of *The Jaws Log*, or the famous interviewees in the documentaries. They supposedly ensure each narrative's credibility. In addition to that, certain characteristic defence strategies against rival narratives are detectable in each making-of. For example, Peter Benchley's praise for Carl Gottlieb's *The Jaws Log* involves depreciation of differing making-of versions online, when he emphasizes: 'In sheer, raw volume, of course, the Internet overwhelms everyone, but it's unreliable: too many so-called facts go out into cyberspace unchecked and, often, dead wrong.'[58]

The making-ofs' fear of losing their prerogative of interpretation explains such fierce attacks on different narrations, though, admittedly, Carl Gottlieb, in his preface to *The Jaws Log*, emphasizes the subjectivity of memory and, consequently, of his version of events. However, this hardly comports with the making-of genre's usual claim that it discloses a production's process objectively. Thus, it is Benchley's preface to *The Jaws Log* rather than Gottlieb's which expresses the characteristic attitude of many making-of narratives, when he concludes apodictically: 'Carl says of his story, "This was how I saw it". Well, as far as I'm concerned, this is how it *was*.'[59]

Notes

This chapter is a revised translation of my 'Martha's Vineyard Revisited. Die Making-ofs und ihre Erzählstrategien', in Wieland Schwanebeck, ed., *Der weiße Hai revisited. Steven Spielbergs 'Jaws' und die Geburt eines amerikanischen Alptraums* (Berlin: Bertz+Fischer, 2015), 24–39. I thank Dorine Schellens, Claire Amanda Ross and Jannis Funk for their valuable remarks.

1   Joseph McBride, *Steven Spielberg: A Biography* (New York: Faber & Faber, 1997), 254.
2   In his behind-the-scenes account, *The Jaws Log*, Carl Gottlieb points out that the success of Peter Benchley's novel was apparent before the shooting started. This makes it highly probable that those responsible conjectured a lucrative outcome from the filming of *Jaws* from the very beginning. See Carl Gottlieb, *The Jaws Log Expanded Edition* (New York: HarperCollins, 2012), 17–18.
3   Georg Seeßlen therefore concludes: '[T]he great white shark not only depicts its poor biological role models; it is the manifestation of catastrophe as such, the right image for a crisis situation.' [In the original: '[D]er weiße Hai bildet ja nicht nur seine armen biologischen Vorbilder ab. Er ist der Ausdruck der Katastrophe schlechthin, das passende Bild für eine Krisensituation']. Georg Seeßlen, *Steven Spielberg und seine Filme* (Marburg: Schüren, 2016), 37; see also Seeßlen, *Steven Spielberg und seine Filme*, 31–40; Wieland Schwanebeck, Der Haifisch, der hat Zähne. Zur Einführung', in Schwanebeck, ed., *Der weiße Hai revisited*, 12–16; Christian Keathley, 'Trapped in the Affection Image. Hollywood's Post-traumatic Cycle (1970–1976)', in Thomas Elsaesser, Alexander Horwath and Noel King, eds, *The Last Great American Picture Show: New Hollywood Cinema in the 1970s* (Amsterdam: Amsterdam University Press, 2004), 305.
4   See, e.g., William Baer, 'Jaws (1975): A Conversation with Carl Gottlieb', in William Baer, ed., *Classic American Films. Conversations with the Screenwriters* (Westport, CT: Praeger, 2008), 196–214. In this interview, Gottlieb tries to invalidate (among other things) the legend of the actors improvising freely on set, which is meanwhile even spread by Spielberg himself (see ibid., 201).
5   What Paul Arthur states regarding film reception since the age of DVD in general is therefore also true for *Jaws*: 'It has become commonplace to say that media's

self-reflexive loop has made us all vicarious Hollywood insiders, and that the boundaries separating gossip, studio flackery, and genuine historiography have undergone considerable erosion.' Paul Arthur, '(In)Dispensable Cinema. Confessions of a "Making-of" Addict', *Film Comment* (July/August 2004): 39.

6 Ibid.

7 For a short overview of the history and characteristics of, as well as academic approaches to the (movie) making-of genre, see, e.g. Vinzenz Hediger, 'Spaß an harter Arbeit. Der Making-of-Film', in Vinzenz Hediger and Patrick Vonderau, eds, *Demnächst in Ihrem Kino. Grundlagen der Filmwerbung und Filmvermarktung* (Marburg: Schüren, 2005), 332–41; Craig Hight, 'Making-of Documentaries on DVD: *The Lord of the Rings* Trilogy and Special Editions', *The Velvet Light Trap: A Critical Journal of Film and Television*, 56 (2005): 4–17; Andreas Rauscher: 'Making-of', in Thomas Koebner, ed., *Reclams Sachlexikon des Films* (Stuttgart: Reclam jun., 2007), 411–14; Wieland Schwanebeck, 'Making-of, klassisches', in Amelie Buchinger, Jannis Funk, Laura Hindelang, Felix Lempp, Stephan Porombka, Jens Roselt, Wieland Schwanebeck and Lukas Stopczynski, eds, *Making-of. Ein Lexikon*, http://making-of- lexikon.de/#text=klassisches-making-of (accessed 12 July 2018); Volker Wortmann, 'DVD-Kultur und "Making-of"', *Rabbit Eye. Zeitschrift für Filmforschung*, 1 (2010): 95–108.

8 Noteworthy in this context is the first volume of Joseph McBride's series *Filmmakers on Filmmaking*, in which several team members report on the production process of *Jaws*. See Joseph McBride, ed., *Filmmakers on Filmmaking. The American Film Institute. Seminars on Motion Pictures and Television*, 1 (Los Angeles: J. P. Tarcher, 1983).

9 Edith Blake, *On Location ... On Martha's Vineyard: The Making of the Movie Jaws* (New York: Ballatine Books, 1975); Matt Taylor, *Jaws: Memories from Martha's Vineyard* (Martha's Vineyard: Moonrise Media, 2011).

10 See Taylor, *Jaws. Memories from Martha's Vineyard*, 75–6.

11 Arthur, '(In)Dispensable Cinema', 39.

12 See ibid.; Wortmann, 'DVD-Kultur', 95–108.

13 See Laurent Vachaud, 'Entretien avec Laurent Bouzereau. Faire un making of, c'est raconter une historie', *Positif. Revue mensuelle de Cinéma*, 634 (2013): 98. Acknowledging the important role of the DVD format for the reception of films leads Volker Wortmann to a new way of looking at movies. He concludes that, as the paratexts provided by the DVD alter the way the viewer perceives the 'original' movie, one must no longer think of movies as artefacts that are independent of their mediality. See Wortmann, 'DVD-Kultur', 98.

14 See Hight, 'Making-of Documentaries on DVD', 4–17.

15 See Wortmann, 'DVD-Kultur', esp. 98f.

16 Hight, 'Making-of Documentaries', 5.

17 See Wieland Schwanebeck, 'Making-of, klassisches'.

18 Hight, 'Making-of Documentaries', 7. Nowadays, a producer of making-ofs sometimes even has to meet both claims and provide a short making-of predominantly for the promotion of the movie as well as a significantly elaborated documentary for the Blu-ray disc; see Vachaud, 'Entretien avec Laurent Bouzereau', 99.

19 The online encyclopaedia *Making-of. Ein Lexikon* (predominantly German-speaking, but open to English-language submissions) offers basic approaches towards an interdisciplinary and multimedia exploration of the phenomenon of 'making-ofs'. Its constantly extensible web of headwords aims for a new perspectivation of concepts

and terms from a variety of disciplines with respect to the making-of genre. See Amelie Buchinger, Jannis Funk, Laura Hindelang et al., eds, *Making-of. Ein Lexikon*, http://making-of-lexikon.de (accessed 12 July 2018).

20 Gottlieb, *The Jaws Log*, 9.

21 Ibid., 11–14.

22 Ibid., 14.

23 Ibid., 76.

24 Ibid., 75.

25 Ibid., 76.

26 Ibid., 78–9.

27 Ibid., 80–4.

28 Even for an instant of time, when the production schedule had already been far overrun, Gottlieb actually goes so far as to speak of a *'laissez-faire* time' (157) without any pressure from the studio.

29 Ibid., 169–73.

30 Ibid., 153–4.

31 Ibid., 217.

32 Ibid., 43.

33 Ibid., 33–4.

34 Ibid., 169.

35 Ibid., 155.

36 Ibid., 146.

37 Ibid., 148–9.

38 Ibid., 156–7.

39 Arthur, '(In)Dispensable Cinema', 40; see also Wortmann, 'DVD-Kultur', 100–4.

40 Gottlieb, *The Jaws Log*, 153.

41 Ibid., 36.

42 According to Peter Lev, the disaster movies of the early 1970s are characterized by their tendency 'to displace contemporary problems into simple, physical confrontations .... [which] are generally resolved via old-fashioned virtues: hard work, individual initiative, group cooperation'. Peter Lev, *American Films of the 70s. Conflicting Visions* (Austin: University of Texas Press, 2000), 49. Complementary to this, Maurice Yacowar describes the 'idea of isolation', the fact that '[n]o help can be expected from the outside' as one of the crucial conventions of disaster movies. Maurice Yacowar, 'The Bug in the Rug: Notes on the Disaster Genre', in Barry Keith Grant, ed., *Film Genre Reader IV* (Austin: University of Texas Press, 1986), 322.

43 Gottlieb's concentration on Steven Spielberg's importance for the success of the movie can be identified as one of the making-of genre's conventions: 'the validation of directorial artistry' is one of the most prominent 'intrinsic principles' for all making-of narrations, as Paul Arthur puts it. Arthur, '(In)Dispensable Cinema', 40.

44 Thereby, Gottlieb's narration – taken with a grain of salt – covers the four elements which Vinzenz Hediger argues [is there a 'to' missing?] have characterized the typical (filmic) making-of since the time of New Hollywood: technology, stars, the (enjoyable) industrial production in the studio system and the director as auteur. See Hediger, 'Spaß an harter Arbeit', 332–41.

45 Gottlieb, *The Jaws Log*, 185–6.

46 The assumption that it is the invisibility of the dangerous predator which constitutes both the terrifying impact and the success of *Jaws* is widely shared down to the

present day. See Lev, *American Films of the 70s*, 45–6; Seeßlen, *Steven Spielberg und seine Filme*, 37.

47 See McBride, *Steven Spielberg*, 243–4.

48 The interview structure of Bouzereau's making-of allows Spielberg to constitute himself as an auteur-director. His screen time by far surpasses that of the other interviewees, and it is striking that he presents himself as directly responsible for the smallest elements of the shooting from script writing through to detailed questions of scenography.

49 Gottlieb, *The Jaws Log*, 30.

50 See McBride, *Steven Spielberg*, 240.

51 Arthur, '(In)Dispensable Cinema', 40.

52 These are 'Martha's Vineyard, 1974', 'The Shark Is Not Working', 'I Love Sharks … I Love Them', and 'Call me Ishmael'.

53 Among other things, these chapters of the documentary focus on *Jaws'* commercialization, its fan culture and score together with the movie's influence on later directors and producers.

54 Arthur, '(In)Dispensable Cinema', 41.

55 Laurent Bouzereau describes the challenge for every making-of producer who has to deal with the former film-makers precisely: 'Sometimes you have to be their aide-mémoire without forgetting that they are the persons to give you the information, which will constitute the documentary later on.' [In the original: "Il faut parfois être leur aide-mémoire, sans oublier que c'est ce qu'elles vous donneront qui constituera le documentaire"]; Vachaud, 'Entretien avec Laurent Bouzereau', 99.

56 Arthur, 'Indispensable Cinema', 42.

57 See, e.g., the fan-driven project, *Inside Jaws: A Filmumentary* (2013), hosted on and downloadable from *vimeo.com*: Jamie Benning: 'Inside *Jaws*. A Filmumentary', uploaded 14 June 2013, https://vimeo.com/68400837 (accessed 12 July 2018).

58 Gottlieb, *The Jaws Log*, 10.

59 Ibid., 10.

15

Ben Gardner's head is missing: Notes on *Jaws: The Sharksploitation Edit*

Neil Jackson

A conventional critical enquiry into *Jaws: The Sharksploitation Edit* (2009; henceforth *Jaws TSE*) would be an odd proposition.[1] As an example of the phenomenon of fan editing, it might at best be looked upon as an impressively playful, but ultimately meaningless confection. At worst, it might be construed as a mindless degradation of concept and premise, whereupon an achieved condition of (post)-classical poise has been upturned by larkish artistic vandalism. Either way, *Jaws TSE* tends to resist any form of interpretive critical methodology that aspires to claims for textual coherence, complexity or singular artistic vision. Instead, evaluation is necessarily informed by knowledge of an *unauthorized* editorial intervention that upsets form, structure and multiple levels of possible meaning.

Consequently, while I will highlight some of the key changes visited upon the original film, it is clear that cataloguing all of its often bewildering alterations would soon descend into a taxonomic blur. Proper appreciation of *Jaws TSE* therefore demands both a cognitive and imaginative leap, a process best pursued through observance of three key perspectives: its status as a fan-conceived (but expertly rendered) form of adaptation; its relationship to oft-confused, ill-defined and, in this case, superficially imposed stylistic and material properties of exploitation cinema; and its processes of textual desecration and transformation. Taken together, these lay bare not only *Jaws'* secure position within the canon of the so-called 'New Hollywood' but also its relationship to cinematic trends and tendencies to which its original creative and executive team might prefer to maintain a respectable distance.

Thomas Schatz has argued perhaps just a little contentiously that 'if any single film marked the arrival of the New Hollywood, it was *Jaws*'.[2] While one could just as easily construct a case for (among many others) *The Godfather* (1972), *The Exorcist* (1973) or *The Towering Inferno* (1974), this positions *Jaws TSE* immediately as part of a broader creative dialogue with what is now commonly accepted as a vibrant period of commercial and creative renaissance. In this light, altering *Jaws* so obsessively might be construed as an extreme symptom of what Joli Jensen identifies as 'excessive, bordering on deranged behaviour', characterizing the singularly committed fan as a potentially 'deviant' figure.[3] However, Joshua Wille has defined fan edits as essentially alternative versions of feature films and television shows created by fans using desktop editing software ... often to refine or expand a narrative, to shift genres through aesthetic and structural changes, or even to recreate recombinant story lines using multiple films and television episodes.[4]

Beyond story-centred changes, such software also offers possibilities for visual effects and colour manipulation that can radically alter the tone, ambience and visual schemata of any film, a possibility that *Jaws TSE* pursues to an extreme degree. Prioritizing the bare mechanics of narrative progression, while coarsening an occasional reliance upon affective sensation, *Jaws TSE* removes much character detail, severely diminishes many layers of dramatic and thematic nuance, and reduces the original running time of 124 minutes to just 102. However, this does nothing to indicate the greater degree of pruning that has occurred, with a further twenty minutes excised from the original film partly in favour of scenes originally consigned to the cutting room floor. Other replacement footage is taken from exterior textual sources, including two of *Jaws'* own sequels, a selection of documentaries and several examples of the subgenre/rip-off cycle it inevitably spawned. At the expense of several dramatic set pieces that have come to define the film's identity, approximately one-third of *Jaws* has been removed in its entirety.

The opening section of *Jaws TSE* provides a neat encapsulation of its dense network of alterations. Against imagery depicting serene, dark blue ocean depths (extracted from *Atlantis* [1991]) and to the strains of Nana Mouskouri's romantic ballad, 'Deep and Silent Sea', the film now commences as cast and major production credits appear in a swirling font evocative of the ocean waves above the surface. These substitute respectively for the famed shark POV shot of the ocean floor (which now exists as a momentary fragment), and the ubiquitous John Williams score (which itself now only appears as a brief extract after the ballad has played out). Listing all key creative contributors before and behind the camera, the instantly ironic effect is to assign credit for work which has been significantly compromised. Excising the brief beach party sequence which perfunctorily introduces the first shark victim, Chrissie Watkins (Susan Backlinie), immediate character emphasis is placed instead upon an unidentified, naked female form, running into the ocean before her fatal encounter with the shark. The addition of digital blood to the water's surface during her nocturnal death throes renders the corporeal spectacle more crudely explicit. Then, before the attack has even climaxed, the original film's lap dissolve from night to early daylight shimmering across the ocean surface is obliterated by the sudden clamping shut of a crudely animated set of shark teeth, blacking out the image as the title logo is emblazoned on-screen. This is followed immediately by the shot of the silhouetted head of Chief Brody (Roy Scheider), peering over the ocean from his bedroom window as a title-card ('Day 1') initiates the breakdown of the film into a nine-day structure (Figure 15.1).

Besides this immediate series of curtailments and embellishments, other significant amendments include: the reduction of the dinner table sequence between Brody and his infant son to a barely rendered vignette; the complete elimination of the underwater

Figure 15.1 The film's temporal structure is transformed through the imposition of on-screen text.

discovery of Ben Gardner (Craig Kingsbury)'s corpse and replacing it with a 'Missing Reel' intertitle, thus depriving the film of its most infamous jump-shock moment; the fingers on chalkboard introduction of Quint (Robert Shaw) at the town hall meeting arranged to discuss the capture of the shark; and the ultimate destruction of the shark, which in its original form already stretched the bounds of verisimilitude, but is transformed here into self-reflexive meta-commentary.

Such startling irreverence for the tonal and structural design of the film immediately signals *Jaws TSE*'s intent, and other significant changes are characterized not by excision but by alternately elegant and crude interpolations. John Williams's orchestral flourishes fall particularly foul of this tendency, his work frequently replaced by artists such as The Beach Boys, Townes Van Zandt, Metallica, Iggy Pop and Manowar. In a particularly wry touch, Lalo Schifrin's jazz-funk rendition of the famous main theme[5] is utilized for one of the extended set-piece encounters between the main protagonists and the shark.[6] However, this also affects two sequences which have on very different levels served as signature moments for the original film: Peter Benchley's cameo as a television news reporter is now rendered as a fuzzy black and white television image before transforming into an informational fragment on the hunting and feeding proclivities of great white sharks (extracted from *Blue Water White Death* [1971]). This offers a perspective upon the author of the original novel and his position amid the mythology of *Jaws*, his brief on-screen presence transformed into an educational vignette via a knowing nod to his later efforts as a shark preservationist; Quint's monologue on the sinking of the *USS Indianapolis* is also rendered through a switch to monochrome, but is intercut/overlapped with a documentary reconstruction of the event created originally for the National Geographic channel. This de-emphasizes the intimacy of Robert Shaw's performative subtleties and gestures, and is underpinned by the brief but patently ridiculous superimposition of a visual effect approximating the view through a periscope.

All of this de-centres and debilitates Steven Spielberg's authorial control of *Jaws*, privileging an editing process that can just as readily obliterate rather than enhance directorial intent and offering tacit commentary on the film's narrative construction. While credited screenwriter Carl Gottlieb has insisted that *Jaws* adopts a two-act structure,[7] critic Nigel Andrews has suggested that the film adheres to a three-act progression.[8] When screenwriters and professional critics can't even seem to agree upon basic storytelling design, the imposition of alternative structural markers demonstrates just how malleable even the most familiar film narratives can be, actively undoing the widely accepted tenets of modern screenwriting orthodoxy that have taken hold since the film's original release. However, the newly created on-screen credits also signal an affectionate awareness of *Jaws'* production lore, privileging the notoriously malfunctioning mechanical shark – famously nicknamed 'Bruce' during shooting – with its own screen credit – as 'Himself'. The fan editor has also inscribed his own presence amid the original professional participants, his onscreen credit appearing alongside that of editor Verna Fields, who was (like composer John Williams and sound mixers John R. Carter, Roger Herman Jr., Robert L. Hoyt and Earl Madery) honoured with an Academy Award in 1976 (Figure 15.2).

As an independent creative endeavour, *Jaws TSE* is founded immediately in a proclamation of ersatz collaboration, the skills of a fan editor of primary importance to the new work, but unavoidably to the detriment of the original's stylistic and thematic integrity. As a result, authorial provenance is blurred further through the manipulations of a fresh post-production process with little regard for the directorial anxieties infamously endured by Spielberg during principal photography.

An auteurist perspective would bemoan the destruction of any early evidence of Spielberg's subsequent directorial tics and tendencies, but these changes imaginatively position *Jaws* as an utterly compromised artistic failure, the very antithesis of the fine-tuned blockbuster prototype it came to embody. In achieving this, *Jaws TSE* allows us to reflect upon the fine line between acceptance and rejection that the film traversed prior to its domestic and international domination in 1975. Indeed, its modern historical status as commercial and creative watershed has overridden what many contemporaneous observers felt to be an undesirable interface with the less reputable underside of the popular cinema.

This was regardless of Carl Gottlieb's observation that its production problems were 'insurmountable to a low budget operation, which is where a quickie rip-off might come from'.[9] None other than Roger Corman has observed somewhat ruefully that

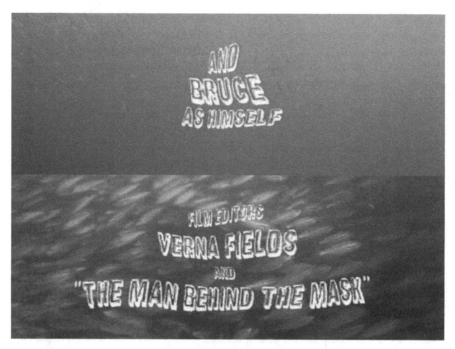

Figure 15.2 A new title sequence credits the film's malfunctioning mechanical shark, while aligning the fan editor's credit with that of his Oscar-winning predecessor.

> when I first saw *Jaws,* I thought I've *made* this picture. The first picture I ever made was *Monster from the Ocean Floor* [1954]. This is the first time a major had gone into the type of picture that was bread and butter for me and the other independents.[10]

Even Spielberg seemed acutely aware of *Jaws'* schlocky intersections, initially fearful of being typecast as 'a shark and truck director',[11] but stating in retrospect that after 'Bruce' started to fail on set

> I had to think fast and make a movie that didn't rely on the effects to tell the story … I threw out most of my storyboards and just suggested the shark. My movie went from William Castle to Alfred Hitchcock.[12]

Such self-comparison tends to affirm an often spurious dialectic of art and entertainment that has plagued Spielberg's career from the outset. Castle's shameless attachment to innovative, but gimmicky immersive experiences such as 'Emergo' and 'Percepto' is antithetical to Spielberg's somewhat self-conscious struggle to reconcile the affective pleasures of his fantasy blockbuster films with the austere responsibility of his self-adopted role as popular cinematic historian. Indeed, there has often been a sense that the spectacle and excess of Spielberg's nominal 'entertainments' have been granted licence through the status and respectability acquired via the Academy Award endorsement for his more avowedly 'serious' work. Spielberg's barely concealed implication is that favouring Hitchcock's artistic influence over Castle's commercial hucksterism was a wholly desirable necessity, eliminating much associative detritus from the popular cinema's carnivalesque shadow.

Jaws TSE takes up these critical and creative concerns as a conceptual base, bringing together the prestige of the once highest grossing film of all time with the commercial cinema's less salubrious underbelly. Acute awareness of a trash culture legacy informs its distinct identity, casting light upon the lower forms of genre production from which *Jaws* partially plundered its identity. The mythology of the film's development has repeatedly stressed the fear of artistic failure, the possibility of financial catastrophe and the prospect of audience ridicule at the revelation of its patently fake and persistently malfunctioning beast. But while the affective sensations of exploitation have always been far more integral to mainstream production and marketing trends than studios would like to admit, *Jaws* is notable for its combination of both high *and* low cultural reference points. Antonia Quirke argues that it 'belongs to a mixture of low genres',[13] but Nigel Andrews sees providence in sacred literary texts such as Coleridge's *The Rime of the Ancient Mariner*, Melville's *Moby-Dick* and Ibsen's *An Enemy of the People*.[14] Lester D. Friedman (categorizing it as a 'monster movie') calls it 'a cross between horror and adventure films [with] echoes of the western',[15] which encourages critical readings that are variously 'psychoanalytic, feminist, Marxist, nationalistic, historical, ecological, generational, economic, moralistic, legalistic, classist, auteurist, psychosocial, and sociological'.[16] With this eclectic interpretive range, *Jaws* would appear to be a notable case study in the collapsing notions of 'high' and 'low' cultural production, which *Jaws TSE* actively negotiates through its editorial strategies.

Wille concentrates his attention upon the efforts of fan editors to redeem the perceived sins of the contentious trilogy of *Star Wars* (1977) prequels – *The Phantom Menace* (1999), *Attack of the Clones* (2002) and *Revenge of the Sith* (2005). Arguing that these are far from petulant, destructive acts by overly proprietorial enthusiasts, Wille sees fan editors as the cinematic equivalent of DJs and remixers, 'experimenting with cinematic media in the digital age'.[17] This has been achieved largely on locked, clandestine websites, a self-imposed measure designed to avoid potential legal repercussions for the appropriation, alteration and dissemination of copyrighted material. Nevertheless, while a strictly non-profit pursuit, fan editing is unavoidably tainted by the notion of artistic theft. Wille again disputes this position, arguing that the best examples of the form are not 'poorly executed, reactionary works [but] the products of talented people who creatively reinterpret existing media in the spirit of narrative and aesthetic experimentation'.[18] There is no suggestion, implicit or otherwise, that *Jaws TSE* has been designed as some form of 'improvement' over its source material. Rather, it has been conceived explicitly as an alternative narrative construct, the same story told differently while retaining the fundamental shape of its primary textual wellspring.

Even a cursory glance at the Internet Fan Edit Database (for such a thing actually exists[19]) reveals that much fan editing takes place in the realm of science fiction/fantasy-oriented genres, where film enthusiasts have usually operated at their most determinedly committed. While the box office figures for such films indicate a distinct level of crossover between fan adoration and mass acceptance, the very moniker of *Jaws TSE*'s creator encourages a sense of the furtive that often informs notions of subcultural cachet. Using widely available tools such as Premier Pro and After Effects, 'The Man Behind The Mask' has created reductions or abridgements of titles such as *The Good, The Bad and The Ugly* (1966), *Once Upon a Time in the West* (1968) and *Conan the Barbarian* (1982). His version of *Jaws* is complemented most obviously by a similar treatment of *Star Wars* (retitled *The War of the Stars*) which repeats many of the same editorial strategies and retaining a similar awareness of its source material's intersection with 'trash' or 'pulp' cinema modes and practices.[20] Taken together, these offer another implicit critical commentary, stripping away the slick veneer that each film adopts to reveal the often simple structural mechanisms that underlie their elegantly rendered surfaces. Besides offering alternative layers of narrative experience, these revisions of signature New Hollywood works from two of its chief creative constituents position 'The Man Behind The Mask' as a revelatory figure. Based in France, he is in a tradition of creative cinephilia harking back to the auteurist aspirations of the *Cahiers du cinéma* critics of the 1950s, and it is far from ridiculous to align his appropriations of existing film footage with those of Jean-Luc Godard in his *Histoire(s) du cinéma* (1988–98). However, instead of Godard's poetic and often determinedly oblique critical-historical essays, these fan edits frequently accentuate the sensational or the maladroit, offering a highly skilled commentary upon the presumed gap between the respectable and disreputable poles of commercial film practice.

This also characterizes fan edits as another link in the historical chain of participatory culture among niche audience groups. The layers of critical and historical commentary embedded within *Jaws TSE* offer variation upon John Fiske's contention that fandom has often consumed mass-produced entertainment in a proactive manner, reworking it 'into an intensely pleasurable, intensely signifying popular culture'.[21] Writing prior to the widespread development of the internet, Fiske identified a proliferation of what he called 'textual productivity ... wherein fans produce and circulate amongst themselves texts which are often crafted with production values as high as any in the official culture'.[22] This has encompassed (but is not necessarily limited to) fanzines, fan fiction, art and posters, websites, social media groups or even independently produced documentary and fiction films. Alternatively, performative activities such as tribute acts or cosplay have allowed participants to embody their object of devotion through both vocal/musical impersonation and physical mimicry. However, none of these activities indulged in extensive alterations to the raw material of original texts. If the fan edit has any kind of rough antecedent, it is the fan recreation or re-enactment amateur video productions that revel in amateur imperfections while articulating a deep devotion to the source material. With creative impulses founded in imitation and reproduction regardless of budgetary or technical constraints, they are relatively rare, but are exemplified by *Raiders of the Lost Ark: The Adaptation* (1989) or latterly by *Star*

Wars Uncut (2010), both of which point again to the ubiquity of Spielberg and Lucas as key inspirational figures in this particular sphere of fan activity.

Of course, *Jaws TSE* is not a mere imitation of its source, which supports Matt Hills's argument that Fiske's concept of textual productivity is 'a singular, monolithic entity' that does not account adequately for gradations of competence and skill in the fan-creative process.[23] By its very nature, fan editing is a process conflating amateur and professional creative judgements, the new work unavoidably passing tacit or even explicit critical commentary upon the original. This itself is an unofficial step in a process of development and adaptation that began in 1973 upon the purchase of *Jaws* as a literary property by producers David Brown and Richard Zanuck. As is the norm, this encompassed numerous stages, including an initial screenplay by Peter Benchley, uncredited amendments by Howard Sackler and John Milius, and the final contributions of credited screenwriter Carl Gottlieb. This collective process scythed away the novel's bitterness and moral cynicism, typified by such elements as the adulterous affair of Ellen Brody and Matt Hooper and clear allusions to the mob connections of Mayor Vaughn. Andrew Britton argues that the novel exhibits 'an immitigable contempt for everyone and everything … a novel of complete disillusionment, cynicism, and despair'.[24] Such characteristics are in stark contrast to the recuperative possibilities expressed in the film and which are evident as a frequent element within Spielberg's subsequent oeuvre. Through its own process of adaptation, *Jaws TSE* restores an equally cynical opportunism, corrupting those modifications to the film that were deemed necessary to eliminate the novel's unpalatable tone. While this fan edit cannot reinstate un-filmed sequences, it amplifies melodramatic excesses of sex and violence and restores a level of prurience that the original film sought so steadfastly to avoid.

Both the narrative possibilities and the presentational qualities of fan edits have been accommodated significantly by the inclusion of deleted/alternative scenes as extra features on official DVD and Blu-ray releases of feature films. These have been utilized ingeniously in *Jaws TSE*, offering not just a blank variation upon the familiar release version of *Jaws* but also a sense of a film steeped even deeper in exploitation modes and practices. Having been consigned to editorial oblivion in the final stages of *Jaws*' completion, *Jaws TSE* now includes Quint's introduction via a shot of his feet (rather than his hand) as he emerges from a motor vehicle; Quint playfully mimicking a young boy attempting to play Beethoven's 'Ode to Joy' on a clarinet; Hooper's (Richard Dreyfuss) short anecdote to Brody about the sexual proclivities of a former girlfriend; and a short outtake in which Brody's pistol fails to discharge, an on-set mishap now absorbed into the narrative as Roy Scheider's frustrated exclamation of 'Ahhh fuck!' introduces profanity not otherwise present in the film. The degraded, unfinished visual quality of this cut material on the DVD supplements has the ironic effect of perfectly servicing the creative rationale of *Jaws TSE*, seamlessly aligning with the deliberately coarsened visuals elsewhere. As a consequence, they avoid the visual disjuncture that would be unavoidable in an attempt to reintegrate them into a pristine rendition.

The very deliberate transformation evident in *Jaws TSE* evinces not only an advanced cinephilia but also a tacit academicism, a quality evident in the end-credit list identifying where external footage and replacement music derived. Yet regardless of the creative and critical intelligence on display here, fan edits remain limited to a narrowcast online audience, whose viewing habits are far removed from *Jaws'* original entry into mass audience acceptance. Britton argued that *Jaws* was originally

> inconceivable without an enormous audience, without that exhilarating, jubilant explosion of cheers and hosannas which greet the annihilation of the shark, and which transform the cinema, momentarily, into a temple.[25]

This observation is borne of the film's overt gestures to audience participation, but the consumption of fan edits is far removed from the quasi-religious rite observed by Britton. Fan editors are embroiled in activity that could only have been meaningfully achieved in the twenty-first century, as the production and exhibition of cinema shifted from being a mechanical to predominantly digital medium which serves the stay-at-home viewer more faithfully than the frequent cinemagoer. *Jaws TSE* was not conceived for, nor has it ever been consumed within, a legally sanctioned theatrical viewing environment. In counterpoint to the mass experience of the original film, its reception has been selective and points to the increased significance of the internet as a repository for the increasingly fragmented attitudes that have developed within cineaste cultures. As meta-textual markers of technological access, participation and spectatorship, fan edits have liberated a small coterie of engaged audience members from previous levels of ownership, distribution, consumption and appreciation. Fan edits utilize their source material in ways which allow individual creators to present their work to a scattered, fragmented audience that is global in reach but limited in numbers, its constituents more often than not watching in isolation and more than willing to indulge such brazen tampering with the film's epochal status.

If one cherishes the communal aspect of cinema-going, *Jaws TSE* could only be perceived as a work of diminution, marking a journey from object of mass experience to that of specialized (and often highly fetishized) fan adoration. Its incorporation of footage from 'lesser' sources only compounds this feeling, with such textual displacement focalizing the relationship to a 'trash' sensibility even more acutely. Schatz stresses *Jaws'* hybridization of action film, thriller and monster movie, before noting certain affinities with the soon-to-be-popularized slasher film cycle.[26] This latter observation takes on particular resonance in light of *Jaws 2* (1978), which was released a full five months before the October 1978 release of *Halloween* and foregrounded precisely the type of youthful cast that would become familiar prey in the subgenre that soon followed in *Halloween's* wake. The typical emphasis in slasher films upon victim quantification is something which *Jaws TSE* shamelessly replicates, boosting the shark's body count initially by incorporating the attack upon a female water-skier from *Jaws 2*, before the Fourth of July set piece plunders additional action footage from *The Last Shark* (1981), *Jaws: The Revenge* (1987) and *Spring Break Shark Attack* (2005). All of this increases further the number of victims claimed by the shark, while characteristically paying little heed to the implications of extending and altering the editorial rhythms of a key transitory point. This is also particularly evident in the incorporation of the sequence depicting a beached, mutilated killer whale from *Jaws 2*, which now serves as the motivating event foreshadowing the shark's ultimate fate. Replacing the explosive man-versus-beast climax, the great white's demise is now presented as a revenge attack by another killer whale. This utterly preposterous deus ex machina utilizes documentary footage alongside a close up of the title creature from *Orca, Killer Whale* (1977), now intercut with Brody's delirious laughter to create the impression they are united in a victory celebration over their joint foe (Figure 15.3).

These might seem like cheap, albeit skilfully inserted intertextual jokes, but the inclusion of moments from both the official and unofficial progeny of *Jaws* forges direct, almost seamless links to the disparate sub-cycle that it inevitably spawned. This encompassed everything from official sequels seemingly determined to affirm the oft-stated law of diminishing artistic returns to a slew of nature amok titles set on dry land and deep water alike.[27] While *Jaws* has been critically segregated from its varied and less well-regarded offspring, *Jaws TSE* literally conjoins and collapses the culturally enshrined with the critically reviled. Of course, this appeal to the lowest cultural common denominator is a notion embedded in the very title of *Jaws TSE*.

Figure 15.3 In the film's amended climax, Chief Brody (Roy Scheider) and a killer whale exchange joyful wails at the destruction of the great white shark.

'Sharksploitation' crudely and very obviously hybridizes 'shark' and 'exploitation', evoking a basic subject matter and theme while implying a litany of disrepute encompassing cheapness, derivation and incompetence underpinned by vulgar representations of sex, violence and social deviance. However, despite the titular implication, it would of course be wholly inaccurate to describe *Jaws TSE* as typical 'sharksploitation' product. I. Q. Hunter has argued that, in its twenty-first-century guise, 'sharksploitation' follows '*Jaws*ploitation' as the second wave of the original film's subgeneric legacy, a phenomenon he suggests 'is virtually a horror sub-genre in its own right'.[28] Outlining the dizzying global array of films in which the animal kingdom teaches humankind lessons in evolutionary humility, Hunter contests that *Jaws* very naturally 'lends itself to [a] cinephiliac, intertextual *dérive* …certainly, few movies have given rise to such an extravagant surfeit of imitations'.[29] 'Sharksploitation' is a phrase applied to an ongoing spate of direct to DVD/streaming titles that gradually developed in the wake of *Deep Blue Sea* (1999), a twenty-first-century home viewing phenomenon which has evolved into increasingly more outlandish sci-fi/fantasy hybrids such as the *Mega Shark* (2009–2015), *Dino Shark* (2010), *Sharktopus* (2010) and *Sharknado* (2012–2018) films, to name but a few. These have been supplemented by titles such as *Jurassic Shark* (2012), *Shark Exorcist* (2015) and *Raiders of the Lost Shark* (2015), all of which (through their titles if not their budgets, ambition or achievement) allude to the enduring influence of work produced by varied alumni of New Hollywood's formative period. Curiously, the cycle appears to have come full circle back to the multiplex following the $385 million international box office gross for *The Meg* (2018).

Hollywood's history is scattered with the mutilated remains of creative compromise and executive interference, but regardless of its troubled shooting period, *Jaws* was never subject to unwelcome post-production tinkering. This has blighted (among many others) landmarks such as *Greed* (1924) and *The Magnificent Ambersons* (1942), whose integral forms are seemingly lost forever, or *Heaven's Gate* (1980) and *Once Upon a Time in America* (1984), whose ruinous truncations were eventually lovingly restored. Therefore, as a work of historical experimentation, *Jaws TSE* also serves as a fanciful imagining of the kind of film it might have become had it been re-fashioned by a coterie of unscrupulous producers and distributors intent on capitalizing upon its baser elements. In reality, such an elaborate plundering of a major studio's property is highly unlikely, but 'The Man Behind The Mask' also functions in this regard as an independent *producer* unencumbered by any economic responsibilities. His particular approach to *Jaws* aligns him with a long-standing tradition of often insensitive reconstruction by exploitation distributors handling countless films in Anglo-American territories. Just like those more illustrious examples above, external interference has affected the reception of titles as diverse as *Godzilla* (1954), *Lisa and the Devil* (1973), *Possession* (1981), *Shogun Assassin* (1980) and *Phenomena* (1985), all of which were alternatively re-titled, re-arranged and re-scored for their international release, often radically altering the design, intent and purpose of their original form. However, all of these films (and increasingly more besides) now exist in DVD or high-definition Blu-ray formats, often restored and approved by key creative participants, and frequently festooned with an array of supplemental features which contextualize their respective production histories and critical afterlives. *Jaws TSE* mischievously inverts this process both through its plundering of the material that archival restoration and digital video formats have made widely available and its artistic debasement of a work that has a proven record of studio, producer and audience endorsement.

The most obvious exploitation element of *Jaws TSE* is its intensification of gruesome violence. This includes the digital addition of blood to the water's surface during several shark attacks; a musical 'sting' to accentuate the discovery of Chrissie Watkins's dismembered remains; gruesome flash cut images of mutilated flesh and exposed organs during the post-mortem examination of her corpse; and the reinstatement of excised imagery depicting the gory demise of both the lifeguard victim (Ted Grossman) and Quint. The latter's death scene utilizes another out-take in which a messy excess of blood was vomited from the actor's mouth (embellished further by the effect of digital blood splattering the lens). The inclusion of the former's death throes in the shark's maw deliberately defies Spielberg's act of self-censorship prior to submission for an MPAA rating submission, a decision founded in his belief that the imagery was in 'bad taste'.[30] Here, the restoration of violent deleted material undercuts conscious creative and ethical decisions of the nominal auteur, shifting the film into the realms of a dubious 'taste' more befitting its transformation into a 'bad' cinematic object. While far less pronounced, this strategy is also applied in order to boost the film's sexual suggestiveness, an element restricted in the original film to very brief, discrete female nudity prior to the opening shark attack. Now, as Brody surveys the beach prior to the Alex Kintner attack, shot/reverse-shot pattern intercutting Brody's point of view of potential shark victims with increasingly closer images of his anxious reactions reveals him to be observing the bikini-clad bottoms of female bathers.

These editorial jokes accentuate the sense of *Jaws TSE* as a *deliberately* crass, inferior – and hence highly self-reflexive – bastard object. Such changes are all in the service of what 'The Man Behind the Mask' himself described as an attempt to 'turn *Jaws* into a grindhouse movie'.[31] He has commented elsewhere that he 'added grain and scratches to the picture to match a grindhouse feeling', imitating the natural vulnerability of film materials subjected to both archival neglect and the hazardous route through the sprockets, wheels and bulbs of past-their-best projection systems.[32] This convention of the battered, worn celluloid surface as an instant visual signifier of exploitation very rapidly slid into cliché in the wake of its extensive deployment in Robert Rodriguez and Quentin Tarantino's *Grindhouse* (2007). Despite its underwhelming commercial performance in the United States, *Grindhouse* was instrumental in generating a broader interest in exploitation legacies of a bygone age. Fuelled by nostalgia and experimentation in equal measure, this attempt to replicate a typical theatrical double bill of low-budget horror and action films was a creative manifestation of what David Church has called an 'implanted nostalgia [that] spurs longing for a sense of sub-cultural community that *perhaps never truly existed* [author's italics]'.[33] A side effect of this has been the popularizing of the very set of assumptions that characterize the above comments by 'The Man Behind the Mask'.[34] Like *Grindhouse*, *Jaws TSE* relies upon a superficial, second-hand adoption of various material deficiencies of the theatrical experience, romanticizing a period and exhibitory space without any first-hand referent through which it can be verified. As Glenn Ward has commented, 'grind houses once existed but "grindhouse cinema" and "grindhouse films" as they are imagined today never did ... for that we may have to thank or blame Quentin Tarantino'.[35]

As a deliberate aesthetic choice, the digital addition of visible marks, scratches, splices, focus loss, image roll and missing reel cards renders 'safe' and familiar one aspect of a supposedly dangerous and exotic theatrical experience which is consigned to history, but now assumed (however reliably) to be an integral element of the experience of such films. The already overplayed image of battered reels unspooling as unruly patrons indulge in all manner of activity in the auditorium below is part of the founding assumptions of the typical grindhouse experience, something which *Grindhouse* and its surrounding publicity discourse was so keen to emphasize.[36]

Of course, *Jaws TSE* has been achieved not through utilization of a degraded print, but through a mere affectation of that form. Unlike *Grindhouse*, instead of offering a pastiche of an already marginalized and despised cinematic form, it takes a familiar Hollywood object in an attempt to obliterate its varied signifiers of quality. Effectively, the digital grafting of those shortcomings now commonly ascribed to exploitation product suggests that *all* films, regardless of their perceived historical status and artistic value, are now subject potentially to an equalizing process of fan-imposed erosion which might manifest in all manner of bizarre and seemingly incongruous forms. In this context, *Jaws TSE* works very effectively as an audiovisual critical essay on both the textual *and* textural properties of this set of assumptions, its in-built conflation of 'grindhouse' and 'sharksploitation' perhaps inadvertently highlighting the historical and material disjuncture between the two terms. The former refers directly to a historically spent theatrical experience and exhibition space; the latter is more readily applicable to a cycle of films that never enjoyed widespread theatrical exposure, and which have been experienced via DVD or streaming platforms in the relative comfort of the domestic environment. Material decay hardly speaks of the now-taken-for-granted luxuries of the modern home-viewing experience and certainly does not evoke the historical narrative of *Jaws* and its record-breaking box office performance. While *Grindhouse* is a film to which *Jaws TSE* is obviously both indebted and in thrall, the Rodriguez/Tarantino team-up has had a largely deleterious effect as far as fuller understanding of its titular cinematic phenomenon is concerned. However, a specific 'feeling' was clearly being invoked to define both a generic form and a consumption process, one utterly alien to audiences born into the digital age. This is irrespective of the fact that 'grindhouse' itself is essentially meaningless as a generic descriptor, being more usefully deployed to identify historically fixed theatrical phenomena than as an indicator of specific textual or generic expectations. Just as low-budget exploitation films played in relatively respectable theatrical outlets as they moved into global distribution, then bigger studio productions would often unspool in the so-called grindhouses as their first-run capital diminished over the months and even years of the pre-video exhibition cycle.

This faux aesthetic of decay is adopted as one more adjunct to *Jaws TSE*'s imposition of a battery of technical and creative shortcomings. *Jaws* was never representative of the same sector of film culture upon which *Grindhouse* centred its allusion and pastiche, but its importance to that production sector is evident in its highly variable subgeneric progeny. Enhancing the sense of *Jaws TSE* as a severe artistic devaluation, one anonymous online observer argues that

> [if *Jaws TSE* evinces] missteps in pacing, narrative cohesion, or consistency in tone, then they can be accepted as the vagaries endemic to exploitation cinema generally and failures are converted into successes in the name of industrial and generic fidelity.[37]

Through such appropriations, *Jaws TSE* fashions a critical sleight of hand: instead of offering a pastiche of an already marginalized and critically derided form, it takes a culturally enshrined object and subjects it to the same level of faux textural decay. Through its appropriation of a litany of devices and features deemed endemic to the exploitation film, *Jaws TSE* gleefully reinscribes the trash cultural elements which the original film so consciously eliminated in its appeal to mass acceptance.

The foregoing analysis has offered some formative answers to the question of why we should afford serious attention to anything that tampers so extensively with a canonized object such as *Jaws*. Its seeming imitation of the varied conceits of *Grindhouse* actually serves as a point of conceptual departure, transforming both the narrative and technical professionalism of the source material from the original film. Going beyond the established conventions of the fan edit, *Jaws TSE* simultaneously celebrates and satirizes the placement of Spielberg's film in the pantheon of the New Hollywood renaissance of the 1970s, the apparent destruction of a cherished text actually achieved with a significant degree of skill, critical acumen and intuitive insight. As a sophisticated mode of historical and critical commentary, *Jaws TSE* goes beyond conventional fan-critical discourse, achieving an alternative identity for a film whose ubiquity and familiarity might easily beget an uncritical complacency among its adherents and admirers. While at first glance a wholly flippant enterprise, its creative practice supports a critical reflection upon internal coherence, helping to identify and exaggerate those 'low' cultural influences visible on various levels in the original film. While it may elicit an amused admiration for the invention and imagination on display, its textual transformation simultaneously draws attention to the formal elegance of the original film's deceptively simple architecture. As a form of meta-textual criticism, *Jaws TSE* highlights the presumed dichotomies of mainstream and exploitation films, and how they are often encouraged by institutions and individuals mindful of their place in the cultural and economic hierarchy. In turn, it allows for reflection upon the place of a popular entertainment such as *Jaws* amid the realm of marginalized pop culture objects, focalizing its status as *urtext* for a largely derided subgenre that is still regenerating almost half a century after its initial release. In its efficient and imaginative gutting of Spielberg's first big fish, *Jaws TSE* acknowledges its elite standing amid Hollywood's 1970s revival while locating it squarely within the mini-ocean of cinematic flotsam it unwittingly begat.

Notes

1   Until 6 December 2018, the film (among many others) was available to view on the Vimeo page attributed to 'The Man Behind the Mask'. Alas, this resource has succumbed in its entirety to the demands of copyright protection law. His full filmography is listed on his web page, *The Man Behind the Mask Fanedits*, http://tmbtm-fanedits.blogspot. com/. At the time of writing this does not host any of the actual work itself.

2   Thomas Schatz, 'The New Hollywood', in Jim Collins, Hilary Radner and Ava Preacher Collins, eds, *Film Theory Goes to the Movies* (New York: Routledge, 1993), 17.

3   Joli Jenson, 'Fandom as Pathology: The Consequences of Characterization', in Lisa A. Lewis, ed., *The Adoring Audience: Fan Culture and Popular Media* (London: Routledge, 1992), 9.

4   Joshua Wille, 'Dead Links, Vaporcuts, and Creativity in Fan Edit Replication', *Transformative Works and Cultures*, 20 (2015), https://journal.transformativeworks. org/index.php/twc/article/view/663/537) (accessed 29 March 2017).

5   Recorded for Schifrin's 1976 album, *Black Widow*.

6   This ironic touch is compounded by knowledge that Schifrin himself saw his original score for *The Exorcist* completely rejected by its director William Friedkin just two years previously.

7   Carl Gottlieb, *The Jaws Log* (London: Faber & Faber, 2001), 211.

8   Nigel Andrews, *Jaws Pocket Movie Guide* (London: Bloomsbury, 1999), 123.

9   Gottlieb, *The Jaws Log*, 50.

10 Quoted in Steven Kurutz, 'Why Did B-Movies Vanish from Theaters?', *Wall Street Journal*, 18 September 2010, https://blogs.wsj.com/speakeasy/2010/09/18/film-school-roger-corman-explains-why-b-movies-vanished-from-theaters/ (accessed 14 March 2018).

11 Quoted in Gottlieb, *The Jaws Log*, 30.

12 Quoted in Peter Biskind, *Easy Riders, Raging Bulls* (London: Bloomsbury, 1998), 277.

13 Antonia Quirke, *Jaws BFI Modern Classic* (London: BFI, 2002), 7.

14 Nigel Andrews, *Jaws Pocket Movie Guide* (London: Bloomsbury, 1999), 5.

15 Lester D. Friedman, *Citizen Spielberg* (Chicago: University of Illinois Press, 2006), 164.

16 Ibid.

17 Joshua Wille, 'Fan Edits and the Legacy of the Phantom Menace', *Transformative Works and Cultures*, 17 (2014), https://journal.transformativeworks.org/index.php/twc/article/view/575/466 (accessed 25 March 2017).

18 Wille, 'Fan Edits, Vapor Cuts', *Transformative Works and Cultures*, 20 (2015) https://journal.transformativeworks.org/index.php/twc/article/view/663/537 (accessed 26 March 2017).

19 See https://www.fanedit.org/ for a comprehensive overview of the fan-editing community and its creative efforts.

20 For first-hand insight into his creative methods see 'Meet the Fan Editor Transforming Hollywood Greats', in *Sabotage Times*, April 2015, https://sabotagetimes.com/tv-film/meet-the-fan-editor-transforming-hollywood-greats (accessed 17 June 2019).

21 John Fiske, 'The Cultural Economy of Fandom', in *The Adoring Audience*, 30.

22 Ibid., 39.

23 Matt Hills, 'Fiske's Textual Productivity and Digital Fandom: Web 2.0 Democratization versus Fan Distinction?', *Participations: Journal of Audience and Reception Studies*, 10, no. 1, 2013, http://www.participations.org/Volume%2010/Issue%201/9%20Hills%2010.1.pdf (accessed 9 July 2018).

24 Andrew Britton, Review of *Jaws* in *Movie*, 23 (1976): 27.

25 Ibid.

26 Schatz, 'The New Hollywood', 18.

27 For a lively and comprehensive overview of this nature amok subgenre before *and* after *Jaws*, see Lee Gambin, *Massacred by Mother Nature: Exploring the Natural Horror Film* (Baltimore, MD: Midnight Marquee Press, 2012).

28 I. Q. Hunter, *Cult Movies as a Guide to Life: Fandom, Adaptation, Identity* (London: Bloomsbury, 2016), 77.

29 Ibid.

30 Quoted in the documentary *The Making of Steven Spielberg's Jaws* (1995).

31 Quoted on the now deleted Vimeo page.

32 *The Man behind the Mask Fanedits* blog, http://tmbtm-fanedits.blogspot.com/search?updated-max=2016-01-25T00:44:00%2B01:00&max- results=7&start=7&by-date=false (accessed 3 May 2017).

33 David Church, *Grindhouse Nostalgia: Memory, Home Video and Exploitation Film Fandom* (Edinburgh: Edinburgh University Press, 2015), 4.

34 This visual affectation was also present in *Grindhouse*'s own spin-off feature *Machete* (2010), as well as *Smash Cut* (2009).

35 Glenn Ward, 'Grinding Out the Grind House: Exploitation, Myth, and Memory', in Austin Fisher and Johnny Walker, eds, *Grindhouse: Cultural Exchange on 42nd Street, and Beyond* (London: Bloomsbury, 2016), 13.

36 See BillLandis, *Sleazoid Express* (New York: Fireside, 2002) for the most expansive, but equally self-mythologizing, first-hand accounts of New York theatres in the 1970s and 1980s.

37 Anonymous reviewer, *Make Mine Criterion!*, https://makeminecriterion.wordpress.com/2013/06/29/jaws-the-sharksploitation-edit-steven-spielbergthe-man-behind-the-mask-19752009/ (accessed 23 June 2018).

16

Live every week like it's shark week: *Jaws* and natural history documentary

Vincent Campbell

Introduction

In the shark documentary *Great White Serial Killer Lives* (2017), broadcast by the Discovery Channel as part of its annual Shark Week event, a team of marine biologists are shown attempting to place a radio tracker onto a great white shark. As the team gets close to a shark and try to tag it, one of them takes control of their vessel and says in passing to colleagues, with a grin, 'Hooper drives the boat' (Figure 16.1). The programme this scene occurs in is structured around a series of accounts of great white shark attacks off the coast of California and a theory that an apparent pattern of attacks might suggest a single shark is responsible. While the marine biologists shown in this scene, who are researching great white shark populations in the area, explicitly refute the idea of a 'serial killer' shark, the programme's overarching structure, and that pithy aside, is indicative of the continuing resonance of *Jaws* (1975) in the mediated representation of great white sharks.

Science documentaries in general have not attracted a great deal of academic attention, despite often being among the most popularly lauded television genres, such as Carl Sagan's *Cosmos* (1980) and virtually the entire output of David Attenborough.[1] Natural history documentaries have garnered comparatively more critical attention, and a common theme in such work is a largely critical take on such programmes' validity, in terms of both their scientific (or lack of scientific) representations of the natural world and their claims to be documentary.[2] The influence of commercial companies and entertainment-oriented production imperatives on natural history film-making, such as the influential role of Disney in US wildlife films from the late 1940s onwards, is argued by many to offer fundamentally distorted narrative frameworks for the natural world and the organisms in it.[3] Add in critiques of production practices commonly used that would be regarded as unacceptable, even unethical, in documentaries on human subjects and some go as far as to deny that natural history films and television programmes are documentaries in any substantive sense.[4] What is particularly interesting is how the relationship between *Jaws* and documentary is noticeably absent from these accounts, when it is arguably a particularly strong example of the concerns

Figure 16.1 Dr Michael Domeier saying 'Hooper Drives the Boat' in *Great White Serial Killer Lives* (2013).

they raise, especially with regard to possible impacts on public attitudes and public policy regarding shark welfare. The relationship between popular attitudes and screen representations of sharks has actually been discussed more fully in the marine sciences literature in this sense but only on rare occasions in literature on documentary[5] and very rarely as the specific focus of discussion.[6] This is curious since, as suggested by the opening example, the influence of *Jaws* persists in the structure and contents of documentaries on sharks, on public perceptions and cultural attitudes, and even as frames of reference for shark scientists themselves, some forty-five years after the feature film appeared.

Within the marine science literature, there is the view that media representations and *Jaws* in particular continue to dominate both public perceptions and political decision-making with negative consequences for shark conservation, as illustrated by the statement by Friedrich et al. that 'the image of sharks as fearsome predators, cultural representation in movies such as *Jaws* and sensationalist media reports of shark attacks all contribute to frame sharks negatively in the public image'.[7] Even in coastal communities where shark encounters are comparatively frequent, research suggests that in some communities at least people 'feel that the media we consume, especially since the movie *Jaws*, continually feed community fear of sharks'.[8] Neff argues that *Jaws'* fictional construction of sharks has directly influenced policy decision-making and the political narratives used to justify them as well, amounting to what he calls 'the *Jaws* Effect'.[9] As this chapter will show, the relationship between *Jaws* and documentary offers an ideal focus for the kinds of discussions of the relationship between science, entertainment and television documentary that dominate writing on natural history films and the mediation of science more widely.[10] Through discussing a range of examples of shark documentaries produced in the years since *Jaws* hit the screen, as well as considering their representation prior to *Jaws*, the chapter will explore some of the ways in which the film continues to cast its shadow over the depiction of sharks, and marine life more widely, in screen documentaries. In the wider context of perceptions among marine biologists that media representations contribute to public and political attitudes and behaviour towards sharks, the persistence of *Jaws*' influence on documentary may also be consequential beyond screen representations, making it additionally worthy of closer scrutiny.

Sharks in documentary before *Jaws*

The depiction of wildlife in film stretches back pretty much to the earliest uses of film cameras (e.g. Muybridge's famous photographic sequences of horses), but for marine wildlife in particular it was largely the work of Jacques-Yves Cousteau who started and significantly shaped the marine world's representation on-screen from the 1950s onwards. Developing the first aqualung, and later having a role in the first specialist underwater film camera designs, Cousteau shot to international prominence with the release of *The Silent World* in 1956. While Cousteau would later become a world-famous conservationist and spokesperson for the marine environment, his early work and views, particularly about sharks, were reflective of a set of attitudes common at the time, and in turn a product of attitudes evolving over time.[11] These attitudes essentially centred on sharks as mindless killing machines, with great whites in particular as man-eaters, a narrative framing of sharks that reached their zenith, or nadir depending on your point of view, in *Jaws* itself. In *The Silent World* book that preceded the film, published in 1953, a chapter on sharks offers a number of statements that stand somewhat at odds with Cousteau's later conservation attitudes. Cousteau writes, for instance, of sharks as 'the savage population of the open ocean' and more specifically of great white sharks as 'the only shark species that all specialists agree is a confirmed maneater'.[12] His accounts of diving with sharks of a variety of species include incidents of harpooning them – for no evident purpose other than testing a super-harpoon gun.[13] Interestingly, he comments on interacting with sharks to get shots on film, stating, 'We saw three sharks sleeping in rocky caverns. The camera demanded lively sharks. Dumas and Taillez swam into the caves and pulled their tails to wake them.'[14]

This notion of the camera needing dynamism and action in its shark subjects is an important, and persistent, element in the documentary representations of sharks that do not originate with *Jaws*, as is the placing of humans into the shot as part of the action which is arguably distinctive from at least some strands of natural history film-making. Among a variety of styles of natural history film among the most long-standing are, on the one hand, those which try to reduce human presence in the natural world to that of omniscient narrator as seen in many of David Attenborough's award-winning series such as *Blue Planet 2* (2017), and often referred to as 'blue chip' programmes, and those which foreground on-screen presenters often engaging directly with animals, perhaps typified by the 'crocodile hunter' Steve Irwin (who was infamously killed during filming by being stung in the chest by a sting ray). Criticisms of the blue chip, narration-led programmes are of essentially misrepresenting the natural world as pristine and unaffected by human activity.[15] Meanwhile, presenter-led programmes are critiqued as being overly centred on the human explorers and their disruption of the natural world for sensationalist entertainment and focusing on constructing the natural world as a space of risk to be contained and enjoyed like a theme park.[16] From Cousteau onwards, the explicit presence of camera-people in shark documentaries, including extended sequences of the acts of preparing to film and scenes of filming people filming sharks, has been a consistent feature of shark documentaries.

In the 1960s, a number of marine film-makers began to emerge, and the popularity of natural history films on international television markets enhanced their activity. Australian spear-fishing champions Ben Cropp and Ron Taylor produced a black-and-white film in 1961/2 called *The Shark Hunters* which was sold to both Australian and US television. Ron and his wife Valerie Taylor, also a spear-fishing specialist, developed a long career as marine film-makers, particularly in relation to sharks. While they too would later become noted conservationists, their early marine careers were not imbued with a conservationist mind-set. Some accounts of Ron Taylor credit his films as being direct influences on Peter Benchley's writing of *Jaws* the novel,[17] but unquestionably the biggest influence on both Benchley's 1974 novel and the *Jaws* movie was the documentary film *Blue Water, White Death* (1971), led by wealthy explorer Peter Gimbel and with filmed contributions from the Taylors, who went on to film the live shark sequences for Spielberg's film.

Blue Water, White Death

Given the significant symbiotic relationship between the book, the film and marine documentary it is interesting that the core precursor documentary text *Blue Water, White Death* (hereafter *BWWD*) hasn't been subject to more than passing mention in studies of either the fictional work or natural history documentary (a rare exception is Horak who briefly refers to it).[18] The film reflects many of the established narrative tropes of natural history documentaries, still very much extant today, albeit reflecting the markedly different attitudes towards representations of animal life and the natural world of the time it was filmed in compared to later decades. The structure of the film as a first-of-a-kind quest, to film something never filmed before and/or never filmed in a particular way before, is now a common framework for natural history films both at the blue chip and presenter-led ends of the spectrum of programme types. Like many wildlife films, the actual money shots of the great white sharks don't occur until the very end of the film and consist of maybe ten minutes or so of footage at the end of a film around ninety minutes in total length. Much the same occurs in *Jaws*, though in the fiction film the brief glimpses of fins in the water can be justified as building audience tension for the eventual climactic reveal (as well as reflecting the practical problems of the mechanical shark simply not working sufficiently well or convincingly enough to be seen on-screen for long). In documentaries, however, the tendency is to work at 'very high shooting ratios',[19] producing lots of raw footage, and it is in the editing that the narrative is constructed, mixing together images with no necessary spatiotemporal relationship, indeed even cutting images of different animals together to build a single sequence (like a hunt for instance). It is this kind of practice that underpins Bousé's denial of wildlife films' claims to be documentary.[20] So, to position the shark hunters at the centre of the majority of the film, as *BWWD* does, particularly highlights it as a film about the shark hunters more than about the sharks themselves. Horak's claims of increasing trends towards this being far more common by the 2000s might be correct,[21] but in the specific case of marine documentaries it arguably has been the archetypal narrative since at least Cousteau's films of the 1950s. Possibly this is at least partly due to the comparative restrictions of filming in the water compared to filming on land. Great white shark documentaries today can feature multiple high-definition, slow-motion shots of the creatures engaged in a variety of behaviours as both much more is known about them to be able to find and film them (even to the point of several tourist trips operating now to swim with them), and film technologies have continued to develop offering a wider range of ways of filming them. Nonetheless, the construction of the narrative around the explorers more than the targets of the exploration is foregrounded particularly strongly in *BWWD*, with many lengthy sequences of preparations on-board the expedition's ship. Much of the opening segment involves setting up in port, and then, once out in the ocean, presenting at length various aspects of preparing to try and film, such as following a whaling fleet to see sharks feeding on whale carcasses, rigging diving cages with lights for some night filming and rigging tether lines to a Second World War British wreck off the coast of Sri Lanka causing significant problems for the divers due to the depth and risk of the bends. Locations on the coast of South Africa, near Madagascar, and off Sri Lanka all prove fruitless for capturing images of great whites, though filming other shark species and a variety of other sea creatures is provided. The comparatively leisurely pace of these sequences, compared to more recent documentaries, especially the length of sequences in places where no great whites are seen at all, is distinctive, but the more general structural narrative remains a dominant framework today (Figure 16.2).

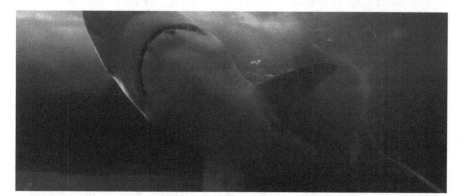

Figure 16.2 *Blue Water, White Death* (1971).

Two things are particularly interesting about *BWWD*'s narrative construction of the marine environment and the visual representation of sharks in general and great whites in particular. In terms of the narrative construction and framing of the marine world, the film is notable by being almost entirely devoid of scientific discussion, information and framing of the expedition or what it encounters. Some sequences are entirely devoid of either dialogue or narration. For instance, the first part of the expedition involves following a whaling vessel off the coast of South Africa, showing whales being harpooned, and then, back in harbour, the whale carcasses being cut up on land for processing. A key criticism of much natural history film-making stems from the typical elision of such scenes of human destruction and exploitation of the natural world, with blue chip programmes typically eschewing graphic images like these altogether. In recent trends for environmental advocacy-oriented films such as *Sharkwater* (2007) and *The Cove* (2009), such sequences often constitute key scenes as part of narratives centred on human exploitation of the marine world. In *BWWD*, however, while the sequence is a few minutes long, there is only a single comment from expedition leader Peter Gimbel that the rate of whale culling might mean that 'they'll be extinct before we come to understand them'. Otherwise, the responses of the crew that are shown are essentially pragmatic and even indifferent, the carcasses being simply the means by which sharks are to be attracted. What Horak refers to as a structuring theme of the need for 'rescue' of endangered species,[22] or what Papson identifies as an 'ecological paradigm',[23] focusing on respect, preservation and balance in the natural world seen in later wildlife documentaries, is essentially entirely absent here. In later sequences, a relative apparent indifference to animal life is displayed, such as Ron Taylor scaring a sleeping seal on the Australian coast, Val Taylor riding the back of a sea turtle off Madagascar and one of the team on an island commenting on a tortoise that 'something on it says made in Japan!'. Even when in the water with sharks, there are aspects of the team's behaviour that are suggestive more of fear than say respect or privilege in the proximity to the sharks. In an early sequence, a shark swimming past a diving cage – not trying to bite or get in the cage – is punched, with narration stating 'these brutes can't stand this kind of treatment'. In a sequence where the team films outside their cages, a lot of shots show them punching or hitting sharks to keep them away. In one instance, Val Taylor tests a cartridge shot containing prod on a shark that sends it into a constant spinning loop, and whether that was fatal for the shark is not commented upon. While outright hostility to the sharks is not particularly present, even though great whites as killers of humans are referred to, the wider attitudes seem not to reflect any particular goal or objective, such as tracking their behaviour to better warn people, for instance, or to better understand sharks generally. There's almost a vacuum of motive, beyond filming great whites for the first time. Apart from a brief opening sequence listing some basic information about great whites, little to no scientific information about sharks is provided across the rest of the film (save a comment about how they have to keep swimming from lacking air bladders). Much more information is given about the risks of the bends, which becomes evident when one of the team has a brief bout of them. The performances of a folk singer, whose songs accompany montages of the ship moving locations, feature more prominently as a framing device than any kind of scientist/expert input.

The second significant feature, which perhaps stems from this apparent lack of particular motive for engagement with the sharks other than for filming purposes, is how the sequences of sharks are constructed. The film tends to use quite long sequences of several minutes in length for each part, and for the underwater sequences these are almost entirely without voice-over narration. The sound mix is particularly interesting, with sounds essentially of gurgling water (suggested as diegetic, though it's not entirely clear whether it is or not), mixed in with bursts of overlaid whale song, and atonal, discordant and arrhythmic electronic sounds, not unlike the sounds of 1950s sci-fi B movies, to suggest alien life and alien worlds. Something not dissimilar is used to open *The Silent World*, reflecting what Mitman suggests was a common perception of the ocean in the 1950s and 1960s as being akin to outer space, as an alien, unexplored frontier.[24] In the climactic scenes of great whites in the waters of Dangerous Reef, Australia, this technique of long shots with other-worldly music is repeated, the only addition being the use of still frames in sequences showing a stills photographer inside the diving cages. The use of music is particularly important in the context of marine wildlife films, as Cousteau's film indicates that the notion of the marine world being largely 'silent' means that audio contributes a significant component to its representational framing. Narration and dialogue are crucial as in documentaries generally, but the role of music is arguably even more important,[25] and will be returned to later in the chapter.

Looking at *BWWD* in the wake of *Jaws*, it is interesting how its narrative, visual and musical construction of the sharks offers something quite distinctive from the predominant representational frames that have decisively shaped their representation in documentaries in the wake of Spielberg's film. Although *BWWD* sets up great whites as man killers in its opening sequences, and in its closing sequences shows their ferocity in attacking the shark cages, neither of these aspects are constructed in a particularly heightened or dramatic manner akin to *Jaws*, either visually or in terms of musical framing. The absence of an apparent agenda in the expedition, coupled with the visual and aural construction of sharks as primarily other-worldly and alien, is in stark contrast with the shark documentaries that followed *Jaws*. The hyperbolic framing in *Jaws* of great whites as serial killers of humans has overridden the capacity of documentary film-makers to represent sharks without some kind of reference to Spielberg's film, including even those which claim to be trying to dispel mythologies created by *Jaws*' lurid framing of great whites.

Shark documentaries after *Jaws*: The rise of *Shark Week*

Among the many consequences of *Jaws*' success was a, perhaps inevitable, plethora of shark documentaries. *Jaws* had arguably given the great white shark not only 'celebrity status' but also 'both personality and internationality',[26] amounting to what Pierson calls a 'gradual aesthetization of the shark' through the 1970s.[27] Quite quickly, shark documentaries were noticeable in signalling a relationship to the fiction film. In the long-running British natural history strand *Survival*, for instance, *Survival: Shark!* (1979) screened only a few years after *Jaws*, revealed its influence in the voice-over narration of the opening sequences, which focus immediately on the great white shark:

> If any species deservedly gives sharks a bad name, it is this monster – otherwise known as the great white shark and sometimes as the white death. This is the beast that wields those famous jaws … It is impossible to pretend the great white is anything but what it is, a killer of fish, turtles, sealions and men … no-one takes chances with the great white.

As well as images of great whites biting boats and diving cages, the narration is accompanied by images of victims' wounds, and the sequence on great whites concludes with the sentence 'so much for the arch villain of the shark scene'.

Just over a decade after *Jaws*' release there were enough shark documentaries in circulation for the relatively new specialist science channel Discovery to launch *Shark Week*. Shark Week started in 1988 and has continued every year since, celebrating its thirtieth anniversary at the time of writing. For its first few years it was just a branded collation of mostly acquired, rather than commissioned, shark documentaries. A clear ratings winner for Discovery, *Shark Week* has become an ever more prominent piece of annual event television, with increasing proportions of directly commissioned programmes devoted to it, reflecting an emergent Discovery Channel style that is much criticized for its tendency towards sensationalist, infotainment approaches to science documentary.[28] Mitman, for instance, refers to *Shark Week* as an example of trends in wildlife channels to engage 'new generations of enthusiasts with graphic, close-up scenes of animals copulating or predators killing prey'.[29] Peter Benchley himself was the first *Shark Week* host in 1994,[30] and the event has also become part of US popular culture – the title of this chapter coming from a line from comedian Tracy Jordan on the comedy series about television *30 Rock* (and now found on posters, mugs and in online vernacular).

Commentaries on *Shark Week* output directly link it to *Jaws* to criticize the style and tone of shark programmes shown in the event, such as Stockton's comment that

> the serial killer shark trope is a throwback to *Jaws*, and a free square on the Shark Week bingo card. It is an outgrowth of the most persistent theme of Shark Week programming – and the biggest gripe among Shark Week critics: Shark Week casts sharks as objects of fear.[31]

Despite persistent concerns about the kinds of programmes shown, research on public knowledge about sharks seems to suggest that viewers of *Shark Week* typically have more knowledge about sharks than non-viewers, particularly around issues of shark conservation, though such data is caveated with the assertion that *Shark Week* programmes need to 'provide accurate and scientifically sound information' and treat their subjects in a 'non-sensationalised' manner.[32]

Shark Week so dominates the production and viewing of shark documentaries that those shown during the event constitute the primary texts analysed by critical studies of the 'genre'.[33] Papson's 1992 study has been the only one to look at shark documentaries systematically with a focus on their narrative framing and compositional techniques in the context of documentary theory and practice.[34] Evans's more recent study concentrates on aspects of shark information/behaviour from a science communication perspective and not in terms of narrative composition or form.[35] Neither of these studies explicitly looks for relationships to *Jaws* or precursor documentaries like *BWWD* and they are both solely concerned with programmes screened as part of *Shark Week*. Thanks to a variety of sources now available, such as online streaming services, online broadcasting archives, video websites and DVDs, it's possible to get a non-systematic but illustrative sample of documentaries on great white sharks. These stretch from documentaries that directly influenced *Jaws*' production to the present day, heavily centred around but not exclusive to programmes screened as part of *Shark Week*, and give a sense of the extent and nature of the influence of *Jaws* on how documentaries represent great white sharks. Having already explored some key features of sharks in documentaries before *Jaws*, the rest of the chapter examines a range of documentaries whose representation of great whites is 'anchored' by *Jaws*.

Jaws as an archetypal anchor for shark documentaries

Roland Barthes's concept of anchorage is particularly well exemplified in shark documentaries in the wake of *Jaws*.[36] The concept refers to how captioning in things like advertisements and newspaper photographs serves to anchor or frame the range of possible readings available to audiences of the imagery on display, and the explicit presence of *Jaws* as an anchoring frame of reference persists across many shark documentaries. In Papson's study,[37] for instance, which looked at *Shark Week*'s output in 1990, one of the screened documentaries was *Jaws: The True Story* (originally released in 1984). The first of what became a running series of *Shark Week* documentaries branded *Air Jaws* appeared in 2001, while one of 2016's batch of programmes was entitled *Jaws of the Deep*. Name-checking *Jaws* persistently occurs in the contents of programmes as well, in some more overtly than in others, but regularly and through both narration/presentation and the contributions of experts. The passage of time doesn't seem to have dimmed the value of *Jaws* as a narrative point of reference whether to enhance or debunk the film's mythologization of the killer great white. For instance, just as *Survival: Shark!* alludes to *Jaws* in its opening sequence in 1979, later programmes still seem compelled to it in opening sequences. Thirty seconds into *The Great White Shark Hunt* (1994), the narration states, 'This is the domain of *Jaws* itself.' An episode on great whites of *The Adventures of Jacques Cousteau* from 1992 features Cousteau's son, Jean-Michel, expressing concern that public perception of the sharks has been shaped by 'fictional scare movies designed to entertain', films which offer 'white death in blue water' (it's not clear if this is an intentional swipe at *BWWD* or not). A Discovery film from 1992, *Great White!*, includes a sequence of images of media representations of

Figure 16.3 *Air Jaws* (2001).

great whites as killers and some brief shots from *Jaws* itself, though it isn't explicitly referred to in narration or dialogue. The year 2001's *White Sharks: Outside the Cage* has an opening narration that describes the focal expert featured in the show, Mark Marks, as someone who 'challenges the Hollywood image of sharks as merciless killers', and one of Marks's first statements in the film is 'look at these sharks – they're not the big maneaters or *Jaws*'. In *Air Jaws* (2001) (Figure 16.3), which focuses on great whites off the coast of South Africa known for jumping out of the water while hunting seals, the impact of *Jaws* is referred to viscerally in narration: 'Spurred on by the movie *Jaws*, trophy-hunting great white fishermen combed the waters around seal island in the 1970s [avoiding] the ring of death ... for fear of having their boat attacked.' In *Deep White: The Shark Behind the Myth* (2013) the film is referenced in expert dialogue on two occasions. First, the organizer of tourist trips to swim with great whites talks about how below surface level great whites 'move slowly and you get to see the white shark as they truly are, as opposed to the white shark that's most often portrayed on TV and in movies like *Jaws*'. Later in the programme, a professional marine photographer says, 'If anyone associates danger underwater, they think of this massive white zeppelin-looking shark, bristling with teeth coming straight towards them with *Jaws* music playing.'

One of the most overt examples of *Jaws* as an anchoring device in great white shark documentaries occurs in a 2010 *Inside Nature's Giants* episode on a great white shark. An award-winning British series, screened by PBS in the United States, it might be expected to offer a fundamentally different approach to the dominant representational modes offered by *Shark Week*. Its unique premise was to build a programme around an actual dissection of an animal, with explanation of the animal's distinctive characteristics offered by a team of experts in the animal's behaviour, anatomy and evolution (the last of these explained in sequences featuring internationally renowned zoologist Richard Dawkins). The great white shark episode begins with an opening narration by the presenter, Mark Evans, that refers to 'the deadly nature of its infamous jaws'. Later in the show Evans comments that 'since the film *Jaws* most people see these animals as mindless assassins of the sea, hell bent on eating anything that comes in their way, and that includes us'. The programme is a good illustration of the tension in great white shark documentaries between trying to use the reference point of *Jaws* as a narrative framework to engage audiences and dispelling the myths the film embodied, but rarely being able to move beyond that point of reference. Papson identified this in the early 1990s commenting that despite 'criticising the misconceptions which Hollywood creates, shark documentaries use the same structures and devices to create salience',[38] and it seems not a great deal has changed a generation on from Papson's study. In *Inside Nature's Giants*, a sequence of tagging great whites includes a piece of corrective dialogue from a biologist saying, 'Sharks don't swim like in the movie *Jaws* with the dorsal fin out all the time and music in the background', but then the narration immediately switches to another member of the team saying, 'after hours of waiting I hear that music', and as a great white shark approaches the boat the *Jaws* music itself is used.

Da dum, da dum, da dum …: Musical framing of great white sharks

The use of the actual *Jaws* theme in *Inside Nature's Giants* is an exception, but the influence of Williams's iconic score has been substantial on the musical framing of great whites in documentary. As indicated earlier, in *BWWD* the soundtrack for shark encounters was other-worldly and alien, but after *Jaws* the consistent musical framing of sharks is with orchestral arrangements, switching between magisterial and ominous tonalities, largely produced through arrangements of strings and with prominent drum-beats. In *Jaws* 'the assignment of an ominous musical motif to its presence gave a shark a personality', an important aspect given that it was unseen for most of the film.[39] Arguably, the use of similar music in documentaries meant 'sharks quickly became eating machines devoid of personality with musical gestures as sinister companions'.[40] The role of music in these programmes is reflected in concerns around a trend where 'soundtracks for nature documentaries are now dominated by music at the expense of sounds of wild nature'.[41] The rarity of public criticisms of the use of music in wildlife films, indeed the celebration of some series' scores (particularly Attenborough's series, which have had Proms performances built around some of them) elides the obvious reality that most organisms in the natural world don't engage in behaviour with a musical backdrop. Choices of music used to frame animals and environments matter.

For instance, the alien soundtrack of *BWWD* serves to contribute to the othering of the sharks as themselves alien, in spite of their otherwise being shown in their natural habitat. Williams's score in *Jaws* frames the sharks within a more conventional sonic landscape, that of the orchestral cinematic score, but at the same time in culturally recognizable motifs of power, danger and so on. Similar kinds of music tend to accompany other great predators in wildlife films like lions and crocodiles, but the association between great whites and an ominous piece of string music is arguably the strongest of all. For some marine scientists, this type of music is not just of incidental interest to the discussion of the use of music in documentary, but might impact on public perceptions of sharks. In one experimental study that tested the apparent impact of ominous versus uplifting background music accompanying shark footage, evidence suggested a possible negative impact of ominous music on public attitudes towards sharks.[42] Whether or not such data points to a substantive negative impact on public attitudes and behaviour towards great white sharks, it is certain that their musical framing has essentially been delimited by the ominous 'da dum da dum da dum' of Williams's score for *Jaws*.

'You're going to need a bigger boat': Sharks and subjunctive documentary

One of the notable trends in science documentary over time and apparent in shark documentaries as well has been the role of documentary technologies.[43] Particularly in marine documentaries from Cousteau onwards, the foregrounding of the filming process has been an explicit part of such films' narratives – in contrast to blue chip programmes that tend to present such material as 'making-of' extras – at least in part because of the constant pushing of boundaries of filming strategies and techniques. Jean-Michel Cousteau's 1992 episode mentioned earlier, for instance, features a cylindrical, clear shark cage to get clear shots and uses a robot shark to test whether great whites are cannibalistic or not. In the National Geographic programme *Shark Sonics* (2003), the unique feature is a device that produces sonic vibrations that attract sharks so that they can be filmed outside of shark cages. In an overt instance of the symbiosis between marine documentary and marine science, in *Air Jaws* a contributor mentions an unnamed 1993 shark documentary that influenced their tactics for trying to attract great white sharks with a seal-shaped decoy. In *Deep White: The Shark Behind the Myth* (2013) submersible shark cages that go deeper than the traditional kinds depicted in *Jaws* are used to observe the different behaviour mentioned earlier that occurs below the surface. In *Jaws of the Deep* (2016), a robotic, submersible camera dubbed 'shark cam' is used to follow tagged great whites at distance and at depth, not only revealing previously unseen behaviour but generating substantially different footage from the typical boat-side feeding frenzies seen in many earlier programmes.

Alongside these technical developments, including improvements in the visual quality of cameras, the use of slow-motion imagery and so on, a few programmes have begun to use one of the biggest influences on modern factual entertainment programmes – computer-generated imagery (CGI).[44] *Air Jaws* (2001), for instance, features an opening sequence of a crude CGI representation of a shark hunt of seals. Dawkins's sequences in *Inside Nature's Giants* (2010) uses CGI to highlight the nature of the shark's highly evolved and aquadynamic skin, and the 2017 programme *Rise of the Great White Shark* has a brief use of CGI to comparatively depict the great white's prehistoric relative: the Megalodon.

Documentaries using CGI to depict things impossible to capture with conventional photography have been described rather critically as 'subjunctive documentaries', where what is being depicted is not the documenting of events that have happened but 'what *could be, would be,* or *might have been*'.[45] Exemplified by series like *Walking with Dinosaurs* (1998), which brought extinct animals back to life through CGI, and heavily influenced by Spielberg's *Jurassic Park* (1993), there are instances of the intersection of the rise of subjunctive documentaries and the dominance of *Jaws* as a framing device for shark documentaries. The focus for these intersections is the Megalodon, a prehistoric shark several times larger than a great white. Pre-dating the Megalodon-featuring shark movie *The Meg* (2018) by several years, Megalodons have featured in factual entertainment for some time. In the *Walking with Dinosaurs* follow-up series *Sea Monsters* (2003), for example, whose conceit is that an expedition travels into prehistory, one sequence depicts the presenter being nearly eaten by a Megalodon that crashes into a shark cage. More notoriously, a *Shark Week* mock-documentary, *Megalodon: The Monster Shark Lives* (2013), attracted nearly 5 million viewers with an account of Megalodons alive in the present day. The pull of the *Jaws* narrative of the dramatic, scary and dangerous shark persists and extends into the subjunctive imaginings of what a Megalodon could do to us, if it were alive today, freed from the constraints of scientific verisimilitude of the conventional documentary.

Conclusion

The shadow of *Jaws* hanging over cultural representations and perceptions of great white sharks is long and continues to be an explicit frame of reference for documentaries on the species. The arguably negative impact of fictional representations of animals on their narrative construction in wildlife films and natural history documentaries more generally has been well documented and critiqued in the literature, but it is surprising that *Jaws'* impact has drawn very little attention within studies of natural history documentary. Given the symbiotic relationship between documentary and *Jaws* since its release, it should have arguably garnered more critical attention, as should *Blue Water, White Death* in particular. *Jaws'* demonstrable and continuing influence on documentary representations of great white sharks exemplifies concerns over the tensions between cultural perceptions and scientific realities. Documentaries on great white sharks continue to reference *Jaws* in a variety of different ways – explicitly in programme titles, narration and dialogue – and more implicitly in terms of use of music, narrative structure and visual focus. Even as a combination of continuing changes in attitudes towards sharks (focused around respect and conservation rather that hatred and hunting), knowledge about the sharks themselves (from ever more research) and tools and techniques for filming them (e.g. 'shark cams' and submersible cages) broaden the range of *potential* ways to represent them, *Jaws* continues to define the representations that typically emerge. Just as the marine biologist in *Great White Serial Killer Lives* finds himself unable to resist quoting *Jaws* ('Hooper drives the boat') so Spielberg's libel against great whites seems to have become an anchoring archetype for great white shark representation on-screen that shows little sign of disappearing anytime soon.

Notes

1   See Vincent Campbell, *Science, Entertainment and Television Documentary* (Basingstoke: Palgrave Macmillan, 2016).
2   See Gregg Mitman, *Reel Nature: America's Romance with Wildlife on Film* (Cambridge, MA: Harvard University Press, 1999); Derek Bousé, *Wildlife Films* (Philadelphia: University of Pennsylvania Press, 2000); Cynthia Chris, *Watching Wildlife* (Minneapolis: University of Minnesota Press, 2006); Jan-Christopher Horak, 'From Classical Forms to Reality TV', *Film History*, 18, no. 4 (2006): 459–75.
3   Horak, 'From Classical Forms', 467.
4   Derek Bousé, 'Are Wildlife Films Really Nature Documentaries?', *Critical Studies in Mass Communication*, 5, no. 2 (2000): 116–40.
5   Horak, 'From Classical Forms'; Helen Hughes, 'Humans, Sharks and the Shared Environment in the Contemporary Eco-doc', *Environmental Education Research*, 17, no. 6 (2011): 735–49.
6   Stephen Papson, '"Cross the Fin Line of Terror": Shark Week on the Discovery Channel', *Journal of America Culture*, 15, no. 4 (1992): 67–81.
7   Laura A. Friedrich, Rebecca Jefferson and Gillian Glegg, 'Public Perceptions of Sharks: Gathering Support for Shark Conservation', *Marine Policy*, 47 (2014): 2.
8   Peter Simmons and MichaelMehmet, 'Feeding Frenzy: Public Accuse the Media of Deliberately Fuelling Shark Fear', *The Conversation*, 22 June 2018, https://theconversation.com/feeding-frenzy-public-accuse-the-media-of-deliberately-fuelling- shark-fear-95858 (accessed 23 May 2019).
9   Christopher Neff, 'The *Jaws* Effect: How Movie Narratives Are Used to Influence Policy Responses to Shark Bites in Western Australia', *Australian Journal of Political Science*, 50, no. 1 (2015): 114–27.
10   Campbell, *Science, Entertainment and Television Documentary*.
11   Christopher Neff and Robert Hueter, 'Science, Policy, and the Public Discourse of Shark "Attack": A Proposal for Reclassifying Human–Shark Interactions', *Journal of Environmental Studies and Sciences*, 3 (2013): 65–73.
12   Jacques-Yves Cousteau, *The Silent World* (Washington, DC: National Geographic Society, 1953), 128.
13   Ibid.
14   Ibid.
15   Bousé, *Wildlife Films*.
16   Horak, 'From Classical Forms'.

17 Anna, Hart, 'The Most Glamorous Shark Hunter in the World', *Daily Telegraph*, 28 June 2018, https://www.telegraph.co.uk/culture/film/11700946/The-most-glamorous-shark-hunter- in-the-world.html (accessed 23 May 2019).

18 Horak, 'From Classical Forms'.

19 Ibid., 462.

20 Bousé, 'Are Wildlife Films'.

21 Horak, 'From Classical Forms'.

22 Ibid.

23 Papson, 'Cross the Fin Line'.

24 Mitman, 'Reel Nature', 174.

25 Isabelle Delmotte, 'Losing Sight of Atmospheric Sounds in Televised Nature Documentary', *The New Soundtrack*, 7, no. 1 (2017): 67–82.

26 Papson, 'Cross the Fin Line', 68.

27 David P. Pierson, ' "Hey, They're Just Like Us!" Representations of the Animal World in the Discovery Channel's Nature Programming', *The Journal of Popular Culture*, 38, no. 4 (2005): 704.

28 Pierson, 'Hey They're Just Like Us'; Campbell, *Science, Entertainment and Television Documentary*.

29 Mitman, 'Reel Nature', 205.

30 Lorena Blas, 'Shark Week Encounters through the Years', *USA Today*, 1 July 2015, https://eu.usatoday.com/story/life/tv/2015/07/01/shark-week-through-the-years/29485167/ (accessed 23 May 2019).

31 Nick Stockton, 'The Ethics of Why You Should Definitely Watch Shark Week', *Wired*, 29 June 2016, https://www.wired.com/2016/06/ethics-definitely-watch-shark-week/?mbid=email_onsiteshare (accessed 23 May 2019).

32 Jason R. O'Bryhim, and E. C. M. Parsons, 'Increased Knowledge about Sharks Increases Public Concern about Their Conservation', *Marine Policy*, 56 (2015): 46.

33 Papson, 'Cross the Fin Line'; Suzannah Evans, 'Shark Week and the Rise of Infotainment in Science Documentaries', *Communication Research Reports*, 32, no. 3 (2015): 265–71.

34 Papson, 'Cross the Fin Line'.

35 Evans, 'Shark Week'.

36 Roland Barthes, *Image-Music-Text* (London: Fontana, 1977).

37 Papson, 'Cross the Fin Line'.

38 Ibid.

39 Delmotte, 'Losing Sight of Atmospheric Sounds', 72.

40 Ibid.

41 Ibid., 73.

42 Andrew P. Nosal, Elizabeth A. Keenan, Philip A. Hastings and AyeletGneezy, 'The Effect of Background Music in Shark Documentaries on Viewers' Perceptions of Sharks', *PLoS ONE*, 11, no. 8 (2016): 1–15. doi:10.1371/journal.pone.0159279.

43 Campbell, *Science, Entertainment and Television Documentary*.

44 Ibid.

45 Mark J. P. Wolf, 'Subjunctive Documentary: Computer Imaging and Simulation', in Jane M. Gaines and Michael Renov, eds, *Collecting Visible Evidence* (Minneapolis: University of Minnesota Press, 1999), 274; Campbell, *Science, Entertainment and Television Documentary*.

Index

NOTE: Page numbers in **bold** and *italics* refer to tables and figures, respectively.

CPSIA information can be obtained
at www.ICGtesting.com
Printed in the USA
LVHW082049110522
718381LV00012B/405

9 781501 373862